Edmund Spenser

SELECTED POETRY

Edited by A. C. Hamilton

The Signet Classic Poetry Series
GENERAL EDITOR: JOHN HOLLANDER

PUBLISHED BY
THE NEW AMERICAN LIBRARY, NEW YORK AND TORONTO,
AND
THE NEW ENGLISH LIBRARY LIMITED, LONDON

Library of Congress Catalog Card Number: 66-24518

First Printing, August, 1966

SIGNET TRADEMARK REG. U.S. PAT. OFF. AND FOREIGN COUNTRIES
REGISTERED TRADEMARK—MARCA REGISTRADA
HECHO EN CHICAGO, U.S.A.

SIGNET CLASSICS are published in the United States
by The New American Library, Inc.,
1301 Avenue of the Americas, New York, New York 10019,
in Canada by The New American Library of Canada Limited,
295 King Street East, Toronto 2, Ontario,
in the United Kingdom by The New English Library Limited,
Barnard's Inn, Holborn, London, E.C. 1, England

PRINTED IN THE UNITED STATES OF AMERICA

Contents

v

Introduction

1579, the year in which Spenser's *Shepheardes Calender* was published, is recognized as the turning point in English literary history. It marks the beginning of Renaissance English literature: the birth of a new literary tradition that was also its rebirth, for it realigns English literature with both the classical tradition of the pastoral and the native traditions of satire and complaint that derive respectively from Chaucer and Langland. Surprisingly, the age realized the significance of the moment. Nashe was prepared to uphold "divine Master *Spencer,* the miracle of wit, to bandie line by line for my life in the honour of England, against Spaine, Fraunce, Italy, and all the world," and Drayton declared that Spenser "had done enough for the immortality of his name had he only given us his *Shepheardes Calender,* a masterpiece if any." Even after Renaissance pastoral had run its course, Pope agreed with Dryden's opinion that Spenser's poem "is the most complete work of this kind which any nation has produced ever since the time of Virgil." In an Epistle to the poem, E. K. daringly proclaims Spenser to be England's new poet who succeeds the old poet, Chaucer, and who aspires to become the English Virgil. In an epilogue to the poem, Spenser himself claims that his poem is eternal: in all succeeding years until the end of the world, his *Calender* will instruct the English nation how to act. Over sixty years later Milton read the poem in this way; and there is no reason why it may not teach us today if we read it as it should be read, as prophecy rather than topical history.

Characteristically, Spenser's high claims in *The Shepheardes Calender* are presented humbly, as an offering. He reveals himself as a poet by hiding his personal identity. While he signs himself "Immerito," the Unworthy One, his signature as a poet is "Colin Clout," one whose art astonishes the Muses. It would seem that Spenser the man hardly matters: what we know of him through his biography contributes little to our knowledge of Colin Clout. While it may help us in reading *Paradise Lost* to learn that Milton composed long verse paragraphs in early-morning bursts of inspiration, it is only distracting to read Spenser's modish letters to Harvey, so that we wonder, as Chaucer's biographers often do, whether we have the wrong man for the name. Keats's remark that "Shakespeare led a life of allegory; his works are the comments on it," applies above all to Spenser. His own life and times, his political opinions and religious beliefs, may be dimly conjectured only by getting behind and outside the poem, or by reducing its allegorical significance to oblique statement. In the Renaissance, poems in the pastoral form become *radically* allegorical: Drayton holds that "the most High, and most Noble Matters of the World may bee shaddowed in them." Consequently, as Petrarch declares, the form needs the author's commentary and a key. For the *Calender,* such commentary is provided by E. K.'s gloss which hints of particular matters alluded to in the eclogues, but the key is given in the work itself which turns particular "historical" matters to their general and universal significance. Throughout the eclogues Spenser labors to conceal a private allusion in order to reveal its public moral significance, in line with Sidney's claim that the pastoral "can include the *whole* considerations of wrong-doing and patience." One result is that a work which is involved most intimately in the immediate political and religious concerns of the age is projected on the impersonal level of poetry, and the poet who brings himself directly into the poem appears as the type of Renaissance poet. In one of his sonnets Spenser praises Harvey as "the happy above happiest men,/. . . sitting like a looker-on/Of this worldes stage," praise that applies oddly to the ambitious time-server revealed in his marginalia or to the buffoon relished by Nashe, but may be applied most appropriately to Spenser himself. In his profoundly comprehensive vision of "the worldes stage," he is personally withdrawn in order to commit himself as a poet who is ready to assume the role of the poet-prophet for the English nation.

In displaying poetry's power to reveal the moral and spiritual condition of his age, Spenser dedicates himself to its high calling. The *Calender* becomes a testimony to his emerging poetic powers. Through his unfailing sense of decorum, each detail becomes fitting to the argument and form of the work. E. K. singles out for praise the rhetorical skill; but more important, there is the architectonical power: "what in most English wryters useth to be loose, and as it were ungyrt, in this Authour is well grounded, finely framed, and strongly trussed up together." Moreover, he displays astonishing originality within traditional forms, and a daring comprehensiveness in his argument. His radical experimenting with various verse forms makes the work a testing ground for the potentialities of the English language in verse. His aim in the work is partly modeled upon what Leland held to be Chaucer's aim: "to render the English speech as polished as possible in all respects. . . . And since poetry had always pleased him above everything else, he devoted himself to it with ardor, he cultivated it religiously. It seemed to him that through its agency it was most easy to lay open the path to the very heights of expression." Where Chaucer fails through his rude age and changes in the language, Spenser hopes to triumph under the patronage of Queen Elizabeth. Consequently, the work is justified and sustained by its promise. As the pastoral version of *The Faerie Queene,* it becomes the means of organizing and absorbing his minor poems into the one greater work.

Traditionally the pastoral treats the theme of wandering in search of identity. The pattern is shown most clearly in Milton's pastoral, *Lycidas,* where the poet, being himself drowned in despair, seeks his drowned counterpart in his friend. Through his quest—his questioning—he finds himself, and leaves the pastoral world renewed. In the *Calender,* the melancholy Colin Clout is dominated by the elusive Rosalind, and seeks to escape. Though in a later poem Spenser criticizes Daniel for remaining "In loves soft laies and looser thoughts delight," his point is not that the poet should forsake the theme of love. As Piers declares in the October eclogue, love aroused by beauty teaches Colin to "climbe so hie" and "rayse [his] mynd above the starry skie." Thus while Spenser's "son," Milton, turns from love to virtue in the epilogue to *Comus* where the Spirit declares that virtue "can teach ye how to clime/Higher then the Spheary chime," Colin Clout finds himself by rejecting only the pastoral disguise with its pursuit of faithless love. At the end of the pastoral, he emerges as England's heroic poet who sings of "Fierce warres and faithfull loves."

By 1579, or within the year, Spenser started to write *The Faerie Queene.* Nothing less than the ideal heroical courage praised by the poem was called upon to project a work of nearly 150,000 lines at a time when the English Parnassus had been so long barren. It puzzled Sidney that England had grown so hard a stepmother to poets, for he found that only parts of the *Mirror for Magistrates,* Surrey's lyrics, and *The Shepheardes Calender* revealed any poetic structure. No major English poet had appeared since Chaucer, and his language had become too corrupt to read as poetry. "Am now enforst" is the simple phrase Spenser uses to explain why he undertakes his heroic quest, and his inspiration carries him until his death through six books of the projected twenty-four. There is no flagging even where he sets himself the epic chore of composing a pageant of most of the rivers of England and Ireland. Though we may be appalled by the sheer labor of the task, Pope found that Spenser's "Variety of Description, and Fruitfulness of Imagination are no where more admirable than in that Part." Spenser's own comment on the pageant reveals the craftsman's joy in the driving energy of his work:

O What an endlesse worke have I in hand,
    To count the seas abundant progeny,
    Whose fruitfull seede farre passeth those in land,
    And also those which wonne in th'azure sky?
    For much more eath to tell the starres on hy,
    Albe they endlesse seeme in estimation,
    Then to recount the Seas posterity:
    So fertile be the flouds in generation,
So huge their numbers, and so numberlesse their nation.

At the end he writes as one who is making a fresh beginning, as though he has arrived at the perfection of craftsmanship which was the goal of his quest. Even in the poem's fragmented state, its 35,000 lines make it the most comprehensive poem by any major English poet.

The scope of *The Faerie Queene* suggests that the poem was carefully planned, while its sheer accomplishment suggests that though he was the inspired poet, he knew what he wanted to do, but he did it better than he knew. By 1579 he had written a critical treatise entitled *The English Poet,* one of its doctrines being mentioned by E. K., that poetry is "no arte, but a divine gift and heavenly instinct not to bee gotten by labour and learning, but adorned with both: and poured into the witte by . . . celestiall inspiration." The emblem to the October eclogue claims, more accurately, that such inspiration comes from the God within us. Even more accurately, his inspiration is his commitment to his poetic intentions, as lines early in the poem suggest:

> The noble hart, that harbours vertuous thought,
> And is with child of glorious great intent,
> Can never rest, untill it forth have brought
> Th'eternall brood of glorie excellent.

Near the end of the poem Spenser traces the source of his inspiration to where it truly belongs, the work itself:

The waies, through which my weary steps I guyde,
    In this delightfull land of Faery,
    Are so exceeding spacious and wyde,

> And sprinckled with such sweet variety,
> Of all that pleasant is to eare or eye,
> That I nigh ravisht with rare thoughts delight,
> My tedious travell doe forget thereby;
> And when I gin to feele decay of might,
> It strength to me supplies, and chears my dulled spright.

For him, inspiration becomes the free play of a liberated imagination in which reason and the emotions, both the conscious and subconscious powers of the mind, are dedicated to the poem's fulfillment.

In 1579 Spenser was in "close familiarity" with Sidney, who was composing his *Apology for Poetry*. Sidney's defense of poetry rests upon the poet's power to create a golden world of fiction that the reader may use as "an imaginative ground-plot of a profitable invention" to move him to virtuous action. This view of fiction that later provides the critical basis of his *Arcadia,* provides some insight into *The Faerie Queene*. Both Arcadia and Fairyland are imaginative worlds that reflect the "real" world through clarifying images. What is confused, perverse, and unsatisfying in ordinary reality is clarified by the poet's "proper embatteling of the virtues and vices," in Jonson's phrase, and given direction by our sense of what should be. The identification of poetry with fiction led both poets to write romance; but while Sidney uses the method of example, Spenser uses the elaborate structure of his continued allegory. To illustrate briefly, after Sidney's hero, Pyrocles, has established his heroic nature in battle, and then falls in love with Philoclea by gazing upon her picture, he must dress as a female warrior, an Amazon, in order to enjoy her company. His transformed state is an emblem of his effeminate condition, and as such is moralized upon at length by his friend Musidorus. In the narrative it leads to an elaborate comedy in which Pyrocles is accepted as a woman by Philoclea, wooed as such by her father, and pursued by her mother, who sees through his disguise. Through suffering for the sake of love, he proves himself "Never more valiant," which is the motto he wears in his transformed state. Sidney's method is essentially static as it elaborates the moral, spiritual, and dramatic possibilities of a given exemplum. Spenser's method differs considerably. After his hero, Guyon, has asserted his heroic nature by destroying the Bower of Bliss, he lectures Acrasia's transformed victims for yielding to love. In the two succeeding episodes, however, he is overcome first by a woman knight, Britomart, and then by the vision of beauty seen in the fleeing Florimell. Then he and the other knights are plunged into "diverse pageants of love" which are treated in Books III and IV. While Sidney's method allows specific moral applications from his fiction, Spenser's method demands that the reader expand the allegorical contexts of any episode until they include the whole poem. Only in terms of the unity of the whole poem may a given episode be understood.

Other broad distinctions follow from this comparison of the two poets. As the aristocrat, Sidney stresses the select group of aristocrats; through the pattern of virtuous conduct that they provide, the ideal society may be achieved. As a poet of the middle class, Spenser stresses society, the English nation as a whole, though he recognizes that its center is the court. W. H. Auden has remarked that "in his heart of hearts the audience he [the English poet] desires and expects are those who govern the country." If so, Spenser alone among English poets could hope that his vision of English society would influence his country's leaders. In 1579 he could regard himself as the right poet who had come at the right time. The rule of Queen Elizabeth fostered a strong apocalyptic faith that the golden age was returning. The moment had come for Spenser to assume the role of the heroic poet who would speak for his nation.

Spenser's role as the heroic poet is supported by a strong humanist faith in an education that leads to virtuous action. Milton expresses that faith when he defines a complete education as that "which fits a man to perform justly, skillfully, and magnanimously all the offices, both private and public, of peace and war." Sidney writes to his friend Languet: "to what purpose should our thoughts be directed to various kinds of knowledge unless room be afforded for putting it into practice, so that public advantage may be the result." Yet being frustrated in his hope for public service, he adds: "which in a corrupt age we cannot hope for." His irritated phrase suggests one reason why Spenser wrote an allegory. Fairyland provides an image to a corrupt age of what must be done to achieve a golden age. There remains the problem which Sidney resolves in the *Apology:* since man's will is corrupt, he must be persuaded to do what he knows is right. He justifies poetry above all other arts because of its power to move man's will. Accordingly, Spenser colors his allegory with the pleasing fiction of the history of Arthur in order that the general end of his poem will be "to fashion a gentleman or noble person in vertuous and gentle discipline." *The Faerie Queene* is meant above all to be a deeply persuasive poem. Persuasion is prior even to understanding.

In the *Letter to Raleigh,* Spenser explains and defends his poetic method with considerable care. He knows that some would prefer him to deliver his discipline plainly in precepts rather than covertly in a historical fiction. In reply, he urges that since the present age regards things only by their outward appearance, an example or pattern of behavior is more persuasive than rules. He admires Plato who in the *Republic* forms a commonwealth as it should be according to rule, yet recognizes that the age prefers Xenophon who in the *Cyropaedia* fashions a government through the example of Cyrus. Since the age prefers doctrine by example rather than by rule, Spenser fashions a government in the person of Arthur. Instead of delivering a sermon, he tells a story, the historical fiction of Arthur. Accordingly, his purpose in his poem is to portray in Arthur "the image of a brave knight, perfected in the twelve private morall vertues," and to make this image sufficiently persuasive that men may be moved by the sight of his goodness to imitate his virtues. Since Arthur illustrates the perfection of all the virtues, both public and private, the fiction of Arthur—"clowdily enwrapped" is Spenser's phrase—contains the discipline that orders man's nature in virtue. He explains his choice of Arthur on the grounds that his history is "furthest from the daunger of envy, and suspition of present time," but Jonson told Drummond a better reason: "for a Heroik poeme he said ther was no such Ground as King Arthurs fiction and that S. P. Sidney had ane intention to have transform'd all his Arcadia to ye stories of King Arthure." The history of Arthur was close enough both to fiction and to fact, and thus served the purposes both of romance in projecting a mythical figure and of a heroic poem that becomes the vehicle for national aspirations.

Spenser's method ranks him with "the antique Poets historicall," Homer and Virgil, and also, for him, Ariosto and Tasso. It places his poem in the heroic tradition in which poems were read as allegories of the life of either the virtuous man or the good governor. He does not seek to rival or supplant the poems in this tradition, though he may include and transcend Homer and Virgil where the actions of the private man or political animal relate to the truth of Holy Scripture, and Ariosto and Tasso where moral and religious doctrine are involved. Chiefly, he places himself in their fellowship. What each did for his age, he will do for England: through him, their Muses speak with the English tongue. Consequently, his poem is projected as the one complete work for his age: its educational treatise, courtesy handbook, moral and spiritual enchiridion, and (in Book I) its Bible, the one work that reveals the vision of life as it should be, and the faith by which men should live.

Spenser defends his use of fiction on the specific grounds that it is "most plausible and pleasing," "profitable and gratious," and what "the most part of men delight to read." His terms are carefully chosen to stress the imaginative possibilities of fiction. Traditionally, fiction differs from history on grounds that Aristotle made clear: the historian deals "not with one action, but with one period and all that happened in that," while the poet treats a single action as a complete whole "with all the organic unity of a living creature." Following him, Spenser writes that the historiographer must recount "as well the times as the action," while the poet historical is free to offer "a pleasing Analysis." In creating his imaginative world, the poet first must delight his reader. Spenser chooses to write romance whose appeal is both primitive and sophisticated. His story is one of "Fierce warres and faithfull loves," of battles with monstrous foes or monsters of the earth, water, air, and fire, of endless quests and sudden flights, of imprisonments and escapes. His setting is the wilderness, the mysterious forest or the sea, deep caves, dark dungeons, and glittering castles. It is a mysterious world of sudden illumination or confused enchantment; the world of dreams, visions, and nightmares. His central story, a hero's quest to slay the monster, is the essential form of all stories. It is too particular and vital to be regarded simply as the vehicle of some intended meaning; yet as a romance it constantly suggests larger meanings. It may hint at such larger meanings by aligning itself with morality, theology, or history while maintaining its own integrity. Its method is to evoke meaning, or rather to awaken many meanings. Dragon-slaying is a literary theme with some precise moral and theological significances, but as a story it is primitive, and surely prehistoric in its appeal to any reader. For example, in the story of how Britomart enters the house of Busyrane to free Amoret who is bound to a brazen pillar with iron bands, the reader becomes aware through the mask of Cupid that the story is the vehicle for a sophisticated allegory of courtly love. When he learns that Amoret was bound on her marriage night, he will recognize that the pillar and the bands have broad erotic significance. Yet the story appeals primarily on the level of folklore, the story of Bluebeard in which the bride enters the room bearing the inscription, "Be Bold," and discovers the mutilated bride. Spenser is not using folklore as a means of conveying an allegory of courtly love: both are means of expressing the impact of marriage on the feminine psyche through a story. Spenser's story is not bound by any of the meanings it suggests, nor do any number of them exhaust the story. They only add to it; and the more one sees in the fiction, the more there is to see.

Since the poem is named "a continued Allegory, or darke conceit," in the *Letter to Raleigh,* it invites our attention to its "other sense" apart from the literal meaning. Coleridge remarks that no reader of *The Faerie Queene* can fail to be concerned with the nature of allegorical writing. Any reader is disturbed to learn that a poem does not mean what it says, but something else. Without some key to the allegory, it means nothing; or if there are many keys, it may mean anything at all. Some help is given by the age in which such a poem could be written and expect to be understood. "Allegory" is commonly described in Renaissance rhetorical manuals as a form of speech that expresses one thing in words and another in sense. Mythological handbooks provide extensive allegorical interpretations of the classical myths, usually into moral, historical, and cosmological meanings. The fourfold medieval exegesis of Holy Scripture suggests its application to profane literature. Many poets wrote allegorical poems, or their poems were read as such despite claims that nothing of the kind was intended. Yet efforts to discover from the Renaissance a way to read Spenser's allegory have been disappointing, and usually a liability. His poem is a more extended allegory than the rhetoricians allow. It cannot be reduced to classical myth, and specific levels of interpretation are only intermittent. The possible influence of medieval scriptural exegesis must be countered with the Protestant's renewed emphasis upon the literal level. Comparison with other poets helps little because only Spenser and Dante have written poems that were conceived and executed as continued allegories. In interpreting the allegorical poems of other poets, there remains the uneasy feeling that an interpretation is being foisted on the work. With Spenser's poem alone, interpretation follows inevitably and continually from careful reading. Yet the age does reveal the sheer energy expended in reading, and a general willingness to respond to complexities of significance in a poem. Chapman's remark that "Poesie is the flower of the sunne and disdaines to open to the eye of a candle" expresses a strong Renaissance belief that poetry demands intensity of response. It is the

one age in which the heroic poet could cast his poem in
the form of a continued allegory.

The critical effort to understand Spenser's poem as a
continued allegory must begin with the work itself, and
not with any conception of what allegory is or should be.
The poem contains many kinds of "allegory," from simple
and direct to complex and subtle. Some kinds make ex-
plicit identifications with traditional morality, Christian
theology, or Elizabethan history; some suggest significant
analogues, or point to what the poem and the analogues
have in common; and some point only to the work itself.
An example of the simplest kind is the Castle of Alma
episode in Book II, Canto X in which details of the castle
may be translated into physical features of the human
body. If we ignore the comic and witty extravagance of
the episode, the correspondences may prove boring. Yet
the presence of Guyon and Arthur in the Castle, as it leads
to Arthur's slaying of Maleger and Guyon's capture of
Acrasia, turns the episode into a different kind of allegory,
one that leads the poet to comment:

> Now gins this goodly frame of Temperance
> Fairely to rise, and her adorned hed
> To pricke of highest praise forth to advance.

Again, the presence both of Alma as a virgin in contrast
to Acrasia, and of Shamefastnesse, who is the fountain of
Guyon's modesty, raises larger questions about the relation of Temperance to Chastity, the subject of the succeeding book. However we approach the poem, we find that
it makes increasing and shifting demands upon us. Our
only general guide is that any understanding of allegory
that limits the poem's range of significance is wrong; if it
extends its significance, it may well be right.

The poem resists any effort to translate it into other
terms. To press any interpretation toward identification,
or at the expense of other interpretations, puts one with
Britomart as she ponders the inscription in the house of
Busyrane:

> she oft and oft it over-red,
> Yet could not find what sence it figured:
> But what so were therein or writ or ment,
> She was no whit thereby discouraged
> From prosecuting of her first intent.

Such interpretation reveals the ingenuity of the reader rather than the poem's complexity. Yet continually the poem invites and sustains our interpretation on many levels, even though one level may dominate the others. The religious significance dominates the Red Cross Knight's adventures, while Una's story in relation to his suggests an ecclesiastical interpretation. The moral significance governs Guyon's adventures, while his adventures in relation to the Red Cross Knight's suggest a theological interpretation. Even when one kind of interpretation is dominant, it must be related to other kinds that are suggested simultaneously. Spenser calls his poem a "rusticke Madrigale," and its music of meaning may be heard only when the voices, or kinds of meaning, sound in concert.

Spenser's poem defines itself as an allegory through its control over allegorical meanings. For a poet who writes an allegory, Spenser proves to be a stubborn literalist. While his poem aspires to the Renaissance ideal that it contain all knowledge, he insists upon the primacy and integrity of the poem's literal level. He controls meaning chiefly through the language of allegory which he employs consistently throughout the poem. Any reader of the poem soon finds that he must compile a dictionary of its special language. While the meanings of most words will be broadly traditional and literary and some will be peculiar to the poem, all are given a defining and particular significance according to their poetic contexts. For example, the Knight's armor is identified in the opening stanzas with the armor of a Christian man, but its significance is determined when the Knight proves himself worthy of the armor by defeating Error, when he lays it aside while he lies with Duessa, and when it harms him through the Dragon's fire. In the opening stanzas again, details such

as the labyrinth, the cave, and the monster have broad
traditional meanings which are used for the particular
purpose of describing the Knight's initiation into his pilgrimage. Or a particular detail, for example, that the
Knight was "too solemne sad," will be defined when he
battles Sansjoy, by his feigned cheer with Duessa, by the
sadness that leads him to become Despair's victim, and by
the experience in the house of Penance through which
finally he learns "himselfe to chearish."

When the reader begins to appreciate the poem's con-
centration and economy of language, there may seem some
loosening of tension in the description of the trees that
the Knight and Una admire in the Wandering Wood:

> Much can they prayse the trees so straight and hy,
>   The sayling Pine, the Cedar proud and tall,
>   The vine-prop Elme, the Poplar never dry,
>   The builder Oake, sole king of forrests all,
> The Aspine good for staves, the Cypresse funerall.
>
> The Laurell, meed of mightie Conquerours
>   And Poets sage, the Firre that weepeth still,
>   The Willow worne of forlorne Paramours,
>   The Eugh obedient to the benders will,
>   The Birch for shaftes, the Sallow for the mill,
>   The Mirrhe sweete bleeding in the bitter wound,
>   The warlike Beech, the Ash for nothing ill,
>   The fruitfull Olive, and the Platane round,
> The carver Holme, the Maple seeldom inward sound.

The passage appears to be a digression in which Spenser
declares himself the heroic poet: the catalogue of trees is
an epic convention that derives from Ovid's account of
Orpheus, the archetype of the inspired poet, who gathers
trees in a forest around him as he plays on his lyre. Yet
one must consider the particular terms and defining con-
text in which the convention is used. The trees are described through the common associations and uses given
them by human society, each in a particular manner. When
we are told that these "loftie trees yclad with sommers
pride" hide heaven's light, each detail will be expanded by

the imagery used throughout the whole book. To define the particular allegorical significance of the Wandering Wood, the reader may seek for analogues such as Dante's Dark Wood, or for Horace's account of the trees which led Upton to comment on Spenser's Wood: "what are these trees and labyrinths, but the various amusements and errors of human life?" Yet the poem itself defines the allegorical significance of the trees, without translation, through other contexts. The monster in the center of the wood vomits books to defeat the Knight: at this point the trees become the tree of the knowledge of good and evil through which mankind falls into sin. Later the Knight falls into the power of Orgoglio when he lies with Duessa in the shade "with greene boughes decking a gloomy glade," and his final victory over the Dragon will be achieved when he is restored by healing balm from the Tree of Life. Later books add larger, and more particular, meanings to the trees, such as the Bower of Bliss in Book II. Or the forest will be given a special significance in contrast to the open plain, the sea coast, or the sea. Gradually the reader becomes aware that each detail in the poem is significant, not on an allegorical level but in the precise terms in which it is given on the literal level.

Spenser controls the meanings of his romance also through the virtues treated in the separate books. While he claims that Arthur is "perfected in the twelve private morall vertues, as Aristotle hath devised," Holiness has little basis in Aristotle, Temperance is Aristotle's Continence, or pagan virtue generally, and the figure "twelve" is imposed by the set number of books for the epic poem. In general, Spenser gives short shrift to moralists: the one point at which he engages their debate, whether mercy is a part of justice, he turns from their "devicefull art" to his inner assurance that mercy is as great as justice. Faith in a golden age that governs the vision behind the poem inverts the customary moral judgments of virtue and vice:

> For that which all men then did vertue call,
> Is now cald vice; and that which vice was hight,
> Is now hight vertue, and so us'd of all:

Right now is wrong, and wrong that was is right,
As all things else in time are chaunged quight.

His method of treating the virtues is suggested in his statement that "In that Faery Queene I meane glory in my
generall intention, but in my particular I conceive the
most excellent and glorious person of our soveraine the
Queene," to which he adds the footnote that the Queen
bears two persons: first, the royal Queen or Empress;
and second, in her own person, a virtuous lady. Accordingly, each book presents two aspects of the hero: in
his actions as patron of a virtue, and in his own person.
In all that he does, the Red Cross Knight seems capable
only of doing wrong: his natural movement is downward
and he must be helped to ascend each step. Yet he is the
patron of Holiness because in his person, judged apart
from his own merit and works, he is a "man of God," as
Una must remind him in his battle against Error when
she urges him to "shew what ye bee," and then against
Despair when she tells him that he is "chosen" by God.
In contrast, Guyon must rely entirely on his own merit.
Accordingly, Book II reveals the virtue of Temperance
instead of the man; or rather, by placing man in the contexts of internal and external nature, it shows their control
by virtue. The limitation of Guyon's virtue is simply that
the person and the virtue remain separate: the chief lesson
he learns is to resist the "natural" impulses to action
through which the Red Cross Knight falls. In Book III
these two halves merge: both in her person and in all her
actions, Britomart manifests Chastity. Her person is not
distinct from her virtue. For this reason the treatment of
her virtue apart from her person must be told through the
stories of Amoret, Florimell, and Belphoebe.

There is a similar structuring of the virtues in the second three books. Spenser uses the notion of traduction,
or sharing of natures between friends, and the hermaphro-
ditic union of man and woman in marriage to reveal the
"personal" nature of Friendship. In Book V, Artegall is
the impersonal patron of Justice: necessarily, his person
is divorced from the virtue he upholds. In Book VI the

person and the virtue are again identified: Calidore manifests Courtesy in his own person and in all his actions.

By relating the virtues treated in the separate books, Spenser further controls the meaning of the whole poem. The relation between Holiness and Temperance is defined by the encounter between the Red Cross Knight and Guyon, and by the careful paralleling of the structure of the first two books. A similar encounter between Guyon and Britomart relates Temperance and Chastity. Later, when the Red Cross Knight and Britomart join forces, the virtues treated in the first three books are shown in a "goodly golden chaine." In the second three books a more complex relation among the virtues is established by the tournament that relates all the knights, but chiefly Britomart and Artegall. Finally, all the virtues are embodied in Arthur, who appears throughout the poem as "the image of a brave knight." He manifests the harmony of the virtues in perfected human nature, both in his own person and in all his actions. Even in his first appearance in the poem, where he is the vehicle of heavenly grace, he does not supplant, but rather supplements, human nature. Through the "lovely court" with which he entertains Una in her despair, he persuades her to accept the reason— not grace—through which faith may be restored. In the divine mission with Una to redeem the fallen Red Cross Knight, both are led by the Dwarf, whose role here corresponds to human reason.

The unity of the poem may be treated even though the poem is not complete. As a Protestant poet, Spenser does not move to an ultimately clarifying vision but begins with one. Book I, which is an imitation of Holy Scripture, becomes the center for the whole poem; and by providing the whole poem's pattern, it contains its larger meanings. According to its story, there are four phases of the quest in Fairyland: the Knight's confused wandering or flight that leads downward to a state of wounding, imprisonment, or death from which he must be rescued by some higher power; then he takes the ordered journey that leads upward to a final triumph. These four phases—downward movement, fall, upward movement, and resolution—form two halves, of which the first parodies the second. In the first, the Red Cross Knight is attacked by external enemies, such as Sansfoy, who belong to a Satanic conspiracy which opposes Una, and then by inner spiritual enemies, such as Sansjoy, who besiege his soul. He is guided on a downward path by Duessa until he is reduced to a pitiful corpse in Orgoglio's dungeon while she rides the Dragon in her triumph over Una. He is redeemed from this state of spiritual death by Arthur, who descends into hell to lift him out in order that he may start on the upward path. In the second half of his adventures, inward meditation of his guilt brings a vision of hell through which he becomes the victim of Despair until Una intercedes and leads him upward to a house of Penance where its vision of hell purges him of sin, and contemplation brings the vision of his salvation. The final battle inverts the midpoint of his quest: the Dragon lies under his feet, Duessa is stripped of her robes, and he is betrothed to Una. The Knight's adventures reveal vertically the entire range of wandering, from the hell that constantly opens before his feet to the vision of heaven that urges him upward.

These four phases of the Red Cross Knight's adventures are explored in the later books, while the sequence of the books shows a change of emphasis from one phase to the next. In this manner the poem takes its point of departure from Book I even while being contained by it.

Book II repeats the full pattern of the quest in Book I on the horizontal level. Guyon's enemies are internal, being aspects of himself. In contrast to the Red Cross Knight, who makes himself the victim of his own wrath and lust, Guyon shows a disciplined ordering of nature through which something other than self-destroying action may be possible. Consequently, Book II becomes the most moral of the books, and the most involved in learning. It engages that end of learning described by Chapman:

> to have skill to throwe
> Reignes on your bodies powres, that nothing knowe,
> And fill the soules powres so with act and art,

That she can curb the bodies angrie part:
All perturbations, all affects that stray
From their one object, which is to obey
Her Sovereigne Empire.

Guyon's actions show the power of man's wisdom or learning to measure a mean between extremes, and to resist the arguments of Mammon. Yet Spenser would agree with Berowne in *Love's Labour's Lost* when he opposes the Platonic faith in learning with the Christian awareness that "every man with his affects is born,/Not by might mast'red, but by special grace." In the cave of Mammon, Guyon must remain passive in the face of its furious activity; and through denying himself food and sleep, he falls under the power of his enemies. In showing the power of Temperance, Guyon reveals its limitations: he resists the self-destroying action only by not acting. Arthur must intercede on his behalf and destroy both the internal enemies, Pyrocles and Cymocles, and the external enemy, Maleger, who besiege the temperate body. In the climactic episode, Guyon may resist the temptations of the Bower of Bliss to eat and rest: he "sees and endures all" (in Milton's phrase), and in a final triumphant action, he destroys the Bower.

This most famous episode in the poem becomes a test of poetry's power to enchant the reader by its vision of beauty, and yet release him through poetry's power to include reason that reflects on the enchantment. Bacon writes that man's reason would become captive to the affections if the poet's eloquence "did not practise and win the imagination from the Affection's part, and contract a confederacy between the Reason and Imagination against the Affections." For all except Grill, the episode joins reason and imagination though it leaves unresolved the role of the affections.

Temperance treats man's nature on the level of rational conduct. Since reason suppresses the passions, the temperate human body is viewed as a castle besieged by temptations from the external world. The utmost power of temperance is to establish a viable equation between human nature and Nature. It must hold the things of the world—chiefly Beauty and Money, the two chief foes of the temperate body—without being held by them. The occasion of Guyon's adventure is his meeting with the dying Amavia whose excessive love for Mortdant, Acrasia's victim, brings her death. While temperance destroys the enchantment that brings Mortdant's death, it cannot cure Amavia. Her plight becomes the central human predicament in the rest of the poem. Its pattern is expressed in Book I in Una's love for the Red Cross Knight, through which she seeks to rescue him from the enchantments of Duessa. Temperance may repress the passions as evil until Acrasia's victims awake from the sensual dream into reality; then it must yield to a higher power which orders the passions into the harmony of chaste love.

Book III explores human nature in depth once passion breaks out. The power of Amavia's love is shown in Amoret's love for Scudamour, Florimell's love for Marinell, and Britomart's love for Artegall. At the beginning of the book, the male knights are overcome by the vision of beauty in the fleeing Florimell while Britomart persists in her quest for Artegall. Led by love, she undertakes a more profound quest than the other knights, one in which she suffers the agony of wounding and imprisonment, and the perils of fire and the sea that overcome Amoret and Florimell. "In my heart I quested for beauty, but God, God hath sent me to sea for pearls." The higher nature that sustains such love is revealed in the Garden of Adonis, the earthly paradise where Venus enjoys her love for Adonis, and where Amoret is trained "In all the lore of love, and goodly womanhead." The virtue that sustains faithful love is Britomart's Chastity, that power through which "the body is sanctified by the sanctification of the will" (the definition is Augustine's), and through which, in Spenser's terms, love leads to its fulfillment in marriage.

Book III treats the second phase of the quest: all the characters fall, wounded by love. Since Chastity becomes the higher power that releases the imprisoned Amoret, Britomart takes the place of Arthur. Like him, she is guided by a vision of her beloved; and in pursuit of her vision, love leads to virtuous action. As the story of Amoret describes her love on the physical level, her imprisonment in the house of Busyrane represents the fears and threats of masculine domination through love. Busyrane himself is the feminine counterpart of the masculine dream of love shown in Acrasia. Through her chaste love, Britomart endures Amoret's agony in order to free her and prepare the way for the curing of love's wounds.

Book IV treats the third phase of the total quest, the upward movement that leads to the final triumph. It shows how love "of honor and all vertue is/The roote, and brings forth glorious flowres of fame." Britomart is aided by Belphoebe, who slays the Lust that would overpower Amoret, and by Arthur, who saves Amoret from the attacks of Slander. The Tournament in Canto IV which arranges the ascending power of maidenhead in Satyrane, manhood in Artegall, and Chastity in Britomart brings Artegall's submission to Britomart. Lovers who have been separated are joined, lovers' debates are resolved, and discord changes to harmony. The diverse pageants of love are resolved when Arthur and Britomart join forces to bring all the lovers into harmony. The Temple of Venus serves as an emblematic statement of the inspiring power of love throughout the world. While love's dangers to manhood and its shock to womanhood must be endured, the Temple displays the higher paradise that true lovers enjoy and shows their reward in its vision of beauty. That the higher powers in nature support love is shown after the seas' posterity gathers at the marriage of the Thames and the Medway: through the intercession of Neptune, Marinell and Florimell, who represent the powers of the sea and land, are joined in marriage.

Book V treats the fourth and final phase of the quest by projecting upon the Red Cross Knight's role as St. George, the patron saint of England, an apocalyptic vision of England's victory over her enemies, and by showing the resolution of Britomart's quest in her betrothal to Artegall. The whole book projects "the image of the antique world," and on this level of significance, Canto VII, which recounts

Britomart's sojourn in the Temple of Isis and her rescue of Artegall from Radigund's power, resolves the action of the whole poem. Britomart's dream of her fears of love and yet her submission to her lover gather the complex allegory of love that has been the subject of Books III to V. Since her Chastity shows Arthur's virtue on the natural level, and Artegall's Justice shows Arthur's virtue on the political level, their union in marriage represents a final union and ordering of the private and public virtues. As the instrument of Justice, Artegall translates the virtue of temperance into political terms: the rule of temperance which Guyon imposes over his own body, Artegall extends to the body politic to shape a commonwealth that corresponds to the Castle of Alma. Yet he goes beyond Guyon's rigorous suppression of the passions by yielding to Britomart's chaste love, and remaining faithful to her even though he submits to Radigund's power. When Britomart frees him, she rules Radigund's city as Isis while he fulfills his mission.

The final phase of the quest, the resolution, is not an achieved state but one that leads to a renewed quest. For Spenser, passivity is always evil. The ideal state is ordered, active, and ascending, such as the heavenly city which rises from the earth and to which angels descend from heaven, the healthy powers of the temperate body, the ceaseless creation in the Garden of Adonis, the lovers' joy in the Temple of Venus, and the vigorous justice in Mercilla's court. Such a state is best expressed in the harmony of the dance. In the climactic vision in the poem, Calidore sees

> An hundred naked maidens lilly white,
> All raunged in a ring, and dauncing in delight.

On the level of the virtues, this ideal state is realized in Calidore. His virtue, Courtesy, is best defined as the delight in virtuous action for its own sake. For him, such action is spontaneous, gracious, and natural. As the law to regenerate man is not imposed from without but arises from the heart, virtue becomes a state of being, the expression of what is fitting to human nature. Inevitably, Calidore's world becomes a romance in which the happy dream of pastoral innocence is realized in his discovery of Pastorella.

The Mutability Cantos become a fitting climax to the whole poem by presenting the cosmic stage on which its various quests are acted. Mutability displays her power throughout creation and her power in time. Yet at the end Nature affirms that time is redemptive: in the cyclical nature of continual change, mutable things seek their perfection. The poem's matter is testimony to Mutability's power: the endless adventures, the repeated quests, and the evil powers continually renewed. Yet the poem's structure supports Nature's testimony: the pattern of the quest separates the downward path from one that leads upward toward man's perfection. In this way the Mutability Cantos, and thus the whole poem, return to the vertical perspective of Book I.

A. C. HAMILTON
University of Washington

A General Note on the Text

The overall textual policy for the Signet Classic Poetry series attempts to strike a balance between the convenience and dependability of total modernization, on the one hand, and the authenticity of an established text on the other. Starting with the Restoration and Augustan poets, the General Editor has set up the following guidelines for the individual editors:

Modern American spelling will be used, although punctuation may be adjusted by the editor of each volume when he finds it advisable. In any case, syllabic final "ed" will be rendered with grave accent to distinguish it from the silent one, which is written out without apostrophe (e.g., "to gild refinèd gold," but "asked" rather than "ask'd"). Archaic words and forms are to be kept, naturally, whenever the meter or the sense may require it.

In the case of poets from earlier periods, the text is more clearly a matter of the individual editor's choice, and the type and degree of modernization has been left to his decision. But in any event, archaic typographical conventions ("i," "j," "u," "v," etc.) have all been normalized in the modern way.

JOHN HOLLANDER

A Note on this Edition

For the text of Spenser's poetry, I keep closely to the first editions, except for the selections from the first three books of *The Faerie Queene* which are based on the second edition in 1596. However, I have silently emended the text both where a later edition provides a preferable reading and where there seems to be an obvious misprint or error in the original. I have adopted modern printer's conventions for "i," "u," "j," and ampersand. The text for the selections from *The Shepheardes Calender* and *Epithalamion* is based with permission on photostats of first editions of the poems in the Huntington Library. Selections from *The Faerie Queene* are based on the copy of the 1596 edition in the University of Washington Library. I am indebted to Robert D. Monroe, Curator of Rare Books at the University of Washington Library, for his courteous assistance.

—A. C. HAMILTON

Chronology

1552	Probable date of his birth in London.
1561	Enters the newly founded Merchant Taylors' School.
1569	Publication of Van der Noodt's *Theatre of Voluptuous Worldlings,* containing verse translations by Spenser.
1569	Proceeds to Pembroke Hall, Cambridge, where he is a *sizar,* or impecunious student.
1572	B.A. degree.
1576	M.A. degree.
1577	Possibly in Ireland.
1578	Secretary to the Bishop of Rochester in Kent.
1579	Publication of *The Shepheardes Calender.* Servant of the Earl of Leicester in London; associated with Sidney, Dyer, and Gabriel Harvey. Marriage to Machabyas Chylde.
1580	Publication of *Three Proper, and Wittie, Familiar Letters,* his correspondence with Harvey.
1580	Secretary to Lord Grey, Lord Deputy of Ireland. Living in Dublin, and later present at the massacre of Irish soldiers at Smerwick.
1582	Lease of New Abbey, County Kildare, where he is a county commissioner.
1584–88	Deputy to Lodowick Bryskett.
1588	Occupies Kilcolman Castle and its estate.
1589	Returns to England with Sir Walter Raleigh.
1590	Publication of the first three books of *The Faerie Queene*. Returns to Ireland.

1591   Publication of *Complaints* and *Daphnaida*.

1595   Publication of *Colin Clouts Come Home
          Again* (probably written in 1591), *Amoretti*
          and *Epithalamion* (to celebrate his marriage
          to Elizabeth Boyle).

1596   Publication of *The Faerie Queene,* Books I to
          VI; *Fowre Hymnes; and Prothalamion.* In En-
          gland during part of the year.

1598   Entry of his prose tract, *Vewe of the Present
          State of Irelande,* published in 1633.

1599   An Irish insurrection causes Spenser's flight to
          England where he dies, "for lack of bread"
          according to Jonson, though he received a pen-
          sion from the Queen. Buried in Westminster
          Abbey.

1609   Publication of *The Faerie Queene* together
          with the two *Cantos of Mutabilitie.*

Selected Bibliography

Editions of the Works

The Complete Poetical Works of Spenser. R. E. Neil Dodge (ed.). Cambridge Edition, 1908.

The Poetical Works of Edmund Spenser. J. C. Smith and E. de Selincourt (eds.). London: Oxford University Press, 1909–10. Reprinted by Oxford in paperback in 1960.

A Variorum Edition of The Works of Edmund Spenser. E. Greenlaw, C. G. Osgood, F. M. Padelford, et al. (eds.). 9 vols. Baltimore: Johns Hopkins University Press, 1932–1949; London: Oxford University Press, 1950.

Bibliographies

Atkinson, Dorothy R. *Edmund Spenser: A Bibliographical Supplement*. Baltimore: Johns Hopkins University Press; London: Oxford University Press, 1937. A supplement to Carpenter, covering the period from 1923 to 1937.

Carpenter, Frederic Ives. *A Reference Guide to Edmund Spenser*. Chicago: University of Chicago Press, 1923. Gloucester, Mass.: Peter Smith, National Bibliophile Service, 1950. The standard bibliography up to 1923.

McNeir, Waldo F., and Foster Provost. *Annotated Bibliography of Edmund Spenser, 1937–1960*. Duquesne

Studies, Philological Series 3. Pittsburgh: Duquesne University Press, 1962.

Criticism

Arthos, John. *On the Poetry of Spenser and the Form of Romances.* New York: The Macmillan Company; London: George Allen & Unwin, Ltd., 1956.

Bennett, J. W. *The Evolution of "The Faerie Queene."* Chicago: University of Chicago Press, 1942; New York: Burt Franklin, 1960.

Berger, Harry. *The Allegorical Temper, Vision and Reality in Book II of Spenser's "Faerie Queene."* New Haven, Conn.: Yale University Press; London: Oxford University Press, 1957.

Bradner, L. *Edmund Spenser and "The Faerie Queene."* Chicago: University of Chicago Press; London: Cambridge University Press, 1948.

Davis, B. E. C. *Edmund Spenser: A Critical Study.* New York: The Macmillan Company; London: Cambridge University Press, 1933.

Fowler, Alastair. *Spenser and the Numbers of Time.* London: Routledge & Kegan Paul, Ltd., 1964.

Freeman, Rosemary. *Edmund Spenser.* British Council, Writers and Their Work, No. 89, London, 1957. Revised edition, 1962.

Hamilton, A. C. *The Structure of Allegory in "The Faerie Queene."* New York and London: Oxford University Press, 1961.

Hough, Graham G. *A Preface to "The Faerie Queene."* London: Gerald Duckworth & Co., Ltd., 1962; New York: W. W. Norton & Company, Inc., 1963.

Jones, H. S. V. *A Spenser Handbook.* New York: F. S. Crofts and Co., 1930; London: George Bell & Sons, Ltd., 1947.

Lewis, C. S. *The Allegory of Love: A Study in Medieval Tradition.* New York and London: Oxford University Press, 1936.

Mueller, W. R., and D. C. Allen (eds.). *"That Soveraine Light": Essays in Honor of Edmund Spenser, 1552–*

1952. Baltimore: Johns Hopkins University Press; London: Oxford University Press, 1953.

Nelson, William (ed.). *Form and Convention in the Poetry of Edmund Spenser.* English Institute Essays. New York: Columbia University Press, 1961.

Nelson, William. *The Poetry of Edmund Spenser: A Study.* New York: Columbia University Press, 1963.

Parker, M. Pauline. *The Allegory of "The Faerie Queene."* London: Oxford University Press, 1960.

Renwick, W. L. *Edmund Spenser: An Essay on Renaissance Poetry.* London: Longmans, Green & Co., Ltd., 1925.

Roche, Thomas P. *The Kindly Flame: A Study of the Third and Fourth Books of Spenser's "Faerie Queene."* Princeton, N. J.: Princeton University Press, 1964.

Spens, Janet. *Spenser's "Faerie Queene": An Interpretation.* London: Edward Arnold & Co., 1934.

Whitaker, Virgil K. *The Religious Basis of Spenser's Thought.* Stanford, Calif.: Stanford University Press; London: Oxford University Press, 1950.

THE SHEPHEARDES CALENDER

Conteyning twelve Æglogues proportionable to the twelve monethes, 1579.

Januarye. Ægloga prima.

ARGUMENT.

In this fyrst Æglogue Colin cloute *a shepheardes boy complaineth him of his unfortunate love, being but newly* (*as semeth*) *enamoured of a countrie lasse called* Rosalinde: *with which strong affection being very sore traveled,° he compareth his carefull case° to the sadde season of the yeare, to the frostie ground, to the frosen trees, and to his owne winterbeaten flocke. And lastlye, fynding himselfe robbed of all former pleasaunce and delights, hee breaketh his Pipe in peeces, and casteth him selfe to the ground.*

COLIN CLOUTE.

A shepeheards boys (no better doe him call)
When Winters wastful° spight was almost spent,
All in a sunneshine day, as did befall,
Led forth his flock, that had bene long ypent.°
So faynt they woxe,° and feeble in the folde,   5
That now unnethes their feete could them uphold.

Arg. **traveled** travailed.   Arg. **his carefull case** his state being full of care.   2 **wastful** causing desolation.   4 **ypent** pent, shut in. 5 **woxe** grew.

All as the Sheepe, such was the shepeheards looke,
For pale and wanne he was, (alas the while,)
May seeme he lovd, or els some care he tooke:°
10 Well couth he tune his pipe, and frame his stile.°
Tho° to a hill his faynting flocke he ledde,
And thus him playnd,° the while his shepe there fedde.

Ye Gods of love, that pitie lovers payne,
(If any gods the paine of lovers pitie:)
15 Looke from above, where you in joyes remaine,
And bowe your eares unto my dolefull dittie.
And *Pan* thou shepheards God, that once didst love,
Pitie the paines, that thou thy selfe didst prove.

Thou barrein ground, whome winters wrath hath
       wasted,
20 Art made a myrrhour, to behold my plight:
Whilome° thy fresh spring flowrd, and after hasted
Thy sommer prowde with Daffadillies dight.°
And now is come thy wynters stormy state,
Thy mantle mard, wherein thou maskedst late.

25 Such rage as winters, reigneth in my heart,
My life bloud friesing with unkindly° cold:
Such stormy stoures do breede my balefull smart,
As if my yeare were wast, and woxen old.
And yet alas, but now my spring begonne,
30 And yet alas, yt is already donne.

You naked trees, whose shady leaves are lost,
Wherein the byrds were wont to build their bowre:
And now are clothd with mosse and hoary frost,
Instede of bloosmes, wherwith your buds did flowre:
35 I see your teares, that from your boughes doe raine,
Whose drops in drery ysicles remaine.

9 **tooke** was affected by.   10 **frame his stile** shape his composition,
i.e., compose.   11 **Tho** then.   12 **playnd** complained, lamented.
21 **Whilome** once.   22 **dight** adorned.   26 **unkindly** unnatural.

All so my lustfull° leafe is dry and sere,
My timely° buds with wayling all are wasted:
The blossome, which my braunch of youth did beare,
With breathed sighes is blowne away, and blasted, 40
And from mine eyes the drizling teares descend,
As on your boughes the ysicles depend.°

Thou feeble flocke, whose fleece is rough and rent,
Whose knees are weake through fast and evill fare:
Mayst witnesse well by thy ill governement,° 45
Thy maysters mind is overcome with care.
Thou weake, I wanne: thou leane, I quite forlorne:
With mourning pyne I, you with pyning mourne.

A thousand sithes I curse that carefull hower,
Wherein I longd the neighbour towne to see: 50
And eke tenne thousand sithes I blesse the stoure,°
Wherein I sawe so fayre a sight, as shee.
Yet all for naught: such sight hath bred my bane.
Ah God, that love should breede both joy and payne.

It is not *Hobbinol*, wherefore I plaine, 55
Albee my love he seeke with dayly suit:
His clownish gifts and curtsies° I disdaine,
His kiddes, his cracknelles,° and his early fruit.
Ah foolish *Hobbinol*, thy gyfts bene vayne:
Colin them gives to *Rosalind* againe. 60

I love thilke° lasse, (alas why doe I love?)
And am forlorne, (alas why am I lorne?)
Shee deignes not° my good will, but doth reprove,
And of my rurall musick holdeth scorne.
Shepheards devise° she hateth as the snake, 65
And laughes the songes, that *Colin Clout* doth make.
Wherefore my pype, albee° rude *Pan* thou please,

37 **lustfull** lusty, vigorous.   38 **timely** seasonable.   42 **depend** hang.
45 **by thy ill governement** by being ill governed.   51 **stoure** occasion.   57 **curtsies** courtesies.   58 **cracknelles** biscuits.   61 **thilke** this.
63 **deignes not** does not condescend to accept.   65 **devise** invention.   67 **albee** although.

Yet for thou pleasest not, where most I would:
And thou unlucky Muse, that wontst to ease
70 My musing mynd, yet canst not, when thou should:
Both pype and Muse, shall sore the while abye.°
So broke his oaten pype, and downe dyd lye.

By that, the welked *Phœbus*° gan° availe,
His weary waine,° and nowe the frosty *Night*
75 Her mantle black through heaven gan overhaile.
Which seene, the pensife boy halfe in despight
Arose, and homeward drove his sonned sheepe,
Whose hanging heads did seeme his carefull case to
weepe.

COLINS EMBLEME.
Anchôra speme.

GLOSSE

Colin Cloute is a name not greatly used, and yet have I sene a Poesie
of M. Skeltons under that title. But indeede the word Colin is
Frenche, and used of the French Poete Marot (if he be worthy of
the name of a Poete) in a certein Æglogue. Under which name
this Poete secretly shadoweth himself, as sometime did Virgil
under the name of Tityrus, thinking it much fittr, then such
Latine names, for the great unlikelyhoode of the language.
6 *unnethes* scarcely.   10 *couthe* commeth of the verbe Conne, that
is, to know or to have skill. As well interpreteth the same the worthy
Sir Tho. Smith in his booke of government: wherof I have a perfect
copie in wryting, lent me by his kinseman, and my verye singular
good freend, M. Gabriel Harvey: as also of some other his most
grave and excellent wrytings.   37 *Sere* withered.   49 *Sythe* time.
50 *Neighbour towne* the next towne: expressing the Latine Vicina.
51 *Stoure* a fitt.   57 *His clownish gyfts* imitateth Virgils verse,
Rusticus es Corydon, nec munera curat Alexis.   59 *Hobbinol* is a
fained country name, whereby, it being so commune and usuall,
seemeth to be hidden the person of some his very speciall and most
familiar freend, whom he entirely and extraordinarily beloved, as
peradventure shall be more largely declared hereafter. In thys place
seemeth to be some savour of disorderly love, which the learned call
pæderastice: but it is gathered beside his meaning. For who that hath
red Plato his dialogue called Alcybiades, Xenophon and Maximus
Tyrius of Socrates opinions, may easily perceive, that such love is
muche to be alowed and liked of, specially so meant, as Socrates

---

71 **shall . . . abye** shall sorely pay for the time that they failed him.
73 **the welked Phœbus** the setting sun.   73 **gan** did.   74 **waine**
wagon.

used it: who sayth, that in deede he loved Alcybiades extremely, yet not Alcybiades person, but hys soule, which is Alcybiades owne selfe. And so is pæderastice much to be præferred before gynerastice, that is the love whiche enflameth men with lust toward womankind. But yet let no man thinke, that herein I stand with Lucian or hys develish disciple Unico Aretino, in defence of execrable and horrible sinnes of forbidden and unlawful fleshlinesse. Whose abominable errour is fully confuted of Perionius, and others. 60 *Rosalinde* is also a feigned name, which being wel ordered, wil bewray the very name of hys love and mistresse, whom by that name he coulereth. So as Ovide shadoweth hys love under the name of Corynna, which of some is supposed to be Julia, themperor Augustus his daughter, and wyfe to Agryppa. So doth Aruntius Stella every where call his Lady Asteris and Janthis, albe it is wel knowen that her right name was Violantilla: as witnesseth Statius in his Epithalamium. And so the famous Paragone of Italy, Madonna Cœlia in her letters envelopeth her selfe under the name of Zima: and Petrona under the name of Bellochia. And this generally hath bene a common custome of counterfeicting the names of secret Personages. 61 *I love* a prety Epanorthosis in these two verses, and withall a Parono-masia or playing with the word, where he sayth (I love thilke lasse (alas etc. 73 *Avail* bring downe. 75 *Overhaile* drawe over.

Embleme.

His Embleme or Poesye is here under added in Italian, Anchóra speme: the meaning wherof is, that notwithstande his extreme passion and lucklesse love, yet leaning on hope, he is some what recomforted.

THE SHEPHEARDES CALENDER

October. Ægloga decima.

ARGUMENT.

In Cuddie is set out the perfecte paterne of a Poete, whiche finding no maintenance of his state and stud-ies, complayneth of the contempte of Poetrie, and the causes thereof: Specially having bene in all ages, and even amongst the most barbarous alwayes of singular accounpt and honor, and being indede so worthy and commendable an arte: or rather no arte, but a divine

*gift and heavenly instinct not to bee gotten by laboure
and learning, but adorned with both: and poured into
the witte by a certaine ἐνθουσιασμὸς, and celestiall inspiration, as the Author hereof els where at large discourseth, in his booke called the English Poete, which
booke being lately come to my hands, I mynde also by
Gods grace upon further advisement to publish.*

PIERCE.   CUDDIE.

Cuddie, for shame hold up thy heavye head,
And let us cast° with what delight to chace:
And weary thys long lingring *Phœbus* race.
Whilome thou wont° the shepheards laddes to leade,
5   In rymes, in ridles, and in bydding base:°
Now they in thee, and thou in sleepe art dead.

CUDDYE.

Piers, I have pyped erst so long with payne,
That all mine Oten reedes bene rent and wore:
And my poore Muse hath spent her spared store,
10 Yet little good hath got, and much lesse gayne.
Such pleasaunce makes the Grashopper so poore,
And ligge so layd, when Winter doth her straine:°

The dapper ditties, that I wont devise,
To feede youthes fancie, and the flocking fry,
15 Delighten much: what I the bett for thy?°
They han° the pleasure, I a sclender prise.
I beate the bush, the byrds to them doe flye:
What good thereof to Cuddie can arise?

PIERS.

Cuddie, the prayse is better, then the price,
20 The glory eke much greater then the gayne:
O what an honor is it, to restraine
The lust of lawlesse youth with good advice:

2 **cast** contrive.   4 **wont** used.   5 **bydding base** the game of prisoner's base.   12 **straine** constrain.   15 **what . . . thy** what am I the
better for that?   16 **han** have.

Or pricke them forth with pleasaunce of thy vaine,°
Whereto thou list their trayned willes entice.°

Soone as thou gynst to sette thy notes in frame,°   25
O how the rurall routes to thee doe cleave:
Seemeth thou dost their soule of sence bereave,
All as° the shepheard, that did fetch his dame
From *Plutoes* balefull bowre withouten leave:
His musicks might the hellish hound did tame.   30

CUDDIE.

So praysen babes the Peacoks spotted traine,
And wondren at bright *Argus* blazing eye:
But who rewards him ere the more for thy?°
Or feedes him once the fuller by a graine?
Sike° prayse is smoke, that sheddeth° in the skye,   35
Sike words bene wynd, and wasten soone in vayne.

PIERS.

Abandon then the base and viler° clowne,
Lyft up thy selfe out of the lowly dust:
And sing of bloody Mars, of wars, of giusts,
Turne thee to those, that weld° the awful° crowne,   40
To doubted° Knights, whose woundlesse armour rusts,
And helmes unbruzed wexen° dayly browne.

There may thy Muse display her fluttryng wing,
And stretch her selfe at large from East to West:
Whither thou list in fayre *Elisa* rest,   45
Or if thee please in bigger notes to sing,
Advaunce°the worthy whome shee loveth best,
That first the white beare to the stake did bring.

And when the stubborne° stroke of stronger stounds,°

23 **pricke . . . vaine** incite with the pleasure aroused by your talent
or "divine gift" (Argument).   24 **Whereto . . . entice** To whatever
you desire to entice their wills that are allured by your poetry.
25 **frame** order.   28 **All as** even as.   33 **ere . . . thy** ever the more
for that.   35 **Sike** such.   35 **sheddeth** is dispersed.   37 **viler** too
vile or mean.   40 **weld** wield.   40 **awful** awesome.   41 **doubted**
redoubted, dreaded.   42 **wexen** grow.   47 **Advaunce** extol.   49
stubborne hard.   49 **stounds** times of trial.

50 Has somewhat slackt the tenor° of thy string:
    Of love and lustihead° tho mayst thou sing,
    And carrol lowde, and leade the Myllers rownde,
    All° were *Elisa* one of thilke same ring.
    So mought° our *Cuddies* name to Heaven sownde.

                        CUDDYE.

55 Indeede the Romish *Tityrus,* I heare,
    Through his *Mecænas* left his Oaten reede,
    Whereon he earst had taught his flocks to feede,
    And laboured lands° to yield the timely eare,
    And eft° did sing of warres and deadly drede,
60 So as the Heavens did quake his verse to here.

    But ah *Mecænas* is yclad in claye,
    And great *Augustus* long ygoe is dead:
    And all the worthies liggen° wrapt in leade,
    That matter made for Poets on to play:
65 For ever, who in derring doe° were dreade,
    The loftie verse of hem was loved aye.

    But after vertue gan for age to stoupe,
    And mighty manhode brought a bedde° of ease:
    The vaunting Poets found nought worth a pease,°
70 To put in preace among the learned troupe.°
    Tho gan the streames of flowing wittes to cease,
    And sonnebright honour pend in shamefull coupe.

    And if that any buddes of Poesie,
    Yet of the old stocke gan to shoote agayne,
75 Or° it mens follies mote be forst to fayne,
    And rolle with rest in rymes of rybaudrye.
    Or as it sprong, it wither must agayne:
    Tom Piper makes us better melodie.

---

50 **slackt the tenor** lowered the pitch.   51 **lustihead** lustiness.
53 **All** although.   54 **mought** might.   58 **laboured lands** lands being labored.   59 **eft** afterward.   63 **liggen** lie.   65 **derring doe**
daring action.   68 **a bedde** to bed.   69 **pease** pea.   70 **To put . . .
troupe** To present among the throng of poets before the Muses.
Cf. the prologue to *The Faerie Queene,* Book I: "To blazon broad
emongst her learned throng."   75 **Or** either.

PIERS.

O pierlesse Poesye, where is then the place?
If nor in Princes pallace thou doe sitt: 80
(And yet is Princes pallace the most fitt)
Ne brest of baser birth doth thee embrace.
Then make thee winges of thine aspyring wit,
And, whence thou camst, flye backe to heaven apace.

CUDDIE.

Ah *Percy* it is all to weake and wanne,
So high to sore, and make so large a flight: 85
Her peeced pyneons bene not so in plight,°
For *Colin* fittes such famous flight to scanne:°
He, were he not with love so ill bedight,°
Would mount as high, and sing as soote as Swanne.

90

PIERS.

Ah fon,° for love does teach him climbe so hie,
And lyftes him up out of the loathsome myre:
Such immortall mirrhor, as he doth admire,
Would rayse ones mynd above the starry skie.
And cause a caytive corage to aspire,   95
For lofty love doth loath a lowly eye.

[CUDDIE.]

All otherwise the state of Poet stands,
For lordly love is such a Tyranne fell:
That where he rules, all power he doth expell.
The vaunted verse a vacant head demaundes.   100
Ne wont with crabbed care the Muses dwell,
Unwisely weaves, that takes two webbes in hand.

Who ever casts to compasse° weightye prise,
And thinks to throwe out thondring words of threate:
Let powre in lavish cups and thriftie° bitts of meate,   105
For *Bacchus* fruite is frend to *Phœbus* wise.
And when with Wine the braine begins to sweate,
The nombers flowe as fast as spring doth ryse.

87 **plight** condition. 88 **scanne** attempt. 89 **bedight** arrayed.
91 **fon** fool. 103 **compasse** attain. 105 **thriftie** abundant.

Thou kenst not *Percie* howe the ryme should rage.
110 O if my temples were distaind° with wine,
And girt in girlonds of wild Yvie twine,
How I could reare the Muse on stately stage,
And teache her tread aloft in buskin fine,
With queint *Bellona* in her equipage.

115 But ah my corage cooles ere it be warme,
For thy,° content us in thys humble shade:
Where no such troublous tydes han us assayde,°
Here we our slender pipes may safely charme.

PIERS.

And when my Gates shall han their bellies layd:°
120 *Cuddie* shall have a Kidde to store his farme.

Cuddies Embleme.
Agitante calescimus illo etc.

GLOSSE

This Æglogue is made in imitation of Theocritus his xvi. Idilion,
   wherein hee reproved the Tyranne Hiero of Syracuse for his
   nigardise towarde Poetes, in whome is the power to make men
   immortal for theyr good dedes, or shameful for their naughty lyfe.
   And the lyke also is in Mantuane, The style hereof as also that in
   Theocritus, is more loftye then the rest, and applyed to the
   heighte of Poeticall witte.
1 *Cuddie* I doubte whether by Cuddie be specified the authour selfe,
or some other. For in the eyght Æglogue the same person was
brought in, singing a Cantion of Colins making, as he sayth. So that
some doubt, that the persons be different. 4 *Whilome* sometime.
8 *Oaten reedes* Avena. 12 *Ligge so layde* lye so faynt and unlustye.
13 *Dapper* pretye. 14 *Frye* is a bold Metaphore, forced from the
spawning fishes. For the multitude of young fish be called the frye.
21 *To restraine* This place seemeth to conspyre with Plato, who in
his first booke de Legibus sayth, that the first invention of Poetry
was of very vertuous intent. For at what time an infinite number
of youth usually came to theyr great solemne feastes called Pane-
gyrica, which they used every five yeere to hold, some learned man
being more hable then the rest, for speciall gyftes of wytte and
Musicke, would take upon him to sing fine verses to the people,
in prayse eyther of vertue or of victory or of immortality or such

110 **distaind** stained.   116 **For thy** therefore.   117 **han us assayde**
have assailed us.   119 **han their bellies layd** shall have reduced the
swelling of their bellies, i.e., delivered of their young.

like. At whose wonderful gyft al men being astonied and as it were ravished, with delight, thinking (as it was indeed) that he was inspired from above, called him vatem: which kinde of men afterwarde framing their verses to lighter musick (as of musick be many kinds, some sadder, some lighter, some martiall, some heroical: and so diversely eke affect the mynds of men) found out lighter matter of Poesie also, some playing wyth love, some scorning at mens fashions, some powred out in pleasures, and so were called Poetes or makers.   27 *Sence bereave* what the secrete working of Musick is in the myndes of men, aswell appeareth hereby, that some of the auncient Philosophers, and those the moste wise, as Plato and Pythagoras held for opinion, that the mynd was made of a certaine harmonie and musicall nombers, for the great compassion and likenes of affection in thone and in the other as also by that memorable history of Alexander: to whom when as Timotheus the great Musitian playd the Phrygian melodie, it is said, that he was distraught with such unwonted fury, that streight way rysing from the table in great rage, he caused himselfe to be armed, as ready to goe to warre (for that musick is very war like:) And immediatly whenas the Musitian chaunged his stroke into the Lydian and Ionique harmony, he was so furr from warring, that he sat as styl, as if he had bene in matters of counsell. Such might is in musick. Wherefore Plato and Aristotle forbid the Arabian Melodie from children and youth. For that being altogither on the fyft and vii, tone, it is of great force to molifie and quench the kindly courage, which useth to burne in yong brests. So that it is not incredible which the Poete here sayth, that Musick can bereave the soule of sence.   28 *The shepheard that* Orpheus: of whom is sayd, that by his excellent skil in Musick and Poetry, he recovered his wife Eurydice from hell.   32 *Argus eyes* of Argus is before said, that Juno to him committed hir husband Jupiter his Paragon Iô, bicause he had an hundred eyes: but afterwarde Mercury wyth hys Musick lulling Argus aslepe, slew him and brought Iô away, whose eyes it is sayd that Juno for his eternall memory placed in her byrd the Peacocks tayle. For those coloured spots indeede resemble eyes. 41 *Woundlesse armour* unwounded in warre, doe rust through long peace.   43 *Display* A poeticall metaphore: whereof the meaning is, that if the Poet list showe his skill in matter of more dignitie, then is the homely Æglogue, good occasion is him offered of higher veyne and more Heroicall argument, in the person of our most gratious soveraign, whom (as before) he calleth Elisa. Or if mater of knighthoode and chevalrie please him better, that there be many Noble and valiaunt men, that are both worthy of his payne in theyr deserved prayses, and also favourers of hys skil and faculty.   47 *The worthy* he meaneth (as I guesse) the most honorable and renowmed the Erle of Leycester, whom by his cognisance (although the same be also proper to other) rather then by his name he bewrayeth, being not likely, that the names of noble princes be known to country clowne.   50 *Slack* that is when thou chaungest thy verse from stately discourse, to matter of more pleasaunce and delight.   52 *The Millers* a kind of daunce.   53 *Ring* company of dauncers.   55 *The Romish Tityrus* wel knowen to be Virgile, who by Mecænas means was brought into the favour of the Emperor Augustus, and by him moved to write in loftier kinde, then he erst had doen.   57 *Whereon* in these three verses are the three severall workes of Virgile intended. For in teaching his flocks to feede, is meant his Æglogues.

In labouring of lands, is hys Bucoliques. In singing of wars and deadly dreade, is his divine Æneis figured. 65 *For ever* He sheweth the cause, why Poetes were wont be had in such honor of noble men; that is, that by them their worthines and valor shold through theyr famous Posies be commended to al posterities. Wherfore it is sayd, that Achilles had never bene so famous, as he is, but for Homeres immortal verses. which is the only advantage, which he had of Hector. And also that Alexander the great comming to his tombe in Sigeus, with naturall teares blessed him, that ever was his hap to be honoured with so excellent a Poets work: as so renowned and ennobled onely by hys meanes. Which being declared in a most eloquent Oration of Tullies, is of Petrarch no lesse worthely sette forth in a sonet

> Giunto Alexandro a la famosa tomba
> Del fero Achille sospírando disse
> O fortunato che si chiara tromba.   Trovasti etc.

And that such account hath bene alwayes made of Poetes, aswell sheweth this that the worthy Scipio in all his warres against Carthage and Numantia had evermore in his company, and that in a most familiar sort the good olde Poet Ennius: as also that Alexander destroying Thebes, when he was enformed that the famous Lyrick Poet Pindarus was borne in that citie, not onely commaunded streightly, that no man should upon payne of death do any violence to that house by fire or otherwise: but also specially spared most, and some highly rewarded, that were of hys kinne. So favoured he the only name of a Poete. Whych prayse otherwise was in the same man no lesse famous, that when he came to ransacking of king Darius coffers, whom he lately had overthrowen, he founde in a little coffer of silver the two bookes of Homers works, as layd up there for speciall jewells and richesse, which he taking thence, put one of them dayly in his bosome, and thother every night layde under his pillowe. Such honor have Poetes alwayes found in the sight of princes and noble men. Which this autor here very well sheweth, as els where more notably. 65 *In derring doe* In manhoode and chevalrie. 67 *But after* he sheweth the cause of contempt of Poetry to be idlenesse and basenesse of mynd. 72 *Pent* shut up in slouth, as in a coope or cage. 78 *Tom Piper* An Ironicall Sarcasmus, spoken in derision of these rude wits, whych make more account of a ryming rybaud, then of skill grounded upon learning and judgment. 82 *Ne brest* the meaner sort of men. 87 *Her peeced pineons* unperfect skil. Spoken wyth humble modestie. 90 *As soote as Swanne* The comparison seemeth to be strange: for the swanne hath ever wonne small commendation for her swete singing: but it is sayd of the learned that the swan a little before hir death, singeth most pleasantly, as prophecying by a secrete instinct her neere destinie. As well sayth the Poete elswhere in one of his sonetts.

> The silver swanne doth sing before her dying day
> As shee that feeles the deepe delight that is in death etc.

93 *Immortall myrrhour* Beauty, which is an excellent object of Poeticall spirites, as appeareth by the worthy Petrarchs saying.

Fiorir faceva il mio debile ingegno
A la sua ombra, et crescer ne gli affanni.

95 *A caytive corage* a base and abject minde. 96 *For lofty love*
I think this playing with the letter to be rather a fault then a figure, aswel in our English tongue, as it hath bene alwayes in the
Latine, called Cacozelon.   100 *A vacant* imitateth Mantuanes saying. vacuum curis divína cerebrum Poscit.   105 *Lavish cups* Resembleth that comen verse Fæcundi calices quem non fecere diser-
tum.   110 *O if my* He seemeth here to be ravished with a Poetical
furie. For (if one rightly mark) the numbers rise so ful, and the
verse groweth so big, that it seemeth he hath forgot the meanenesse
of shepheards state and stile. 111 *Wild yvie* for it is dedicated to
Bacchus and therefore it is sayd that the Mænades (that is Bacchus
franticke priestes) used in theyr sacrifice to carry Thyrsos, which
were pointed staves or Javelins, wrapped about with yvie.   113 *In
buskin* it was the maner of Poetes and plaiers in tragedies to were
buskins, as also in Comedies to use stockes and light shoes. So that
the buskin in Poetry is used for tragical matter, as it said in Virgile.
Sola sophocleo tua carmina digna cothurno. And the like in Horace,
Magnum loqui, nitique cothurno.   114 *Queint* strange Bellona; the
goddesse of battaile, that is Pallas, which may therefore wel be
called queint for that (as Lucian saith) when Jupiter hir father was
in traveile of her, he caused his sonne Vulcane with his axe to hew
his head. Out of which leaped forth lustely a valiant damsell armed
at all poyntes, whom Vulcane seeing so faire and comely, lightly
leaping to her, proferred her some cortesie, which the Lady dis-
deigning, shaked her speare at him, and threatned his saucinesse.
Therefore such straungenesse is well applyed to her.   114 *Æquipage*
order.   117 *Tydes* seasons.   118 *Charme* temper and order. For
Charmes were wont to be made by verses as Ovid sayth. Aut si
carminibus.

Embleme.

Hereby is meant, as also in the whole course of this Æglogue, that
Poetry is a divine instinct and unnatural rage passing the reache
of comen reason. Whom Piers answereth Epiphonematicos as admiring the excellencye of the skyll whereof in Cuddie hee hadde
alreadye hadde a taste.

THE SHEPHEARDES CALENDER

December. Ægloga Duodecima.

ARGUMENT.

*This Æglogue (even as the first beganne) is ended
with a complaynte of Colin to God Pan, wherein as
weary of his former wayes, he proportioneth his life
to the foure seasons of the yeare, comparing hys
youthe to the spring time, when he was fresh and free
from loves follye. His manhoode to the sommer, which
he sayth, was consumed with greate heate and excessive drouth caused throughe a Comet or blasinge
starre, by which hee meaneth love, which passion is
comenly compared to such flames and immoderate
heate. His riper yeares hee resembleth to an unseason-
able harveste wherein the fruites fall ere they be rype.
His latter age to winters chyll and frostie season, now
drawing neare to his last ende.*

The gentle shepheard satte beside a springe,
All in the shadowe of a bushye brere,
That *Colin* hight,° which wel could pype and singe,
For he of *Tityrus* his songs did lere.°
5   There as he satte in secreate shade alone,
     Thus gan he make of love his piteous mone.

O soveraigne *Pan* thou God of shepheards all,
Which of our tender Lambkins takest keepe:°
And when our flocks into mischaunce mought fall,
10   Doest save from mischiefe the unwary sheepe:
     Als° of their maisters hast no lesse regarde,

---

3 **hight** was called.   4 **lere** learn.   8 **keepe** care.   11 **Als** also.

Then° of the flocks, which thou doest watch and
    ward:°

I thee beseche (so be° thou deigne to heare,
Rude ditties tund to shepheards Oaten reede,
Or if I ever sonet song so cleare,   15
As it with pleasaunce mought thy fancie feede)
    Hearken awhile from thy greene cabinet,°
    The rurall song of carefull Colinet.

Whilome in youth, when flowrd my joyfull spring,
Like Swallow swift I wandred here and there: 20
For heate of heedlesse lust° me so did sting,
That I of doubted° daunger had no feare.
    I went° the wastefull° woodes and forest wyde,
    Withouten dreade of Wolves to bene espyed.

I wont° to raunge amydde the mazie thickette,   25
And gather nuttes to make me Christmas game:
And joyed oft to chace the trembling Pricket,°
Or hunt the hartlesse° hare, til shee were tame.
    What wreaked° I of wintrye ages waste,
    Tho deemed I, my spring would ever laste.   30

How often have I scaled the craggie Oke,
All to dislodge the Raven of her neste:
Howe have I wearied with many a stroke,
The stately Walnut tree, the while the rest
    Under the tree fell all for nuts at strife: 35
    For ylike° to me was libertee and lyfe.

And for I was in thilke° same looser yeares,
(Whether the Muse, so wrought me from my birth,
Or I tomuch beleeved my shepherd peres)
Somedele ybent° to song and musicks mirth.   40

12 **Then** than.   12 **watch and ward** keep continual lookout.   13 **so
be** if.   17 **cabinet** bower.   21 **lust** desire.   22 **doubted** dreaded.
23 **went** wended.   23 **wastefull** desolate.   25 **wont** was accustomed.
27 **Pricket** buck.   28 **hartlesse** timid.   29 **wreaked** recked, heeded.
36 **ylike** alike.   37 **thilke** those.   40 **Somedele ybent** somewhat inclined.

A good olde shephearde, *Wrenock* was his name,
Made me by arte more cunning in the same.

Fro thence I durst in derring doe° compare
With shepheards swayne, what ever fedde in field:
45 And if that *Hobbinol* right judgement bare,
To *Pan* his owne selfe pype° I neede not yield.
     For if the flocking Nymphes did folow *Pan,*
     The wiser Muses after *Colin* ranne.

But ah such pryde at length was ill repayde,
50 The shepheards God (perdie° God was he none)
My hurtlesse° pleasaunce did me ill upbraide,
My freedome lorne,° my life he lefte to mone.
     Love they him called, that gave me checkmate,
     But better mought they have behote° him Hate.

55 Tho gan my lovely Spring bid me farewel,
And Sommer season sped him to display
(For love then in the Lyons house did dwell)
The raging fyre, that kindled at his ray.
     A comett stird up that unkindly heate,
60   That reigned (as men sayd) in *Venus* seate.

Forth was I ledde, not as I wont afore,
When choise I had to choose my wandring waye:
But whether luck and loves unbridled lore°
Would leade me forth on Fancies bitte to playe.
65   The bush my bedde, the bramble was my bowre,
     The Woodes can witnesse many a wofull stowre.°

Where I was wont to seeke the honey Bee,
Working her formall rowmes in Wexen frame:
The grieslie Todestoole growne there mought I se
70 And loathed Paddocks lording on the same.

43 **derring doe** daring invention. 46 **To Pan . . . pype** to Pan's
own pipe. 50 **perdie** truly. 51 **My hurtlesse** for my harmless.
52 **lorne** lost. 54 **behote** called. 63 **lore** teaching. 66 **stowre**
time of affliction.

And where the chaunting birds luld me a sleepe,
The ghastlie Owle her grievous ynne doth keepe.

Then as the springe gives place to elder time,
And bringeth forth the fruite of sommers pryde:
All so my age now passed youngthly pryme,   75
To thinges of ryper reason self applyed.
    And learnd of lighter timber cotes to frame,
    Such as might save my sheepe and me fro shame.

To make fine cages for the Nightingale,
And Baskets of bulrushes was my wont: 80
Who to entrappe the fish in winding sale
Was better seene,° or hurtful beastes to hont?
    I learned als the signes of heaven to ken,°
    How *Phœbe* fayles, where *Venus* sittes and when.

And tryed° time yet taught me greater thinges,   85
The sodain rysing of the raging seas:
The soothe of byrds by beating of their wings,
The power of herbs, both which can hurt and ease:
    And which be wont t'enrage the restlesse sheepe,
    And which be wont to worke eternall sleepe.   90

But ah unwise and witlesse *Colin cloute,*
That kydst the hidden kinds of many a wede:
Yet kydst not ene° to cure thy sore hart roote,
Whose ranckling wound as yet does rifelye° bleede.
    Why livest thou stil, and yet hast thy deathes
        wound?   95
    Why dyest thou stil, and yet alive art founde?

Thus is my sommer worne away and wasted,
Thus is my harvest° hastened all to rathe:°
The eare that budded faire, is burnt and blasted,
And all my hoped gaine is turnd to scathe.   100

82 **seene** versed, skilled.   83 **ken** know.   85 **tryed** tested by experience.   93 **ene** any.   94 **rifelye** abundantly.   98 **harvest** autumn.
98 **to rathe** too early.

Of all the seede, that in my youth was sowne,
Was nought but brakes and brambles to be mowne.

My boughes with bloosmes that crowned were at
     firste,
And promised of timely fruite such store,
105 Are left both bare and barrein now at erst:°
The flattring fruite is fallen to grownd before,
     And rotted, ere they were halfe mellow ripe:
     My harvest wast,° my hope away dyd wipe.

The fragrant flowres, that in my garden grewe,
110 Bene withered, as they had bene gathered long.
Theyr rootes bene dryed up for lacke of dewe,
Yet dewed with teares they han be ever among.
     Ah who has wrought my *Rosalind* this spight
     To spil° the flowres, that should her girlond dight?

115 And I, that whilome wont to frame my pype,
Unto the shifting of the shepheards foote:
Sike follies nowe have gathered as too ripe,
And cast hem out, as rotten and unsoote.°
     The loser° Lasse I cast° to please nomore,
120 One if I please, enough is me° therefore.

And thus of all my harvest hope I have
Nought reaped but a weedye crop of care:
Which, when I thought have thresht in swelling
     sheave,
Cockel for corne, and chaffe for barley bare.
125 Soone as the chaffe should in the fan be fynd,°
     All was blowne away of the wavering wynd.

So now my yeare drawes to his latter terme,
My spring is spent, my sommer burnt up quite:
My harveste hasts to stirre up winter sterne,
130 And bids him clayme with rigorous rage hys right.

105 **at erst** already.   108 **wast** wasted.   114 **spil** spoil, destroy.
118 **unsoote** unsweet.   119 **loser** looser.   119 **cast** contrive.   120
me to me.   125 **fynd** refined.

So nowe he stormes with many a sturdy stoure,
So now his blustring blast eche coste doth scoure.

The carefull cold hath nypt my rugged rynde,
And in my face deepe furrowes eld hath pight:°
My head besprent with hoary frost I fynd,   *135*
And by myne eie the Crow his clawe dooth wright.
  Delight is layd abedde, and pleasure past,
  No sonne now shines, cloudes han all overcast.

Now leave ye shepheards boyes your merry glee,
My Muse is hoarse and weary of thys stounde:°   *140*
Here will I hang my pype upon this tree,
Was never pype of reede did better sounde.
  Winter is come, that blowes the bitter blaste,
  And after Winter dreerie death does hast.

Gather ye together my little flocke,   *145*
My little flock, that was to me so liefe:°
Let me, ah lette me in your folds ye lock,
Ere the breme Winter breede you greater griefe.
  Winter is come, that blowes the balefull° breath,
  And after Winter commeth timely death.   *150*

Adieu delightes, that lulled me asleepe,
Adieu my deare, whose love I bought so deare:
Adieu my little Lambes and loved sheepe,
Adieu ye Woodes that oft my witnesse were:
  Adieu good *Hobbinol,* that was so true,   *155*
  Tell *Rosalind,* her *Colin* bids her adieu.

          Colins Embleme.

                GLOSSE

4 *Tityrus* Chaucer: as hath bene oft sayd. 8 *Lambkins* young
lambes. 11 *Als of their* Semeth to express Virgils verse

134 **eld hath pight** age has placed. 140 **stounde** time of trial,
i.e., the effort to write the poem. 146 **liefe** dear. 149 **balefull**
injurious.

Pan curat oves oviumque magistros.

13 *Deigne* voutchsafe.   17–18 *Cabinet . . . Colinet* diminutives.
25 *Mazie* For they be like to a maze whence it is hard to get out
agayne.   39 *Peres* felowes and companions.   40 *Musick* that is
Poetry as Terence sayth Qui artem tractant musicam, speking of
Poetes.   43 *Derring doe* aforesayd.   57 *Lions house* He imagineth
simply that Cupid, which is love, had his abode in the whote signe
Leo, which is in middest of somer; a pretie allegory, whereof the
meaning is, that love in him wrought an extraordinarie heate of
lust.   58 *His ray* which is Cupides beame or flames of Love.   59 *A
Comete* a blasing starre, meant of beautie, which was the cause of
his whote love.   60 *Venus* the goddesse of beauty or pleasure. Also
a signe in heaven, as it is here taken. So he meaneth that beautie,
which hath alwayes aspect to Venus, was the cause of all his un-
quietnes in love.   67 *Where I was* a fine discription of the chaunge
of hys lyfe and liking; for all things nowe seemed to hym to have
altered their kindly course.   70 *Lording* Spoken after the maner
of Paddocks and Frogges sitting which is indeed Lordly, not re-
moving nor looking once a side, unlesse they be sturred.   73 *Then
as* The second part. That is his manhoode.   77 *Cotes* sheepecotes.
For such be the exercises of shepheards.   81 *Sale* or Salow a kind
of woodde like Wyllow, fit to wreath and bynde in leapes to catch
fish withall.   84 *Phœbe fayles* The Eclipse of the Moone, which is
alwayes in Cauda or Capite Draconis, signes in heaven.   84 *Venus*
Venus starre otherwise called Hesperus and Vesper and Lucifer,
both because he seemeth to be one of the brightest starres, and also
first ryseth and setteth last. All which skill in starres being convenient for shepheardes to knowe as Theocritus and the rest use.
86 *Raging seaes* The cause of the swelling and ebbing of the sea
commeth of the course of the Moone, sometime encreasing, sometime wayning and decreasing.   87 *Sooth of byrdes* A kind of sooth
saying used in elder tymes, which they gathered by the flying of
byrds; First (as is sayd) invented by the Thuscanes, and from them
derived to the Romanes, who (as is sayd in Livie) were so super-
sticiously rooted in the same, that they agreed that every Noble
man should put his sonne to the Thuscanes, by them to be brought
up in that knowledge.   88 *Of herbes* That wonderous thinges be
wrought by herbes, aswell appeareth by the common working of
them in our bodies, as also by the wonderful enchauntments and
sorceries that have bene wrought by them; insomuch that it is sayde
that Circe a famous sorceresse turned men into sondry kinds of
beastes and Monsters, and onely by herbes: as the Poete sayth Dea
sæva potentibus herbis etc.   92 *Kidst* knewest.   97–98 *Thus is my*
The thyrde parte wherein is set forth his ripe yeres as an untimely
harvest, that bringeth little fruite.   99 *Eare* of corne.   100 *Scathe*
losse hinderaunce.   109 *The fragraunt flowres* sundry studies and
laudable partes of learning, wherein how our Poete is seene, be they
witnesse which are privie to his study.   112 *Ever among* Ever and
anone.   127 *So now my yeere* The last part, wherein is described
his age by comparison of wyntrye stormes.   133 *Carefull cold* for
care is sayd to coole the blood.   135 *Hoary frost* A metaphore
of hoary heares scattred lyke to a gray frost.   139 *Glee* mirth.
148 *Breeme* sharpe and bitter.   151 *Adiew delights* is a conclusion
of all. Where in sixe verses he comprehendeth briefly all that was
touched in this booke. In the first verse his delights of youth gen-

erally. In the second, the love of Rosalind, in the thyrd, the keeping of sheepe, which is the argument of all Æglogues. In the fourth his complaints. And in the last two his professed frendship and good will to his good friend Hobbinoll.

Embleme.

The meaning wherof is that all thinges perish and come to theyr last end, but workes of learned wits and monuments of Poetry abide for ever. And therefore Horace of his Odes a work though ful indede of great wit and learning, yet of no so great weight and importaunce boldly sayth.

> Exegi monimentum ære perennius,
> Quod nec imber nec aquilo vorax etc.

Therefore let not be envied, that this Poete in his Epilogue sayth he hath made a Calendar, that shall endure as long as time etc. folowing the ensample of Horace and Ovid in the like.

> Grande opus exegi quae nec Iovis ira nec ignis,
> Nec ferum poterit nec edax abolere vetustas etc.

THE SHEPHEARDES CALENDER

Epilogue

Loe I have made a Calender for every yeare,
That steele in strength, and time in durance shall
    outweare:
And if I marked well the starres revolution,
  It shall continewe till the worlds dissolution.
To teach the ruder shepheard how to feede his sheepe,   5
And from the falsers fraud his folded° flocke to keepe.
  Goe lyttle Calender, thou hast a free passeporte,
Goe but a lowly gate° emongste the meaner sorte.°
Dare not to match thy pype with Tityrus hys° style,
    Nor with the Pilgrim° that the Ploughman playde
    a whyle: 10
But followe them farre off, and their high steppes
    adore,

6 **folded** shut in the fold. 8 **gate** manner. 8 **sorte** company.
9 **Tityrus hys** Chaucer's. 10 **the Pilgrim** Langland.

The better please, the worse despise,° I aske
nomore.

Merce non mercede.

EPITHALAMION

Ye learned sisters° which have oftentimes
Beene to me ayding,° others to adorne:
Whom ye thought worthy of your gracefull° rhymes,
That even the greatest did not greatly scorne
5 To heare theyr names sung in your simple layes,
But joyed° in theyr prayse.
And when ye list your owne mishaps to mourne,°
Which death, or love, or fortunes wreck did rayse,
Your string could soone to sadder tenor° turne,
10 And teach the woods and waters to lament
Your dolefull dreriment.°
Now lay those sorrowfull complaints aside,
And having all your heads with girland crownd,
Helpe me mine owne loves prayses to resound,
15 Ne let the same of any be envide:°
So Orpheus° did for his owne bride,
So I unto my selfe alone will sing,
The woods shall to me answer and my Eccho ring.

Early before the worlds light giving lampe,
20 His golden beame upon the hils doth spred,
Having disperst the nights unchearefull dampe,
Doe you awake, and with fresh lusty hed,°
Go to the bowre° of my beloved love,

12 **despise** cause to despise.
1 **sisters** the nine Muses who inspire poets. 2 **Beene . . . ayding**
helped me. 3 **gracefull** conferring favor. 6 **joyed** rejoiced.
7 **your . . . mourne** i.e., in Spenser's *Tears of the Muses.* 9 **tenor**
tone. 11 **dreriment** grief. 15 **envide** begrudged. 16 **Orpheus** see
note to IV.x.58. 22 **lusty hed** lustiness, vigor. 23 **bowre** bed-
chamber.

My truest turtle dove,
Bid her awake; for Hymen° is awake,   25
And long since ready forth his maske° to move,
With his bright Tead° that flames with many a flake,°
And many a bachelor to waite on him,
In theyr fresh garments trim.
Bid her awake therefore and soone her dight,°   30
For lo the wished day is come at last,
That shall for al the paynes and sorrowes past,
Pay to her usury of long delight,
And whylest she doth her dight,
Doe ye to her of joy and solace sing,   35
That all the woods may answer and your eccho ring.

Bring with you all the Nymphes that you can heare°
Both of the rivers and the forrests greene:
And of the sea that neighbours to her neare,
Al with gay girlands goodly wel beseene.°   40
And let them also with them bring in hand,
Another gay girland
For my fayre love of lillyes and of roses,
Bound truelove wize° with a blew silke riband.
And let them make great store of bridale poses,°   45
And let them eeke° bring store of other flowers
To deck the bridale bowers.
And let the ground whereas° her foot shall tread,
For feare the stones her tender foot should wrong
Be strewed with fragrant flowers all along,   50
And diapred lyke the discolored mead.°
Which done, doe at her chamber dore awayt,
For she will waken strayt,°
The whiles doe ye this song unto her sing,
The woods shall to you answer and your Eccho ring.   55

25 **Hymen** the god of marriage. 26 **his maske** the wedding pro-
cession. 27 **Tead** nuptial torch. 27 **flake** spark. 30 **her dight**
dress herself. 37 **that . . . heare** that can hear you. 40 **beseene**
appearing. 44 **truelove wize** a double-knot that is a symbol of
true love. 45 **poses** posies. 46 **eeke** also. 48 **whereas** where.
51 **diapred . . . mead** and ornately patterned like the variously colored meadow. 53 **strayt** at once.

Ye Nymphes of Mulla° which with carefull heed,
The silver scaly trouts doe tend full well,
And greedy pikes which use therein to feed,
(Those trouts and pikes all others doo excell)
60 And ye likewise which keepe the rushy lake,
Where none doo fishes take,
Bynd up the locks the which hang scatterd light,
And in his waters which your mirror make,
Behold your faces as the christall bright,
65 That when you come whereas my love doth lie,
No blemish she may spie.
And eke ye lightfoot mayds which keepe the deere,
That on the hoary mountayne use to towre,°
And the wylde wolves which seeke them to devoure,
70 With your steele darts doo chace from comming neer,
Be also present heere,
To helpe to decke her and to help to sing,
That all the woods may answer and your eccho ring.

Wake, now my love, awake; for it is time,
75 The Rosy Morne° long since left Tithones bed,
All ready to her silver coche to clyme,
And Phœbus° gins to shew his glorious hed.
Hark how the cheerefull birds do chaunt theyr laies
And carroll of loves praise.
80 The merry Larke hir mattins° sings aloft,
The thrush replyes, the Mavis° descant° playes,
The Ouzell° shrills, the Ruddock° warbles soft,
So goodly all agree with sweet consent,°
To this dayes merriment.
85 Ah my deere love why doe ye sleepe thus long,
When meeter were° that ye should now awake,
T'awayt the comming of your joyous make,°
And hearken to the birds lovelearned song,

56 **Mulla** the river Awbeg, in Ireland near Spenser's home. 68 **use**
to towre are accustomed to climb. 75 **the Rosy Morne** Aurora,
the goddess of dawn, married to the aged Tithonus, a mortal who
suffers eternal life without perpetual youth. 77 **Phœbus** the sun
god. 80 **mattins** morning song. 81 **Mavis** song-thrush. 81 **des-**
cant accompaniment. 82 **Ouzell** blackbird. 82 **Ruddock** robin.
83 **consent** harmony. 86 **meeter** **were** it were more fitting.
87 **make** mate.

The deawy leaves among.
For they of joy and pleasance to you sing,   90
That all the woods them answer and theyr eccho ring.

My love is now awake out of her dreame,
And her fayre eyes like stars that dimmed were
With darksome cloud, now shew theyr goodly beams
More bright then Hesperus° his head doth rere.   95
Come now ye damzels,° daughters of delight,
Helpe quickly her to dight,
But first come ye fayre houres which were begot
In Joves sweet paradice, of° Day and Night,
Which doe the seasons of the yeare allot,   100
And al that ever in this world is fayre
Doe make and still° repayre.
And ye three handmayds of the Cyprian Queene,°
The which doe still adorne her beauties pride,
Helpe to addorne my beautifullest bride   105
And as ye her array, still throw betweene
Some graces to be seene,
And as ye use to Venus, to her sing,
The whiles the woods shal answer and your eccho
     ring.

Now is my love all ready forth to come,   110
Let all the virgins therefore well awayt,
And ye fresh boyes that tend upon her groome
Prepare your selves; for he is comming strayt.
Set all your things in seemely good aray
Fit for so joyfull day,   115
The joyfulst day that ever sunne did see.
Faire Sun, shew forth thy favourable ray,
And let thy lifull° heat not fervent be
For feare of burning her sunshyny face,
Her beauty to disgrace.°   120
O fayrest Phœbus, father of the Muse,

95 **Hesperus** the evening star.   96 **damzels** bridesmaids.   99 **of** by.
102 **still** always.   103 **three . . . Queene** the three graces in the
service of Venus. See VI.x.21.   118 **lifull** life-giving.   120 **disgrace**
mar.

If ever I did honour thee aright,
Or sing the thing, that mote thy mind delight,
Doe not thy servants simple boone° refuse,
125 But let this day let this one day be myne,
Let all the rest be thine.
Then I thy soverayne prayses loud wil sing,
That all the woods shal answer and theyr eccho ring.

Harke how the Minstrels gin to shrill aloud
130 Their merry Musick that resounds from far,
The pipe, the tabor,° and the trembling Croud,°
That well agree withouten breach or jar.°
But most of all the Damzels doe delite,
When they their tymbrels° smyte,
135 And thereunto doe daunce and carrol sweet,
That all the sences they doe ravish quite,
The whyles the boyes run up and downe the street,
Crying aloud with strong confused° noyce,
As if it were one voyce.
140 Hymen io Hymen,° Hymen they do shout,
That even to the heavens theyr shouting shrill
Doth reach, and all the firmament doth fill,
To which the people standing all about,
As in approvance° doe thereto applaud
145 And loud advaunce her laud,°
And evermore they Hymen Hymen sing,
That al the woods them answer and theyr eccho ring.

Loe where she comes along with portly pace,°
Lyke Phœbe° from her chamber of the East,
150 Arysing forth to run her mighty race,
Clad all in white, that seemes° a virgin best.
So well it her beseemes that ye would weene
Some angell she had beene.

124 **boone** prayer.   131 **tabor** a small drum.   131 **Croud** crowd, a
fiddle.   132 **withouten . . . jar** without break or discord.   134 **tymbrels** tambourines.   138 **confused** blended.   140 **Hymen io Hymen**
ritual cry of the marriage ceremony.   144 **approvance** approval.
145 **advaunce her laud** extol her praises.   148 **portly pace** stately
step.   149 **Phœbe** the goddess of the moon.   151 **seemes** befits.

Her long loose yellow locks lyke golden wyre,
Sprinckled with perle, and perling flowres° a tweene,   155
Doe lyke a golden mantle her attyre,
And being crowned with a girland greene,
Seeme lyke some mayden Queene.
Her modest eyes abashed to behold
So many gazers, as on her do stare,   160
Upon the lowly ground affixed are.
Ne dare lift up her countenance too bold,
But blush to heare her prayses sung so loud,
So farre from being proud.
Nathlesse° doe ye still loud her prayses sing,   165
That all the woods may answer and your eccho ring.

Tell me ye merchants daughters did ye see
So fayre a creature in your towne before,
So sweet, so lovely, and so mild as she,
Adornd with beautyes grace and vertues store,   170
Her goodly eyes lyke Saphyres shining bright,
Her forehead yvory white,
Her cheekes lyke apples which the sun hath rudded,°
Her lips lyke cherryes charming men to byte,
Her brest like to a bowle of creame uncrudded,°   175
Her paps lyke lyllies budded,
Her snowie necke lyke to a marble towre,
And all her body like a pallace fayre,
Ascending uppe with many a stately stayre,
To honors seat° and chastities sweet bowre.   180
Why stand ye still ye virgins in amaze,
Upon her so to gaze,
Whiles ye forget your former lay to sing,
To which the woods did answer and your eccho ring.

But if ye saw that which no eyes can see,   185
The inward beauty of her lively spright,°
Garnisht with heavenly guifts of high degree,

---

155 **perling flowres** lace flowers, after "perling," a kind of lace.
165 **Nathlesse** nevertheless.   173 **rudded** reddened.   175 **uncrudded**
uncurdled, smooth.   180 **honors seat** the head.   186 **lively spright**
living spirit.

Much more then would ye wonder at that sight,
And stand astonisht lyke to those which red°
190 Medusaes mazeful hed.°
There dwels sweet love and constant chastity,
Unspotted fayth and comely womanhood,
Regard of honour and mild modesty,
There vertue raynes as Queene in royal throne,
195 And giveth lawes alone.
The which the base affections° doe obay,
And yeeld theyr services unto her will,
Ne thought of thing uncomely ever may
Thereto approch to tempt her mind to ill.
200 Had ye once seene these her celestial threasures,°
And unrevealed pleasures,
Then would ye wonder and her prayses sing,
That al the woods should answer and your echo ring.

Open the temple gates unto my love,
205 Open them wide that she may enter in,
And all the postes° adorne as doth behove,°
And all the pillours deck with girlands trim,
For to recyve this Saynt with honour dew,
That commeth in to you.
210 With trembling steps and humble reverence,
She commeth in, before th'almighties vew,
Of her ye virgins learne obedience,
When so ye come into those holy places,
To humble your proud faces
215 Bring her up to th'high altar that she may,
The sacred ceremonies there partake,
The which do endlesse matrimony make,
And let the roring Organs loudly play
The praises of the Lord in lively notes,
220 The whiles with hollow throates
The Choristers the joyous Antheme sing,
That al the woods may answere and their eccho ring.

189 **red** saw.   190 **Medusaes mazeful hed** Medusa was one of the
Gorgons whose head, covered with a maze of serpents, transformed
the amazed beholder to stone.   196 **base affections** lower emotions.
200 **threasures** treasures.   206 **postes** doorposts.   206 **doth behove**
is fitting.

Behold whiles she before the altar stands
Hearing the holy priest that to her speakes
And blesseth her with his two happy hands, 225
How the red roses flush up in her cheekes,
And the pure snow with goodly vermill° stayne,
Like crimsin dyde in grayne,°
That even th'Angels which continually,
About the sacred Altare doe remaine, 230
Forget their service and about her fly,
Ofte peeping in her face that seemes more fayre,
The more they on it stare.
But her sad eyes still fastened on the ground,
Are governed with goodly modesty, 235
That suffers not one looke to glaunce awry,
Which may let in a little thought unsownd.°
Why blush ye love to give to me your hand,
The pledge of all our band?°
Sing ye sweet Angels, Alleluya sing, 240
That all the woods may answere and your eccho ring.

Now al is done; bring home the bride againe,
Bring home the triumph of our victory,
Bring home with you the glory of her gaine,°
With joyance bring her and with jollity. 245
Never had man more joyfull day then this,
Whom heaven would heape with blis.
Make feast therefore now all this live long day,
This day for ever to me holy is,
Poure out the wine without restraint or stay, 250
Poure not by cups, but by the belly° full,
Poure out to all that wull,°
And sprinkle all the postes and wals with wine,
That they may sweat, and drunken be withall.°
Crowne ye God Bacchus° with a coronall,° 255
And Hymen also crowne with wreathes of vine,
And let the Graces daunce unto the rest;

227 **vermill** vermilion. 228 **dyde in grayne** fast dyed. 237 **un-sownd** wicked. 239 **band** bond. 244 **her gaine** having gained her. 251 **belly** wine bag. 252 **wull** will. 254 **withall** as well. 255 **Bacchus** the god of wine. 255 **coronall** garland.

For they can doo it best:
The whiles the maydens doe theyr carroll sing,
260 To which the woods shal answer and theyr eccho ring.

Ring ye the bels, ye yong men of the towne,
And leave your wonted labors for this day:
This day is holy; doe ye write it downe,
That ye for ever it remember may.
265 This day the sunne is in his chiefest hight,
With Barnaby the bright,°
From whence declining daily by degrees,
He somewhat loseth of his heat and light,
When once the Crab° behind his back° he sees.
270 But for this time it ill ordained was,
To chose the longest day in all the yeare,
And shortest night, when longest fitter weare:
Yet never day so long, but late° would passe.
Ring ye the bels, to make it weare away,
275 And bonefiers make all day,
And daunce about them, and about them sing:
That all the woods may answer, and your eccho ring.

Ah when will this long weary day have end,
And lende me leave to come unto my love?
280 How slowly do the houres theyr numbers spend?°
How slowly does sad Time his feathers move?
Hast thee O fayrest Planet° to thy home
Within the Westerne fome:
Thy tyred steedes long since have need of rest.
285 Long though it be, at last I see it gloome,°
And the bright evening star with golden creast
Appeare out of the East.
Fayre childe of beauty, glorious lampe of love
That all the host of heaven° in rankes doost lead,

266 **Barnaby the bright** St. Barnabas' Day, the longest day of the
year in the "Old Style" calendar.   269 **Crab** fourth sign of the
zodiac.   269 **behind his back** because the sun enters Leo, the fifth
sign of the zodiac, in June.   273 **late** at last.   280 **spend** waste
away.   282 **O fayrest Planet** the sun, according to the Ptolemaic
system.   285 **gloome** grow dark.   289 **the host of heaven** the stars.

And guydest lovers through the nights dread,   290
How chearefully thou lookest from above,
And seemst to laugh atweene thy twinkling light
As joying° in the sight
Of these glad many which for joy doe sing,
That all the woods them answer and their echo ring.   295

Now ceasse ye damsels your delights forepast;
Enough is it, that all the day was youres:
Now day is doen,° and night is nighing fast:
Now bring the Bryde into the brydall boures.
Now night is come, now soone her disaray,°   300
And in her bed her lay;
Lay her in lillies and in violets,
And silken courteins over her display,
And odourd sheetes, and Arras° coverlets.
Behold how goodly my faire love does ly   305
In proud humility;
Like unto Maia,° when as Jove her tooke,
In Tempe, lying on the flowry gras,
Twixt sleepe and wake, after she weary was,
With bathing in the Acidalian brooke.   310
Now it is night, ye damsels may be gon,
And leave my love alone,
And leave likewise your former lay to sing:
The woods no more shal answere, nor your echo ring.

Now welcome night, thou night so long expected,   315
That long daies labour doest at last defray,
And all my cares, which cruell love collected,
Hast sumd in one, and cancelled for aye:
Spread thy broad wing over my love and me,
That no man may us see,   320
And in thy sable mantle us enwrap,
From feare of perrill and foule horror free.
Let no false treason seeke us to entrap,

293 **As joying** as if rejoicing.   298 **doen** done.   300 **disaray** undress.   304 **Arras** a rich tapestry fabric.   307 **Maia** one of the
seven daughters of Atlas, on whom Jove begot Mercury, though not
in Tempe.

Nor any dread disquiet once annoy
325 The safety of our joy:
But let the night be calme and quietsome,
Without tempestuous storms or sad afray:°
Lyke as when Jove with fayre Alcmena lay,
When he begot the great Tirynthian groome:
330 Or lyke as when he with thy selfe° did lie,
And begot Majesty.°
And let the mayds and yongmen cease to sing:
Ne let the woods them answer, nor theyr eccho ring.

Let no lamenting cryes, nor dolefull teares,
335 Be heard all night within nor yet without:
Ne let false whispers breeding hidden feares,
Breake gentle sleepe with misconceived dout.°
Let no deluding dreames, nor dreadful sights
Make sudden sad affrights;
340 Ne let housefyres, nor lightnings helpelesse harmes,
Ne let the Pouke,° nor other evill sprights,
Ne let mischivous witches with theyr charmes,
Ne let hob Goblins, names whose sence we see not,
Fray° us with things that be not.
345 Let not the shriech Oule, nor the Storke be heard:
Nor the night Raven that still deadly yels,
Nor damned ghosts cald up with mighty spels,
Nor griesly vultures make us once affeard:
Ne let th'unpleasant Quyre of Frogs still croking
350 Make us to wish theyr choking.
Let none of these theyr drery accents sing;
Ne let the woods them answer, nor theyr eccho ring.

But let stil Silence trew night watches keepe,
That sacred peace may in assurance rayne,
355 And tymely sleep, when it is tyme to sleepe,

327 **afray** fear.   330 **thy selfe** i.e., the goddess of night. The myth
is Spenser's.   328–331 **as when Jove . . . Majesty** Jove assumed
the person and place of Amphitryon, the husband of Alcmena, and
on her, during a much-extended night, begot Hercules, whom Spenser calls the "Tirynthian groome" because he was born in the city
of Tiryns, and for his labor in cleansing the stables of Augeas, king
of Elis.   337 **misconceived dout** false fear.   341 **Pouke** Puck or
Robin Goodfellow.   344 **Fray** frighten.

May poure his limbs forth on your pleasant playne,
The whiles an hundred little winged loves,
Like divers fethered doves,
Shall fly and flutter round about your bed,
And in the secret darke, that none reproves,   360
Their prety stealthes shal worke, and snares shal
    spread
To filch away sweet snatches of delight,
Conceald through covert night.
Ye sonnes of Venus, play your sports at will,
For greedy pleasure, carelesse of your toyes,°   365
Thinks more upon her paradise of joyes,
Then what ye do, albe it good or ill.
All night therefore attend your merry play,
For it will soone be day:
Now none doth hinder you, that say or sing,   370
Ne will the woods now answer, nor your Eccho ring.

Who is the same, which at my window peepes?
Or whose is that faire face, that shines so bright,
Is it not Cinthia,° she that never sleepes,
But walkes about high heaven al the night?   375
O fayrest goddesse, do thou not envy
My love with me to spy:
For thou likewise didst love, though now unthought,°
And for a fleece of woll, which privily,
The Latmian shephard° once unto thee brought,   380
His pleasures with thee wrought.
Therefore to us be favorable now;
And sith of wemens labours° thou hast charge,
And generation goodly dost enlarge,°
Encline thy will t'effect our wishfull vow,   385
And the chast wombe informe with timely seed,
That may our comfort breed:
Till which we cease our hopefull hap° to sing,
Ne let the woods us answere, nor our Eccho ring.

365 **toyes** amorous games.   374 **Cinthia** the goddess of the moon.
378 **now unthought** not thought of now.   380 **Latmian shephard**
Endymion, who fell in love with the moon.   383 **labours** the pains
of childbirth.   384 **enlarge** give birth to.   388 **our hopefull hap** the
happening that we hope for.

390 And thou great Juno,° which with awful° might
    The lawes of wedlock still dost patronize,
    And the religion° of the faith first plight
    With sacred rites hast taught to solemnize:
    And eeke for comfort often called art
395 Of women in their smart,°
    Eternally bind thou this lovely band,
    And all thy blessings unto us impart.
    And thou glad Genius,° in whose gentle hand,
    The bridale bowre and geniall bed° remaine,
400 Without blemish or staine,
    And the sweet pleasures of theyr loves delight
    With secret ayde doest succour and supply,
    Till they bring forth the fruitfull progeny,
    Send us the timely fruit of this same night.
405 And thou fayre Hebe,° and thou Hymen free,
    Grant that it may so be.
    Til which we cease your further prayse to sing,
    Ne any woods shal answer, nor your Eccho ring.

    And ye high heavens, the temple of the gods,
410 In which a thousand torches flaming bright
    Doe burne, that to us wretched earthly clods,
    In dreadful darknesse lend desired light;
    And all ye powers which in the same remayne,
    More then we men can fayne,
415 Poure out your blessing on us plentiously,
    And happy influence° upon us raine,
    That we may raise a large posterity,
    Which from the earth, which they may long possesse,
    With lasting happinesse,
420 Up to your haughty pallaces may mount,
    And for the guerdon of theyr glorious merit
    May heavenly tabernacles there inherit,
    Of blessed Saints for to increase the count.
    So let us rest, sweet love, in hope of this,

390 **Juno** goddess and patroness of marriage.   390 **awful** awesome.
392 **religion** sanctity.   395 **smart** labors of childbirth.   398 **Genius**
See *F.Q.*, II.xii.47.   399 **geniall bed** generative or marriage bed.
405 **Hebe** the goddess of youth.   416 **influence** stellar influence
that determines man's fortune.

And cease till then our tymely joyes to sing,   425
The woods no more us answer, nor our eccho ring.

Song made in lieu of many ornaments,
With which my love should duly have bene dect,°
Which cutting off through hasty accidents,°
Ye would not stay your dew time to expect,°   430
But promist both to recompens,
Be unto her a goodly ornament,
And for short time an endlesse moniment.°

THE LETTER TO RALEIGH

A LETTER OF THE AUTHORS EXPOUNDING HIS WHOLE INTENTION IN THE COURSE OF THIS WORKE: WHICH FOR THAT IT GIVETH GREAT LIGHT TO THE READER, FOR THE BETTER UNDERSTANDING IS HEREUNTO ANNEXED.

To the Right noble, and Valorous, Sir Walter Raleigh knight, Lo. Wardein of the Stanneryes, and her Majesties liefetenaunt of the County of Cornewayll.

Sir knowing how doubtfully all Allegories may be construed, and this booke of mine, which I have entituled the Faery Queene, being a continued Allegory, or darke conceit, I have thought good aswell for avoyding of gealous opinions and misconstructions, as also for your better light in reading therof, (being so by you commanded,) to discover unto you the general intention and meaning, which in the whole course thereof I have fashioned, with-

428 **dect** adorned.   429 **cutting . . . accidents** having been cut off through accidental circumstances caused by haste.   430 **expect** await.   433 **endlesse moniment** eternal memorial.

out expressing of any particular purposes or by-accidents therein occasioned. The generall end therefore of all the booke is to fashion a gentleman or noble person in vertuous and gentle discipline: Which for that I conceived shoulde be most plausible and pleasing, being coloured with an historicall fiction, the which the most part of men delight to read, rather for variety of matter, then for profite of the ensample: I chose the historye of king Arthure, as most fitte for the excellency of his person, being made famous by many mens former workes, and also furthest from the daunger of envy, and suspition of present time. In which I have followed all the antique Poets historicall, first Homere, who in the Persons of Agamemnon and Ulysses hath ensampled a good governour and a vertuous man, the one in his *Ilias,* the other in his *Odysseis:* then Virgil, whose like intention was to doe in the person of Aeneas: after him Ariosto comprised them both in his Orlando: and lately Tasso dissevered them againe, and formed both parts in two persons, namely that part which they in Philosophy call Ethice, or vertues of a private man, coloured in his Rinaldo: The other named Politice in his Godfredo. By ensample of which excellente Poets, I labour to pourtraict in Arthure, before he was king, the image of a brave knight, perfected in the twelve private morall vertues, as Aristotle hath devised, the which is the purpose of these first twelve bookes: which if I finde to be well accepted, I may be perhaps encoraged, to frame the other part of polliticke vertues in his person, after that hee came to be king. To some I know this Methode will seeme displeasaunt, which had rather have good discipline delivered plainly in way of precepts, or sermoned at large, as they use, then thus clowdily enwrapped in Allegoricall devises. But such, me seeme, should be satisfide with the use of these dayes, seeing all things accounted by their showes, and nothing esteemed of, that is not delightfull and pleasing to commune sence. For this cause is Xenophon preferred before Plato, for that the one in the exquisite depth of his judgement, formed a Commune welth such as it should be, but the other in the person of Cyrus and the Persians fashioned a governement such as might best be: So much more profitable and gratious is doctrine by ensample, then by rule. So have I laboured to doe in the person of Arthure: whome I conceive after his long education by Timon, to whom he was by Merlin delivered to be brought up, so soone as he was borne of the Lady Igrayne, to have seene in a dream or vision the Faery Queen, with whose excellent beauty ravished, he awaking resolved to seeke her out, and so being by Merlin armed, and by Timon throughly instructed, he went to seeke her forth in Faerye land. In that Faery Queene I meane glory in my generall intention, but in my particular I conceive the most excellent and glorious person of our soveraine the Queene, and her kingdome in Faery land. And yet in some places els, I doe otherwise shadow her. For considering she beareth two persons, the one of a most royall Queene or Empresse, the other of a most vertuous and beautifull Lady, this latter part in some places I doe expresse in Belphœbe, fashioning her name according to your owne excellent conceipt of Cynthia, (Phœbe and Cynthia being both names of Diana.) So in the person of Prince Arthure I sette forth magnificence in particular, which vertue for that (according to Aristotle and the rest) it is the perfection of all the rest, and conteineth in it them all, therefore in the whole course I mention the deedes of Arthure applyable to that vertue, which I write of in that booke. But of the xii. other vertues, I make xii. other knights the patrones, for the more variety of the history: Of which these three bookes contayn three. The first of the knight of the Redcrosse, in whome I expresse Holynes: The seconde of Sir Guyon, in whome I sette forth Temperaunce: The third of Britomartis a Lady knight, in whome I picture Chastity. But because the beginning of the whole worke seemeth abrupte and as depending upon other antecedents, it needs that ye know the occasion of these three knights severall adventures. For the Methode of a Poet historical is not such, as of an Historiographer. For an Historiographer discourseth of affayres orderly as they were donne, accounting as well the times as the actions, but a Poet thrusteth into the middest, even where it most concerneth him, and there recoursing to the thinges forepaste, and divining of thinges to come, maketh a pleasing Analysis of all. The beginning therefore of my history, if it were to be told by an Historiographer, should be the twelfth booke, which is the last, where I devise that the Faery Queene kept her Annuall feaste xii. dayes, uppon which xii. severall dayes, the occasions of the xii. severall adventures hapned, which being undertaken by xii. severall knights, are in these xii books severally handled and discoursed. The first was this. In the beginning of the feast, there presented him selfe a tall clownishe younge man, who falling before the Queen of Faries desired a boone (as the manner then was) which during that feast she might not refuse: which was that hee might have the atchievement of any adventure, which during that feaste should happen, that being graunted, he rested him on the floore, unfitte through his rusticity for a better place. Soone after entred a faire Ladye in mourning weedes, riding on a white Asse, with a dwarfe behind her leading a warlike steed, that bore the Armes of a knight, and his speare in the dwarfes hand. Shee falling before the Queene of Faeries, complayned that her father and mother an ancient King and Queene, had bene by an huge dragon many years shut up in a brasen Castle, who thence suffred them not to yssew: and therefore besought the Faery Queene to assygne her some one of her knights to take on him that exployt. Presently that clownish person upstarting, desired that adventure: whereat the Queene much wondering, and the Lady much gainesaying, yet he earnestly importuned his desire. In the end the Lady told him that unlesse that armour which she brought, would serve him (that is the armour of a Christian man specified by Saint Paul v. Ephes.) that he could not succeed in that enterprise, which being forthwith put upon him with dewe furnitures thereunto, he seemed the goodliest man in al that company, and was well liked of the Lady. And eftesoones taking on him knighthood, and mounting on that straunge Courser, he went forth with her on that adventure: where beginneth the first booke, vz.

A gentle knight was pricking on the playne. etc.

The second day ther came in a Palmer bearing an Infant with bloody hands, whose Parents he complained to have bene slayn by an Enchaunteresse called Acrasia: and therfore craved of the Faery Queene, to appoint him some knight, to performe that adventure, which being assigned to Sir Guyon, he presently went forth with that same Palmer: which is the beginning of the second booke and the whole subject thereof. The third day there came in, a Groome who complained before the Faery Queene, that a vile Enchaunter called Busirane had in hand a most faire Lady called Amoretta, whom he kept in most grievous torment, because she would not yield him the pleasure of her body. Whereupon Sir Scudamour the lover of that Lady presently tooke on him that adventure. But being unable to performe it by reason of the hard Enchauntments, after long sorrow, in the end met with Britomartis, who succoured him, and reskewed his love.

But by occasion hereof, many other adventures are intermedled, but rather as Accidents, then intendments. As the love of Britomart, the overthrow of Marinell, the misery of Florimell, the vertuousnes of Belphœbe, the lasciviousnes of Hellenora, and many the like.

Thus much Sir, I have briefly overronne to direct your understanding to the wel-head of the History, that from thence gathering the whole intention of the conceit, ye may as in a handfull gripe al the discourse, which otherwise may happily seeme tedious and confused. So humbly craving the continuance of your honorable favour towards me, and th'eternall establishment of your happines, I humbly take leave.

23. January. 1589.
Yours most humbly affectionate.
ED. SPENSER.

The First Booke

OF THE FAERIE QUEENE.

Contayning

THE LEGENDE OF THE

KNIGHT OF THE RED CROSSE,

OR

Of Holinesse

1

Lo I the man, whose Muse whilome° did maske,°
    As time her taught in lowly Shepheards weeds,°
    Am now enforst a far unfitter taske,
    For trumpets sterne to chaunge mine Oaten
        reeds,°
5   And sing of Knights and Ladies gentle° deeds;

1 **whilome** formerly. 1 **Lo . . . maske** an imitation of verses pre-
fixed to Virgil's *Aeneid* in Renaissance editions. It announces the
change from the pastoral to the heroic poem. 2 **As time . . . weeds**
a reference to *The Shepheardes Calender* where, fitting his ap-
renticeship to poetry, he appears as the shepherd, Colin Clout.
weeds dress. 4 **Oaten reeds** The Muse forces him to change the
shepherd's pipe of the pastoral for the trumpet of the heroic poem.
5 **gentle** noble.

Whose prayses having slept in silence long,
Me, all too meane, the sacred Muse areeds°
To blazon broad° emongst her learned throng:
Fierce warres and faithfull loves shall moralize my
    song.

2

Helpe then, O holy Virgin° chiefe of nine,   10
Thy weaker Novice° to performe thy will,
Lay forth out of thine everlasting scryne°
The antique rolles, which there lye hidden still,
Of Faerie knights and fairest *Tanaquill,*°
Whom that most noble Briton Prince° so long   15
Sought through the world, and suffered° so much
    ill,
That I must rue° his undeserved wrong:
O helpe thou my weake wit, and sharpen my dull tong.

3

And thou most dreaded impe° of highest *Jove,*
Faire *Venus* sonne, that with thy cruell dart   20
At that good knight so cunningly° didst rove,°
That glorious fire it kindled in his hart,
Lay now thy deadly Heben° bow apart,
And with thy mother milde come to mine ayde:
Come both, and with you bring triumphant
    Mart,°   25
In loves and gentle jollities arrayd,
After his murdrous spoiles and bloudy rage allayd.

4

And with them eke,° O Goddesse heavenly bright,
Mirrour of grace and Majestie divine,

7 **areeds** counsels. 8 **To blazon broad** to proclaim. 10 **O holy
Virgin** Clio, the Muse of History, and first of the nine Muses.
11 **Thy weaker Novice** that is, "too weak" as he is "too meane"
to be enforced to the Muse's task. 12 **scryne** a desk or chest.
14 **Tanaquill** Gloriana, or Queen Elizabeth. 15 **that most noble
Briton Prince** Arthur. 16 **suffered** i.e., for whom he suffered.
17 **rue** pity. 19 **impe** offspring, i.e., Cupid, son of Jove and Venus.
21 **cunningly** skillfully. 21 **rove** shoot. 23 **Heben** made of ebony.
25 **Mart** Mars, the god of war. 28 **eke** also.

30   Great Lady° of the greatest Isle, whose light
      Like *Phœbus* lampe throughout the world doth
          shine,
      Shed thy faire beames into my feeble eyne,°
      And raise my thoughts too humble and too vile,°
      To thinke of that true glorious type° of thine,
35   The argument° of mine afflicted° stile:
The   which to heare, vouchsafe, O dearest dred°
          a-while.

CANTO I

The Patron of true Holinesse,
    Foule Errour doth defeate:
Hypocrisie him to entrape,
    Doth to his home entreate.

1

A Gentle° Knight was pricking° on the plaine,
    Y cladd° in mightie armes° and silver shielde,
    Wherein old dints of deepe wounds did remaine,
    The cruell markes of many' a bloudy fielde;
5   Yet armes till that time did he never wield:
    His angry steede did chide his foming bitt,
    As much disdayning to the curbe to yield:
    Full jolly° knight he seemd, and faire did sitt,
As one for knightly giusts° and fierce encounters fitt.

30 **Great Lady** Queen Elizabeth.   32 **eyne** eyes.   33 **vile** mean.
34 **true glorious type** Elizabeth being the type or pattern of glory,
as Spenser explains in the *Letter to Raleigh*.   35 **argument** the subject of the poem.   35 **afflicted** humble or mean.   36 **dred** object
of reverence.
1 **Gentle** well-born, noble.   1 **pricking** spurring his horse.   2
Y cladd clothed.   2 **mightie armes** "that is the armour of a Christian man specified by Saint Paul v. Ephes." (*Letter to Raleigh*).
The reference is to Ephesians vi.11–17.   8. **jolly** brave, gallant.
9 **giusts** jousts.

2

But on his brest a bloudie Crosse he bore,   10
    The deare remembrance of his dying Lord,
    For whose sweete sake that glorious badge he
        wore,
    And dead as living ever° him ador'd:
    Upon his shield the like was also scor'd,
    For soveraine hope, which in his helpe° he had: 15
    Right faithfull true° he was in deede and word,
    But of his cheere° did seeme too solemne sad;°
Yet nothing did he dread, but ever was ydrad.°

3

Upon a great adventure he was bond,°
    That greatest *Gloriana* to him gave,   20
    That greatest Glorious Queene of *Faerie* lond,
    To winne him worship,° and her grace to have,
    Which of all earthly things he most did crave;
    And ever as he rode, his hart did earne°
    To prove his puissance in battell brave   25
    Upon his foe, and his new force to learne;
Upon his foe, a Dragon° horrible and stearne.

4

A lovely Ladie rode him faire beside,
    Upon a lowly Asse more white then° snow,
    Yet she much whiter, but the same did hide   30
    Under a vele, that wimpled° was full low,
    And over all a blacke stole she did throw,
    As one that inly° mournd: so was she sad,
    And heavie sat upon her palfrey° slow;
    Seemed° in heart some hidden care she had,   35
And by her in a line° a milke white lambe she lad.°

---

13 **dead as living ever** See Rev. i.18: "I was dead, and behold,
I am alive for evermore." 15 **his helpe** i.e., the cross's help.
16 **Right faithfull true** See Rev. xix.11. 17 **cheere** countenance.
17 **sad** grave. 18 **ydrad** dreaded. 19 **bond** bound. 22 **worship**
honor. 24 **earne** yearn. 27 **a Dragon** "that old Dragon" (Argument to Canto xi). Cf. Rev. xx.2. 29 **then** than. 31 **wimpled**
lying in folds. 33 **inly** inwardly. 34 **palfrey** a small saddle-horse.
35 **Seemed** It seemed that. 36 **in a line** on a line. 36 **lad** led.

5

So pure an innocent, as that same lambe,
    She was in life and every vertuous lore,
    And by descent from Royall lynage° came
40   Of ancient Kings and Queenes, that had of yore
    Their scepters stretcht from East to Westerne
        shore,
    And all the world in their subjection held;
    Till that infernall feend with foule uprore°
    Forwasted° all their land, and them expeld:
Whom to avenge, she had this Knight from far
45   compeld.°

6

Behind her farre away a Dwarfe did lag,
    That lasie seemd in being ever last,
    Or wearied with bearing of her bag
    Of needments° at his backe. Thus as they past,
50   The day with cloudes was suddeine overcast,
    And angry *Jove* an hideous storme of raine
    Did poure into his Lemans lap° so fast,
    That every wight to shrowd° it did constrain,°
And this faire couple eke to shroud themselves were
    fain.

7

55 Enforst to seeke some covert° nigh at hand,
    A shadie grove not far away they spide,
    That promist ayde the tempest to withstand:
    Whose loftie trees yclad with sommers pride,
    Did spred so broad, that heavens light did hide,
60   Not perceable° with power of any starre:°
    And all within were pathes and alleies wide,

39 **from Royall lynage** Her parents are Adam and Eve. 43 **uprore**
insurrection. 44 **Forwasted** utterly wasted, ruined. 45 **compeld**
called to her aid. 49 **needments** needs. 52 **his Lemans lap** the
lap of his mistress, the earth. 53 **to shrowd** to shelter himself.
53 **constrain** force. 55 **covert** covering. 60 **perceable** penetrable.
60 **power of any starre** i.e., the influence or emanation from the
stars.

With footing° worne, and leading inward farre:
Faire harbour° that them seemes; so in they entred
   arre.

8

And foorth they passe, with pleasure forward led,
   Joying to heare the birdes sweete harmony,   65
   Which therein shrouded from the tempest dred,
   Seemd in their song to scorne the cruell sky.
   Much can° they prayse the trees so straight and
      hy,
   The sayling Pine,° the Cedar proud and tall,°
   The vine-prop Elme,° the Poplar never dry,°   70
   The builder° Oake, sole king of forrests all,
The Aspine good for staves, the Cypresse funerall.°

9

The Laurell, meed° of mightie Conquerours
   And Poets sage, the Firre that weepeth still,°
   The Willow worne of° forlorne Paramours,   75
   The Eugh° obedient to the benders will,
   The Birch for shaftes, the Sallow° for the mill,
   The Mirrhe sweete bleeding in the bitter wound,°
   The warlike Beech, the Ash for nothing ill,°
   The fruitfull Olive, and the Platane° round,   80
The carver Holme,° the Maple seeldom inward sound.

---

62 **footing** footsteps.   63 **harbour** shelter, with a pun on "arbor"
(Latin for "tree").   68 **can** did.   69 **sayling Pine** so called because
ships were made out of pine.   69 **the Cedar proud and tall** from
the Biblical "cedars of Lebanon, that are high and lifted up"
(Isaiah ii.13).   70 **The vine-prop Elme** because the elm supports
the vine.   70 **the Poplar never dry** because the poplar grows near
water.   71 **builder** for building.   72 **the Cypresse funerall** In I.vi.17
Spenser recounts the legend of Cyparissus who was changed into
a cypress through grief for his slain hind. Hence the cypress was
used to adorn graves.   73 **meed** reward.   74 **the Firre that weepeth
still** because the Pine continually exudes resin.   75 **of** by.   76 **Eugh**
The yew was used to make bows.   77 **Sallow** "a kind of woodde
like Wyllow" (E. K.'s note to *S. C.* Dec., 81).   78 **The Mirrhe . . .
wound** because the myrrh has a bitter taste though its gum has a
sweet smell.   79 **the Ash for nothing ill** because it is good for all
uses (?).   80 **the Platane** the plane-tree.   81 **The carver Holme** because the holly is suitable for carving.

10

Led with delight, they thus beguile the way,
  Untill the blustring storme is overblowne;
  When weening° to returne, whence they did
    stray,
  They cannot finde that path, which first was
    showne,
  But wander too and fro in wayes unknowne,
  Furthest from end then, when they neerest
    weene,
  That makes them doubt,° their wits be not their
    owne:
  So many pathes, so many turnings seene,
That which of them to take, in diverse° doubt they
  been.

11

At last resolving forward still to fare,°
  Till that some end they finde or in or out,
  That path they take, that beaten seemd most
    bare,
  And like to lead the labyrinth about;°
  Which when by tract° they hunted had through-
    out,
  At length it brought them to a hollow cave,
  Amid the thickest woods. The Champion stout°
  Eftsoones° dismounted from his courser brave,
And to the Dwarfe a while his needlesse spere° he
  gave.

12

Be well aware, quoth then that Ladie milde,
  Least suddaine mischiefe° ye too rash provoke:
  The danger hid, the place unknowne and wilde,
  Breedes dreadfull doubts: Oft fire is without
    smoke,

84 **weening** thinking. 88 **doubt** fear. 90 **diverse** distracting.
91 **fare** go. 94 **And . . . about** And would be likely to lead out
of the labyrinth. 95 **tract** track. 97 **stout** brave. 98 **Eftsoones**
forthwith. 99 **his needlesse spere** because the spear is used on
horseback. 101 **mischiefe** misfortune.

And perill without show: therefore your stroke
Sir knight with-hold, till further triall made. *105*
Ah Ladie (said he) shame were to revoke
The forward footing for° an hidden shade:
Vertue gives her selfe light, through darkenesse for to
wade.°

13

Yea but (quoth she) the perill of this place
I better wot° then you, though now too late *110*
To wish you backe returne with foule disgrace,
Yet wisedome warnes, whilest foot is in the gate,
To stay the steppe, ere forced to retrate.
This is the wandring wood,° this *Errours den,*
A monster vile, whom God and man does hate: *115*
Therefore I read° beware. Fly fly (quoth then
The fearefull Dwarfe:) this is no place for living men.

14

But full of fire and greedy hardiment,°
The youthfull knight could not for ought° be
staide,
But forth unto the darksome hole he went, *120*
And looked in: his glistring° armor made
A litle glooming light, much like a shade,
By which he saw the ugly monster plaine,
Halfe like a serpent horribly displaide,°
But th'other halfe did womans shape retaine, *125*
Most lothsom, filthie, foule, and full of vile disdaine.°

15

And as she lay upon the durtie ground,
Her huge long taile her den all overspred,
Yet was in knots and many boughtes° upwound,
Pointed with mortall sting. Of her there bred *130*

107 **for** because of.   108 **wade** go.   110 **wot** know.   114 **the wan-dring wood** i.e., the wood of wandering.   116 **read** advise.
118 **hardiment** boldness.   119 **for ought** for aught or anything.
121 **glistring** shining with light, for "Vertue gives her selfe light."
124 **displaide** extended.   126 **disdaine** i.e., what arouses disdain in
others.   129 **boughtes** folds.

A thousand yong ones, which she dayly fed,
Sucking upon her poisonous dugs, eachone
Of sundry shapes, yet all ill favored:°
Soone as that uncouth° light upon them shone,
135 Into her mouth they crept, and suddain all were gone.

16

Their dam upstart,° out of her den effraide,
And rushed forth, hurling her hideous taile
About her cursed head, whose folds displaid
Were stretcht now forth at length without en-
    traile.°
140 She lookt about, and seeing one in mayle
Armed to point,° sought backe to turne againe;
For light she hated as the deadly bale,°
Ay wont° in desert darknesse to remaine,
Where plaine none might her see, nor she see any
    plaine.

17

145 Which when the valiant Elfe° perceiv'd, he lept
As Lyon fierce upon the flying pray,
And with his trenchand° blade her boldly kept
From turning backe, and forced her to stay:
Therewith enrag'd she loudly gan to bray,
150 And turning fierce, her speckled taile advaunst,
Threatning° her angry sting, him to dismay:°
Who nought aghast,° his mightie hand en-
    haunst:°
The stroke down from her head unto her shoulder
    glaunst.

18

Much daunted with that dint,° her sence was dazd,

---

133 **ill favored** evil-looking. 134 **uncouth** strange. 136 **upstart**
started up. 139 **without entraile** unfolded. 141 **Armed to point**
i.e., completely armed. 142 **deadly bale** deadly injury, i.e., death.
143 **Ay wont** ever accustomed. 145 **Elfe** i.e., as he is supposed to be "a Faeries sonne" (I.x.64). 147 **trenchand** sharp.
151 **Threatning** i.e., threatening him with. 151 **dismay** defeat.
152 **aghast** frightened. 152 **enhaunst** raised. 154 **dint** blow.

Yet kindling rage, her selfe she gathered round, 155
And all attonce her beastly body raizd
With doubled forces high above the ground:
Tho° wrapping up her wrethed sterne arownd,
Lept fierce upon his shield, and her huge traine
All suddenly about his body wound, 160
That hand or foot to stirre he strove in vaine:
God helpe the man so wrapt in *Errours* endlesse
traine.°

19

His Lady sad to see his sore constraint,
Cride out, Now now Sir knight, shew what ye
bee,
Add faith unto your force, and be not faint: 165
Strangle her, else she sure will strangle thee.
That when he heard, in great perplexitie,
His gall° did grate° for griefe° and high disdaine,
And knitting° all his force got one hand free,
Wherewith he grypt her gorge° with so great
paine, 170
That soone to loose her wicked bands did her con-
straine.°

20

Therewith° she spewd out of her filthy maw
A floud of poyson horrible and blacke,
Full of great lumpes of flesh and gobbets° raw,
Which stunck so vildly, that it forst him slacke 175
His grasping hold, and from her turne him
backe:
Her vomit full of bookes and papers was,
With loathly frogs and toades, which eyes did
lacke,

---

158 **Tho** then.   162 **traine** the duplication of the rhyme word iden-
tifies the literal and allegorical senses of "traine" as "tail" and
"snare."   168 **His gall** i.e., his gall bladder as the source of his
anger.   168 **grate** fret.   168 **griefe** anger.   169 **knitting** concen-
trating.   170 **gorge** throat or maw.   171 **constraine** force.   172
Therewith with that.   174 **gobbets** pieces.

And creeping sought way in the weedy gras:
180 Her filthy parbreake° all the place defiled has.

21

As when old father *Nilus* gins to swell
    With timely pride° above the *Aegyptian* vale,
    His fattie° waves do fertile slime outwell,
    And overflow each plaine and lowly dale:
185   But when his later spring gins to avale,°
    Huge heapes of mudd he leaves, wherein there
        breed
    Ten thousand kindes of creatures, partly male
    And partly female of his fruitfull seed;
Such ugly monstrous shapes elswhere may no man
        reed.°

22

190 The same so sore annoyed has the knight,
    That welnigh choked with the deadly stinke,
    His forces faile, ne° can no longer fight.
    Whose corage when the feend perceiv'd to
        shrinke,
    She poured forth out of her hellish sinke
195   Her fruitfull cursed spawne of serpents small,
    Deformed monsters, fowle, and blacke as inke,
    Which swarming all about his legs did crall,
And him encombred sore, but could not hurt at all.

23

As gentle Shepheard in sweete even-tide,
200   When ruddy *Phœbus* gins to welke° in west,
    High on an hill, his flocke to vewen wide,
    Markes which do byte their hasty supper best;
    A cloud of combrous° gnattes do him molest,
    All striving to infixe their feeble stings,
205   That from their noyance he no where can rest,

---

180 **parbreake** vomit.   182 **timely pride** seasonable swelling.   183
fattie fat, i.e., fertile, being supplied with what is needed.   185 **But
. . . avale** But later when the flood begins to ebb.   189 **reed** see.
192 **ne** nor.   200 **welke** fade.   203 **combrous** harassing.

But with his clownish° hands their tender wings
He brusheth oft, and oft doth mar their murmurings.

24

Thus ill bestedd,° and fearefull more of shame,
    Then° of the certaine perill he stood in,
    Halfe furious unto his foe he came,   *210*
    Resolv'd in minde all suddenly to win,
    Or soone to lose, before he once would lin;°
    And strooke at her with more then manly force,
    That from her body full of filthie sin
    He raft° her hatefull head without remorse;   *215*
A streame of cole black bloud forth gushed from her
    corse.

25

Her scattred brood, soone as their Parent deare
    They saw so rudely° falling to the ground,
    Groning full deadly, all with troublous feare,
    Gathred themselves about her body round,   *220*
    Weening their wonted entrance to have found
    At her wide mouth: but being there withstood
    They flocked all about her bleeding wound,
    And sucked up their dying mothers blood,
Making her death their life, and eke her hurt their
    good.   *225*

26

That detestable sight him much amazde,
    To see th'unkindly Impes° of heaven accurst,
    Devoure their dam; on whom while so he gazd,
    Having all satisfide their bloudy thurst,
    Their bellies swolne he saw with fulnesse burst,   *230*
    And bowels gushing forth: well worthy end
    Of such as drunke her life, the which them nurst;

206 **clownish** belonging to a rustic. Cf. the *Letter to Raleigh* in which
the Red Cross Knight is described as "a tall clownishe younge man"
who sits on the floor, "unfitte through his rusticity for a better place."
208 **bestedd** placed.   209 **Then** than.   212 **lin** cease.   215 **raft** reft.
218 **rudely** violently.   227 **th'unkindly Impes** the unnatural off-
spring.

Now needeth him no lenger labour spend,
His foes have slaine themselves, with whom he should
contend.

27

235 His Ladie seeing all, that chaunst, from farre
Approcht in hast to greet his victorie,
And said, Faire knight, borne under happy°
starre,
Who see your vanquisht foes before you lye:
Well worthy be you of that Armorie,°
240 Wherein ye have great glory wonne this day,
And proov'd your strength on a strong enimie,
Your first adventure: many such I pray,
And henceforth ever wish, that like succeed it may.

28

Then mounted he upon his Steede againe,
245 And with the Lady backward sought to wend;°
That path he kept, which beaten was most plaine,
Ne ever would to any by-way bend,
But still did follow one unto the end,
The which at last out of the wood them brought.
250 So forward on his way (with God to frend)°
He passed forth, and new adventure sought;
Long way he travelled, before he heard of ought.

29

At length they chaunst to meet upon the way
An aged Sire, in long blacke weedes° yclad,
255 His feete all bare, his beard all hoarie gray,
And by his belt his booke he hanging had;
Sober he seemde, and very sagely sad,
And to the ground his eyes were lowly bent,
Simple in shew, and voyde of malice bad,
260 And all the way he prayed, as he went,
And often knockt his brest, as one that did repent.

---

237 **happy** of good hap or fortune, auspicious.   239 **Armorie** armor.
245 **wend** go.   250 **to frend** for a friend.   254 **weedes** clothes.

30

He faire the knight saluted, louting° low,
 Who faire him quited,° as that° courteous was:
 And after° asked him, if he did know
 Of straunge adventures, which abroad did pas. *265*
 Ah my deare Sonne (quoth he) how should, alas,
 Silly° old man, that lives in hidden cell,
 Bidding his beades° all day for his trespas,
 Tydings of warre and worldly trouble tell?
With holy father sits not° with such things to mell.° *270*

31

But if of daunger which hereby doth dwell,
 And homebred evill ye desire to heare,
 Of a straunge man I can you tidings tell,
 That wasteth° all this countrey farre and neare.
 Of such (said he) I chiefly do inquere, *275*
 And shall you well reward to shew the place,
 In which that wicked wight° his dayes doth weare:°
 For to all knighthood it is foule disgrace,
That such a cursed creature lives so long a space.

32

Far hence (quoth he) in wastfull° wildernesse *280*
 His dwelling is, by which no living wight
 May ever passe, but thorough° great distresse.
 Now (sayd the Lady) draweth toward night,
 And well I wote,° that of your later° fight
 Ye all forwearied° be: for what so strong, *285*
 But wanting rest will also want of might?
 The Sunne that measures heaven all day long,

---

262 **louting** bowing. 263 **quited** requited, i.e., returned the salutation. 263 **as that** as. 264 **after** afterward. 267 **Silly** simple. 268
Bidding his beades saying his prayers. 270 **sits not** it is not fitting.
270 **mell** meddle. 274 **wasteth** destroys. 277 **wight** creature. 277
weare spend. 280 **wastfull** waste. 282 **thorough** through. 284
wote know. 284 **later** late, last. 285 **forwearied** utterly wearied.

At night doth baite° his steedes the *Ocean* waves
    emong.

33

Then with the Sunne take Sir, your timely rest,
    And with new day new worke at once begin:
    Untroubled night they say gives counsell best.
    Right well Sir knight ye have advised bin,
    (Quoth then that aged man;) the way to win
    Is wisely to advise: now day is spent;
    Therefore with me ye may take up your In°
    For this same night. The knight was well con-
        tent:
So with that godly father to his home they went.

34

A little lowly Hermitage it was,
    Downe in a dale, hard by a forests side,
    Far from resort of people, that did pas
    In travell to and froe: a little wyde°
    There was an holy Chappell edifyde,°
    Wherein the Hermite dewly wont to say
    His holy things° each morne and eventyde:
    Thereby a Christall streame did gently play,
Which from a sacred fountaine welled forth alway.°

35

Arrived there, the little house they fill,
    Ne looke for entertainment, where none was:
    Rest is their feast, and all things at their will;
    The noblest mind the best contentment has.
    With faire discourse the evening so they pas:
    For that old man of pleasing wordes had store,
    And well could file° his tongue as smooth as
        glas;

---

288 **baite** rest.   295 **In** inn, paralleling their earlier "harbour" in the
Wandering Wood where "in they entred arre."   301 **wyde** distant.
302 **edifyde** built.   304 **things** offices.   306 **alway** always.   313 **file**
polish.

He told of Saintes and Popes, and evermore
He strowd° an *Ave-Mary* after and before.   *315*

36

The drouping° Night thus creepeth on them fast,
    And the sad humour° loading their eye liddes,
    As messenger of *Morpheus*° on them cast
Sweet slombring° deaw, the which to sleepe them
    biddes.
    Unto their lodgings then his guestes he riddes: *320*
    Where when all drownd in deadly sleepe he
    findes,
    He to his study goes, and there amiddes
    His Magick bookes and artes of sundry kindes,
He seekes out mighty charmes, to trouble sleepy°
    mindes.

37

Then choosing out few wordes most horrible,   *325*
    (Let none them read) thereof did verses frame,
    With which and other spelles like terrible,
    He bad awake blacke *Plutoes* griesly° Dame,°
    And cursed heaven, and spake reprochfull shame
Of highest God, the Lord of life and light;   *330*
    A bold bad man, that dar'd to call by name
    Great *Gorgon,*° Prince of darknesse and dead
    night,
At which° *Cocytus* quakes, and *Styx*° is put to flight.

38

And forth he cald out of deepe darknesse dred
    Legions of Sprights,° the which like little flyes   *335*
    Fluttring about his ever damned hed,

---

315 **strowd** strewed. 316 **drouping** drooping. 317 **humour** moisture, the dew of sleep. Cf. the house of Morpheus washed by the
Ocean in stanza 39. 318 **Morpheus** the god of sleep. 319 **slombring** causing sleep. 324 **sleepy** sleeping. 328 **griesly** horrible.
328 **blacke Plutoes griesly Dame** Proserpina, the wife of Pluto, who
is the god of hell. 332 **Gorgon** Demogorgon; see I.v.22. 333 **At
which** at whose name. 333 **At which . . . Styx** Cocytus and Styx are
rivers of hell. 335 **Sprights** spirits.

A-waite whereto their service he applyes,
    To aide his friends, or fray° his enimies:
    Of those he chose out two, the falsest twoo,
340   And fittest for to forge true-seeming lyes;
    The one of them he gave a message too,
The other by him selfe staide° other worke to doo.

39

He making speedy way through spersed° ayre,
    And through the world of waters wide and
        deepe,
345   To *Morpheus* house doth hastily repaire.
    Amid the bowels of the earth full steepe,
    And low, where dawning day doth never peepe,
    His dwelling is; there *Tethys*° his wet bed
    Doth ever wash, and *Cynthia*° still doth steepe
350   In silver deaw his ever-drouping hed,
Whiles sad Night over him her mantle black doth
        spred.

40

Whose double gates he findeth locked fast,
    The one faire fram'd of burnisht Yvory,
    The other all with silver overcast;°
355   And wakefull dogges before them farre do lye,
    Watching to banish Care their enimy,
    Who oft is wont to trouble gentle Sleepe.
    By them the Sprite doth passe in quietly,
    And unto *Morpheus* comes, whom drowned
        deepe
360 In drowsie fit° he findes: of nothing he takes keepe.°

41

And more, to lulle him in his slumber soft,
    A trickling streame from high rocke tumbling
        downe

---

338 **fray** frighten.   342 **staide** stayed.   343 **spersed** dispersed, thin.
348 **Tethys** the sea, or the wife of Oceanus, the ocean.   349 **Cynthia**
the goddess of the moon.   354 **overcast** covered.   360 **drowsie fit**
attack of drowsiness.   360 **keepe** heed.

And ever-drizling raine upon the loft,
Mixt with a murmuring winde, much like the
    sowne°
Of swarming Bees, did cast him in a swowne:°   365
No other noyse, nor peoples troublous cryes,
As still° are wont t'annoy the walled towne,
Might there be heard: but carelesse° Quiet lyes,
Wrapt in eternall silence farre from enemyes.

42

The messenger approching to him spake,   370
    But his wast° wordes returnd to him in vaine:
So sound he slept, that nought mought° him
    awake.
Then rudely he him thrust, and pusht with
    paine,°
Whereat he gan to stretch: but he againe
Shooke him so hard, that forced him to speake.   375
As one then in a dreame, whose dryer° braine
Is tost with troubled sights and fancies weake,
He mumbled soft, but would not all° his silence
    breake.

43

The Sprite then gan more boldly him to wake,
    And threatned unto him the dreaded name   380
Of *Hecate:*° whereat he gan to quake,
    And lifting up his lumpish° head, with blame
Halfe angry asked him, for what he came.
Hither (quoth he) me *Archimago* sent,
He that the stubborne Sprites can wisely tame,   385
He bids thee to him send for his intent°
A fit false dreame, that can delude the sleepers sent.°

364 **sowne** sound.   365 **swowne** swoon.   367 **still** ever.   368 **carelesse** free from cares.   371 **wast** wasted.   372 **mought** might.   373 **paine** effort.   376 **dryer** too dry, not being loaded with the dew of sleep.   378 **all** altogether.   381 **Hecate** an infernal deity and the female counterpart to Demogorgon.   382 **lumpish** heavy.   386 **intent** purpose.   387 **the sleepers sent** the sleeper's senses.

44

The God obayde, and calling forth straight way
   A diverse° dreame out of his prison darke,
390   Delivered it to him, and downe did lay
   His heavie head, devoide of carefull carke,°
   Whose sences all were straight benumbd and
     starke.°
   He backe returning by the Yvorie dore,°
   Remounted up as light as chearefull Larke,
395   And on his litle winges the dreame he bore
In hast unto his Lord, where he him left afore.°

45

Who all this while with charmes and hidden artes,
   Had made a Lady of that other Spright,
   And fram'd of liquid ayre her tender partes
400   So lively,° and so like in all mens sight,
   That weaker° sence it could have ravisht
     quight:°
   The maker selfe for all his wondrous witt,
   Was nigh beguiled with so goodly sight:
   Her all in white he clad, and over it
405 Cast a blacke stole, most like to seeme for *Una* fit.

46

Now when that ydle° dreame was to him brought,
   Unto that Elfin knight he bad him fly,
   Where he slept soundly void of evill thought,
   And with false shewes abuse his fantasy,°
410   In sort as he him schooled privily:
   And that new creature borne without her dew,°
   Full of the makers guile, with usage sly
   He taught to imitate that Lady trew,
Whose semblance she did carrie under feigned hew.°

---

389 **diverse** diverting. 391 **carke** anxiety. 392 **starke** rigid. 393
the Yvorie dore the door through which false dreams ascend. 396
afore before. 400 **lively** lifelike. 401 **weaker** too weak. 401
quight entirely. 406 **ydle** frivolous. 409 **abuse his fantasy** deceive
his fancy. 411 **without her dew** without her due, being miscreated.
414 **hew** shape.

47

Thus well instructed, to their worke they hast,   *415*
    And comming where the knight in slomber lay,
    The one upon his hardy head him plast,
    And made him dreame of loves and lustfull play,
    That nigh his manly hart did melt away,
    Bathed in wanton blis and wicked joy: *420*
    Then seemed him° his Lady by him lay,
    And to him playnd,° how that false winged boy°
Her chast hart had subdewd, to learne Dame plea-
    sures toy.

48

And she her selfe of beautie soveraigne Queene,
    Faire *Venus* seemde unto his bed to bring   *425*
    Her, whom he waking evermore did weene
    To be the chastest flowre, that ay° did spring
    On earthly braunch, the daughter of a king,
    Now a loose Leman° to vile service bound:
    And eke the *Graces* seemed all to sing,   *430*
    Hymen io Hymen,° dauncing all around,
Whilst freshest *Flora*° her with Yvie girlond°
    crownd.

49

In this great passion of unwonted° lust,
    Or wonted feare of doing ought amis,
    He started up, as seeming to mistrust   *435*
    Some secret ill, or hidden foe of his:
    Lo there before his face his Lady is,
    Under blake stole hyding her bayted hooke,
    And as halfe blushing offred him to kis,
    With gentle blandishment and lovely looke,   *440*
Most like that virgin true, which for her knight him
    took.

---

421 **seemed him** it seemed to him.   422 **playnd** complained.   422
that false winged boy Cupid.   427 **ay** ever.   429 **Leman** mistress.
431 **Hymen io Hymen** i.e., part of the ritual in praise of **Hymen,** the
god of marriage, as in *Epith.* 140.   432 **Flora** the goddess of flowers.
432 **girlond** garland.   433 **unwonted** unaccustomed.

50

All cleane° dismayd to see so uncouth° sight,
 And halfe enraged at her shamelesse guise,°
 He thought have slaine her in his fierce de-
  spight:°
445 But hasty heat tempring with sufferance wise,
 He stayde his hand, and gan himselfe advise
 To prove his sense, and tempt her faigned truth.
 Wringing her hands in wemens pitteous wise,°
 Tho can she weepe,° to stirre up gentle ruth,°
450 Both for her noble bloud, and for her tender youth.

51

And said, Ah Sir, my liege Lord and my love,
 Shall I accuse the hidden cruell fate,
 And mightie causes wrought in heaven above,
 Or the blind God, that doth me thus amate,°
455 For hoped love to winne me certaine hate?
 Yet thus perforce° he bids me do, or die.
 Die is my dew: yet rew my wretched state
 You, whom my hard avenging destinie
Hath made judge of my life or death indifferently.

52

460 Your owne deare sake forst me at first to leave
 My Fathers kingdome, There she stopt with
  teares;
 Her swollen hart her speach seemd to bereave,
 And then againe begun, My weaker° yeares
 Captiv'd to fortune and frayle worldly feares,
465 Fly to your faith for succour and sure ayde:
 Let me not dye in languor and long teares.
 Why Dame (quoth he) what hath ye thus dis-
  mayd?
What frayes° ye, that were wont to comfort me
 affrayd?

---

442 **cleane** entirely.   442 **uncouth** unseemly.   443 **guise** manner.
444 **despight** anger.   448 **wise** manner.   449 **Tho can she weepe**
Then she began to weep.   449 **ruth** pity.   454 **amate** dismay.   456
perforce of necessity.   463 **weaker** too weak.   468 **frayes** frightens.

53

Love of your selfe, she said, and deare° constraint
 Lets me not sleepe, but wast the wearie night   *470*
 In secret anguish and unpittied plaint,
 Whiles you in carelesse sleepe are drowned quight.
 Her doubtfull words made that redoubted° knight
 Suspect her truth: yet since no'untruth he knew,
 Her fawning love with foule disdainefull spight *475*
 He would not shend,° but said, Deare dame I rew,
That for my sake unknowne such griefe unto you grew.

54

Assure your selfe, it fell not all to ground;°
 For all so deare as life is to my hart,
 I deeme your love, and hold me to you bound; *480*
 Ne let vaine feares procure your needlesse smart,
 Where cause is none, but to your rest depart.
 Not all content, yet seemd she to appease°
 Her mournefull plaintes, beguiled of her art,
 And fed with words, that could not chuse but please, *485*
So slyding softly forth, she turnd as to her ease.

55

Long after lay he musing at her mood,
 Much griev'd to thinke that gentle Dame so light,
 For whose defence he was to shed his blood.
 At last dull wearinesse of former fight *490*
 Having yrockt a sleepe° his irkesome spright,°
 That troublous° dreame gan freshly tosse his braine,

---

469 **deare** dire. 473 **redoubted** dreaded. 476 **shend** reprove. 478 **fell . . . ground** did not come to nothing. 483 **appease** stop. 491 **yrockt a sleepe** rocked asleep. 491 **irksome spright** troubled mind. 492 **troublous** troublesome.

With bowres, and beds, and Ladies deare de-
        light:
But when he saw his labour all was vaine,
495 With that misinformed spright he backe returnd againe.

CANTO II

The guilefull great Enchaunter parts
    The Redcrosse Knight from Truth:
Into whose stead faire falshood steps,
    And workes him wofull ruth.°

1

By this° the Northerne wagoner° had set
        His sevenfold teme° behind the stedfast starre,°
        That was in Ocean waves yet never wet,
        But firme is fixt, and sendeth light from farre
5   To all, that in the wide deepe wandring arre:
        And chearefull Chaunticlere° with his note shrill
        Had warned once, that *Phœbus* fiery carre°
        In hast was climbing up the Easterne hill,
Full envious that night so long his roome did fill.

2

10 When those accursed messengers of hell,
        That feigning dreame, and that faire-forged
            Spright
        Came to their wicked maister, and gan tell°
        Their bootelesse° paines, and ill succeeding
            night:
        Who all in rage to see his skilfull might
15   Deluded so, gan threaten hellish paine
        And sad *Proserpines* wrath, them to affright.

Arg. **ruth** mischief.   1 **By this** by this time.   1 **the Northerne wag-
oner** the constellation Boötes.   2 **His sevenfold teme** stars of the
Plough or Big Dipper.   2 **the stedfast starre** the pole star.   6
Chaunticlere the cock.   7 **Phœbus fiery carre** the chariot of the
sun.   12 **gan tell** began to tell.   13 **bootelesse** unprofitable.

But when he saw his threatning was but vaine,
He cast about, and searcht his balefull° bookes againe.

3

Eftsoones° he tooke that miscreated faire,
    And that false other Spright, on whom he spred   20
    A seeming body of the subtile° aire,
    Like a young Squire, in loves and lusty-hed°
    His wanton dayes that ever loosely led,
    Without regard of armes and dreaded fight:
    Those two he tooke, and in a secret bed,   25
    Covered with darknesse and misdeeming night,°
Them both together laid, to joy in vaine delight.

4

Forthwith he runnes with feigned faithfull hast
    Unto his guest, who after troublous sights
    And dreames, gan now to take more sound
        repast,°   30
    Whom suddenly he wakes with fearefull frights,
    As one aghast with feends or damned sprights,
    And to him cals, Rise rise unhappy Swaine,
    That here wex° old in sleepe, whiles wicked
        wights
    Have knit themselves in *Venus* shamefull chaine;   35
Come see, where your false Lady doth her honour
        staine.

5

All in amaze he suddenly up start
    With sword in hand, and with the old man went;
    Who soone him brought into a secret part,
    Where that false couple were full closely ment°   40
    In wanton lust and lewd embracement:
    Which when he saw, he burnt with gealous fire,
    The eye of reason was with rage yblent,°

18 **balefull** deadly. 19 **Eftsoones** forthwith. 21 **subtile** thin. 22
lusty-hed lust. 26 **misdeeming night** night that causes unjust
thoughts. 30 **repast** repose. 34 **wex** wax, grow. 40 **ment** joined.
43 **yblent** blinded.

And would have slaine them in his furious ire,
45 But hardly° was restreined of that aged sire.

6

Returning to his bed in torment great,
    And bitter anguish of his guiltie sight,
    He could not rest, but did his stout heart eat,°
    And wast his inward gall with deepe despight,
50   Yrkesome° of life, and too long lingring night.
    At last faire *Hesperus*° in highest skie
    Had spent his lampe, and brought forth dawning
        light,
    Then up he rose, and clad him hastily;
The Dwarfe him brought his steed: so both away do
    fly.

7

55 Now when the rosy-fingred Morning° faire,
    Weary of aged *Tithones* saffron bed,
    Had spred her purple robe through deawy aire,
    And the high hils *Titan*° discovered,°
    The royall virgin shooke off drowsy-hed,°
60   And rising forth out of her baser° bowre,
    Lookt for her knight, who far away was fled,
    And for her Dwarfe, that wont to wait each
        houre;
Then gan she waile and weepe, to see that woefull
    stowre.°

8

And after him she rode with so much speede
65   As her slow beast could make; but all in vaine:
    For him so far had borne his light-foot steede,
    Pricked with wrath and fiery fierce disdaine,
    That him to follow was but fruitlesse paine;

---

45 **hardly** with difficulty.   48 **did his stout heart eat** i.e., suffered from vexation.   50 **Yrkesome** tired.   51 **Hesperus** the morning star. 55 **Morning** Aurora, the goddess of dawn.   58 **Titan** the sun.   58 **discovered** revealed.   59 **drowsy-hed** drowsiness.   60 **baser** base. 63 **stowre** time of turmoil.

Yet she her weary limbes would never rest,
  But every hill and dale, each wood and plaine   70
  Did search, sore grieved in her gentle brest,
He so° ungently left her, whom she loved best.

9

But subtill *Archimago,* when his guests
  He saw divided into double parts,
  And *Una* wandring in woods and forrests,°   75
  Th'end of his drift,° he praisd his divelish arts,
  That had such might over true meaning harts;
  Yet rests not so, but other meanes doth make,°
  How he may worke unto her further smarts:
  For her he hated as the hissing snake,   80
And in her many troubles did most pleasure take.

10

He then devisde himselfe how to disguise;
  For by his mightie science° he could take
  As many formes and shapes in seeming wise,°
  As ever *Proteus°* to° himselfe could make: 85
  Sometime a fowle, sometime a fish in lake,
  Now like a foxe, now like a dragon fell,°
  That of himselfe he oft for feare would quake,
  And oft would flie away. O who can tell
The hidden power of herbes, and might of Magicke
    spell?   90

11

But now seemde best, the person to put on°
  Of that good knight, his late beguiled guest:
  In mighty armes he was yclad anon,
  And silver shield: upon his coward brest
  A bloudy crosse, and on his craven crest   95
  A bounch of haires discolourd diversly:°

72 **He so** because he so.   75 **And . . . forrests** The broken scansion
of the line indicates her wandering.   76 **drift** plot.   78 **make** devise.
83 **mightie science** knowledge capable of producing miracles.   84
in seeming wise in ways of seeming.   85 **Proteus** a sea god who
could change himself into any shape.   85 **to** of.   87 **fell** fierce.   91
the person to put on to assume the appearance.   96 **discolourd diversly** of many different colors.

Full jolly knight he seemde, and well addrest,°
And when he sate upon his courser free,°
Saint George himself ye would have deemed him to
    be.

12

100 But he the knight, whose semblaunt° he did beare,
The true *Saint George* was wandred far away,
Still flying from his thoughts and gealous feare;
Will was his guide, and griefe led him astray.
At last him chaunst to meete upon the way
105 A faithlesse Sarazin° all arm'd to point,°
In whose great shield was writ with letters gay
Sans foy:° full large of limbe and every joint
He was, and cared not for God or man a point.°

13

He had a faire companion of his way,
110 A goodly Lady clad in scarlot red,
Purfled° with gold and pearle of rich assay,°
And like° a *Persian* mitre° on her hed
She wore, with crownes and owches° garnished,
The which her lavish lovers to her gave;
115 Her wanton palfrey all was overspred
With tinsell trappings, woven like a wave,
Whose bridle rung with golden bels and bosses brave.°

14

With faire disport° and courting dalliaunce
She intertainde her lover all the way:
But when she saw the knight his speare ad-
120   vaunce,
She soone left off her mirth and wanton play,
And bad her knight addresse him to° the fray:

97 **addrest** armed. 98 **free** willing. 100 **semblaunt** resemblance.
105 **Sarazin** Saracen. 105 **to point** completely. 107 **Sans foy** Faith-
lessness. 108 **not . . . a point** not . . . a bit. 111 **Purfled** embroidered. 111 **of rich assay** of great value. 112 **like** what was like.
112 **mitre** headdress. 113 **owches** jewels. 117 **brave** handsome.
118 **disport** diversion. 122 **addresse him to** prepare himself for.

His foe was nigh at hand. He prickt with pride
   And hope to winne his Ladies heart that day,
   Forth spurred fast: adowne his coursers side   *125*
The red bloud trickling staind the way, as he did ride.

15

The knight of the *Redcrosse* when him he spide,
   Spurring so hote with rage dispiteous,°
   Gan fairely couch his speare,° and towards
     ride:°
   Soone meete they both, both fell and furious,   *130*
   That daunted with their forces hideous,
   Their steeds do stagger, and amazed stand,
   And eke themselves too rudely rigorous,
   Astonied° with the stroke of their owne hand,
Do backe rebut,° and each to other yeeldeth land.   *135*

16

As when two rams stird with ambitious pride,
   Fight for the rule of the rich fleeced flocke,
   Their horned fronts so fierce on either side
   Do meete, that with the terrour of the shocke
   Astonied both, stand sencelesse as a blocke,   *140*
   Forgetfull of the hanging° victory:
   So stood these twaine, unmoved as a rocke,
   Both staring fierce, and holding idely
The broken reliques° of their former cruelty.

17

The *Sarazin* sore daunted with the buffe°   *145*
   Snatcheth his sword, and fiercely to him flies;
   Who well it wards, and quyteth° cuff with cuff:
   Each others equall puissaunce envies,°
   And through their iron sides with cruell spies°

---

128 **dispiteous** without pity.   129 **couch his speare** to place his spear
in its rest.   129 **towards ride** ride toward him.   134 **Astonied**
stunned.   135 **backe rebut** recoil.   141 **hanging** i.e., hanging in the
balance.   144 **The broken reliques** the fragments of their broken
spears.   145 **buffe** blow.   147 **quyteth** requites.   148 **Each . . . en-**
vies Each seeks to rival the other's equal power.   149 **spies** darting
thrusts.

150   Does seeke to perce: repining° courage yields
    No foote to foe. The flashing fier flies
    As from a forge out of their burning shields,
 And streames of purple bloud new dies the verdant
    fields.

18

 Curse on that Crosse (quoth then the *Sarazin*)
155   That keepes thy body from the bitter fit;°
    Dead long ygoe° I wote thou haddest bin,
    Had not that charme from thee forwarned° it:
    But yet I warne thee now assured sitt,
    And hide thy head. Therewith upon his crest
160   With rigour so outrageous he smitt,
    That a large share° it hewd out of the rest,
 And glauncing downe his shield, from blame him
    fairely blest.°

19

 Who thereat wondrous wroth, the sleeping spark
    Of native vertue° gan eftsoones revive,
165   And at his haughtie helmet making mark,
    So hugely° stroke, that it the steele did rive,°
    And cleft his head. He tumbling downe alive,
    With bloudy mouth his mother earth did kis,
    Greeting his grave: his grudging° ghost did
     strive
170   With the fraile flesh; at last it flitted° is,
 Whither the soules do fly of men, that live amis.

20

 The Lady when she saw her champion fall,
    Like the old ruines of a broken towre,
    Staid not to waile his woefull funerall,
175   But from him fled away with all her powre;
    Who after her as hastily gan scowre,°

150 **repining** grudging, indignant. 155 **the bitter fit** i.e., death. 156
ygoe ago. 157 **forwarned** guarded. 161 **share** piece. 162 **blest**
preserved. 164 **native vertue** natural power. 166 **So hugely** with
such great power. 166 **rive** split. 169 **grudging** complaining. 170
flitted departed. 176 **scowre** run.

Bidding the Dwarfe with him to bring away
The *Sarazins* shield, signe of the conqueroure.
Her soone he overtooke, and bad to stay,
For present cause was none of dread her to dismay.   *180*

21

She turning backe with ruefull° countenaunce,
Cride, Mercy mercy Sir vouchsafe to show
On silly° Dame, subject to hard mischaunce,
And to your mighty will. Her humblesse° low
In so ritch weedes and seeming glorious show,   *185*
Did much emmove° his stout heroïcke heart,
And said, Deare dame, your suddein overthrow
Much rueth° me; but now put feare apart,
And tell, both who ye be, and who that tooke your
                part.

22

Melting in teares, then gan she thus lament;   *190*
The wretched woman, whom unhappy° howre
Hath now made thrall° to your commandement,
Before that angry heavens list to lowre,°
And fortune false betraide me to your powre,
Was, (O what now availeth that I was!)   *195*
Borne the sole daughter of an Emperour,
He that the wide West under his rule has,
And high hath set his throne, where *Tiberis*° doth pas.

23

He in the first flowre of my freshest age,
Betrothed me unto the onely haire°   *200*
Of a most mighty king, most rich and sage;
Was never Prince so faithfull and so faire,
Was never Prince so meeke and debonaire;°
But ere my hoped day of spousall shone,
My dearest Lord fell from high honours staire,   *205*

181 **ruefull** doleful. 183 **silly** innocent. 184 **humblesse** humbleness. 186 **emmove** move. 188 **rueth** grieves. 191 **unhappy** unfortunate. 192 **thrall** slave. 193 **list to lowre** it pleased to frown.
198 **Tiberis** the Tiber. 200 **haire** heir. 203 **debonaire** gracious.

Into the hands of his accursed fone,°
And cruelly was slaine, that shall I ever mone.

24

His blessed body spoild° of lively° breath,
    Was afterward, I know not how, convaid
210 And fro° me hid: of whose most innocent death
    When tidings came to me unhappy maid,
    O how great sorrow my sad soule assaid.°
    Then forth I went his woefull corse° to find,
    And many yeares throughout the world I straid,
215 A virgin widow, whose deepe wounded mind
With love, long time did languish as the striken hind.

25

At last it chaunced this proud *Sarazin*
    To meete me wandring, who perforce me led
    With him away, but yet could never win
220 The Fort, that Ladies hold in soveraigne dread.
    There lies he now with foule dishonour dead,
    Who whiles he liv'de, was called proud *Sans foy*,
    The eldest of three brethren, all three bred
    Of one bad sire, whose youngest is *Sans joy,*°
And twixt them both was borne the bloudy bold *Sans*
225   *loy.*°

26

In this sad plight, friendlesse, unfortunate,
    Now miserable I *Fidessa*° dwell,
    Craving of you in pitty of my state,
    To do none ill, if please ye not do well.
230 He in great passion all this while did dwell,
    More busying his quicke eyes, her face to view,
    Then his dull eares, to heare what she did tell;
    And said, Faire Lady hart of flint would rew°
The undeserved woes and sorrowes, which ye shew.

---

206 **fone** foes.   208 **spoild** robbed.   208 **lively** living.   210 **fro**
from.   212 **assaid** assailed.   213 **corse** corpse.   224 **Sans joy** Joy-
lessness.   225 **Sans loy** Lawlessness.   227 **Fidessa** Faithful.   233
rew pity.

27

Henceforth in safe assuraunce may ye rest,   235
 Having both found a new friend you to aid,
 And lost an old foe, that did you molest:
 Better new friend then an old foe is said.°
 With chaunge of cheare the seeming simple maid
 Let fall her eyen, as shamefast to the earth,   240
 And yeelding soft, in that she nought gain-said,
 So forth they rode, he feining seemely merth,
And she coy lookes: so dainty they say maketh
  derth.°

28

Long time they thus together traveiled,
 Till weary of their way, they came at last,   245
 Where grew two goodly trees, that faire did
  spred
 Their armes abroad, with gray mosse overcast,°
 And their greene leaves trembling with every
  blast,
 Made a calme shadow far in compasse round:
 The fearefull Shepheard often there aghast   250
 Under them never sat, ne wont° there sound
His mery oaten pipe, but shund th'unlucky ground.

29

But this good knight soone as he them can spie,°
 For the coole shade him thither hastly got:
 For golden *Phœbus* now ymounted hie,   255
 From fiery wheeles of his faire chariot
 Hurled his beame so scorching cruell hot,
 That living creature mote it not abide;
 And his new Lady it endured not.
 There they alight, in hope themselves to hide   260
From the fierce heat, and rest their weary limbs a
  tide.°

---

238 **is said** it is said. 243 **so . . . derth** proverbial, suggesting here
that Fidessa's coyness makes the Knight want her. 247 **overcast**
covered. 251 **ne wont** nor was accustomed to. 253 **can spie** saw.
261 **a tide** for a time.

30

Faire seemely pleasaunce° each to other makes,
    With goodly purposes° there as they sit:
    And in his falsed° fancy he her takes
265   To be the fairest wight, that lived yit;°
    Which to expresse, he bends his gentle wit,
    And thinking of those braunches greene to frame
    A girlond for her dainty forehead fit,
    He pluckt a bough; out of whose rift there came
270 Small drops of gory bloud, that trickled downe the same.

31

Therewith° a piteous yelling voyce was heard,
    Crying, O spare with guilty hands to teare
    My tender sides in this rough rynd embard,°
    But fly, ah fly far hence away, for feare
275   Least° to you hap, that happened to me heare,
    And to this wretched Lady, my deare love,
    O too deare love, love bought with death too deare.
    Astond° he stood, and up his haire did hove,°
And with that suddein horror could no member move.

32

280 At last whenas the dreadfull passion°
    Was overpast, and manhood well awake,
    Yet musing at the straunge occasion,
    And doubting much his sence, he thus bespake;
    What voyce of damned Ghost from *Limbo*° lake,
285   Or guilefull spright wandring in empty aire,
    Both which fraile men do oftentimes mistake,
    Sends to my doubtfull° eares these speaches rare,

---

262 **Faire seemely pleasaunce** courteous pleasantries.   263 **purposes** discourse.   264 **falsed** proven false.   265 **yit** yet.   271 **Therewith** with that.   273 **embard** imprisoned.   275 **Least** lest.   278 **Astond** astonished.   278 **hove** rise.   280 **whenas the dreadfull passion** when the emotion of dread.   284 **Limbo** a dwelling place in hell for restless spirits.   287 **doubtfull** full of fear.

And ruefull plaints, me bidding guiltlesse bloud to
    spare?

33

Then groning deepe, Nor damned Ghost, (quoth he,)
    Nor guilefull sprite to thee these wordes doth
    speake,   *290*
    But once a man *Fradubio,*° now a tree,
    Wretched man, wretched tree; whose nature
    weake,
    A cruell witch her cursed will to wreake,
    Hath thus transformd, and plast in open plaines,
    Where *Boreas*° doth blow full bitter bleake,   *295*
    And scorching Sunne does dry my secret vaines:
For though a tree I seeme, yet cold and heat me
    paines.

34

Say on *Fradubio* then, or man, or tree,
    Quoth then the knight, by whose mischievous
    arts
    Art thou misshaped thus, as now I see?   *300*
    He oft finds med'cine, who his griefe imparts;
    But double griefs afflict concealing harts,°
    As raging flames who striveth to suppresse.
    The author then (said he) of all my smarts,
    Is one *Duessa*° a false sorceresse,   *305*
That many errant° knights hath brought to wretched-
    nesse.

35

In prime of youthly yeares, when corage hot°
    The fire of love and joy of chevalree
    First kindled in my brest, it was my lot
    To love this gentle Lady, whom ye see,   *310*
    Now not a Lady, but a seeming tree;
    With whom as once I rode accompanyde,

291 **Fradubio** Doubtful.   295 **Boreas** the north wind.   302 **conceal-
ing harts** hearts that conceal their grief.   305 **Duessa** two-faced.
306 **errant** wandering.   307 **corage hot** passionate spirit.

Me chaunced of a knight encountred bee,°
That had a like faire Lady by his syde,
315 Like a faire Lady, but did fowle *Duessa* hyde.

36

Whose forged beauty he did take in hand,°
All other Dames to have exceeded farre;
I in defence of mine did likewise stand,
Mine, that did then shine as the Morning starre:
320 So both to battell fierce arraunged arre,
In which his harder° fortune was to fall
Under my speare: such is the dye° of warre:
His Lady left as a prise martiall,
Did yield her comely person, to be at my call.

37

325 So doubly lov'd of Ladies unlike faire,
Th'one seeming such, the other such indeede,
One day in doubt I cast for° to compare,
Whether in beauties glorie did exceede;°
A Rosy girlond was the victors meede:°
Both seemde to win, and both seemde won to
330   bee,
So hard the discord was to be agreede.
Frælissa° was as faire, as faire mote bee,
And ever false *Duessa* seemde as faire as shee.

38

The wicked witch now seeing all this while
335 The doubtfull ballaunce equally to sway,
What not by right, she cast° to win by guile,
And by her hellish science° raisd streight way
A foggy mist, that overcast the day,
And a dull° blast, that breathing on her face,
340 Dimmed her former beauties shining ray,

---

313 **Me . . . bee** It happened that I met a knight.   316 **did take in
hand** maintained.   321 **harder** hard.   322 **dye** chance, as with dice.
327 **cast for** attempted.   328 **Whether . . . exceede** which of the two
was the more beautiful.   329 **meede** reward.   332 **Frælissa** Frailty.
336 **cast** resolved.   337 **science** knowledge.   339 **dull** dulling or
dimming.

And with foule ugly forme did her disgrace:
Then was she faire alone, when none was faire in
    place.°

39

Then cride she out, Fye, fye, deformed wight,
    Whose borrowed beautie now appeareth plaine
    To have before bewitched all mens sight;   345
    O leave her soone, or let her soone be slaine.
    Her loathly visage viewing with disdaine,
    Eftsoones I thought her such, as she me told,
    And would have kild her; but with faigned paine,
    The false witch did my wrathfull hand with-hold;   350
So left her, where she now is turnd to treen mould.°

40

Thens forth I tooke *Duessa* for my Dame,
    And in the witch unweeting° joyd long time,
    Ne ever wist, but that she was the same,
    Till on a day (that day is every Prime,°   355
    When Witches wont do penance for their crime)
    I chaunst to see her in her proper hew,°
    Bathing her selfe in origane° and thyme:
    A filthy foule old woman I did vew,
That ever to have toucht her, I did deadly rew.   360

41

Her neather partes misshapen, monstruous,
    Were hidd in water, that I could not see,
    But they did seeme more foule and hideous,
    Then womans shape man would beleeve to bee.
    Thens forth from her most beastly companie   365
    I gan refraine, in minde to slip away,
    Soone as appeard safe oportunitie:
    For danger great, if not assur'd decay°
I saw before mine eyes, if I were knowne to stray.

342 **in place** i.e., in place of her.   351 **treen mould** the mold or form
of a tree.   353 **unweeting** unwittingly.   355 **Prime** spring.   357
hew shape.   358 **origane** oregano or wild marjoram.   368 **assur'd
decay** certain death.

42

370 The divelish hag by chaunges of my cheare°
  Perceiv'd my thought, and drownd in sleepie
   night,
  With wicked herbes and ointments did besmeare
  My bodie all, through charmes and magicke
   might,
  That all my senses were bereaved quight:
375   Then brought she me into this desert waste,
  And by my wretched lovers side me pight,°
  Where now enclosd in wooden wals full faste,
Banisht from living wights, our wearie dayes we
  waste.

43

But how long time, said then the Elfin knight,
380   Are you in this misformed house to dwell?
  We may not chaunge (quoth he) this evil plight,
  Till we be bathed in a living° well;
  That is the terme prescribed by the spell.
  O how, said he, mote I that well out find,
385   That may restore you to your wonted well?°
  Time and suffised fates° to former kynd°
Shall us restore, none else from hence may us unbynd.

44

The false *Duessa,* now *Fidessa* hight,°
  Heard how in vaine *Fradubio* did lament,
390   And knew well all was true. But the good knight
  Full of sad feare and ghastly dreriment,°
  When all this speech the living tree had spent,°
  The bleeding bough did thrust into the ground,
  That from the bloud° he might be innocent,
395   And with fresh clay did close the wooden wound:
Then turning to his Lady, dead with feare her found.

370 **cheare** countenance. 376 **pight** placed. 382 **living** constantly
flowing. 385 **wonted well** usual well-being. 386 **suffised fates** fulfilled destiny. 386 **kynd** nature. 388 **hight** called. 391 **dreriment**
gloom. 392 **spent** uttered. 394 **bloud** the guilt of bloodshed.

45

Her seeming dead he found with feigned feare,
　　As all unweeting of that well she knew,
　　And paynd himselfe° with busie care to reare
　　Her out of carelesse° swowne. Her eylids blew　400
　　And dimmed sight with pale and deadly hew
　　At last she up gan lift: with trembling cheare
　　Her up he tooke, too simple and too trew,
　　And oft her kist. At length all passed feare,°
He set her on her steede, and forward forth did beare.　405

CANTO III

Forsaken Truth long seekes her love,
　And makes the Lyon mylde,
Marres blind Devotions mart,° and fals
　In hand of leachour vylde.°

1

Nought is there under heav'ns wide hollownesse,
　　That moves more deare compassion of mind,
　　Then beautie brought t'unworthy wretchednesse
　　Through envies snares or fortunes freakes° un-
　　　　kind:
　　I, whether lately through her brightnesse blind,　5
　　Or through alleageance and fast fealtie,
　　Which I do owe unto all woman kind,
　　Feele my heart perst° with so great agonie,
When such I see, that all° for pittie I could die.

2

And now it is empassioned so deepe,　　　　　10
　　For fairest *Unaes* sake, of whom I sing,

399 **paynd himselfe** took pains.　400 **carelesse** unconscious, being
without apprehension.　404 **all passed feare** having passed all fear.
Arg. **mart** trade.　Arg. **vylde** vile.　4 **freakes** sudden changes.　8
perst pierced.　9 **all** just.

That my fraile eyes these lines with teares do
    steepe,
To thinke how she through guilefull handeling,°
Though true as touch,° though daughter of a
    king,
15   Though faire as ever living wight was faire,
Though nor in word nor deede ill meriting,
Is from her knight divorced in despaire
And her due loves deriv'd° to that vile witches share.

3

Yet she most faithfull Ladie all this while
20   Forsaken, wofull, solitarie mayd
Farre from all peoples prease,° as in exile,
In wildernesse and wastfull deserts strayd,
To seeke her knight; who subtilly betrayd
Through that late vision, which th'Enchaunter
    wrought,
25   Had her abandond. She of nought affrayd,
Through woods and wastnesse wide him daily
    sought;
Yet wished tydings none of him unto her brought.°

4

One day nigh wearie of the yrkesome way,
From her unhastie beast she did alight,
30   And on the grasse her daintie limbes did lay
In secret shadow, farre from all mens sight:
From her faire head her fillet she undight,°
And laid her stole aside. Her angels face
As the great eye of heaven shyned bright,
35   And made a sunshine in the shadie place;
Did never° mortall eye behold such heavenly grace.

5

It fortuned out of the thickest wood

13 **handeling** treatment.   14 **true as touch** i.e., tested in truth, as
gold is tested by touchstone.   18 **her due loves deriv'd** the love due
to her diverted.   21 **prease** press, crowd.   27 **Yet . . . brought** None
brought her tidings of him that she wished.   32 **her fillet she undight**
her headband she took off.   36 **Did never** never did.

A ramping° Lyon rushed suddainly,
    Hunting full greedie after salvage blood;°
    Soone as the royall virgin he did spy,   40
    With gaping mouth at her ran greedily,
    To have attonce° devour'd her tender corse:
    But to the pray when as he drew more ny,
    His bloudie rage asswaged with remorse,
And with the sight amazd, forgat his furious forse.   45

6

In stead thereof he kist her wearie feet,
    And lickt her lilly hands with fawning tong,
    As° he her wronged innocence did weet.°
    Oh how can beautie maister the most strong,
    And simple truth subdue avenging wrong?   50
    Whose yeelded pride and proud submission,
    Still dreading death, when she had marked long,
    Her hart gan melt in great compassion,
And drizling teares did shed for pure affection.°

7

The Lyon Lord of every beast in field,   55
    Quoth she, his princely puissance° doth abate,
    And mightie proud to humble weake° does yield,
    Forgetfull of the hungry rage, which late
    Him prickt, in pittie of my sad estate:°
    But he my Lyon, and my noble Lord,   60
    How does he find in cruell hart to hate
    Her that him lov'd, and ever most adord,
As the God of my life? why hath he me abhord?

8

Redounding° teares did choke th'end of her plaint,
    Which softly ecchoed from the neighbour wood;   65
    And sad to see her sorrowfull constraint°
    The kingly beast upon her gazing stood;

38 ramping raging.   **39 salvage blood** the blood of wild animals.
42 attonce at once.   **48 As** as if.   **48 weet** know.   **54 affection** passion.   **56 puissance** power.   **57 mightie proud to humble weake** proud might to humble weakness.   **59 estate** state.   **64 Redounding** overflowing.   **66 constraint** affliction.

With pittie calmd, downe fell his angry mood.
At last in close hart shutting up her paine,
Arose the virgin borne of heavenly brood,°
And to her snowy Palfrey got againe,
To seeke her strayed Champion, if she might attaine.°

9

The Lyon would not leave her desolate,
But with her went along, as a strong gard
Of her chast person, and a faithfull mate
Of her sad troubles and misfortunes hard:
Still° when she slept, he kept both watch and
ward,°
And when she wakt, he waited diligent,
With humble service to her will prepard:°
From her faire eyes he tooke commaundement,
And ever by her lookes conceived her intent.

10

Long she thus traveiled through deserts wyde,
By which she thought her wandring knight shold
pas,
Yet never shew of living wight espyde;
Till that at length she found the troden gras,
In which the tract° of peoples footing was,
Under the steepe foot of a mountaine hore;
The same she followes, till at last she has
A damzell spyde slow footing her before,
That on her shoulders sad° a pot of water bore.

11

To whom approching she to her gan call,
To weet, if dwelling place were nigh at hand;
But the rude° wench her answer'd nought at all,
She could not heare, nor speake, nor understand;
Till seeing by her side the Lyon stand,
With suddaine feare her pitcher downe she threw,

70 **brood** parentage.   72 **attaine** overtake him.   77 **Still** always.
77 **both watch and ward** continual lookout.   79 **prepard** ready.   86
tract track.   90 **sad** heavy with the weighte.   93 **rude** ignorant.

And fled away: for never in that land
  Face of faire Ladie she before did vew,
And that dread Lyons looke her cast in deadly hew.°

12

Full fast she fled, ne° ever lookt behynd,   *100*
  As if her life upon the wager lay,°
  And home she came, whereas° her mother blynd
  Sate in eternall night: nought could she say,
  But suddaine catching hold, did her dismay
  With quaking hands, and other signes of feare: *105*
  Who full of ghastly fright and cold affray,°
  Gan shut the dore. By this° arrived there
Dame *Una,* wearie Dame, and entrance did requere.°

13

Which when none yeelded, her unruly Page
  With his rude clawes the wicket open rent, *110*
  And let her in; where of his cruell rage
  Nigh dead with feare, and faint° astonishment,
  She found them both in darkesome corner pent;°
  Where that old woman day and night did pray
  Upon her beades devoutly penitent;   *115*
  Nine hundred *Pater nosters* every day,
And thrise nine hundred *Aves* she was wont to say.

14

And to augment her painefull pennance more,
  Thrise every weeke in ashes she did sit,
  And next her wrinkled skin rough sackcloth
    wore,   *120*
  And thrise three times did fast° from any bit:°
  But now for feare her beads she did forget.
  Whose needlesse dread for to remove away,
  Fair *Una* framed words and count'nance fit:

99 **And . . . hew** The sight of the lion made her look as though she were dead. 100 **ne** nor. 101 **upon the wager lay** was at stake. 102 **whereas** where. 106 **affray** fear. 107 **By this** at this time. 108 **requere** request. 112 **faint** i.e., causing a faint. 113 **pent** confined. 121 **And . . . fast** And fasted three meals a day for three days of the week. 121 **bit** bite.

125   Which hardly doen,° at length she gan them pray,
    That in their cotage small, that night she rest her may.

15

The day is spent, and commeth drowsie night,
    When every creature shrowded is in sleepe;
    Sad *Una* downe her laies in wearie plight,
130   And at her feet the Lyon watch doth keepe:
    In stead of rest, she does lament, and weepe
    For the late losse of her deare loved knight,
    And sighes, and grones, and evermore does
        steepe
    Her tender brest in bitter teares all night,
 All night she thinks too long, and often lookes for
135   light.

16

Now when *Aldeboran*° was mounted hie
    Above the shynie *Cassiopeias* chaire,°
    And all in deadly sleepe did drowned lie,
    One knocked at the dore, and in would fare;°
140   He knocked fast, and often curst, and sware,
    That readie entrance was not at his call:
    For on his backe a heavy load he bare
    Of nightly stelths and pillage severall,°
Which he had got abroad by purchase° criminall.

17

145 He was to weete° a stout and sturdie thiefe,
    Wont to robbe Churches of their ornaments,
    And poore mens boxes of their due reliefe,
    Which given was to them for good intents;
    The holy Saints of their rich vestiments
150   He did disrobe, when all men carelesse slept,
    And spoild the Priests of their habiliments,

---

125 **Which hardly doen** which having been done with difficulty.   136
Aldeboran a star that forms the eye of the constellation Taurus.
137 **the shynie Cassiopeias chaire** the constellation Cassiopeia, called
"The Woman in the Chair" by the Romans.   139 **fare** go.   143
severall many different kinds.   144 **purchase** acquisition.   145 **to
weete** to wit.

   Whiles none the holy things in safety kept;
Then he by cunning sleights in at the window crept.

18

And all that he by right or wrong could find,
   Unto this house he brought, and did bestow   *155*
   Upon the daughter of this woman blind,
   Abessa° daughter of *Corceca*° slow,
   With whom he whoredome usd,° that few did
      know,
   And fed her fat with feast of offerings,
   And plentie, which in all the land did grow;   *160*
   Ne spared he to give her gold and rings:
And now he to her brought part of his stolen things.

19

Thus long the dore with rage and threats he bet,°
   Yet of those fearefull women none durst° rize,
   The Lyon frayed° them, him in to let: *165*
   He would no longer stay him to advize,°
   But open breakes the dore in furious wize,°
   And entring is; when that disdainfull beast
   Encountring fierce, him suddaine doth surprize,
   And seizing cruell clawes on trembling brest,   *170*
Under his Lordly foot him proudly hath supprest.

20

Him booteth not resist,° nor succour call,
   His bleeding hart is in the vengers° hand,
   Who streight him rent in thousand peeces small,
   And quite dismembred hath: the thirstie land   *175*
   Drunke up his life; his corse left on the strand.°
   His fearefull friends weare out the wofull night,
   Ne dare to weepe, nor seeme to understand

---

157 **Abessa** The name suggests abbeys.   157 **Corceca** blindness of
heart.   158 **With . . . usd** whom he used as a whore.   163 **bet** beat.
164 **durst** dare.   165 **frayed** frightened.   166 **stay him to advize**
stop to consider.   167 **wize** manner.   172 **Him booteth not resist**
It does not avail him to resist.   173 **vengers** avenger's.   176 **strand**
ground.

The heavie hap,° which on them is alight,°
180 Affraid, least to themselves the like mishappen might.°

21

Now when broad day the world discovered° has,
Up *Una* rose, up rose the Lyon eke,
And on their former journey forward pas,
In wayes unknowne, her wandring knight to
        seeke,
With paines farre passing that long wandring
185   *Greeke,*°
That for his love refused deitie;
Such were the labours of this Lady meeke,
Still seeking him, that from her still did flie,
Then furthest from her hope, when most she weened
        nie.°

22

190 Soone as she parted thence, the fearefull twaine,
        That blind old woman and her daughter deare
        Came forth, and finding *Kirkrapine*° there slaine,
        For anguish great they gan to rend their heare,
        And beat their brests, and naked flesh to teare.
        And when they both had wept and wayld their
195   fill,
        Then forth they ranne like two amazed deare,
        Halfe mad through malice, and revenging will,°
To follow her, that was the causer of their ill.

23

Whom overtaking, they gan loudly bray,
200   With hollow howling, and lamenting cry,
        Shamefully at her rayling all the way,
        And her accusing of dishonesty,°

---

179 **hap** happening.   179 **is alight** had fallen.   180 **to themselves
. . . might** They meet with the like mishap.   181 **discovered** revealed.
185 **that long wandring Greeke** Ulysses, who refused Calypso's offer
of immortality in order to return to Penelope.   189 **weened nie** believed near.   192 **Kirkrapine** church plunderer.   197 **revenging will**
desire for revenge.   202 **dishonesty** unchastity.

That was the flowre of faith and chastity;
   And still amidst her rayling, she° did pray,
   That plagues, and mischiefs, and long misery   *205*
   Might fall on her, and follow all the way,
And that in endlesse error° she might ever stray.

24

But when she saw her prayers nought prevaile,
   She backe returned with some labour lost;
   And in the way as she did weepe and waile,   *210*
   A knight her met in mighty armes embost,°
   Yet knight was not for all his bragging bost,°
   But subtill *Archimag,* that *Una* sought
   By traynes° into new troubles to have tost:
   Of that old woman tydings he besought,   *215*
If that of such a Ladie she could tellen ought.°

25

Therewith she gan her passion to renew,
   And cry, and curse, and raile, and rend her
      heare,
   Saying, that harlot she too lately° knew,
   That causd her shed so many a bitter teare,   *220*
   And so forth told the story of her feare:
   Much seemed he to mone her haplesse chaunce,
   And after for that Ladie did inquere;
   Which being taught, he forward gan advaunce
His faire enchaunted steed, and eke his charmed launce.   *225*

26

Ere long he came, where *Una* traveild slow,
   And that wilde Champion wayting her besyde:
   Whom seeing such, for dread he durst not show
   Himselfe too nigh at hand, but turned wyde°
   Unto an hill; from whence when she him spyde,   *230*
   By his like seeming shield,° her knight by name°

---

204 **she** i.e., Corceca.   207 **error** wandering.   211 **embost** decked
out.   212 **bost** boast.   214 **traynes** stratagems.   216 **ought** anything.   219 **too lately** only too lately.   229 **wyde** away.   231 **like
seeming shield** seeming like the shield of her knight.   231 **her knight
by name** her particular knight.

She weend it was, and towards him gan ryde:
Approching nigh, she wist° it was the same,
And with faire fearefull humblesse° towards him shee
came.

27

235 And weeping said, Ah my long lacked Lord,
Where have ye bene thus long out of my sight?
Much feared I to have bene quite abhord,
Or ought have° done, that ye displeasen might,
That should as death unto my deare hart light:°
240 For since mine eye your joyous sight° did mis,
My chearefull day is turnd to chearelesse night,
And eke my night of death the shadow is;
But welcome now my light, and shining lampe of blis.

28

He thereto meeting° said, My dearest Dame,
245 Farre be it from your thought, and fro my will,
To thinke that knighthood I so much should
shame,
As you leave, that have me loved still,
And chose in Faery court of meere° goodwill,
Where noblest knights were to be found on earth:
250 The earth shall sooner leave her kindly skill°
To bring forth fruit, and make eternall derth,
Then I leave you, my liefe,° yborne of heavenly berth.

29

And sooth° to say, why I left you so long,
Was for to seeke adventure in strange place,
255 Where *Archimago* said a felon strong
To many knights did daily worke disgrace;
But knight he now shall never more deface:°

---

233 **wist** believed.   234 **humblesse** humility.   238 **ought have** something to have.   239 **That . . . light** That should strike my grievous heart like death.   240 **your joyous sight** the joyous sight of you.   244 **thereto meeting** responding accordingly, i.e., with kindness.   248 **meere** pure.   250 **kindly skill** natural power.   252 **liefe** beloved.   253 **sooth** truth.   257 **deface** defame.

      Good cause of mine excuse;° that mote ye please
      Well to accept, and evermore embrace°
      My faithfull service, that by land and seas   260
Have vowd you to defend, now then your plaint
    appease.

      30

His lovely° words her seemd due recompence
      Of all her passed paines: one loving howre
      For many yeares of sorrow can dispence:°
      A dram of sweet is worth a pound of sowre: 265
      She has forgot, how many a wofull stowre°
      For him she late endur'd; she speakes no more
      Of past: true is, that true love hath no powre
      To looken backe; his eyes be fixt before.
Before her stands her knight, for whom she toyld so
    sore.   270

      31

Much like, as when the beaten marinere,
      That long hath wandred in the *Ocean* wide,
      Oft soust° in swelling *Tethys* saltish teare,°
      And long time having tand his tawney hide
      With blustring breath of heaven, that none can
    bide,   275
      And scorching flames of fierce *Orions* hound,°
      Soone as the port from farre he has espide,
      His chearefull whistle merrily doth sound,
And *Nereus* crownes with cups;° his mates him pledg
    around.

      32

Such joy made *Una,* when her knight she found;   280
      And eke th'enchaunter joyous seemd no lesse,

258 **Good cause . . . excuse** good reason why I should be excused.
259 **embrace** accept.   262 **lovely** loving.   264 **dispence** make amends
for.   266 **stowre** encounter.   273 **soust** drenched.   273 **swelling
Tethys saltish teare** the ocean.   276 **fierce Orions hound** Sirius, the
dogstar, whose rising marks the hottest time of the year. It lies in the
constellation Orion.   279 **Nereus crownes with cups** With full cups
he honors Nereus, a sea god.

Then the glad marchant, that does vew from
    ground
His ship farre come from watrie wildernesse,
He hurles out vowes, and *Neptune* oft doth
    blesse:
285   So forth they past, and all the way they spent
Discoursing of her dreadfull late distresse,
In which he askt her, what the Lyon ment:
Who told her all that fell in journey as she went.°

33

They had not ridden farre, when they might see
290   One pricking towards them with hastie heat,
Full strongly armd, and on a courser° free,
That through his fiercenesse fomed all with sweat,
And the sharpe yron° did for anger eat,
When his hot ryder spurd his chauffed° side;
295   His looke was sterne, and seemed still to threat
Cruell revenge, which he in hart did hyde,
And on his shield *Sans loy* in bloudie lines was dyde.

34

When nigh he drew unto this gentle payre
And saw the Red-crosse, which the knight did
    beare,
300   He burnt in fire,° and gan eftsoones prepare
Himselfe to battell with his couched speare.°
Loth was that other, and did faint through feare,
To taste th'untryed dint° of deadly steele;
But yet his Lady did so well him cheare,
305   That hope of new good hap he gan to feele;
So bent his speare, and spurnd° his horse with yron
    heele.

35

But that proud Paynim° forward came so fierce,

---

288 **Who . . . went** Who told as she went all that befell her.   291
courser horse used in tournaments; a charger.   293 **yron** bit.   294
chauffed heated.   300 **fire** rage.   301 **his couched speare** his spear
ready for charging.   303 **th'untryed dint** the blow that he had not
experienced.   306 **spurnd** spurred.   307 **Paynim** pagan.

And full of wrath, that with his sharp-head speare
   Through vainely crossed° shield he quite did
      pierce,
   And had his staggering steede not shrunke for
      feare,   *310*
   Through shield and bodie eke he should him
      beare:°
   Yet so great was the puissance of his push,
   That from his saddle quite he did him beare:
   He tombling rudely downe to ground did rush,
And from his gored wound a well of bloud did gush. *315*

36

Dismounting lightly from his loftie steed,
   He to him lept, in mind to reave° his life,
   And proudly said, Lo there the worthie meed
   Of him, that slew *Sansfoy* with bloudie knife;
   Henceforth his ghost freed from repining° strife, *320*
   In peace may passen over *Lethe* lake,°
   When morning altars° purgd with enemies life,
   The blacke infernall *Furies*° doen aslake:°
Life from *Sansfoy* thou tookst, *Sansloy* shall from thee
      take.

37

Therewith in haste his helmet gan unlace,   *325*
   Till *Una* cride, O hold that heavie° hand,
   Deare Sir, what ever that thou be in place:°
   Enough is, that thy foe doth vanquisht stand
   Now at thy mercy: Mercie not withstand:°
   For he is one the truest° knight alive,   *330*
   Though conquered now he lie on lowly land,°

---

309 **vainely crossed** i.e., without the charm that protects the Red
Cross Knight in I. ii. 18.   311 **he should him beare** he (Sansloy)
should have thrust himself.   317 **in mind to reave** intending to take
away.   320 **repining** fretful. Cf. his "grudging ghost" (ii. 19).   321
Lethe lake the river of forgetfulness in hell.   322 **morning altars**
altars erected for mourning.   323 **Furies** spirits of revenge.   323
aslake assuage.   326 **heavie** cruel.   327 **what ever . . . place** i.e.,
whoever you are.   329 **Mercie not withstand** do not oppose mercy.
330 **one the truest** the one truest.   331 **lie on lowly land** lie lowly
on the ground.

And whilest him fortune favourd, faire did thrive
In bloudie field: therefore of life him not deprive.

38

Her piteous words might not abate his rage,
335   But rudely rending up his helmet, would
        Have slaine him straight: but when he sees his
          age,
        And hoarie head of *Archimago* old,
        His hastie hand he doth amazed hold,
        And halfe ashamed, wondred at the sight:
340   For that old man well knew he, though untold,°
        In charmes and magicke to have wondrous might,
Ne ever wont in field, ne in round lists° to fight.

39

And said, Why *Archimago,* lucklesse syre,
        What doe I see? what hard mishap is this,
345   That hath thee hither brought to taste mine yre?
        Or thine the fault, or mine the error is,
        In stead of foe to wound my friend amis?
        He answered nought, but in a traunce still lay,
        And on those guilefull dazed eyes of his
350   The cloud of death did sit. Which doen away,°
He left him lying so, ne would no lenger stay.

40

But to the virgin comes, who all this while
        Amased stands, her selfe so mockt° to see
        By him, who has the guerdon° of his guile,
355   For so misfeigning° her true knight to bee:
        Yet is she now in more perplexitie,
        Left in the hand of that same Paynim bold,
        From whom her booteth not° at all to flie;

---

340 **untold** not informed. The line suggests an instinctive kinship between evil characters.   342 **round lists** enclosed lists of a tournament.   350 **Which doen away** i.e., when the cloud of death passed.
353 **mockt** duped.   354 **guerdon** reward.   355 **misfeigning** evilly
feigning.   358 **her booteth not** it does not avail her.

Who by her cleanly° garment catching hold,
Her from her Palfrey pluckt, her visage to behold. 360

41

But her fierce servant full of kingly awe
 And high disdaine, whenas° his soveraine Dame
 So rudely handled by her foe he sawe,
 With gaping jawes full greedy at him came,
 And ramping° on his shield, did weene the same 365
 Have° reft away with his sharpe rending clawes:
 But he was stout, and lust did now inflame
 His corage more, that from his griping pawes
He hath his shield redeem'd,° and foorth his swerd
  he drawes.

42

O then too weake and feeble was the forse 370
 Of salvage beast, his puissance to withstand:
 For he was strong, and of so mightie corse,
 As ever wielded speare in warlike hand,
 And feates of armes did wisely° understand.
 Eftsoones he perced through his chaufed° chest 375
 With thrilling° point of deadly yron brand,°
 And launcht° his Lordly hart: with death opprest°
He roar'd aloud, whiles life forsooke his stubborne°
  brest.

43

Who now is left to keepe° the forlorne maid
 From raging spoile of lawlesse victors will?° 380
 Her faithfull gard remov'd, her hope dismaid,°
 Her selfe a yeelded pray to save or spill.°
 He now Lord of the field, his pride to fill,
 With foule reproches, and disdainfull spight

359 **cleanly** always clean. 362 **whenas** when. 365 **ramping** standing on his hind feet, with forepaws extended. 366 **Have** to have. 369 **redeem'd** recovered. 374 **wisely** skillfully. 375 **chaufed** angry. 376 **thrilling** piercing. 376 **brand** sword. 377 **launcht** pierced. 377 **opprest** overpowered. 378 **stubborne** unyielding. 379 **keepe** guard. 380 **From . . . will** from being the spoil of lawless victor's raging will. 381 **dismaid** defeated. 382 **spill** destroy.

385   Her vildly entertaines, and will or nill,°
     Beares her away upon his courser light:
Her prayers nought prevaile, his rage is more of might.

44

And all the way, with great lamenting paine,°
    And piteous plaints she filleth his dull° eares,
390   That stony hart could riven have in twaine,
    And all the way she wets with flowing teares:
    But he enrag'd with rancor, nothing heares.
    Her servile beast yet would not leave her so,
    But followes her farre off, ne ought° he feares,
395   To be partaker of her wandring woe,
More mild in beastly kind,° then that her beastly foe.

CANTO IV

To sinfull house of Pride, Duessa
   guides the faithfull knight,
Where brothers death to wreak° Sansjoy
   doth chalenge him to fight.

1

Young knight, what ever° that dost armes professe,
    And through long labours huntest after fame,
    Beware of fraud, beware of ficklenesse,
    In choice, and change of thy deare loved Dame,
5   Least thou of her beleeve too lightly blame,
    And rash misweening° doe thy hart remove:
    For unto knight there is no greater shame,
    Then° lightnesse and inconstancie in love;

---

385 **Her . . . nill** treats her vilely, and whether she was willing or un-
willing. 388 **lamenting paine** laments full of suffering. 389 **dull**
i.e., not hearing her. 394 **ne ought** not at all. 396 **beastly kind** as a
beast by nature. Arg. **wreak** avenge. 1 **what ever** whoever. 6
rash misweening rashly misunderstanding. 8 **Then** than.

That doth this *Redcrosse* knights ensample° plainly
    prove.

2

Who after that he had faire *Una* lorne,°   10
    Through light misdeeming° of her loialtie,
    And false *Duessa* in her sted had borne,
    Called *Fidess'*, and so supposd to bee;
    Long with her traveild, till at last they see
    A goodly building, bravely garnished,   15
    The house of mightie Prince it seemd to bee:
    And towards it a broad high way that led,
All bare through peoples feet, which thither traveiled.

3

Great troupes of people traveild thitherward
    Both day and night, of each degree and place,°   20
    But few returned, having scaped hard,°
    With balefull° beggerie, or foule disgrace,
    Which ever after in most wretched case,°
    Like loathsome lazars,° by the hedges lay.
    Thither *Duessa* bad him bend his pace:°   25
    For she is wearie of the toilesome way,
And also nigh consumed is the lingring day.

4

A stately Pallace built of squared bricke,
    Which cunningly was without morter laid,
    Whose wals were high, but nothing° strong, nor
        thick,   30
    And golden foile all over them displaid,°
    That purest skye with brightnesse they dismaid:
    High lifted up were many loftie towres,
    And goodly galleries farre over° laid,

---

9 **ensample** example. 10 **lorne** forsaken. 11 **misdeeming** thinking
evil. 20 **of . . . place** i.e., all orders of society. 21 **scaped hard** escaped with difficulty. 22 **balefull** painful. 23 **case** condition. 24
lazars lepers. 25 **bend his pace** turn his step. 30 **nothing** not at all.
31 **displaid** spread out. 34 **farre over** far above.

35   Full of faire windowes, and delightfull bowres;
And on the top a Diall told the timely° howres.

          5

It was a goodly heape° for to behould,
          And spake the praises of the workmans wit;°
          But full great pittie, that so faire a mould°
40   Did on so weake foundation ever sit:
          For on a sandie hill, that still did flit,°
          And fall away, it mounted was full hie,
          That every breath of heaven shaked it:
          And all the hinder° parts, that few could spie,
45   Were ruinous and old, but painted cunningly.

          6

Arrived there they passed in forth right;°
          For still to all the gates stood open wide,
          Yet charge of them was to a Porter hight°
          Cald *Malvenù,*° who entrance none denide:
50   Thence to the hall, which was on every side
          With rich array and costly arras dight:°
          Infinite sorts° of people did abide
          There waiting long, to win the wished sight
Of her, that was the Lady of that Pallace bright.

          7

55   By them they passe, all gazing on them round,°
          And to the Presence° mount; whose glorious vew
          Their frayle amazed senses did confound:
          In living Princes court none ever knew
          Such endlesse richesse, and so sumptuous shew;
60   Ne *Persia* selfe, the nourse of pompous pride
          Like ever saw. And there a noble crew
          Of Lordes and Ladies stood on every side,

36 **timely** passing.   37 **goodly heape** magnificent pile.   38 **wit** skill.
39 **mould** structure.   41 **flit** give way.   44 **hinder** hind.   46 **forth
right** straightway.   48 **hight** committed.   49 **Malvenù** The name
suggests an ominous arrival.   51 **dight** decked.   52 **sorts** companies.   55 **all . . . round** all those around gazing on them.   56 **the
Presence** the presence-chamber in which a sovereign receives guests.

Which with their presence faire, the place much
    beautifide.

8

High above all a cloth of State was spred,
    And a rich throne, as bright as sunny day,   *65*
    On which there sate most brave embellished°
    With royall robes and gorgeous array,
    A mayden Queene, that shone as *Titans* ray,
    In glistring gold, and peerelesse pretious stone:
    Yet her bright blazing beautie did assay°   *70*
    To dim the brightnesse of her glorious throne,
As envying her selfe, that too exceeding shone.

9

Exceeding shone, like *Phœbus* fairest childe,°
    That did presume° his fathers firie wayne,°
    And flaming mouthes of steedes unwonted° wilde   *75*
    Through highest heaven with weaker° hand to
        rayne;
    Proud of such glory and advancement vaine,
    While flashing beames do daze his feeble eyen,
    He leaves the welkin way° most beaten plaine,
    And rapt° with whirling wheeles, inflames the
        skyen,°   *80*
With fire not made to burne, but fairely for to shyne.

10

So proud she shyned in her Princely state,
    Looking to heaven; for earth she did disdayne,
    And sitting high; for lowly° she did hate:
    Lo underneath her scornefull feete, was layne   *85*
    A dreadfull Dragon with an hideous trayne,°
    And in her hand she held a mirrhour bright,

---

66 **brave embellished** splendidly adorned.   70 **assay** try.   73 **Phœbus fairest childe** Phaeton, who borrowed the horses of the sun from
his father. When his erratic driving threatened to burn the world,
Jupiter killed him with a bolt of lightning.   74 **presume** usurp.   74
wayne wagon.   75 **unwonted** unusually.   76 **weaker** too weak.   79
the welkin way the sun's path in the heavens.   80 **rapt** carried away.
80 **skyen** skies.   84 **lowly** lowliness.   86 **trayne** tail.

Wherein her face she often vewed fayne,°
And in her selfe-lov'd semblance tooke delight;
90 For she was wondrous faire, as any living wight.

11

Of griesly *Pluto*° she the daughter was,
　　And sad *Proserpina* the Queene of hell;
　　Yet did she thinke her pearelesse worth to pas
　　That parentage, with pride so did she swell,
　　And thundring *Jove,* that high in heaven doth
95　　　dwell,
　　And wield the world, she claymed for her syre,
　　Or if that any else did *Jove* excell:
　　For to the highest she did still aspyre,
Or if ought higher were then that, did it desyre.

12

100 And proud *Lucifera*° men did her call,
　　That made her selfe a Queene, and crownd to be,
　　Yet rightfull kingdome she had none at all,
　　Ne heritage of native° soveraintie,
　　But did usurpe with wrong and tyrannie
105　　Upon the scepter, which she now did hold:
　　Ne ruld her Realmes with lawes, but pollicie,°
　　And strong advizement of six wisards old,
That with their counsels bad her kingdome did uphold.

13

Soone as the Elfin knight in presence came,
110　　And false *Duessa* seeming Lady faire,°
　　A gentle Husher,° *Vanitie* by name
　　Made rowme, and passage for them did prepaire:°
　　So goodly° brought them to the lowest staire
　　Of her high throne, where they on humble knee

88 **she often vewed fayne** often she rejoiced to view.   91 **Pluto** king
of hell.   100 **Lucifera** the feminine form of Lucifer which, from
Isaiah xiv. 12, denotes Pride.   103 **native** by right of birth.   106
pollicie political cunning.   110 **seeming Lady faire** seeming to be a
fair lady.   111 **Husher** usher.   112 **prepaire** provide.   113 **goodly**
courteously.

Making obeyssance,° did the cause declare,   *115*
Why they were come, her royall state to see,
To prove the wide report of her great Majestee.

14

With loftie° eyes, halfe loth to looke so low,
She thanked them in her disdainefull wise,
Ne other grace vouchsafed them to show   *120*
Of Princesse worthy, scarse them bad arise.
Her Lordes and Ladies all this while devise
Themselves to setten forth to straungers sight:
Some frounce° their curled haire in courtly guise,
Some prancke° their ruffes, and others trimly
    dight   *125*
Their gay attire: each others greater pride does
    spight.°

15

Goodly they all that knight do entertaine,
Right glad with him to have increast their crew:
But to *Duess'* each one himselfe did paine°
All kindnesse and faire courtesie to shew;   *130*
For in that court whylome° her well they knew:
Yet the stout Faerie mongst the middest crowd°
Thought all their glorie vaine in knightly vew,
And that great Princesse too exceeding prowd,
That to strange knight no better countenance allowd.   *135*

16

Suddein upriseth from her stately place
The royall Dame, and for her coche doth call:
All hurtlen° forth, and she with Princely pace,
As faire *Aurora* in her purple pall,
Out of the East the dawning day doth call: *140*
So forth she comes: her brightnesse brode doth
    blaze;

115 **obeyssance** obeisance, homage or submission. 118 **loftie** haughty. 124 **frounce** braid. 125 **prancke** make display of. 126 **each . . . spight** Each spites the others' greater pride. 129 **paine** take pains. 131 **whylome** formerly. 132 **mongst . . . crowd** in the middle of the crowd. 138 **hurtlen** rush.

The heapes of people thronging in the hall,
Do ride each other, upon her to gaze:
Her glorious glitter and light doth all mens eyes
    amaze.

17

145 So forth she comes, and to her coche does clyme,
        Adorned all with gold, and girlonds gay,
        That seemd as fresh as *Flora* in her prime,°
        And strove to match, in royall rich array,
        Great *Junoes* golden chaire,° the which they say
150   The Gods stand gazing on, when she does ride
        To *Joves* high house through heavens bras-paved
            way
        Drawne of faire Pecocks, that excell in pride,°
And full of *Argus* eyes° their tailes dispredden° wide.

18

But this was drawne of six unequall beasts,
155   On which her six sage Counsellours did ryde,
        Taught to obay their bestiall beheasts,
        With like conditions to their kinds applyde:°
        Of which the first, that all the rest did guyde,
        Was sluggish *Idlenesse* the nourse of sin;
160   Upon a slouthfull Asse he chose to ryde,
        Arayd in habit blacke, and amis° thin,
Like to an holy Monck, the service to begin.°

19

And in his hand his Portesse° still he bare,
        That much was worne, but therein little red,
165   For of devotion he had little care,
        Still drownd in sleepe, and most of his dayes
            ded;

147 **Flora in her prime** the goddess of flowers in springtime. 149
Junoes golden chaire the queen of heaven's golden chariot. 152
pride splendor. 153 **Argus eyes** When Argus, who had a hundred
eyes, was slain by Mercury, Juno set the eyes in the peacock's
feathers. 153 **dispredden** spread. 157 **With . . . applyde** i.e., the
bestial commands given by the six deadly sins suited each beast's
nature. 161 **amis** amice, a religious hood. 162 **to begin** about to
begin. 163 **Portesse** breviary.

Scarse could he once uphold his heavie hed,
To looken, whether it were night or day:
May seeme° the wayne was very evill led,
When such an one had guiding of the way,   *170*
That knew not, whether right he went, or else astray.

20

From worldly cares himselfe he did esloyne,°
And greatly shunned manly exercise,
From every worke he chalenged essoyne,°
For contemplation sake: yet otherwise,°   *175*
His life he led in lawlesse riotise;°
By which he grew to grievous malady;
For in his lustlesse° limbs through evill guise°
A shaking fever raignd continually:
Such one was *Idlenesse,* first of this company.   *180*

21

And by his side rode loathsome *Gluttony,*
Deformed creature, on a filthie swyne,
His belly was up-blowne with luxury,
And eke with fatnesse swollen were his eyne,
And like a Crane his necke was long and fyne,°   *185*
With which he swallowd up excessive feast,
For want whereof poore people oft did pyne;
And all the way, most like a brutish beast,
He spued up his gorge,° that all did him deteast.

22

In greene vine leaves he was right fitly clad;   *190*
For other clothes he could not weare for heat,
And on his head an yvie girland had,
From under which fast trickled downe the sweat:
Still as he rode, he somewhat° still did eat,
And in his hand did beare a bouzing can,°   *195*

---

169 **May seeme** it may seem that.   172 **esloyne** eloign, withdraw.
174 **chalenged essoyne** pleaded excuse.   175 **otherwise** in another
way.   176 **riotise** riotousness.   178 **lustlesse** listless.   178 **evill
guise** bad living.   185 **fyne** slender.   189 **gorge** what he had swal-
lowed.   194 **somewhat** something.   195 **bouzing can** drinking cup.

Of which he supt so oft, that on his seat
His dronken corse he scarse upholden can,
In shape and life more like a monster, then a man.

23

Unfit he was for any worldly thing,
200   And eke unhable° once to stirre or go,°
Not meet to be of counsell to a king,
Whose mind in meat and drinke was drowned
        so,
That from his friend he seldome knew his fo:
Full of diseases was his carcas blew,°
205   And a dry dropsie through his flesh did flow:
Which by misdiet daily greater grew:
Such one was *Gluttony*, the second of that crew.

24

And next to him rode lustfull *Lechery*,
Upon a bearded Goat, whose rugged haire,
210   And whally eyes° (the signe of gelosy,)
Was like the person selfe, whom he did beare:
Who rough, and blacke, and filthy did appeare,
Unseemely man to please faire Ladies eye;
Yet he of Ladies oft was loved deare,
215   When fairer faces were bid standen by:°
O who does know the bent of womens fantasy?

25

In a greene gowne he clothed was full faire,
Which underneath did hide his filthinesse,
And in his hand a burning hart he bare,
220   Full of vaine follies, and new fanglenesse:°
For he was false, and fraught° with ficklenesse,
And learned had to love with secret lookes,
And well could daunce, and sing with rueful-
        nesse,

200 **unhable** unable. 200 **go** walk. 204 **blew** livid. 210 **whally
eyes** wall-eyed. 215 **bid standen by** asked to keep away. 220 **new
fanglenesse** fond of novelties. 221 **fraught** filled.

And fortunes tell, and read in loving bookes,
And thousand other wayes, to bait his fleshly hookes. 225

26

Inconstant man, that loved all he saw,
  And lusted after all, that he did love,
  Ne would his looser° life be tide to law,
  But joyd weake wemens hearts to tempt and
    prove
  If from their loyall loves he might them move; 230
  Which lewdnesse fild him with reprochfull°
    paine
  Of that fowle evill,° which all men reprove,
  That rots the marrow, and consumes the braine:
Such one was *Lecherie,* the third of all this traine.

27

And greedy *Avarice* by him did ride, 235
  Upon a Camell loaden all with gold;
  Two iron coffers hong on either side,
  With precious mettall full, as they might hold,
  And in his lap an heape of coine he told;°
  For of his wicked pelfe° his God he made, 240
  And unto hell him selfe for money sold;
  Accursed usurie was all his trade,
And right and wrong ylike in equall ballaunce waide.°

28

His life was nigh unto deaths doore yplast,°
  And thred-bare cote, and cobled shoes he ware, 245
  Ne scarse good morsell all his life did tast,
  But both from backe and belly still did spare,
  To fill his bags, and richesse to compare;°
  Yet chylde ne kinsman living had he none
  To leave them to; but thorough daily care 250

228 **looser** too loose. 231 **reprochfull** shameful. 232 **that fowle evill** syphilis. 239 **told** counted. 240 **wicked pelfe** filthy lucre. 243 **And . . . waide** i.e., he did not distinguish between right and wrong. 244 **yplast** brought. 248 **compare** get.

To get, and nightly feare to lose his owne,
He led a wretched life unto him selfe unknowne.

29

Most wretched wight, whom nothing might suffise,
      Whose greedy lust° did lacke in greatest store,
255   Whose need had end, but no end covetise,°
      Whose wealth was want, whose plenty made him
            pore,
      Who had enough, yet wished ever more;
      A vile disease, and eke in foote and hand
      A grievous gout tormented him full sore,
260   That well he could not touch, nor go, nor stand:
Such one was *Avarice,* the fourth of this faire band.

30

And next to him malicious *Envie* rode,
      Upon a ravenous wolfe, and still did chaw°
      Betweene his cankred° teeth a venemous tode,
265   That all the poison ran about his chaw;°
      But inwardly he chawed his owne maw°
      At neighbours wealth, that made him ever sad;
      For death it was, when any good he saw,
      And wept, that cause of weeping none he had,
But when he heard of harme, he wexed wondrous
270   glad.

31

All in a kirtle° of discolourd say°
      He clothed was, ypainted full of eyes;
      And in his bosome secretly there lay
      An hatefull Snake, the which his taile uptyes°
275   In many folds, and mortall sting implyes.°
      Still as he rode, he gnasht his teeth, to see
      Those heapes of gold with griple Covetyse,°

254 **lust** desire.   255 **covetise** covetousness.   263 **chaw** chew.   264
cankred infected.   265 **chaw** jaw.   266 **maw** stomach   271 **kirtle**
tunic;   271 **discolourd say** a kind of cloth of various colors.   274
uptyes twists.   275 **implyes** enfolds.   277 **with griple Covetyse**
owned by grasping Avarice.

And grudged at the great felicitie
Of proud *Lucifera,* and his owne companie.

32

He hated all good workes and vertuous deeds,   280
    And him no lesse, that any like did use,°
    And who with gracious bread the hungry feeds,°
    His almes for want of faith he doth accuse;
    So every good to bad he doth abuse:
    And eke the verse of famous Poets witt   285
    He does backebite, and spightfull poison spues
    From leprous mouth on all, that ever writt:
Such one vile *Envie* was, that fifte in row did sitt.

33

And him beside rides fierce revenging *Wrath,*
    Upon a Lion, loth for to be led;   290
    And in his hand a burning brond he hath,
    The which he brandisheth about his hed;
    His eyes did hurle forth sparkles° fiery red,
    And stared sterne on all, that him beheld,
    As ashes pale of hew and seeming ded;°   295
    And on his dagger still° his hand he held,
Trembling through hasty rage, when choler in him
        sweld.

34

His ruffin° raiment all was staind with blood,
    Which he had spilt, and all to rags yrent,°
    Through unadvized° rashnesse woxen wood;°   300
    For of his hands he had no governement,°
    Ne car'd for° bloud in his avengement:
    But when the furious fit was overpast,
    His cruell facts° he often would repent;
    Yet wilfull man he never would forecast,°   305

281 **that ... use** that practiced such works.   282 **with ... feeds** with
bread .. graciously feeds.   293 **sparkles** sparks.   295 **seeming ded**
seemed like one dead.   296 **still** always.   298 **ruffin** befitting a
ruffian.   299 **yrent** torn.   300 **unadvized** rash.   300 **woxen wood**
grown mad.   301 **governement** management.   302 **car'd for** took
heed of shedding.   304 **facts** deeds.   305 **forecast** consider before-
hand.

How many mischieves° should ensue° his heedlesse
     hast.

35

Full many mischiefes follow cruell *Wrath;*
     Abhorred bloudshed, and tumultuous strife,
     Unmanly murder, and unthrifty scath,°
310   Bitter despight, with rancours rusty° knife,
     And fretting° griefe the enemy of life;
     All these, and many evils moe° haunt° ire,
     The swelling Splene, and Frenzy raging rife,
     The shaking Palsey, and Saint *Fraunces* fire:°
315 Such one was *Wrath,* the last of this ungodly tire.°

36

And after all, upon the wagon beame
     Rode *Sathan,* with a smarting whip in hand,
     With which he forward lasht the laesie teme,
     So oft as *Slowth* still in the mire did stand.
320   Huge routs° of people did about them band,
     Showting for joy, and still before their way
     A foggy mist had covered all the land;
     And underneath their feet, all scattered lay
Dead sculs and bones of men, whose life had gone
     astray.

37

325 So forth they marchen in this goodly sort,°
     To take the solace of the open aire,
     And in fresh flowring fields themselves to sport;
     Emongst the rest rode that false Lady faire,
     The fowle *Duessa,* next unto the chaire
330   Of proud *Lucifera,* as one of the traine:
     But that good knight would not so nigh re-
          paire,°

---

306 **mischieves** misfortunes;   306 **ensue** result from.   309 **unthrifty
scath** wasteful harm.   310 **rusty** red with blood.   311 **fretting** gnawing.   312 **moe** more.   312 **haunt** run after.   314 **Saint Fraunces
fire** a fever that brings inflammation of the skin.   315 **tire** proces-
sion.   320 **routs** companies.   325 **sort** company.   331 **repaire** go.

Him selfe estraunging from their joyaunce°
    vaine,
Whose fellowship seemd far unfit for warlike swaine.

38

So having solaced themselves a space
    With pleasaunce of the breathing fields° yfed,°   335
    They backe returned to the Princely Place;
    Whereas° an errant knight in armes ycled,°
    And heathnish shield, wherein with letters red
    Was writ *Sans joy,* they new arrived find:
    Enflam'd with fury and fiers hardy-hed,°   340
    He seemd in hart to harbour thoughts unkind,
And nourish bloudy vengeaunce in his bitter mind.

39

Who when the shamed° shield of slaine *Sans foy*
    He spide with that same Faery champions page,
    Bewraying° him, that did of late destroy   345
    His eldest brother, burning all with rage
    He to him leapt, and that same envious gage°
    Of victors glory from him snatcht away:
    But th'Elfin knight, which ought° that warlike
        wage,°
    Disdaind to loose the meed he wonne in fray,   350
And him rencountring° fierce, reskewd the noble
    pray.

40

Therewith they gan to hurtlen greedily,
    Redoubted° battaile ready to darrayne,°
    And clash their shields, and shake their swords
        on hy,

332 **joyaunce** enjoyment.   335 **breathing fields** the fields in which
they smelled the flowers.   335 **yfed** refreshed.   337 **Whereas** where.
337 **ycled** clad.   340 **hardy-hed** hardihood, boldness.   343 **shamed**
being reversed.   345 **Bewraying** revealing.   347 **envious gage** the
pledge of victory which he envied him.   349 **which ought** who
owned.   349 **wage** pledge, reward.   351 **rencountring** engaging in
battle.   353 **Redoubted** dreaded.   353 **darrayne** prepare.

That with their sturre° they troubled all the
355   traine;
      Till that great Queene upon eternall paine
      Of high displeasure, that ensewen might,
      Commaunded them their fury to refraine,°
      And if that either to that shield had right,
360 In equall lists they should the morrow next it fight.°

          41

Ah dearest Dame, (quoth then the Paynim bold,)
      Pardon the errour of enraged wight,
      Whom great griefe made forget the raines to hold
      Of reasons rule, to see° this recreant knight,
365   No knight, but treachour° full of false despight
      And shamefull treason, who through guile hath
        slayn
      The prowest° knight, that ever field did fight,
      Even stout *Sans foy* (O who can then refrayn?)
Whose shield he beares renverst,° the more to heape
      disdayn.

          42

370 And to augment the glorie of his guile,
      His dearest love the faire *Fidessa* loe
      Is there possessed of the traytour vile,
      Who reapes the harvest sowen by his foe,
      Sowen in bloudy field, and bought with woe:
375   That brothers hand shall dearely well requight
      So be, O Queene, you equall° favour showe.
      Him litle answerd th'angry Elfin knight;
He never meant with words, but swords to plead his
      right.

          43

But threw his gauntlet as a sacred pledge,
380   His cause in combat the next day to try:

---

355 **sturre** tumult.   358 **refraine** restrain.   360 **it fight** fight for the right.   364 **to see** upon seeing.   365 **treachour** traitor.   367 **prowest** most valiant.   369 **renverst** reversed, in sign of disgrace.   376 **equall** impartial.

So been they parted both, with harts on edge,°
    To be aveng'd each on his enimy.
    That night they pas in joy and jollity,
    Feasting and courting both in bowre and hall;
    For Steward was excessive *Gluttonie,*   385
    That of his plenty poured forth to all;
Which doen,° the Chamberlain *Slowth* did to rest
    them call.

44

Now whenas darkesome night had all displayd
    Her coleblacke curtein over brightest skye,
    The warlike youthes on dayntie couches layd,   390
    Did chace away sweet sleepe from sluggish eye,
    To muse on meanes of hoped victory.
    But whenas *Morpheus* had with leaden mace
    Arrested all that courtly company,
    Up-rose *Duessa* from her resting place,   395
And to the Paynims lodging comes with silent pace.

45

Whom broad awake she finds, in troublous fit,°
    Forecasting, how his foe he might annoy,°
    And him amoves° with speaches seeming fit:
    Ah deare *Sans joy,* next dearest to *Sans foy,*   400
    Cause of my new griefe, cause of my new joy,
    Joyous, to see his ymage in mine eye,
    And greev'd, to thinke how foe did him destroy,
    That was the flowre of grace and chevalrye;
Lo his *Fidessa* to thy secret faith I flye.   405

46

With gentle wordes he can° her fairely greet,
    And bad say on the secret of her hart.
    Then sighing soft, I learne that litle sweet
    Oft tempred is (quoth she) with muchell° smart:

---

381 **on edge** full of eagerness.   387 **Which doen** which having been
done.   397 **troublous fit** troubled mood.   398 **annoy** injure.   399
amoves stirs up.   406 **can** did.   409 **muchell** mickle, much.

For since my brest was launcht° with lovely
dart°
Of deare *Sansfoy,* I never joyed howre,°
But in eternall woes my weaker° hart
Have wasted, loving him with all my powre,
And for his sake have felt full many an heavie
stowre.°

47

At last when perils all I weened past,
And hop'd to reape the crop° of all my care,
Into new woes unweeting° I was cast,
By this false faytor,° who unworthy ware
His worthy shield, whom he with guilefull snare
Entrapped slew, and brought to shamefull grave.
Me silly maid away with him he bare,
And ever since hath kept in darksome cave,
For that° I would not yeeld, that° to *Sans-foy* I gave.

48

But since faire Sunne hath sperst° that lowring clowd,
And to my loathed life now shewes some light,
Under your beames I will me safely shrowd,
From dreaded storme of his disdainfull spight:
To you th'inheritance belongs by right
Of brothers prayse, to you eke longs° his love.
Let not his love, let not his restlesse spright
Be unreveng'd, that calles to you above
From wandring *Stygian* shores,° where it doth end-
lesse° move.

49

Thereto said he, faire Dame be nought dismaid

---

410 **launcht** pierced. 410 **lovely dart** Cupid's dart. 411 **howre**
for an hour. 412 **weaker** too weak. 414 **stowre** time of turmoil.
416 **crop** harvest. 417 **unweeting** unwittingly. 418 **faytor** impostor.
423 **For that** because. 423 **that** that which. 424 **sperst** dispersed.
429 **longs** belongs. 432 **wandring Stygian shores** banks of the Styx,
a river in hell, where Sansfoy's spirit wanders. 432 **endlesse** forever.

For sorrowes past; their griefe is with them gone:
Ne yet of present perill be affraid;   435
For needlesse feare did never vantage° none,
And helplesse hap it booteth not to mone.°
Dead is *Sans-foy,* his vitall paines° are past,
Though greeved ghost for vengeance deepe do
    grone:
He lives, that shall him pay his dewties last,°   440
And guiltie Elfin bloud shall sacrifice in hast.

    50

O but I feare the fickle freakes° (quoth shee)
    Of fortune false, and oddes° of armes in field.
    Why dame (quoth he) what oddes can ever
      bee,
    Where both do fight alike, to win or yield?   445
    Yea but (quoth she) he beares a charmed shield,
    And eke enchaunted armes, that none can perce,
    Ne none can wound the man, that does them
      wield.
    Charmd or enchaunted (answerd he then ferce)
I no whit reck,° ne you the like need to reherce.°   450

    51

But faire *Fidessa,* sithens° fortunes guile,
    Or enimies powre hath now captived you,
    Returne from whence ye came, and rest a while
    Till morrow next, that° I the Elfe subdew,
    And with *Sans-foyes* dead dowry° you endew.°   455
    Ay me, that is a double death (she said)
    With proud foes sight my sorrow to renew:
    Where ever yet I be, my secret aid
Shall follow you. So passing forth she him obaid.

---

436 **vantage** profit.   437 **And . . . mone** It does no good to lament
what cannot be helped.   438 **vitall paines** pains in life.   440 **pay his
dewties last** pay the last duties owing to Sansfoy's spirit by sacrificing
the one who killed him.   442 **freakes** caprices.   444 **oddes** advantage.   450 **reck** heed.   450 **reherce** describe.   451 **sithens** since.
454 **that** when.   455 **Sans-foyes dead dowry** the dead Sansfoy's
dowry.   455 **endew** endow.

CANTO V

*The faithfull knight in equall field
    subdewes his faithlesse foe,
Whom false Duessa saves, and for
    his cure to hell does goe.*

1

The noble hart, that harbours vertuous thought,
  And is with child of glorious great intent,
  Can never rest, untill it forth have brought
  Th'eternall brood of glorie excellent:
5 Such restlesse passion did all night torment
  The flaming corage of that Faery knight,
  Devizing, how that doughtie turnament°
  With greatest honour he atchieven° might;
Still did he wake, and still did watch for dawning
   light.

2

10 At last the golden Orientall gate
  Of greatest heaven gan to open faire,
  And *Phœbus* fresh, as bridegrome to his mate,
  Came dauncing forth, shaking his deawie haire:
  And hurld his glistring beames through gloomy
   aire.
  Which when the wakeful Elfe perceiv'd, streight
15 way
  He started up, and did him selfe prepaire,
  In sun-bright armes, and battailous° array:
For with that Pagan proud he combat will that day.

3

And forth he comes into the commune hall,

---

7 **that doughtie turnament** the tournament at which he seeks to perform doughty or valiant deeds. 8 **atchieven** finish. 17 **battailous** ready for battle.

Where earely waite him many a gazing eye,   20
To weet what end to straunger knights may fall.°
There many Minstrales maken melody,
To drive away the dull melancholy,
And many Bardes, that to the trembling chord
Can tune their timely voyces cunningly,   25
And many Chroniclers, that can record
Old loves, and warres for Ladies doen by many a
    Lord.

4

Soone after comes the cruell Sarazin,
In woven maile all armed warily,
And sternly lookes at him, who not a pin   30
Does care for looke of living creatures eye.
They bring them wines of *Greece* and *Araby,*
And daintie spices fetcht from furthest *Ynd,*
To kindle heat of corage privily:°
And in° the wine a solemne oth they bynd   35
T'observe the sacred lawes of armes, that are assynd.

5

At last forth comes that far renowmed Queene,
With royall pomp and Princely majestie;
She is ybrought unto a paled greene,°
And placed under stately canapee,°   40
The warlike feates of both those knights to see.
On th'other side in all mens open vew
Duessa placed is, and on a tree
Sans-foy his° shield is hangd with bloudy hew:
Both those the lawrell girlonds to the victor dew.   45

6

A shrilling trompet sownded from on hye,
And unto battaill bad them selves addresse:
Their shining shieldes about their wrestes they
    tye,

---

21 **fall** befall.   34 **privily** secretly, i.e., within their hearts.   35 **in**
with.   39 **a paled greene** grass enclosed by palings; the lists.   40
canapee canopy.   44 **Sans-foy his** Sansfoy's.

And burning blades about their heads do blesse,°
50   The instruments of wrath and heavinesse:°
With greedy force each other doth assayle,
And strike so fiercely, that they do impresse
Deepe dinted furrowes in the battred mayle;
The yron walles to ward their blowes are weake and
     fraile.

7

55   The Sarazin was stout, and wondrous strong,
And heaped blowes like yron hammers great:
For after bloud and vengeance he did long.
The knight was fiers, and full of youthly° heat,
And doubled strokes, like dreaded thunders
     threat:
60   For all for prayse and honour he did fight.
Both stricken strike, and beaten both do beat,
That from their shields forth flyeth firie light,
And helmets hewen deepe, shew marks of eithers
     might.

8

So th'one for wrong, the other strives for right:
65   As when a Gryfon° seized of° his pray,
A Dragon fiers encountreth in his flight,
Through widest ayre making his ydle° way,
That would his rightfull ravine° rend away:
With hideous horrour both together smight,
And souce so sore,° that they the heavens
70   affray:°
The wise Southsayer seeing so sad° sight,
Th'amazed vulgar tels of warres and mortall fight.

9

So th'one for wrong, the other strives for right,

49 blesse brandish. 50 heavinesse anger. 58 youthly youthful.
65 Gryfon vulture; in fable, an animal with the wings of an eagle and
the body of a lion. 65 seized of having seized. 67 ydle indolent.
68 ravine prey. 70 souce so sore strike so severely. 70 affray
frighten. 71 sad ominous.

And each to deadly shame would drive his foe:
The cruell steele so greedily doth bight 75
In tender flesh, that streames of bloud down
  flow,
With which the armes, that earst so bright did
  show,
Into a pure vermillion now are dyde:
Great ruth in all the gazers harts did grow,
Seeing the gored woundes to gape so wyde, 80
That victory they dare not wish to either side.

10

At last the Paynim chaunst to cast his eye,
  His suddein° eye, flaming with wrathfull fyre,
  Upon his brothers shield, which hong thereby:
  Therewith redoubled was his raging yre, 85
  And said, Ah wretched sonne of wofull syre,
  Doest thou sit wayling by black *Stygian* lake,
  Whilest here thy shield is hangd for victors
    hyre,°
  And sluggish german° doest thy forces slake,°
To after-send° his foe, that him may overtake? 90

11

Goe caytive° Elfe, him quickly overtake,
  And soone redeeme from his long wandring woe;
  Goe guiltie ghost, to him my message make,°
  That I his shield have quit° from dying foe.
  Therewith upon his crest he stroke him so, 95
  That twise he reeled, readie twise to fall;
  End of the doubtfull battell deemed tho
  The lookers on, and lowd to him gan call
The false *Duessa,* Thine the shield, and I, and all.

12

Soone as the Faerie heard his Ladie speake, 100
  Out of his swowning dreame he gan awake,

83 **suddein** sharp.   88 **hyre** reward.   89 **german** brother.   89 **slake**
slacken.   90 **after-send** send after.   91 **caytive** vile.   93 **make** offer.
94 **quit** released.

And quickning° faith, that earst was woxen
  weake,
The creeping deadly cold away did shake:
Tho mov'd with wrath, and shame, and Ladies
  sake,
Of all attonce he cast° avengd to bee,
And with so'exceeding furie at him strake,
That forced him to stoupe upon his knee;
Had he not stouped so, he should have cloven bee.

13

And to him said, Goe now proud Miscreant,°
  Thy selfe thy message doe° to german deare,
Alone he wandring thee too long doth want:
Goe say, his foe thy shield with his doth beare.
Therewith his heavie° hand he high gan reare,°
Him to have slaine; when loe a darkesome clowd
Upon him fell: he no where doth appeare,
But vanisht is. The Elfe him cals alowd,
But answer none receives: the darknes him does
  shrowd.

14

In haste *Duessa* from her place arose,
  And to him running said, O prowest° knight,
That ever Ladie to her love did chose,
Let now abate the terror of your might,
And quench the flame of furious despight,°
And bloudie vengeance; lo th'infernall powres
Covering your foe with cloud of deadly night,
Have borne him hence to *Plutoes* balefull
  bowres.
The conquest yours, I yours, the shield, and glory
  yours.

15

Not all so° satisfide, with greedie eye

---

102 **quickning** life-restoring. 105 **cast** resolved. 109 **Miscreant**
infidel. 110 **doe** give. 113 **heavie** cruel. 113 **reare** raise. 119
prowest bravest. 122 **despight** anger. 127 **all so** quite.

He sought all round about, his thirstie blade
　　To bath in bloud of faithlesse enemy;
　　Who all that while lay hid in secret shade: *130*
　　He standes amazed, how he thence should fade.°
　　At last the trumpets Triumph° sound on hie,
　　And running Heralds humble homage made,
　　Greeting him goodly° with new victorie,
And to him brought the shield, the cause of enmitie.   *135*

16

Wherewith he goeth to that soveraine Queene,
　　And falling her before on lowly knee,
　　To her makes present of his service seene:°
　　Which she accepts, with thankes, and goodly
　　　　gree,°
　　Greatly advauncing° his gay chevalree.   *140*
　　So marcheth home, and by her takes the knight,
　　Whom all the people follow with great glee,
　　Shouting, and clapping all their hands on hight,
That all the aire it fils, and flyes to heaven bright.

17

Home is he brought, and laid in sumptuous bed: *145*
　　Where many skilfull leaches° him abide,°
　　To salve his hurts, that yet still freshly bled.
　　In wine and oyle they wash his woundes wide,
　　And softly can embalme° on every side.
　　And all the while, most heavenly melody   *150*
　　About the bed sweet musicke did divide,°
　　Him to beguile of griefe and agony:
And all the while *Duessa* wept full bitterly.

18

As when a wearie traveller that strayes
　　By muddy shore of broad seven-mouthed *Nile,*   *155*

131 **fade** vanish.   132 **Triumph** victory.   134 **goodly** courteously.
138 **To . . . seene** He presents the shield to her as token of his service
which he has shown, and therefore proven.   139 **goodly gree** courteous favor.   140 **advauncing** extolling.   146 **leaches** surgeons.   146
abide attend.   149 **can embalme** did anoint.   151 **divide** descant.

Unweeting of the perillous wandring wayes,
Doth meet a cruell craftie Crocodile,
Which in false griefe hyding his harmefull guile,
Doth weepe full sore, and sheddeth tender teares:
The foolish man, that pitties all this while
His mournefull plight, is swallowd up unwares,°
Forgetfull of his owne, that mindes anothers cares.°

19

So wept *Duessa* untill eventide,
That shyning lampes° in *Joves* high house° were
   light:
Then forth she rose, ne lenger would abide,
But comes unto the place, where th'Hethen
   knight
In slombring swownd° nigh voyd of vitall
   spright,
Lay cover'd with inchaunted cloud all day:
Whom when she found, as she him left in
   plight,°
To wayle his woefull case she would not stay,
But to the easterne coast of heaven makes speedy
   way.

20

Where griesly° *Night,* with visage deadly sad,
That *Phœbus* chearefull face durst never vew,
And in a foule blacke pitchie mantle clad,
She findes forth comming from her darkesome
   mew,°
Where she all day did hide her hated hew.
Before the dore her yron charet° stood,
Alreadie harnessed for journey new;
And coleblacke steedes yborne of hellish brood,°

161 **unwares** suddenly.   162 **Forgetfull . . . cares** Forgetful of his
own care (preservation), that minds another's cares (suffering).   164
That shyning lampes when the stars.   164 **Joves high house** the sky.
167 **swownd** swoon.   169 **as . . . plight** in the same peril as she had
left him.   172 **griesly** horrible.   175 **darkesome mew** dark place of
confinement.   177 **charet** chariot.   179 **brood** extraction.

That on their rustie bits did champ, as they were
  wood.°   180

21

Who when she saw *Duessa* sunny bright,
 Adornd with gold and jewels shining cleare,°
 She greatly grew amazed at the sight,
 And th'unacquainted° light began to feare:
 For never did such brightnesse there appeare,   185
 And would have backe retyred to her cave,
 Untill the witches speech she gan to heare,
 Saying, Yet O thou dreaded Dame, I crave
Abide, till I have told the message, which I have.

22

She stayd, and foorth *Duessa* gan proceede,   190
 O thou most auncient Grandmother of all,
 More old then *Jove,* whom thou at first didst
  breede,
 Or that great house of Gods cælestiall,
 Which wast begot in *Dæmogorgons* hall,
 And sawst the secrets of the world unmade,°   195
 Why suffredst thou thy Nephewes° deare to fall
 With Elfin sword, most shamefully betrade?
Lo where the stout *Sansjoy* doth sleepe in deadly
  shade.

23

And him before,° I saw with bitter eyes
 The bold *Sansfoy* shrinke° underneath his speare; 200
 And now the pray of fowles in field he lyes,
 Nor wayld of friends, nor laid on groning beare,°
 That whylome was to me too dearely deare.
 O what of Gods then boots° it to be borne,
 If old *Aveugles* sonnes so evill heare?°   205

180 **as they were wood** as if they were mad. 182 **cleare** brightly.
184 **th'unacquainted** unfamiliar. 195 **world unmade** i.e., Chaos.
196 **Nephewes** grandchildren. 199 **him before** before he fell. 200
shrinke give way. 202 **groning beare** the bier borne by sorrowing
mourners. 204 **boots** avails. 205 **If . . . heare** If one hears such
evil treatment of the sons of "Aveugle" (Blind), i.e., Night.

Or who shall not great *Nightes* children scorne,
When two of three her Nephews are so fowle for-
        lorne?°

24

Up then, up dreary Dame, of darknesse Queene,
        Go gather up the reliques of thy race,
210   Or else goe them avenge, and let be seene,
        That dreaded *Night* in brightest day hath place,
        And can the children of faire light deface.°
        Her feeling speeches some compassion moved
        In hart, and chaunge in that great mothers face:
215   Yet pittie in her hart was never proved°
Till then: for evermore she hated, never loved.

25

And said, Deare daughter rightly may I rew
        The fall of famous children borne of mee,
        And good successes,° which their foes ensew:°
220   But who can turne the streame of destinee,
        Or breake the chayne of strong necessitee,
        Which fast is tyde to *Joves* eternall seat?
        The sonnes of Day he favoureth, I see,
        And by my ruines thinkes to make them great:
225 To make one great by others losse, is bad excheat.°

26

Yet shall they not escape so freely all;
        For some shall pay the price of others guilt:
        And he the man that made *Sansfoy* to fall,
        Shall with his owne bloud price that° he hath
                spilt.
230   But what art thou, that telst of Nephews kilt?
        I that do seeme not I, *Duessa* am,
        (Quoth she) how ever now in garments gilt,
        And gorgeous gold arayd I to thee came;
Duessa I, the daughter of Deceipt and Shame.

207 **forlorne** forsaken.   212 **deface** destroy.   215 **proved** shown.
219 **successes** results.   219 **ensew** follow.   225 **excheat** escheat,
plunder.   229 **price that** pay the price of that which.

27

Then bowing downe her aged backe, she kist   *235*
    The wicked witch, saying; In that faire face
    The false resemblance of Deceipt, I wist°
    Did closely° lurke; yet so true-seeming grace
    It carried, that I scarse in darkesome place
    Could it discerne, though I the mother bee   *240*
    Of falshood, and root of *Duessaes* race.
    O welcome child, whom I have longd to see,
And now have seene unwares. Lo now I go with thee.

28

Then to her yron wagon she betakes,°
    And with her beares the fowle welfavourd witch: *245*
    Through mirkesome° aire her readie way she
        makes.
    Her twyfold Teme, of which two blacke as pitch,
    And two were browne,° yet each to each un-
        lich,°
    Did softly swim away, ne ever stampe,
    Unlesse she chaunst their stubborne mouths to
        twitch;   *250*
    Then foming tarre,° their bridles they would
        champe,
And trampling the fine element,° would fiercely
    rampe.

29

So well they sped, that they be come at length
    Unto the place, whereas the Paynim lay,
    Devoid of outward sense, and native strength,   *255*
    Coverd with charmed cloud from vew of day,
    And sight of men, since his late luckelesse fray.
    His cruell wounds with cruddy° bloud con-
        gealed,
    They binden up so wisely,° as they may,

237 **wist** knew.   238 **closely** secretly.   244 **betakes** betakes herself.
246 **mirkesome** thick and heavy.   248 **browne** dusky.   248 **unlich**
unlike.   251 **foming tarre** black foam from their mouths.   252 **the
fine element** the air.   258 **cruddy** curdled, clotted.   259 **wisely** skillfully.

260   And handle softly, till they can be healed:
So lay him in her charet, close in night concealed.

30

And all the while she stood upon the ground,
    The wakefull dogs did never cease to bay,
    As giving warning of th'unwonted sound,
265   With which her yron wheeles did them affray,
    And her darke griesly looke them much dismay;
    The messenger of death, the ghastly Owle
    With drearie shriekes did also her bewray;°
    And hungry Wolves continually did howle,
270 At her abhorred face, so filthy and so fowle.

31

Thence turning backe in silence soft they stole,
    And brought the heavie corse with easie pace
    To yawning gulfe of deepe *Avernus* hole.°
    By that same hole an entrance darke and bace°
275   With smoake and sulphure hiding all the place,
    Descends to hell: there creature never past,
    That backe returned without heavenly grace;
    But° dreadfull *Furies,* which their chaines have brast,°
And damned sprights sent forth to make ill men aghast.

32

280 By that same way the direfull dames doe drive
    Their mournefull charet, fild with rusty blood,
    And downe to *Plutoes* house are come bilive:°
    Which passing through, on every side them stood
    The trembling ghosts with sad amazed mood,
285   Chattring their yron teeth, and staring wide
    With stonie eyes; and all the hellish brood
    Of feends infernall flockt on every side,

268 **her bewray** reveal her presence. 273 **deepe Avernus hole** the entrance to hell. 274 **bace** low. 278 **But** except. 278 **brast** burst. 282 **bilive** quickly.

To gaze on earthly wight, that with the Night durst
    ride.

33

They pas the bitter waves of *Acheron,*°
    Where many soules sit wailing woefully,   *290*
    And come to fiery flood of *Phlegeton,*°
    Whereas the damned ghosts in torments fry,
    And with sharpe shrilling shriekes doe bootlesse
      cry,
    Cursing high *Jove,* the which them thither sent.
    The house of endlesse paine is built thereby,   *295*
    In which ten thousand sorts of punishment
The cursed creatures doe eternally torment.

34

Before the threshold dreadfull *Cerberus*°
    His three deformed heads did lay along,
    Curled with thousand adders venemous,   *300*
    And lilled forth° his bloudie flaming tong:
    At them he gan to reare his bristles strong,
    And felly gnarre,° untill dayes enemy
    Did him appease; then downe his taile he hong
    And suffered them to passen quietly: *305*
For she in hell and heaven had power equally.

35

There was *Ixion* turned on a wheele,
    For daring tempt° the Queene of heaven to sin;
    And *Sisyphus* an huge round stone did reele°
    Against an hill, ne might from labour lin;°   *310*
    There thirstie *Tantalus* hong by the chin;
    And *Tityus* fed a vulture on his maw;
    Typhœus joynts were stretched on a gin,°

289 **Acheron** a river in hell associated with woe. 291 **Phlegeton** a
river in hell that flows with fire. 298 **Cerberus** the dog that guards
the entrance to hell. 301 **lilled forth** hung out. 303 **felly gnarre**
fiercely snarl. 308 **tempt** to tempt. 309 **reele** roll. 310 **lin** cease.
313 **gin** rack.

Theseus° condemned to endlesse slouth by law,
315 And fifty sisters° water in leake vessels draw.

36

They all beholding worldly wights in place,°
    Leave off their worke, unmindfull of their smart,
    To gaze on them; who forth by them doe pace,
    Till they be come unto the furthest part:
320   Where was a Cave ywrought° by wondrous art,
    Deepe, darke, uneasie,° dolefull, comfortlesse,
    In which sad *Æsculapius*° farre a part
    Emprisond was in chaines remedilesse,°
For that *Hippolytus* rent corse he did redresse.°

37

325 *Hippolytus* a jolly huntsman was,
    That wont in charet chace the foming Bore;
    He all his Peeres in beautie did surpas,
    But Ladies love as losse of time forbore:°
    His wanton stepdame° loved him the more,
330   But when she saw her offred sweets refused
    Her love she turnd to hate, and him before
    His father° fierce of treason false accused,
And with her gealous termes his open eares abused.

38

Who all in rage his Sea-god syre° besought,
335   Some cursed vengeance on his sonne to cast:
    From surging gulf two monsters straight were
        brought,
    With dread whereof his chasing° steedes aghast,
    Both charet swift and huntsman overcast.

307–314 **Ixion . . . Theseus** sufferers in hell, whose tortures are
described chiefly by Homer, Virgil, and Ovid. For Tantalus, see II.
vii.58 ff. 315 **fifty sisters** the Danaides. 316 **in place** there. 320
ywrought fashioned. 321 **uneasie** without ease. 322 **Aesculapius**
god of the art of medicine. 323 **remedilesse** without hope of release. 324 **redresse** restore. 328 **forbore** avoided. 329 **His wanton stepdame** Phaedra. 332 **His father** Theseus. 334 **his Sea-god
syre** Neptune. 337 **chasing** because used in the chase.

His goodly corps on ragged cliffs yrent,
Was quite dismembred, and his members chast   340
Scattered on every mountaine, as he went,
That of *Hippolytus* was left no moniment.°

39

His cruell stepdame seeing what was donne,
Her wicked dayes with wretched knife did end,
In death avowing th'innocence of her sonne.   345
Which hearing his rash Syre, began to rend
His haire, and hastie tongue, that did offend:
Tho° gathering up the relicks of his smart°
By *Dianes* meanes, who was *Hippolyts* frend,
Them brought to *Æsculape,* that by his art   350
Did heale them all againe, and joyned every part.

40

Such wondrous science in mans wit to raine
When *Jove* avizd,° that could the dead revive,
And fates expired° could renew againe,
Of endlesse life he might him not deprive,   355
But unto hell did thrust him downe alive,
With flashing thunderbolt ywounded sore:
Where long remaining, he did alwaies strive
Himselfe with salves to health for to restore,
And slake the heavenly fire, that raged evermore.   360

41

There auncient Night arriving, did alight
From her nigh wearie waine,° and in her armes
To *Æsculapius* brought the wounded knight:
Whom having softly disarayd of armes,
Tho gan to him discover° all his harmes,   365
Beseeching him with prayer, and with praise,
If either salves, or oyles, or herbes, or charmes

342 **moniment** trace.   348 **Tho** then.   348 **the relicks of his smart**
the record of his affliction, i.e., Hippolytus' remains.   353 **avizd** was
advised.   354 **fates expired** the fated term of life having been fulfilled, as "sufficed fates" (I.ii.43).   362 **waine** wagon.   365 **discover**
reveal.

A fordonne° wight from dore of death mote raise,
He would at her request prolong her nephews daies.

42

370 Ah Dame (quoth he) thou temptest me in vaine,
    To dare the thing, which daily yet I rew,°
    And the old cause of my continued paine
    With like attempt to like end to renew.
    Is not enough, that thrust from heaven dew°
375 Here endlesse penance for one fault I pay,
    But that redoubled crime with vengeance new
    Thou biddest me to eeke?° Can Night defray°
The wrath of thundring *Jove,* that rules both night and
    day?

43

Not so (quoth she) but sith that heavens king
380 From hope of heaven hath thee excluded quight,
    Why fearest thou, that canst not hope for thing,°
    And fearest not, that° more thee hurten might,
    Now in the powre of everlasting Night?
    Goe to then, O thou farre renowmed sonne
385 Of great *Apollo,* shew thy famous might
    In medicine, that else° hath to thee wonne
Great paines, and greater praise, both never to be
    donne.°

44

Her words prevaild: And then the learned leach
    His cunning hand gan to his wounds to lay,°
390 And all things else, the which his art did teach:
    Which having seene, from thence arose away
    The mother of dread darknesse, and let stay
    Aveugles sonne there in the leaches cure,°
    And backe returning tooke her wonted way,

368 **fordonne** completely undone or overcome. 371 **rew** grieve for.
374 **dew** due, fitting for me as an immortal. 377 **eeke** add to. 377
defray settle. 381 **thing** anything. 382 **that** her that, i.e., Night
herself. 386 **else** already. 387 **donne** ended. 389 **lay** apply. 393
cure care.

To runne her timely° race, whilst *Phœbus* pure   *395*
In westerne waves his wearie wagon did recure.°

45

The false *Duessa* leaving noyous° Night,
 Returnd to stately pallace of dame Pride;
 Where when she came, she found the Faery
  knight
 Departed thence, albe° his woundes wide   *400*
 Not throughly° heald, unreadie were to ride.
 Good cause he had to hasten thence away;
 For on a day his wary Dwarfe had spide,
 Where in a dongeon deepe huge numbers lay
Of caytive° wretched thrals,° that wayled night and
  day.   *405*

46

A ruefull sight, as could° be seene with eie;
 Of whom he learned had in secret wise
 The hidden cause of their captivitie,
 How mortgaging their lives to *Covetise,*
 Through wastfull Pride, and wanton Riotise,°   *410*
 They were by law of that proud Tyrannesse°
 Provokt with *Wrath,* and *Envies* false surmise,
 Condemned to that Dongeon mercilesse,°
Where they should live in woe, and die in wretched-
  nesse.

47

There was that great proud king of *Babylon,*°   *415*
 That would compell all nations to adore,
 And him as onely God° to call upon,
 Till through celestiall doome° throwne out of
  dore,

395 **timely** measured. 396 **recure** refresh. 397 **noyous** troublesome. 400 **albe** although. 401 **throughly** thoroughly. 405 **caytive**
captive. 405 **thrals** prisoners. 406 **as could** as ever could. 410
Riotise riotousness. 411 **Tyrannesse** i.e., Lucifera. 413 **mercilesse**
without hope of mercy. 415 **that great proud king of Babylon**
Nebuchadnezzar. The names that follow are drawn from classical
and biblical history. 417 **onely God** the one God. 418 **doome**
sentence.

Into an Oxe he was transform'd of yore:
There also was king *Cræsus,* that enhaunst°
His heart too high through his great riches
    store;
And proud *Antiochus,* the which advaunst°
His cursed hand gainst God, and on his altars daunst.

48

And them long time before, great *Nimrod* was,
That first the world with sword and fire
    warrayd;°
And after him old *Ninus* farre did pas°
In princely pompe, of all the world obayd;
There also was that mightie Monarch° layd
Low under all, yet above all in pride,
That name of native° syre did fowle upbrayd,
And would as *Ammons* sonne be magnifide,
Till scornd of God and man a shamefull death he
    dide.

49

All these together in one heape were throwne,
Like carkases of beasts in butchers stall.
And in another corner wide were strowne
The antique ruines of the *Romaines* fall:
Great *Romulus* the Grandsyre of them all,
Proud *Tarquin,* and too lordly *Lentulus,*
Stout *Scipio,* and stubborne *Hanniball,*
Ambitious *Sylla,* and sterne *Marius,*
High *Cæsar,* great *Pompey,* and fierce *Antonius.*

50

Amongst these mighty men were wemen mixt,
Proud wemen, vaine, forgetfull of their yoke:°
The bold *Semiramis,* whose sides transfixt

---

420 **enhaunst** exalted. 422 **advaunst** raised. 425 **warrayd** made
war against. 426 **pas** surpass. 428 **that mightie Monarch** Alexander the Great. 430 **native** parent. 443 **their yoke** i.e., their proper
subjection to men.

With sonnes owne blade, her fowle reproches
   spoke;°   445
Faire *Sthenobœa,* that her selfe did choke
With wilfull cord,° for wanting of her will;
High minded *Cleopatra,* that with stroke
Of Aspes sting her selfe did stoutly kill:
And thousands moe the like, that did that dongeon
   fill.   450

51

Besides the endlesse routs of wretched thralles,
   Which thither were assembled day by day,
   From all the world after their wofull falles,
   Through wicked pride, and wasted wealthes
     decay.°
   But most of all, which in that Dongeon lay   455
   Fell from high Princes courts, or Ladies bowres,
   Where they in idle pompe, or wanton play,
   Consumed had their goods, and thriftlesse
     howres,
And lastly throwne themselves into these heavy
   stowres.

52

Whose case when as the carefull Dwarfe had tould,   460
   And made ensample° of their mournefull sight°
   Unto his maister, he no lenger would
   There dwell in perill of like painefull plight,
   But early rose, and ere that dawning light
   Discovered had the world to heaven wyde,   465
   He by a privie Posterne° tooke his flight,
   That of no envious eyes he mote be spyde:
For doubtlesse death ensewd, if any him descryde.

---

445 **spoke** disclosed.   447 **With wilfull cord** with a cord willfully.
454 **wasted wealthes decay** destruction caused by wasting their
wealth.   461 **ensample** warning.   461 **of . . . sight** the mournful
sight of them.   466 **privie Posterne** secret back door.

53

Scarse could he footing find in that fowle way,
470   For° many corses, like a great Lay-stall°
      Of murdred men which therein strowed° lay,
      Without remorse,° or decent funerall:
      Which all through that great Princesse pride
        did fall
      And came to shamefull end. And then beside
475   Forth ryding underneath the castell wall,
      A donghill of dead carkases he spide,
The dreadfull spectacle of that sad house of *Pride*.

CANTO VI

From lawlesse lust by wondrous grace
*   fayre Una is releast:*
Whom salvage° nation does adore,
*   and learnes her wise beheast.°*

1

As when a ship, that flyes faire under saile,
      An hidden rocke escaped hath unwares,°
      That lay in waite her wrack for to bewaile,°
      The Marriner yet halfe amazed stares
5   At perill past, and yet in doubt ne dares°
      To joy at his foole-happie° oversight:
      So doubly is distrest twixt joy and cares
      The dreadlesse courage of this Elfin knight,
Having escapt° so sad ensamples in his sight.

2

10 Yet sad he was that his too hastie speed

---

470 **For** because of.   470 **Lay-stall** garbage dump.   471 **strowed** strewn.   472 **remorse** pity.   Arg. **salvage** wild.   Arg. **beheast** command.   2 **unwares** unexpectedly.   3 **her . . . bewaile** that her wreck would be bewailed.   5 **ne dares** does not dare.   6 **foole-happie** "plain" lucky.   9 **Having escapt** i.e., having escaped "like painefull plight" (I.v.52) of.

The faire *Duess'* had forst him leave behind;
And yet more sad, that *Una* his deare dreed°
Her truth had staind with treason so unkind;°
Yet crime° in her could never creature find,
But for his love, and for her owne selfe sake,   *15*
She wandred had from one to other *Ynd,*°
Him for to seeke, ne ever would forsake,
Till her unwares the fierce *Sansloy* did overtake.

3

Who after *Archimagoes* fowle defeat,
Led her away into a forrest wilde,   *20*
And turning wrathfull fire to lustfull heat,
With beastly sin thought her to have defilde,
And made the vassall of his pleasures vilde.°
Yet first he cast by treatie, and by traynes,°
Her to perswade, that stubborne fort to yilde:°   *25*
For greater conquest of hard love° he gaynes,
That workes it to his will, then he that it constraines.

4

With fawning wordes he courted her a while,
And looking lovely,° and oft sighing sore,
Her constant hart did tempt° with diverse
    guile: *30*
But wordes and lookes, and sighes she did
    abhore,
As rocke of Diamond stedfast evermore.
Yet for to feed his fyrie lustfull eye,
He snatcht the vele, that hong her face before;
Then gan her beautie shine, as brightest skye,   *35*
And burnt his beastly hart t'efforce° her chastitye.

5

So when he saw his flatt'ring arts to fayle,

12 **his deare dreed** one whom he holds in love and reverence.
13 **unkind** unnatural to her. 14 **crime** sin. 16 **one to other Ynd**
the East to the West Indies. 23 **vilde** vile. 24 **cast by . . . traynes**
attempted by entreaty and by wiles. 25 **yilde** yield. 26 **hard love**
love that is difficult to gain. 29 **lovely** lovingly. 30 **tempt** seek
to tempt. 36 **t'efforce** to force.

And subtile engines° bet° from batteree,
With greedy force he gan the fort assayle,
40 Whereof he weend possessed soone to bee,
And win rich spoile of ransackt chastetee.°
Ah heavens, that do this hideous act behold,
And heavenly virgin thus outraged° see,
How can ye vengeance just so long withhold
And hurle not flashing flames upon that Paynim°
45   bold?

6

The pitteous maiden carefull° comfortlesse,
Does throw out thrilling° shriekes, and shriek-
    ing cryes,
The last vaine helpe of womens great distresse,
And with loud plaints importuneth° the skyes,
50 That molten starres do drop like weeping eyes;
And *Phœbus* flying so most shameful sight,
His blushing face in foggy cloud implyes,°
And hides for shame. What wit of mortall wight
Can now devise to quit a thrall° from such a plight?

7

55 Eternall providence exceeding thought,°
Where none appeares can make° her selfe a
    way:
A wondrous way it for this Lady wrought,
From Lyons clawes to pluck the griped° pray.
Her shrill outcryes and shriekes so loud did
    bray,
60 That all the woodes and forestes did reswond;
A troupe of *Faunes* and *Satyres*° far away

38 **engines** machines used in warfare; here signifying "wiles."
38 **bet** beaten.   41 **ransackt chastetee** her chastity that he seeks to
plunder.   43 **outraged** violated.   45 **Paynim** pagan.   46 **carefull**
full   of   care.   47 **thrilling**   piercing.   49 **importuneth**   solicits.
52 **implyes** enfolds.   54 **to quit a thrall** to free a captive.   55 **exceeding thought** "passeth all understanding" (Phil. iv.7).   56 **can
make** knows how to make.   58 **griped** grasped.   61 **Faunes and
Satyres** the Latin and Greek wood gods, half man and half goat.

Within the wood were dauncing in a rownd,°
Whiles old *Sylvanus*° slept in shady arber sownd.

8

Who when they heard that pitteous strained voice,
    In hast forsooke their rurall meriment,   65
    And ran towards the far rebownded noyce,
    To weet, what wight so loudly did lament.
    Unto the place they come incontinent:°
    Whom when the raging Sarazin espide,
    A rude, misshapen, monstrous rablement,°   70
    Whose like he never saw, he durst not bide,
But got his ready steed, and fast away gan ride.

9

The wyld woodgods arrived in the place,
    There find the virgin dolefull desolate,
    With ruffled rayments, and faire blubbred face,°   75
    As her outrageous foe had left her late,
    And trembling yet through feare of former hate;
    All stand amazed at so uncouth° sight,
    And gin to pittie her unhappie state,
    All stand astonied° at her beautie bright,   80
In their rude eyes unworthie° of so wofull plight.

10

She more amaz'd, in double dread doth dwell;
    And every tender part for feare does shake:
    As when a greedie Wolfe through hunger fell
    A seely° Lambe farre from the flocke does take,   85
    Of whom he meanes his bloudie feast to make,
    A Lyon spyes fast running towards him,
    The innocent pray in hast he does forsake,
    Which quit° from death yet quakes in every lim
With chaunge of feare, to see the Lyon looke so
        grim.   90

62 **rownd** a dance.   63 **Sylvanus** a god of the forest.   68 **incontinent** hastily.   70 **rablement** rabble.   75 **faire blubbred face** her
beautiful face wet with tears.   78 **uncouth** strange.   80 **astonied**
astonished.   81 **unworthie** undeserving.   85 **seely** innocent.   89
quit freed.

11

Such fearefull fit assaid° her trembling hart,
　　Ne word to speake, ne joynt to move she had:
　　The salvage nation feele her secret smart,
　　And read her sorrow in her count'nance sad;
　　Their frowning forheads with rough hornes
95　　　　yclad,
　　And rusticke horror° all a side doe lay,
　　And gently grenning,° shew a semblance° glad
　　To comfort her, and feare to put away,
Their backward bent° knees teach her humbly to
　　obay.

12

100 The doubtfull° Damzell dare not yet commit
　　Her single° person to their barbarous truth,°
　　But still twixt feare and hope amazd does sit,
　　Late learnd° what harme to hastie trust ensu'th.
　　They in compassion of her tender youth,
105　　And wonder of her beautie soveraine,
　　Are wonne with pitty and unwonted ruth,
　　And all prostrate upon the lowly plaine,
Do kisse her feete, and fawne on her with count'nance
　　faine.°

13

Their harts she ghesseth by their humble guise,
110　　And yieldes her to extremitie of time;°
　　So from the ground she fearelesse doth arise,
　　And walketh forth without suspect of crime:°
　　They all as glad, as birdes of joyous Prime,°

---

91 fearefull fit assaid fit of fear assailed.　**96 horror** roughness.　**97 grenning** grinning.　**97 semblance** appearance.　**99 backward bent** i.e., because they have the legs of a goat. Either (1) their kneeling teaches her to obey humbly their desire that she put away fear; or (2) they teach their knees to kneel, that they may humbly obey her and so put away her fear.　**100 doubtful** fearful.　**101 single** free from duplicity, simple.　**101 truth** allegiance.　**103 Late learnd** lately having been taught.　**108 faine** glad.　**110 And . . . time** And submits herself to the present crisis.　**112 suspect of crime** suspicion or fear of being reproached.　**113 Prime** spring, or morning.

Thence lead her forth, about her dauncing
   round,
Shouting, and singing all a shepheards ryme,   *115*
And with greene braunches strowing all the
   ground,
Do worship her, as Queene, with olive girlond
   cround.

14

And all the way their merry pipes they sound,
   That all the woods with doubled Eccho ring,
   And with their horned° feet do weare° the
     ground,   *120*
   Leaping like wanton kids in pleasant Spring.
   So towards old *Sylvanus* they her bring;
   Who with the noyse awaked, commeth out,
   To weet the cause, his weake steps governing,
   And aged limbs on Cypresse stadle° stout,   *125*
And with an yvie twyne his wast is girt about.

15

Far off he wonders, what them makes so glad,
   Or *Bacchus* merry fruit they did invent,°
   Or *Cybeles* franticke rites° have made them
     mad;
   They drawing nigh, unto their God present   *130*
   That flowre of faith and beautie excellent.
   The God himselfe vewing that mirrhour rare,°
   Stood long amazd, and burnt in his intent;°
   His owne faire *Dryope* now he thinkes not
     faire,
And *Pholoe* fowle, when her to this he doth compaire.   *135*

16

The woodborne people fall before her flat,

120 **horned** horny. 120 **weare** wear away with trampling. 125
stadle staff. 128 **Or . . . invent** whether they had discovered
Bacchus' fruit (that is, grapes) which make men merry. 129 **Cybeles
franticke rites** orgiastic rites associated with Rhea, goddess of
the earth. 132 **mirrhour rare** because she reflects heavenly beauty.
133 **burnt in his intent** i.e., heated with lust through sight of
her.

And worship her as Goddesse of the wood;
And old *Sylvanus* selfe bethinkes not,° what
To thinke of wight so faire, but gazing stood,
140   In doubt to deeme her borne of earthly brood;
Sometimes Dame *Venus* selfe he seemes to see,
But *Venus* never had so sober mood;°
Sometimes *Diana* he her takes to bee,
But misseth bow, and shaftes, and buskins° to her
    knee.

17

145   By vew of her he ginneth° to revive
His ancient love, and dearest *Cyparisse,*
And calles to mind his pourtraiture alive,°
How faire he was, and yet not faire to this,
And how he slew with glauncing dart amisse
150   A gentle Hynd, the which the lovely boy
Did love as life, above all worldly blisse;
For griefe whereof the lad n'ould after joy,°
But pynd away in anguish and selfe-wild annoy.°

18

The wooddy Nymphes, faire *Hamadryades*°
155   Her to behold do thither runne apace,°
And all the troupe of light-foot *Naiades,*°
Flocke all about to see her lovely face:
But when they vewed have her heavenly grace,
They envie her in their malitious mind,
160   And fly away for feare of fowle disgrace:
But all the *Satyres* scorne their woody kind,°
And henceforth nothing faire, but her on earth they
    find.

138 **bethinkes not** cannot decide.   142 **so sober mood** See IV.x.47.
144 **buskins** the high boots traditionally worn by Diana as the
huntress.   145 **ginneth** begins.   147 **pourtraiture alive** his image
when he was alive.   152 **n'ould after joy** would not afterward
feel joy.   153 **selfe-wild annoy** self-willed vexation.   154 **Hamadryades** nymphs of trees.   155 **apace** swiftly.   156 **light-foot
Naiades** light-footed, or nimble, nymphs of fresh water.   161
woody kind wood-born race.

19

Glad of such lucke, the luckelesse lucky maid,
      Did her content° to please their feeble° eyes,
      And long time with that salvage people staid,   *165*
      To gather breath in° many miseries.
      During which time her gentle wit she plyes,
      To teach them truth, which worshipt her in
            vaine,
      And made her th'Image of Idolatryes;
      But when their bootlesse zeale she did restraine   *170*
From her own worship, they her Asse would worship
      fayn.°

20

It fortuned a noble warlike knight°
      By just occasion° to that forrest came,
      To seeke his kindred, and the lignage right,
      From whence he tooke his well deserved name: *175*
      He had in armes abroad wonne muchell fame,
      And fild far landes with glorie of his might,
      Plaine,° faithfull, true, and enimy of shame,
      And ever lov'd to fight for Ladies right,
But in vaine glorious frayes° he litle did delight.   *180*

21

A Satyres sonne yborne in forrest wyld,
      By straunge adventure as it did betyde,°
      And there begotten of a Lady myld,
      Faire *Thyamis* the daughter of *Labryde,*
      That was in sacred bands of wedlocke tyde   *185*
      To *Therion,* a loose unruly swayne;
      Who had more joy to raunge the forrest wyde,
      And chase the salvage beast with busie payne,°

---

164 **Did her content** satisfied herself.   164 **feeble** weak, i.e., lacking strength to resist her appearance which they worship.   166 **in**
after being in.   171 **fayn** gladly.   172 **a noble warlike knight**
i.e., Satyrane.   173 **By just occasion** by well-founded need.
176 **muchell** much.   178 **Plaine** open, free.   180 **vaine glorious
frayes** vainglorious battles.   182 **betyde** befall.   188 **with busie
payne** i.e., taking careful pains.

Then serve his Ladies love, and wast° in pleasures
    vayne.

22

190 The forlorne mayd did with loves longing burne,
    And could not lacke° her lovers company,
    But to the wood she goes, to serve her turne,°
    And seeke her spouse, that from her still does
      fly,
    And followes other game and venery:°
195   A Satyre chaunst her wandring for to find,
    And kindling coles of lust in brutish eye,
    The loyall links of wedlocke did unbind,
And made her person thrall° unto his beastly kind.

23

So long in secret cabin there he held
200   Her captive to his sensuall desire,
    Till that with timely° fruit her belly sweld,
    And bore a boy unto that salvage sire:
    Then home he suffred her for to retire,
    For ransome leaving him the late borne childe;
205   Whom till to ryper yeares he gan aspire,°
    He noursled° up in life and manners wilde,
Emongst wild beasts and woods, from lawes of men
    exilde.

24

For all he taught the tender ymp,° was but
    To banish cowardize and bastard° feare;
210   His trembling hand he would him force to put
    Upon the Lyon and the rugged Beare,
    And from the she Beares teats her whelps to
      teare;
    And eke wyld roring Buls he would him make

---

189 **wast** spend his time. 191 **lacke** do without. 192 **to serve her turne** to satisfy love's longing. 194 **venery** sexual indulgence. 198 **thrall** a prisoner. 201 **timely** occurring in good time. 205 **gan aspire** did reach. 206 **noursled** reared. 208 **ymp** child. 209 **bastard** base.

To tame, and ryde their backes not made to
    beare;
    And the Robuckes° in flight to overtake,   *215*
That every beast for feare of him did fly and quake.

25

Thereby so fearelesse, and so fell he grew,
    That his owne sire and maister of his guise°
    Did often tremble at his horrid vew,°
    And oft for dread of hurt would him advise,   *220*
    The angry beasts not rashly to despise,°
    Nor too much to provoke; for he would learne°
    The Lyon stoup to him in lowly wise,
    (A lesson hard) and make the Libbard° sterne
Leave roaring, when in rage he for revenge did
    earne.°   *225*

26

And for to make his powre approved° more,
    Wyld beasts in yron yokes he would compell;°
    The spotted Panther, and the tusked Bore,
    The Pardale° swift, and the Tigre cruell;
    The Antelope, and Wolfe both fierce and fell;   *230*
    And them constraine in equall teme to draw.°
    Such joy he had, their stubborne harts to quell,
    And sturdie courage tame with dreadfull aw,°
That his beheast they feared, as a tyrans law.

27

His loving mother came upon a day   *235*
    Unto the woods, to see her little sonne;
    And chaunst unwares° to meet him in the way,
    After his sportes, and cruell pastime donne,
    When after him a Lyonesse did runne,

---

215 **Robuckes** roebucks. 218 **maister of his guise** tutor of his behavior. 219 **his horrid vew** the sight of his rough or savage actions. 221 **despise** treat with contempt. 222 **learne** teach. 224
Libbard leopard. 225 **earne** yearn. 226 **approved** demonstrated.
227 **compell** force together. 229 **Pardale** the female pard, or
panther. 231 **in . . . draw** in a team to draw evenly. 233 **dreadfull aw** fear and dread of him. 237 **unwares** unexpectedly.

240   That roaring all with rage, did lowd requere°
       Her children deare, whom he away had wonne:
       The Lyon whelpes she saw how he did beare,
And lull in rugged° armes, withouten childish feare.

28

The fearefull Dame all quaked° at the sight,
245   And turning backe, gan fast to fly away,
          Untill with love revokt° from vaine affright,
          She hardly° yet perswaded was to stay,
          And then to him these womanish words gan
          say;
          Ah *Satyrane,* my dearling,° and my joy,
250   For love of me leave off this dreadfull play;
          To dally thus with death, is no fit toy,
Go find some other play-fellowes, mine own sweet
          boy.

29

In these and like delights of bloudy game
          He trayned was, till ryper yeares he raught,°
255   And there abode, whilst any beast of name
          Walkt in that forest, whom he had not taught
          To feare his force: and then his courage haught°
          Desird of forreine foemen to be knowne,
          And far abroad for straunge adventures sought:
260   In which his might was never overthrowne,
But through all Faery lond his famous worth was
          blown.°

30

Yet evermore it was his manner faire,
          After long labours and adventures spent,°
          Unto those native woods for to repaire,°
265   To see his sire and ofspring° auncient.

240 **requere** demand.   243 **rugged** rough with hair.   244 **all quaked**
quaked all over.   246 **revokt** restrained.   247 **hardly** with difficulty.   249 **dearling** darling.   254 **raught** reached.   257 **haught**
haughty, aspiring.   261 **blown** proclaimed.   263 **spent** passed.
264 **for to repaire** to return.   265 **ofspring** descent, lineage.

And now he thither came for like intent;
    Where he unwares the fairest *Una* found,
    Straunge Lady, in so straunge habiliment,°
    Teaching the Satyres, which her sat around,
Trew sacred lore, which from her sweet lips did
        redound.°   270

31

He wondred at her wisedome heavenly rare,
    Whose like in womens wit he never knew;
    And when her curteous deeds he did compare,
    Gan her admire, and her sad sorrowes rew,
    Blaming of Fortune, which such troubles threw,   275
    And joyd to make proofe of her crueltie
    On gentle Dame, so hurtlesse,° and so trew:
    Thenceforth he kept her goodly company,
And learnd her discipline° of faith and veritie.

32

But she all° vowd unto the *Redcrosse* knight,   280
    His wandring perill closely° did lament,
    Ne in this new acquaintaunce could delight,
    But her deare heart with anguish did torment,
    And all her wit in secret counsels spent,
    How to escape. At last in privie wise°   285
    To *Satyrane* she shewed her intent;°
    Who glad to gain such favour, gan devise,
How with that pensive Maid he best might thence
        arise.°

33

So on a day when Satyres all were gone,
    To do their service to *Sylvanus* old,   290
    The gentle virgin left behind alone
    He led away with courage stout and bold.
    Too late it was, to Satyres to be told,

268 **habiliment** array.   270 **redound** flow.   277 **hurtlesse** harmless.
279 **discipline** teaching.   280 **all** entirely.   281 **closely** secretly.
285 **privie wise** secret manner.   286 **shewed her intent** revealed her
intention.   288 **arise** get up and go.

Or ever hope recover her againe:
In vaine he seekes that having cannot hold.
So fast he carried her with carefull paine,°
That they the woods are past, and come now to the
    plaine.

34

The better part now of the lingring day,
    They traveild had, when as they farre espide
A wearie wight forwandring by the way,°
And towards him they gan in hast to ride,
To weet° of newes, that did abroad betide,
Or tydings of her knight of the *Redcrosse*.
But he them spying, gan to turne aside,
    For feare as seemd,° or for some feigned losse;
More greedy they of newes, fast towards him do
    crosse.°

35

A silly° man, in simple weedes forworne,°
    And soild with dust of the long dried way;
His sandales were with toilesome travell torne,
And face all tand with scorching sunny ray,
As° he had traveild many a sommers day,
Through boyling sands of *Arabie* and *Ynde;*
And in his hand a *Jacobs* staffe,° to stay°
    His wearie limbes upon: and eke behind,
His scrip° did hang, in which his needments he did
    bind.

36

The knight approching nigh, of him inquerd
    Tydings of warre, and of adventures new;
But warres, nor new adventures none he herd.
Then *Una* gan to aske, if ought° he knew,
Or heard abroad of that her champion trew,

296 **paine** pains.   300 **forwandring by the way** wandering from the
way.   302 **weet** learn.   305 **as seemd** as it seemed.   306 **crosse**
come in his way.   307 **silly** simple.   307 **forworne** worn out.
311 **As** as if.   313 **Jacobs staffe** pilgrim's staff.   313 **stay** support.
315 **scrip** small bag.   319 **ought** anything.

That in his armour bare a croslet° red.
    Aye me, Deare dame (quoth he) well may
      I rew
    To tell the sad sight, which mine eies have
      red:°
These eyes did see that knight both living and eke
      ded.

37

That cruell word her tender hart so thrild,°   *325*
    That suddein cold did runne through every
      vaine,
    And stony° horrour all her sences fild
    With dying fit,° that downe she fell for paine.
    The knight her lightly° reared up againe,
    And comforted with curteous kind reliefe: *330*
    Then wonne from death, she bad him tellen
      plaine
    The further processe of her hidden griefe;°
The lesser pangs can° beare, who hath endur'd the
      chiefe.

38

Then gan the Pilgrim thus, I chaunst° this day,
    This fatall° day, that shall I ever rew,°   *335*
    To see two knights in travell on my way
    (A sory sight) arraung'd in battell new,
    Both breathing vengeaunce, both of wrathfull
      hew:
    My fearefull flesh did tremble at their strife,
    To see their blades so greedily imbrew,°   *340*
    That drunke with bloud, yet thristed° after life:
What more? the *Redcrosse* knight was slaine with
      Paynim knife.°

---

321 **croslet** small cross.   323 **red** seen.   325 **thrild** pierced.   327
stony stunned.   328 **dying fit** an attack like death.   329 **lightly**
quickly.   332 **The . . . griefe** The rest of his discourse or story
that caused her inner grief.   333 **can** she can.   334 **I chaunst** it
chanced to me.   335 **fatall** fateful.   335 **rew** grieve.   340 **imbrew**
imbrue, stain with blood.   341 **thristed** thirsted.   342 **knife** sword.

39

Ah dearest Lord (quoth she) how might that bee,
 And he the stoutest knight, that ever wonne?°
345 Ah dearest dame (quoth he) how might I see
 The thing, that might not be, and yet was
  donne?
 Where is (said *Satyrane*) that Paynims sonne,
 That him of life, and us of joy hath reft?
 Not far away (quoth he) he hence doth wonne°
350 Foreby° a fountaine, where I late him left
Washing his bloudy wounds, that through the steele
  were cleft.

40

Therewith° the knight thence marched forth in hast,
 Whiles *Una* with huge heavinesse opprest,
 Could not for sorrow follow him so fast;
355 And soone he came, as he the place had ghest,°
 Whereas° that *Pagan* proud him selfe did rest,
 In secret shadow by a fountaine side:
 Even he it was, that earst would have supprest°
 Faire *Una:* whom when *Satyrane* espide,
360 With fowle reprochfull words he boldly him defide.

41

And said, Arise thou cursed Miscreaunt,°
 That hast with knightlesse° guile and trecherous
  train°
 Faire knighthood fowly shamed, and doest vaunt
 That good knight of the *Redcrosse* to have
  slain:
 Arise, and with like treason° now maintain
365 Thy guilty wrong, or else thee guilty yield.
 The Sarazin this hearing, rose amain,°

---

344 **wonne** won, was victorious. 349 **wonne** remain. 350 **Foreby**
hard by. 352 **Therewith** that having been said. 355 **ghest** guessed.
356 **Whereas** where. 358 **supprest** raped. 361 **Miscreaunt** misbe-
liever. 362 **knightlesse** unknightly. 362 **train** guile. 365 **treason**
treachery. 367 **amain** at once.

And catching up in hast his three square°
   shield,
And shining helmet, soone him buckled to the field.°

42

And drawing nigh him said, Ah misborne° Elfe,   *370*
   In evill houre° thy foes thee hither sent,
   Anothers wrongs to wreake upon thy selfe:°
   Yet ill thou blamest me, for having blent°
   My name with guile and traiterous° intent;
   That *Redcrosse* knight, perdie,° I never slew,   *375*
   But had he beene, where earst° his armes were
      lent,
   Th'enchaunter vaine° his errour° should not
      rew:
But thou his errour shalt, I hope now proven trew.°

43

Therewith they gan, both furious and fell,
   To thunder blowes, and fiersly to assaile   *380*
   Each other bent° his enimy to quell,
   That with their force they perst both plate and
      maile,
   And made wide furrowes in their fleshes fraile,
   That it would pitty° any living eie.
   Large floods of bloud adowne their sides did
      raile;°   *385*
   But floods of bloud could not them satisfie:
Both hungred after death: both chose to win, or die.

44

So long they fight, and fell revenge pursue,

368 **three square** triangular.   369 **him . . . field** made himself ready
for the battle.   370 **misborne** base-born, being born out of wed-
lock.   371 **In evill houre** at an unfortunate time.   372 **Anothers
. . . selfe** To punish yourself for another's wrongs.   373 **blent**
stained.   374 **traiterous** treacherous.   375 **perdie** by God (an oath).
376 **earst** lately.   377 **vaine** i.e., wearing arms in vain.   377 **his
errour** the Red Cross Knight's "wrongs."   378 **now proven trew**
i.e., through trial by combat.   381 **bent** determined.   384 **pitty**
arouse pity in.   385 **raile** flow.

That fainting each, themselves to breathen let,°
390   And oft refreshed, battell oft renue:
As when two Bores with rancling malice met,
Their gory° sides fresh bleeding fiercely fret,°
Til breathlesse both them selves aside retire,
Where foming wrath,° their cruell tuskes they
        whet,
And trample th'earth, the whiles they may
395   respire;
Then backe to fight againe, new breathed and entire.°

        45
So fiersly, when these knights had breathed once,
They gan to fight returne, increasing more
Their puissant° force, and cruell rage attonce,°
400   With heaped strokes more hugely,° then before,
That with their drerie° wounds and bloudy gore
They both deformed, scarsely could be known.
By this sad *Una* fraught with anguish sore,
Led with their noise, which through the aire was
        thrown,
Arriv'd, where they in erth their fruitles bloud had
405   sown.

        46
Whom all so soone as° that proud Sarazin
Espide, he gan revive the memory
Of his lewd lusts, and late attempted sin,
And left the doubtfull° battell hastily,
410   To catch her, newly offred to his eie:
But *Satyrane* with strokes him turning, staid,°
And sternely bad him other businesse plie,
Then hunt the steps of pure unspotted Maid:
Wherewith he all enrag'd, these bitter speaches said.

389 **themselves . . . let** they take breath, pause. 392 **gory** gored.
392 **fret** gnaw. 394 **foming wrath** foaming in wrath. 396 **entire**
fresh. 399 **puissant** mighty. 399 **attonce** at once. 400 **With . . .**
hugely with strokes heaped more violently. 401 **drerie** gory.
406 **all . . . as** as soon as. 409 **doubtfull** being undecided. 411
staid made him stay.

47

O foolish faeries sonne, what furie mad   *415*
   Hath thee incenst, to hast thy dolefull fate?°
   Were it not better, I that Lady had,
   Then that thou hadst repented it too late?
   Most sencelesse man he, that himselfe doth hate,
   To love another. Lo then for thine ayd°   *420*
   Here take thy lovers token on thy pate.
   So they two fight; the whiles the royall Mayd
Fled farre away, of that proud Paynim sore afrayd.

48

But that false *Pilgrim,* which that leasing° told,
   Being in deed old *Archimage,* did stay   *425*
   In secret shadow, all this to behold,
   And much rejoyced in their bloudy fray:
   But when he saw the Damsell passe away
   He left his stond,° and her pursewd apace,
   In hope to bring her to her last decay.°   *430*
   But for to tell her lamentable cace,
And eke this battels end, will need another place.

CANTO VII

The Redcrosse knight is captive made
  By Gyaunt proud opprest,
Prince Arthur meets with Una great-
  ly with those newes distrest.

1

What man so wise, what earthly wit so ware,°
   As to descry° the crafty cunning traine,
   By which deceipt doth maske in visour° faire,

416 **fate** death. 420 **for thine ayd** i.e., as a reward for aiding her.
424 **leasing** untruth. 429 **stond** place. 430 **last decay** final ruin.
1 **ware** wary. 2 **descry** discover. 3 **visour** visor or mask.

And cast° her colours dyed deepe in graine,°
To seeme like Truth, whose shape she well can
faine,
And fitting gestures to her purpose frame,
The guiltlesse man with guile to entertaine?°
Great maistresse of her art was that false Dame,
The false *Duessa,* cloked with *Fidessaes* name.

2

Who when returning from the drery *Night,*
She fownd not in that perilous house of *Pryde,*
Where she had left, the noble *Redcrosse* knight,
Her hoped pray, she would no lenger bide,
But forth she went, to seeke him far and wide.
Ere long she fownd, whereas he wearie sate,
To rest him selfe, foreby a fountaine side,
Disarmed all of yron-coted Plate,
And by his side his steed the grassy forage ate.

3

He feedes upon° the cooling shade, and bayes°
His sweatie forehead in the breathing wind,
Which through the trembling leaves full gently
playes
Wherein the cherefull birds of sundry kind
Do chaunt sweet musick, to delight his mind:
The Witch approching gan him fairely° greet,
And with reproch of carelesnesse° unkind
Upbrayd, for leaving her in place unmeet,
With fowle words tempring° faire, soure gall with
hony sweet.

4

Unkindnesse past, they gan of solace treat,°
And bathe in pleasaunce° of the joyous shade,
Which shielded them against the boyling heat,

4 cast arrange. 4 dyed deepe in graine dyed thoroughly. 7 entertaine treat. 19 feedes upon enjoys. 19 bayes bathes. 24 fairely
becomingly. 25 carelesnesse negligence. 27 tempring mingling.
28 treat discourse. 29 pleasaunce pleasure.

And with greene boughes decking a gloomy
  glade,
About the fountaine like a girlond made;°
Whose bubbling wave did ever freshly well,°
Ne ever would through fervent° sommer fade:
The sacred° Nymph, which therein wont to
  dwell,   35
Was out of *Dianes* favour, as it then befell.

5

The cause was this: one day when *Phœbe°* fayre
  With all her band was following the chace,
  This Nymph, quite tyr'd with heat of scorching
  ayre
  Sat downe to rest in middest° of the race: 40
  The goddesse wroth gan fowly her disgrace,°
  And bad the waters, which from her° did flow,
  Be such as she her selfe was then in place.°
  Thenceforth her waters waxed dull and slow,
And all that drunke thereof, did faint and feeble
  grow.   45

6

Hereof° this gentle knight unweeting was,
  And lying downe upon the sandie graile,°
  Drunke of the streame, as cleare as cristall glas;
  Eftsoones° his manly forces gan to faile,
  And mightie strong was turnd to feeble fraile.°   50
  His chaunged powres at first them selves not
  felt,
  Till crudled° cold his corage gan assaile,
  And chearefull° bloud in faintnesse chill did
  melt,°
Which like a fever fit through all his body swelt.°

32 **made** fashioned itself. 33 **well** well up. 34 **fervent** hot. 35
sacred accursed. 37 **Phœbe** Diana, the goddess of the moon.
40 **middest** the middle. 41 **disgrace** disfigure. 42 **from her** i.e., in
which she dwells. 43 **in place** there. 46 **Hereof** of this. 47 **graile**
gravel. 49 **Eftsoones** immediately. 50 **And . . . fraile** And strong
might was turned to frail feebleness. 52 **crudled** congealing.
53 **chearefull** lively, living. 53 **did melt** changed to water. 54
swelt burned.

7

55 Yet goodly court he made still to his Dame,
      Pourd out in loosnesse° on the grassy grownd,
      Both carelesse of his health, and of his fame:
      Till at the last he heard a dreadfull sownd,
      Which through the wood loud bellowing, did rebownd,
60   That all the earth for terrour seemd to shake,
      And trees did tremble. Th'Elfe therewith astownd,°
      Upstarted lightly° from his looser make,°
And his unready weapons gan in hand to take.

8

But ere he could his armour on him dight,°
65   Or get his shield, his monstrous enimy
      With sturdie steps came stalking in his sight,
      An hideous° Geant horrible and hye,
      That with his talnesse seemd to threat° the skye,
      The ground eke groned under him for dreed;
70   His living like° saw never living eye,
      Ne durst behold:° his stature did exceed
The hight of three° the tallest sonnes of mortall seed.

9

The greatest Earth his uncouth° mother was,
      And blustring _Æolus_° his boasted sire,
      Who with his breath, which through the world
75   doth pas,
      Her hollow womb did secretly inspire,°
      And fild her hidden caves with stormie yre,
      That she conceiv'd; and trebling the dew time,
      In which the wombes of women do expire,°

---

56 **loosnesse** dissoluteness. 61 **astownd** astonished. 62 **lightly**
quickly. 62 **looser make** too loose mate. 64 **on him dight** put
on. 67 **hideous** immense. 68 **threat** threaten, be a source of
danger to. 70 **like** likeness. 71 **behold** hold in sight. 72 **three**
three of. 73 **uncouth** vile. 74 **Æolus** god of the winds. 76 **Inspire** breathe into. 79 **expire** give birth.

Brought forth this monstrous masse of earthly
    slime,   *80*
Puft up with emptie wind, and fild with sinfull crime.

10

So growen great through arrogant delight
    Of th'high descent, whereof he was yborne,
    And through presumption of his matchlesse
      might,
    All other powres and knighthood he did scorne.   *85*
    Such now he marcheth to this man forlorne,
    And left to losse: his stalking steps are stayde
    Upon a snaggy° Oke, which he had torne
    Out of his mothers bowelles, and it made
His mortall mace, wherewith his foemen he dismayde.   *90*

11

That when the knight he spide, he gan advance
    With huge force and insupportable mayne,°
    And towardes him with dreadfull fury praunce;°
    Who haplesse, and eke hopelesse, all in vaine
    Did to him pace, sad battaile to darrayne,°   *95*
    Disarmd, disgrast, and inwardly dismayde,
    And eke so faint in every joynt and vaine,
    Through that fraile° fountaine, which him feeble
      made,
That scarsely could he weeld his bootlesse single°
    blade.

12

The Geaunt strooke so maynly° mercilesse,   *100*
    That could have overthrowne a stony towre,
    And were not heavenly grace, that him did
      blesse,°
He had beene pouldred all,° as thin as flowre:

88 **snaggy** knotty with roots.   92 **insupportable mayne** irresistible
strength.   93 **praunce**   stalk.   95 **darrayne**   maintain.   98 **fraile**
causing him to become weak.   99 **single** alone, because he lacks
armor and shield.   100 **maynly** mightily.   102 **blesse** guard.
103 **pouldred all** entirely reduced to dust.

But he was wary of that deadly stowre,°
105 And lightly lept from underneath the blow:
Yet so exceeding was the villeins powre,
That with the wind it did him overthrow,
And all his sences stound,° that still he lay full low.

13

As when that divelish yron Engin° wrought
110 In deepest Hell, and framd by *Furies* skill,
With windy Nitre° and quick° Sulphur fraught,°
And ramd with bullet round, ordaind to kill,
Conceiveth fire, the heavens it doth fill
With thundring noyse, and all the ayre doth
choke,
115 That none can breath, nor see, nor heare at will,
Through smouldry cloud of duskish° stincking
smoke,
That th'onely breath him daunts,° who hath escapt
the stroke.

14

So daunted when the Geaunt saw the knight,
His heavie° hand he heaved up on hye,
And him to dust thought to have battred
120 quight,
Untill *Duessa* loud to him gan crye;
O great *Orgoglio,*° greatest under skye,
O hold thy mortall° hand for Ladies sake,
Hold for my sake, and do him not to dye,°
125 But vanquisht thine eternall bondslave make,
And me thy worthy meed unto thy Leman° take.

15

He hearkned, and did stay from further harmes,

104 **stowre** encounter. 108 **stound** stunned. 109 **that divelish
yron Engin** the cannon. 111 **Nitre** saltpeter. 111 **quick** inflam-
mable. 111 **fraught** stored. 116 **duskish** dusky. 117 **That . . .
daunts** that the breath (the smoke) alone subdues him. 119 **heavie**
cruel. 122 **Orgoglio** Pride. 123 **mortall** deadly. 124 **do . . . dye**
do not kill him. 126 **unto thy Leman** as your mistress.

To gayne so goodly guerdon, as she spake:°
So willingly she came into his armes,
Who her as willingly to grace° did take,   *130*
And was possessed of his new found make.°
Then up he tooke the slombred° sencelesse
    corse,
And ere he could out of his swowne awake,
Him to his castle brought with hastie forse,
And in a Dongeon deepe him threw without remorse. *133*

16

From that day forth *Duessa* was his deare,
    And highly honourd in his haughtie eye,
He gave her gold and purple pall° to weare,
And triple crowne set on her head full hye,
And her endowd with royall majestye: *140*
Then for to make her dreaded more of men,
And peoples harts with awfull terrour tye,°
A monstrous beast ybred in filthy fen
He chose, which he had kept long time in darksome
    den.

17

Such one it was, as that renowmed Snake°   *145*
    Which great *Alcides* in *Stremona* slew,
Long fostred in the filth of *Lerna* lake,
Whose many heads out budding ever new,
Did breed him endlesse labour to subdew:
But this same Monster much more ugly was;   *150*
For seven great heads out of his body grew,
An yron brest, and backe of scaly bras,
And all embrewd° in bloud, his eyes did shine as glas.

18

His tayle was stretched out in wondrous length,

128 **so . . . spake** such goodly reward as she spoke of.   130 **to grace**
to his favor.   131 **make** mate.   132 **slombred** unconscious.   138
pall robe.   142 **tye** bring into bondage.   145 **that renowmed Snake**
the Lernean hydra slain by Hercules (Alcides). When one of its nine,
or thousand, heads was struck off, two grew in its place.   153 **em-
brewd** stained.

155   That to the house of heavenly gods it raught,°
    And with extorted powre, and borrow'd strength,
    The ever-burning lamps° from thence it brought,
    And prowdly threw to ground, as things of
        nought;
    And underneath his filthy feet did tread
160   The sacred things, and holy heasts foretaught.°
    Upon this dreadfull Beast with sevenfold head
He set the false *Duessa,* for more aw and dread.

19

The wofull Dwarfe, which saw his maisters fall,
    Whiles he had keeping of his grasing steed,
165   And valiant knight become a caytive° thrall,
    When all was past, tooke up his forlorne weed,°
    His mightie armour, missing most at need;°
    His silver shield, now idle maisterlesse;
    His poynant° speare, that many made to bleed,
170   The ruefull moniments° of heavinesse,°
And with them all departes, to tell his great distresse.

20

He had not travaild long, when on the way
    He wofull Ladie, wofull *Una* met,
    Fast flying from the Paynims greedy pray,°
175   Whilest *Satyrane* him from pursuit did let:°
    Who when her eyes she on the Dwarfe had set,
    And saw the signes, that deadly tydings spake,
    She fell to ground for sorrowfull regret,
    And lively° breath her sad brest did forsake,
Yet might her pitteous hart be seene to pant and
180   quake.

---

155 raught reached.   **157 The ever-burning lamps** the stars. See Rev.
xii. 4.   **160 and . . . foretaught** and holy doctrine that had been
taught before.   **165 caytive** captive.   **166 forlorne weed** the armor
abandoned by the Knight.   **167 most at need** when most needed.
169 poynant piercing.   **170 moniments** monuments, records, as line
429.   **170 heavinesse** grief.   **174 pray** preying on her.   **175 let** prevent.   **179 lively** living.

21

The messenger of so unhappie newes,
     Would faine have dyde: dead was his hart°
          within,
     Yet outwardly some little comfort shewes:
     At last recovering hart, he does begin
     To rub her temples, and to chaufe her chin,   185
     And every tender part does tosse and turne:
     So hardly° he the flitted° life does win,°
     Unto her native° prison to retourne:
Then gins her grieved ghost° thus to lament and
     mourne.

22

Ye dreary instruments of dolefull sight,   190
     That doe this deadly spectacle behold,
     Why do ye lenger feed on loathed light,
     Or liking find to gaze on earthly mould,°
     Sith cruell fates° the carefull° threeds unfould,
     The which my life and love together tyde?   195
     Now let the stony dart of senselesse° cold
     Perce to my hart, and pas through every side,
And let eternall night so sad sight fro me hide.

23

O lightsome° day, the lampe of highest *Jove*,
     First made by him, mens wandring wayes to
          guyde,   200
     When darknesse he in deepest dongeon drove,
     Henceforth thy hated face for ever hyde,
     And shut up heavens windowes shyning wyde:
     For earthly sight can nought but sorrow breed,
     And late° repentance, which shall long abyde.   205

---

182 **hart** courage, spirit.   187 **hardly** with difficulty.   187 **flitted** departed.   187 **win** prevail upon.   188 **native** natural.   189 **ghost** spirit.   193 **earthly mould** mortal things.   194 **cruell fates** the three Fates who spin the thread of life, and cut—or unweave ("unfold")—it to cause death.   194 **carefull** full of care.   196 **senselesse** causing loss of sensations.   199 **lightsome** light-giving.   205 **late** too late.

Mine eyes no more on vanitie shall feed,
But seeled up with death, shall have their deadly
    meed.°

24

Then downe againe she fell unto the ground;
    But he her quickly reared up againe:
210   Thrise did she sinke adowne in deadly swownd,°
    And thrise he her reviv'd with busie paine:°
    At last when life recover'd had the raine,°
    And over-wrestled his strong enemie,
    With foltring tong, and trembling every vaine,
215   Tell on (quoth she) the wofull Tragedie,
The which these reliques sad present unto mine eie.

25

Tempestuous fortune hath spent all her spight,
    And thrilling sorrow throwne his utmost° dart;
    Thy sad tongue cannot tell more heavy plight,
220   Then that I feele, and harbour in mine hart:
    Who° hath endur'd the whole, can beare each
        part.
    If death it be, it is not the first wound,
    That launched° hath my brest with bleeding
        smart.
    Begin, and end the bitter balefull stound;°
225 If lesse, then that I feare, more favour I have found.

26

Then gan the Dwarfe the whole discourse declare,
    The subtill traines° of *Archimago* old;
    The wanton loves of false *Fidessa* faire,
    Bought with the bloud of vanquisht Paynim
        bold:
    The wretched payre transform'd to treen
230   mould;°

---

207 **deadly meed** the reward of death.   210 **swownd** swoon.   211
busie paine diligent labor.   212 **raine** rule.   218 **utmost** final.   221
Who he who.   223 **launched** pierced.   224 **stound** time.   227
traines wiles.   230 **treen mould** the mold or form of a tree.

The house of Pride, and perils round about;
The combat, which he with *Sansjoy* did hould;
The lucklesse conflict with the Gyant stout,
Wherein captiv'd, of life or death he stood in doubt.

27

She heard with patience all unto the end,　　　235
　　And strove to maister sorrowfull assay,°
　　Which greater grew, the more she did contend,
　　And almost rent her tender hart in tway;°
　　And love fresh coles unto her fire did lay:
　　For greater love, the greater is the losse.　　　240
　　Was never Ladie loved dearer day,
　　Then she did love the knight of the *Redcrosse;*
For whose deare sake so many troubles her did tosse.

28

At last when fervent sorrow slaked° was,
　　She up arose, resolving him to find　　　245
　　A live or dead: and forward forth doth pas,
　　All° as the Dwarfe the way to her assynd:°
　　And evermore in constant carefull mind
　　She fed her wound with fresh renewed bale;°
　　Long tost with stormes, and bet° with bitter
　　　　wind,　　　250
　　High over hils, and low adowne the dale,
She wandred many a wood, and measurd many a vale.

29

At last she chaunced by good hap to meet
　　A goodly knight, faire marching by the way
　　Together with his Squire, arayed meet:°　　　255
　　His glitterand° armour shined farre away,
　　Like glauncing light of *Phœbus* brightest ray;
　　From top to toe no place appeared bare,
　　That deadly dint of steele endanger may:

---

236 **sorrowfull assay** the affliction of sorrow.　238 **tway** two.　244
slaked abated.　247 **All** just.　247 **assynd** pointed out.　249 **bale**
sorrow.　250 **bet** beaten.　255 **meet** properly.　256 **glitterand** giving light.

260 Athwart his brest a bauldrick brave he ware,
That shynd, like twinkling stars, with stons most
          pretious rare.

          30

And in the midst thereof one pretious stone
          Of wondrous worth, and eke of wondrous
              mights,°
          Shapt like a Ladies head, exceeding shone,
265   Like *Hesperus* emongst the lesser lights,
          And strove for to amaze the weaker° sights;
          Thereby his mortall blade full comely hong
          In yvory sheath, ycarv'd with curious slights;°
          Whose hilts were burnisht gold, and handle
              strong
270 Of mother pearle, and buckled with a golden tong.

          31

His haughtie° helmet, horrid° all with gold,
          Both glorious brightnesse, and great terrour
              bred;
          For all the crest a Dragon did enfold
          With greedie pawes, and over all did spred
275   His golden wings: his dreadfull hideous hed
          Close couched° on the bever, seem'd to throw
          From flaming mouth bright sparkles fierie red,
          That suddeine horror to faint harts did show;
          And scaly tayle was stretcht adowne his backe full
              low.

          32

280 Upon the top of all his loftie crest,
          A bunch of haires discoulourd diversly,°
          With sprincled pearle, and gold full richly drest,
          Did shake, and seem'd to daunce for jollity,
          Like to an Almond tree ymounted hye

---

263 **mights** power.   266 **the weaker** too weak.   268 **curious slights**
elaborate patterns.   271 **haughtie** lofty.   271 **horrid** bristling.   276
couched crouched.   281 **discoulourd diversly** of different colors.

On top of greene *Selinis* all alone,   285
    With blossomes brave bedecked daintily;
    Whose tender locks do tremble every one
At every little breath, that under heaven is blowne.

33

His warlike shield all closely cover'd was,
    Ne might of mortall eye be ever seene;   290
    Not made of steele, nor of enduring bras,
    Such earthly mettals soone consumed bene:
    But all of Diamond perfect pure and cleene°
    It framed was, one massie entire mould,
    Hewen out of Adamant° rocke with engines
      keene,   295
    That point of speare it never percen could,
Ne dint of direfull sword divide the substance would.

34

The same to wight° he never wont disclose,°
    But when as° monsters huge he would dismay,
    Or daunt unequall armies of his foes,   300
    Or when the flying heavens he would affray;°
    For so exceeding shone his glistring ray,
    That *Phœbus* golden face it did attaint,°
    As when a cloud his beames doth over-lay;
    And silver *Cynthia* wexed pale and faint,   305
As when her face is staynd with magicke arts con-
      straint.°

35

No magicke arts hereof° had any might,
    Nor bloudie wordes of bold Enchaunters call,
    But all that was not such, as seemd in sight,
    Before that shield did fade,° and suddeine fall: 310
    And when him list the raskall routes° appall,

---

293 **cleene** clear.   295 **Adamant** suggesting impenetrable hardness.
298 **to wight** to any creature.   298 **disclose** uncover.   299 **But when
as** except when.   301 **affray** frighten.   303 **attaint** obscure, by surpassing in brilliance.   306 **constraint** force.   307 **hereof** concerning
this, the shield.   310 **fade** weaken.   311 **raskall routes** vulgar mobs.

Men into stones therewith he could transmew,°
And stones to dust, and dust to nought at all;
And when him list the prouder lookes subdew,
315 He would them gazing° blind, or turne to other hew.°

36

Ne let it seeme, that credence this exceedes,
    For he that made the same, was knowne right
        well
To have done much more admirable deedes.
It *Merlin* was, which whylome° did excell
320 All living wightes in might of magicke spell:
    Both shield, and sword, and armour all he
        wrought
    For this young Prince, when first to armes he
        fell;°
But when he dyde, the Faerie Queene it brought
To Faerie lond, where yet it may be seene, if sought.

37

325 A gentle youth, his dearely loved Squire
    His speare of heben° wood behind him bare,
    Whose harmefull° head, thrice heated in the fire,
    Had riven many a brest with pikehead square;
    A goodly person, and could menage° faire
330 His stubborne steed with curbed canon bit,°
    Who under him did trample as the aire,°
    And chauft, that any on his backe should sit;
The yron rowels° into frothy fome he bit.

38

When as this knight nigh to the Ladie drew,
335   With lovely° court he gan her entertaine;
    But when he heard her answeres loth, he knew

312 **transmew** transform. 315 **gazing** as they gazed. 315 **other
hew** another expression. 319 **whylome** once. 322 **fell** applied himself. 326 **heben** ebony. Cf. Cupid's bow in Prologue, 3. 327
harmefull capable of inflicting harm. 329 **menage** manège, ride
his horse. 330 **curbed canon bit** a cannon bit (a smooth, round bit)
fastened by a chain under the horse's lower jaw. 331 **did trample
as the aire** i.e., as nimbly as the air. 333 **rowels** knobs on the bit.
335 **lovely** loving.

Some secret sorrow did her heart distraine:°
Which to allay, and calme her storming paine,
Faire feeling words he wisely gan display,
And for her humour fitting purpose faine,°   340
To tempt the cause it selfe for to bewray;°
Wherewith emmov'd,° these bleeding words she gan
    to say.

39

What worlds delight, or joy of living speach
    Can heart, so plung'd in sea of sorrowes deepe,
    And heaped with so huge misfortunes, reach?   345
    The carefull° cold beginneth for to creepe,
    And in my heart his yron arrow steepe,
    Soone as I thinke upon my bitter bale:
    Such helplesse harmes yts° better hidden keepe,
    Then rip up griefe, where it may not availe,   350
My last left comfort° is, my woes to weepe and waile.

40

Ah Ladie deare, quoth then the gentle knight,
    Well may I weene, your griefe is wondrous
        great;
    For wondrous great griefe groneth in my spright,
    Whiles thus I heare you of your sorrowes treat. 355
    But wofull Ladie let me you intrete,
    For to unfold the anguish of your hart:
    Mishaps are maistred by advice discrete,
    And counsell mittigates the greatest smart;
Found never helpe,° who never would his hurts im-
    part.   360

41

O but (quoth she) great griefe will not be tould,
    And can more easily be thought, then said.
    Right so; (quoth he) but he, that never would,

337 **distraine** afflict.   340 **And . . . faine** And for her mood he devised seemly discourse.   341 **bewray** reveal.   342 **emmov'd** moved.
346 **carefull** full of care. See E. K.'s note to *Shep. Cal.*, Dec. 133.
349 **yts** it is.   351 **My last left comfort** the only comfort left to me.
360 **Found never helpe** he never found help.

  Could never: will to might gives greatest aid.
  But griefe (quoth she) does greater grow dis-
365   plaid,°
  If then it find not helpe, and breedes despaire.
  Despaire breedes not (quoth he) where faith is
   staid.°
  No faith so fast (quoth she) but flesh does
   paire.°
Flesh may empaire (quoth he) but reason can repaire.

42

370 His goodly reason, and well guided speach
  So deepe did settle in her gratious thought,
  That her perswaded to disclose the breach,
  Which love and fortune in her heart had wrought,
  And said; faire Sir, I hope good hap hath
   brought
375 You to inquire the secrets of my griefe,
  Or that your wisedome will direct my thought,
  Or that your prowesse can me yield reliefe:
Then heare the storie sad, which I shall tell you
  briefe.

43

The forlorne Maiden, whom your eyes have seene
380 The laughing stocke of fortunes mockeries,
  Am th'only daughter of a King and Queene,
  Whose parents deare, whilest equall destinies
  Did runne about,° and their felicities
  The favourable heavens did not envy,
385 Did spread their rule through all the territories,
  Which *Phison* and *Euphrates* floweth by,
And *Gehons*° golden waves doe wash continually.

44

Till that their cruell cursed enemy,
  An huge great Dragon horrible in sight,

365 **displaid** having been displayed. 367 **staid** fixed. 368 **paire**
impair. 382–383 **whilest . . . about** while the Fates revolved impartially. 386–387 **Phison . . . Gehons** three rivers of Paradise.

Bred in the loathly lakes of *Tartary*,°   *390*
With murdrous ravine,° and devouring might
Their kingdome spoild, and countrey wasted
    quight:°
Themselves, for feare into his jawes to fall,
He forst to castle strong to take their flight,
Where fast embard in mightie brasen wall,   *395*
He has them now foure yeres besiegd to make them
    thrall.

45

Full many knights adventurous and stout°
Have enterprizd° that Monster to subdew;
From every coast that heaven walks about,°
Have thither come the noble Martiall crew,   *400*
That famous hard atchievements still pursew,
Yet never any could that girlond win,
But all still shronke,° and still he greater grew:
All they for want of faith, or guilt of sin,
The pitteous pray of his fierce crueltie have bin.   *405*

46

At last yledd with farre reported praise,
Which flying fame throughout the world had
    spred,
Of doughtie knights, whom Faery land did raise,
That noble order hight° of Maidenhed,
Forthwith to court of *Gloriane*° I sped,   *410*
Of *Gloriane* great Queene of glory bright,
Whose kingdomes seat *Cleopolis*° is red,°
There to obtaine some such redoubted° knight,
That Parents deare from tyrants powre deliver might.

47

It was my chance (my chance was faire and good)   *415*

390 **Tartary** Tartarus, or Hell.   391 **ravine** voracity.   392 **quight**
completely.   397 **stout**   brave.   398 **enterprizd**   attempted.   399
every . . . about every region about which the heavens revolve.   403
shronke collapsed.   409 **hight** called.   410 **Gloriane** the Faery
Queene.   412 **Cleopolis** the city of glory.   412 **red** called.   413 **redoubted** feared.

There for to find a fresh unproved° knight,
　　Whose manly hands imbrew'd in guiltie blood°
　　Had never bene, ne ever by his might
　　Had throwne to ground the unregarded right:
420　　Yet of his prowesse proofe he since hath made
　　(I witnesse am) in many a cruell fight;
　　The groning ghosts of many one dismaide°
Have felt the bitter dint° of his avenging blade.

48

And ye the forlorne° reliques of his powre,
425　　His byting sword, and his devouring speare,
　　Which have endured many a dreadfull stowre,°
　　Can speake° his prowesse, that did earst you
　　　　beare,
　　And well could rule: now he hath left you heare,
　　To be the record of his ruefull losse,
430　　And of my dolefull disaventurous deare:°
　　O heavie record of the good *Redcrosse,*
Where have you left your Lord, that could so well you
　　　　tosse?°

49

Well hoped I, and faire beginnings had,
　　That he my captive langour° should redeeme,
435　　Till all unweeting,° an Enchaunter bad
　　His sence abusd, and made him to misdeeme°
　　My loyalty, not such as it did seeme;
　　That rather death desire, then such despight.°
　　Be judge ye heavens, that all things right esteeme,
440　　How I him lov'd, and love with all my might,
So thought I eke of him, and thinke I thought aright.

---

416 **unproved** untried.　417 **imbrew'd in guiltie blood** wrongly
stained in blood.　422 **many one dismaide** many a one defeated.
423 **bitter dint** cutting stroke.　424 **forlorne** abandoned.　426
stowre encounter.　427 **speake** reveal.　430 **dolefull disaventurous
deare** sad unfortunate harm.　432 **tosse** wield.　434 **my captive
langour** i.e., her parents suffering in captivity.　435 **unweeting** unknown to the Knight.　436 **misdeeme** think evil of.　438 **That . . .
despight** I would desire death rather than such outrage of being dis-
loyal.

50

Thenceforth me desolate he quite forsooke,
 To wander, where wilde fortune would me lead,
 And other bywaies he himselfe betooke,
 Where never foot of living wight did tread, *445*
 That brought not backe the balefull° body dead;°
 In which him chaunced false *Duessa* meete,
 Mine onely° foe, mine onely deadly dread,
 Who with her witchcraft and misseeming sweete,°
Inveigled him to follow her desires unmeete.° *450*

51

At last by subtill sleights she him betraid
 Unto his foe, a Gyant huge and tall,
 Who him disarmed, dissolute,° dismaid,
 Unwares° surprised, and with mightie mall°
 The monster mercilesse him made to fall, *455*
 Whose fall did never foe before behold;
 And now in darkesome dungeon, wretched thrall,
 Remedilesse, for aie° he doth him hold;
This is my cause of griefe, more great, then may be
  told.

52

Ere she had ended all, she gan to faint: *460*
 But he her comforted and faire bespake,
 Certes, Madame, ye have great cause of plaint,
 That stoutest heart, I weene, could cause to
  quake.
 But be of cheare, and comfort to you take:
 For till I have acquit° your captive knight, *465*
 Assure your selfe, I will you not forsake.
 His chearefull words reviv'd her chearelesse
  spright,
So forth they went, the Dwarfe them guiding ever
  right.

446 **balefull** full of pain. 446 **That . . . dead** i.e., he was dead when
he returned. 448 **onely** chief. 449 **misseeming sweete** sweet decep-
tion. 450 **unmeete** unseemly. 453 **dissolute** enfeebled. 454 **Unwares** suddenly. 454 **mall** club, or perhaps blow. 458 **Remedilesse,
for aie** without hope of remedy forever. 465 **acquit** set free.

CANTO VIII

Faire virgin to redeeme her deare
*   brings Arthur to the fight:*
Who slayes the Gyant, wounds the beast,
*   and strips Duessa quight.*

1

Ay me, how many perils doe enfold
    The righteous man, to make him daily fall?
    Were not, that heavenly grace doth him uphold,
    And stedfast truth acquite him out of all.
    Her love is firme, her care continuall,
    So oft as he through his owne foolish pride,
    Or weaknesse is to sinfull bands° made thrall:
    Else should this *Redcrosse* knight in bands have
        dyde,
For whose deliverance she this Prince doth thither
      guide.

2

They sadly traveild thus, untill they came
    Nigh to a castle builded strong and hie:
    Then cryde the Dwarfe, lo yonder is the same,
    In which my Lord my liege doth lucklesse lie,°
    Thrall to that Gyants hatefull tyrannie:
    Therefore, deare Sir, your mightie powres assay.
    The noble knight alighted by and by°
    From loftie steede, and bad the Ladie stay,
To see what end of fight should him befall that day.

3

So with the Squire, th'admirer of his might,
    He marched forth towards that castle wall;

---

7 sinfull bands bonds of sin.   **13 lucklesse lie** lie unlucky.   **16 by and by** straightway.

Whose gates he found fast shut, ne living wight
    To ward° the same, nor answere commers call.
    Then tooke that Squire an horne of bugle small,°
    Which hong adowne his side in twisted gold,
    And tassels gay. Wyde wonders over all°   25
    Of that same hornes great vertues° weren told,
Which had approved° bene in uses manifold.

4

Was never wight, that heard that shrilling sound,
    But trembling feare did feele in every vaine;
    Three miles it might be easie heard around,   30
    And Ecchoes three answerd it selfe againe:
    No false enchauntment, nor deceiptfull traine
    Might once abide the terror of that blast,
    But presently° was voide° and wholly vaine:
    No gate so strong, no locke so firme and fast,   35
But with that percing noise flew open quite, or brast.°

5

The same before the Geants gate he blew,
    That all the castle quaked from the ground,
    And every dore of freewill° open flew.
    The Gyant selfe dismaied with that sownd,   40
    Where he with his *Duessa* dalliance° fownd,
    In hast came rushing forth from inner bowre,
    With staring countenance sterne, as one
        astownd,°
    And staggering steps, to weet° what suddein
        stowre°
Had wrought that horror strange, and dar'd his
        dreaded powre.   45

6

And after him the proud *Duessa* came,
    High mounted on her manyheaded beast,

22 **ward** guard. 23 **bugle small** a small wild ox. 25 **over all** everywhere. 26 **vertues** powers. 27 **approved** proved. 34 **presently** immediately. 34 **voide** ineffective. 36 **brast** burst. 39 **of freewill** freely. 41 **dalliance** amorous play. 43 **astownd** stunned. 44 **to weet** to know. 44 **stowre** tumult.

And every head with fyrie tongue did flame,
And every head was crowned on his creast,
50 And bloudie mouthed with late cruell feast.
That when the knight beheld, his mightie shild
Upon his manly arme he soone addrest,
And at him fiercely flew, with courage fild,
And eger greedinesse° through every member thrild.°

7

55 Therewith the Gyant buckled him° to fight,
Inflam'd with scornefull wrath and high disdaine,
And lifting up his dreadfull club on hight,°
All arm'd with ragged snubbes° and knottie
graine,
Him thought at first encounter to have slaine.
60 But wise and warie was that noble Pere,
And lightly leaping from so monstrous maine,°
Did faire avoide the violence him nere;
It booted nought, to thinke, such thunderbolts to
beare.

8

Ne shame he thought to shunne so hideous might:
65 The idle° stroke, enforcing furious way,
Missing the marke of his misaymed sight
Did fall to ground, and with his heavie sway°
So deepely dinted in the driven clay,
That three yardes deepe a furrow up did throw:
70 The sad° earth wounded with so sore assay,°
Did grone full grievous underneath the blow,
And trembling with strange feare, did like an earth-
quake show.°

9

As when almightie *Jove* in wrathfull mood,
To wreake° the guilt of mortall sins° is bent,

54 **greedinesse** desire. 54 **thrild** penetrated. 55 **buckled him** prepared. 57 **hight** high. 58 **snubbes** root snags. 61 **maine** might.
65 **idle** vain. 67 **sway** momentum. 70 **sad** heavy. 70 **assay** assault. 72 **show** appear. 74 **wreake** revenge. 74 **mortall sins** the
sins of mortals.

Hurles forth his thundring dart with deadly
    food,°   75
Enrold in flames, and smouldring dreriment,°
Through riven cloudes and molten° firmament;
The fierce threeforked engin° making way,
Both loftie towres and highest trees hath rent,
And all that might his angrie passage stay,   80
And shooting in the earth, casts up a mount of clay.

10

His boystrous° club, so buried in the ground,
    He could not rearen up againe so light,°
    But that the knight him at avantage° found,
    And whiles he strove his combred clubbe to
        quight°   85
    Out of the earth, with blade all burning bright
    He smote off his left arme, which like a blocke
    Did fall to ground, depriv'd of native might;°
    Large streames of bloud out of the truncked
        stocke°
Forth gushed, like fresh water streame from riven
    rocke.   90

11

Dismaied with so desperate deadly wound,
    And eke impatient of unwonted° paine,
    He loudly brayd with beastly yelling sound,
    That all the fields rebellowed againe;°
    As great a noyse, as when in Cymbrian plaine   95
    An heard of Bulles, whom kindly rage° doth
        sting,
    Do for the milkie mothers want° complaine,
    And fill the fields with troublous° bellowing,

---

75 **food** feud.   76 **dreriment** darkness.   77 **molten** turned to liquid.
78 **engin** weapon.   82 **boystrous** bulky.   83 **rearen . . . light** lift up
again so quickly.   84 **avantage** advantage.   85 **combred . . . quight**
encumbered club to free.   88 **native might** natural strength.   89
truncked stocke truncated body.   92 **unwonted** unaccustomed.   94
againe back.   96 **kindly rage** natural passion.   97 **the milkie
mothers want** desire for the females.   98 **troublous** troublesome.

The neighbour woods around with hollow murmur
    ring.

12

100 That when his deare *Duessa* heard, and saw
    The evill stownd,° that daungerd her estate,
    Unto his aide she hastily did draw
    Her dreadfull beast, who swolne with bloud of
        late
    Came ramping° forth with proud presumpteous
        gate,
105   And threatned all his heads like flaming brands.
    But him the Squire made quickly to retrate,
    Encountring fierce with single sword° in hand,
And twixt him and his Lord did like a bulwarke stand.

13

The proud *Duessa* full of wrathfull spight,
110   And fierce disdaine, to be affronted° so,
    Enforst her purple beast with all her might
    That stop out of the way to overthroe,
    Scorning the let° of so unequall foe:
    But nathemore° would that courageous swayne
115   To her yeeld passage, gainst his Lord to goe,
    But with outrageous strokes did him restraine,
And with his bodie bard the way atwixt them twaine.

14

Then tooke the angrie witch her golden cup,°
    Which still she bore, replete with magick artes;
120   Death and despeyre did many thereof sup,°
    And secret poyson through their inner parts,
    Th'eternall bale° of heavie wounded harts;
    Which after charmes and some enchauntments
        said,
    She lightly sprinkled on his weaker° parts;

101 **stownd** time. 104 **ramping** prancing. 107 **single sword** sword
alone. 110 **affronted** confronted. 113 **let** hindrance. 114 **nathemore** never the more. 118 **her golden cup** See Rev. xvii. 4. 120
sup drink. 122 **bale** injury. 124 **weaker** too weak.

    Therewith his sturdie courage soone was quayd,° *125*
And all his senses were with suddeine dread dismayd.

15

So downe he fell before the cruell beast,
  Who on his necke his bloudie clawes did seize,°
  That life nigh crusht out of his panting brest:
  No powre he had to stirre, nor will to rize. *130*
  That when the carefull° knight gan well avise,°
  He lightly° left the foe, with whom he fought,
  And to the beast gan turne his enterprise;
  For wondrous anguish in his hart it wrought,
To see his loved Squire into such thraldome brought. *135*

16

And high advauncing his bloud-thirstie blade,
  Stroke one of those deformed heads so sore,
  That of his puissance proud ensample° made;
  His monstrous scalpe° downe to his teeth it tore,
  And that misformed shape mis-shaped more: *140*
  A sea of bloud gusht from the gaping wound,
  That her gay garments staynd with filthy gore,
  And overflowed all the field around;
That over shoes in bloud he waded on the ground.

17

Thereat he roared for exceeding paine, *145*
  That to have heard, great horror would have bred,
  And scourging th'emptie ayre with his long traine,
  Through great impatience of his grieved° hed
  His gorgeous ryder from her loftie sted°
  Would have cast downe, and trod in durtie myre, *150*
  Had not the Gyant soone her succoured;
  Who all enrag'd with smart and franticke yre,

---

125 **was quayd** was quailed, daunted.   128 **seize** fasten.   131 **carefull** full of care or solicitude.   131 **avise** notice.   132 **lightly** swiftly.
138 **ensample** example.   139 **scalpe** skull.   148 **grieved** hurt.   149 **sted** place.

Came hurtling in full fierce, and forst the knight re-
　　tyre.

18

The force, which wont in two to be disperst,
In one alone left hand° he now unites,
　　Which is through rage more strong then both
　　　were erst;
With which his hideous club aloft he dites,°
And at his foe with furious rigour smites,
That strongest Oake might seeme to overthrow:
The stroke upon his shield so heavie lites,
That to the ground it doubleth him full low
What mortall wight could ever beare so monstrous
　　blow?

19

And in his fall his shield, that covered was,
Did loose his vele by chaunce, and open flew:
The light whereof, that heavens light did pas,°
Such blazing brightnesse through the aier threw,
That eye mote not the same endure to vew.
Which when the Gyaunt spyde with staring eye,
He downe let fall his arme, and soft withdrew
His weapon huge, that heaved was on hye
For to have slaine the man, that on the ground did
　　lye.

20

And eke the fruitfull-headed° beast, amaz'd
At flashing beames of that sunshiny shield,
Became starke blind, and all his senses daz'd,°
That downe he tumbled on the durtie field,
And seem'd himselfe as conquered to yield.
Whom when his maistresse proud perceiv'd to
　　fall,
Whiles yet his feeble feet for faintnesse reeld,

155 **one alone left hand** one remaining hand. 157 **dites** makes
ready. 165 **pas** surpass. 172 **fruitfull-headed** many-headed. 174
daz'd dazzled.

Unto the Gyant loudly she gan call,
O helpe *Orgoglio,* helpe, or else we perish all.   *180*

21

At her so pitteous cry was much amoov'd°
        Her champion stout, and for to ayde his frend,
        Againe his wonted angry weapon proov'd:°
        But all in vaine: for he has read his end
        In that bright shield, and all their forces spend   *185*
        Themselves in vaine: for since that glauncing
            sight,
        He hath no powre to hurt, nor to defend;
        As where th'Almighties lightning brond does
            light,
It dimmes the dazed eyen, and daunts the senses
        quight.

22

Whom when the Prince, to battell new addrest,   *190*
        And threatning high his dreadfull stroke did see,
        His sparkling blade about his head he blest,°
        And smote off quite his right leg by the knee,
        That downe he tombled; as an aged tree,
        High growing on the top of rocky clift,   *195*
        Whose hartstrings with keene steele nigh hewen
            be,
        The mightie trunck halfe rent, with ragged rift°
Doth roll adowne the rocks, and fall with fearefull
        drift.°

23

Or as a Castle reared high and round,
        By subtile engins° and malitious slight°   *200*
        Is undermined from the lowest ground,
        And her foundation forst,° and feebled quight,
        At last downe falles, and with her heaped hight

181 **amoov'd** moved.   183 **proov'd** tried.   192 **blest** brandished.
197 **ragged rift** jagged splitting.   198 **drift** impetus.   200 **engins**
machines.   200 **slight** sleight, trickery.   202 **forst** overpowered.

Her hastie ruine does more heavie° make,
205   And yields it selfe unto the victours might;
        Such was this Gyaunts fall, that seemd to shake
The stedfast globe of earth, as° it for feare did quake.

24

The knight then lightly leaping to the pray,
        With mortall steele him smot againe so sore,
210   That headlesse his unweldy bodie lay,
        All wallowd in his owne fowle bloudy gore,
        Which flowed from his wounds in wondrous
            store.
        But soone as breath out of his breast did pas,
        That huge great body, which the Gyaunt bore,
215   Was vanisht quite, and of that monstrous mas
Was nothing left, but like an emptie bladder was.

25

Whose grievous fall, when false *Duessa* spide,
        Her golden cup she cast unto the ground,
        And crowned mitre rudely threw aside;
        Such percing° griefe her stubborne hart did
220   wound,
        That she could not endure that dolefull stound,
        But leaving all behind her, fled away:
        The light-foot Squire her quickly turnd around,
        And by hard meanes enforcing her to stay,
225 So brought unto his Lord, as his deserved pray.

26

The royall Virgin, which beheld from farre,
        In pensive plight, and sad perplexitie,
        The whole atchievement of this doubtfull° warre,
        Came running fast to greet his victorie,
230   With sober gladnesse, and myld modestie,
        And with sweet joyous cheare° him thus be-
            spake;

---

204 **more heavie** i.e., falling with greater force.   207 **as** as if.   220
percing piercing.   228 **doubtfull** arousing apprehensions.   231
cheare countenance.

Faire braunch of noblesse,° flowre of chevalrie,
That with your worth the world amazed make,
How shall I quite° the paines, ye suffer for my sake?

27

And you fresh bud of vertue springing fast,   235
    Whom these sad eyes saw nigh unto deaths dore,
    What hath poore Virgin for such perill past,
    Wherewith you to reward? Accept therefore
    My simple selfe, and service evermore;
    And he that high does sit, and all things see   240
    With equall° eyes, their merites to restore,°
    Behold° what ye this day have done for mee,
And what I cannot quite, requite with usuree.°

28

But sith the heavens, and your faire handeling°
    Have made you maister of the field this day,   245
    Your fortune maister eke with governing,
    And well begun end all so well, I pray,
    Ne let that wicked woman scape away;
    For she it is, that did my Lord bethrall,°
    My dearest Lord, and deepe in dungeon lay,   250
    Where he his better dayes hath wasted all.
O heare, how piteous he to you for ayd does call.

29

Forthwith he gave in charge unto his Squire,
    That scarlot whore to keepen carefully;
    Whiles he himselfe with greedie° great desire   255
    Into the Castle entred forcibly,
    Where living creature none he did espye;
    Then gan he lowdly through the house to call:
    But no man car'd to answere to his crye.
    There raignd a solemne silence over all,   260

---

232 **noblesse** nobility.   234 **quite** requite.   241 **equall** just.   241
restore compensate.   242 **Behold** may he behold.   243 **usuree** interest.   244 **handeling** management.   249 **bethrall** enthrall.   255
greedie eager.

Nor voice was heard, nor wight was seene in bowre
    or hall.

30

At last with creeping crooked pace forth came
    An old old man, with beard as white as snow,
    That on a staffe his feeble steps did frame,°
265   And guide his wearie gate both too and fro:
    For his eye sight him failed long ygo,
    And on his arme a bounch of keyes he bore,
    The which unused rust° did overgrow:
    Those were the keyes of every inner dore,
270 But he could not them use, but kept them still in store.

31

But very uncouth sight was to behold,
    How he did fashion his untoward° pace,
    For as he forward moov'd his footing old,
    So backward still was turnd his wrincled face,
275   Unlike to men, who ever as they trace,°
    Both feet and face one way are wont to lead.
    This was the auncient keeper of that place,
    And foster father of the Gyant dead;
His name *Ignaro*° did his nature right aread.°

32

280 His reverend haires and holy gravitie
    The knight much honord, as beseemed well,°
    And gently askt, where all the people bee,
    Which in that stately building wont to dwell.
    Who answerd him full soft, he could not tell.
285   Againe he askt, where that same knight was layd,
    Whom great *Orgoglio* with his puissaunce fell
    Had made his caytive thrall; againe he sayde,
He could not tell: ne ever other answere made.

---

264 **did frame** directed, shaped his course.　268 **unused rust** because
the keys are not used.　272 **untoward** awkward.　275 **trace** walk.
279 **Ignaro** Ignorance ("He could not tell").　279 **aread** make
known.　281 **as beseemed well** as seemed properly fitting his age.

33

Then asked he, which way he in might pas:
 He could not tell, againe he answered.   *290*
 Thereat the curteous knight displeased was,
 And said, Old sire, it seemes thou hast not red°
 How ill it sits with° that same silver hed
 In vaine to mocke, or mockt in vaine to bee:
 But if thou be, as thou art pourtrahed   *295*
 With natures pen, in ages grave degree,
Aread in graver wise,° what I demaund of thee.

34

His answere likewise was, he could not tell.
 Whose sencelesse speach, and doted° ignorance
 When as the noble Prince had marked well,   *300*
 He ghest his nature by his countenance,
 And calmd his wrath with goodly temperance.
 Then to him stepping, from his arme did reach
 Those keyes, and made himselfe free enterance.
 Each dore he opened without any breach;°   *305*
There was no barre to stop, nor foe him to empeach.°

35

There all within full rich arayd he found,
 With royall arras° and resplendent gold.
 And did with store of every thing abound,
 That greatest Princes presence° might behold.   *310*
 But all the floore (too filthy to be told)
 With bloud of guiltlesse babes, and innocents
  trew,
 Which there were slaine, as sheepe out of the
  fold,
 Defiled was, that dreadfull was to vew,
And sacred° ashes over it was strowed new.   *315*

---

292 **red** perceived. 293 **sits with** suits. 297 **Aread . . . wise** utter
more gravely. 299 **doted** senile. 305 **breach** act of forcing. 306
empeach hinder. 308 **arras** tapestry. 310 **Princes presence** person
of the Prince. 315 **sacred** accursed.

36

And there beside of marble stone was built
　　An Altare, carv'd with cunning° imagery,
　　On which true Christians bloud was often spilt,
　　And holy Martyrs often doen to dye,°
320　With cruell malice and strong tyranny:
　　Whose blessed sprites° from underneath the
　　　　stone
　　To God for vengeance cryde continually,
　　And with great griefe were often heard to grone,
That hardest heart would bleede, to heare their piteous
　　　　mone.

37

325 Through every rowme he sought, and every bowr,
　　But no where could he find that wofull thrall:
　　At last he came unto an yron doore,
　　That fast was lockt, but key found not at all
　　Emongst that bounch, to open it withall;°
330　But in the same a little grate was pight,°
　　Through which he sent his voyce, and lowd did
　　　　call
　　With all his powre, to weet, if living wight
Were housed therewithin, whom he enlargen might.°

38

Therewith° an hollow, dreary, murmuring voyce
335　These piteous plaints and dolours° did resound;
　　O who is that, which brings me happy choyce
　　Of death, that here lye dying every stound,°
　　Yet live perforce in balefull darkenesse bound?
　　For now three Moones have changed thrice their
　　　　hew,°
　　And have beene thrice hid underneath the
340　　　ground,
　　Since I the heavens chearefull face did vew,

317 **cunning** skillful.   319 **doen to dye** were slain.   321 **sprites**
spirits.   329 **withall** with.   330 **pight** placed.   333 **enlargen might**
might free.   334 **Therewith** with that.   335 **dolours** lamentations.
337 **stound** moment.   339 **hew** shape.

O welcome thou, that doest of death bring tydings
    trew.

39

Which when that Champion heard, with percing point
    Of pitty deare° his hart was thrilled sore,
    And trembling horrour ran through every joynt,   *345*
    For ruth of gentle knight so fowle forlore:°
    Which shaking off, he rent that yron dore,
    With furious force, and indignation fell;
    Where entred in, his foot could find no flore,
    But all a deepe descent, as darke as hell,   *350*
That breathed ever forth a filthie banefull° smell.

40

But neither darkenesse fowle, nor filthy bands,°
    Nor noyous° smell his purpose could withhold,
    (Entire affection hateth nicer° hands)
    But that with constant zeale, and courage bold,   *355*
    After long paines and labours manifold,
    He found the meanes that Prisoner up to reare;
    Whose feeble thighes, unhable to uphold
    His pined corse,° him scarse to light could beare,
A ruefull° spectacle of death and ghastly drere.°   *360*

41

His sad dull eyes deepe sunck in hollow pits,
    Could not endure th'unwonted° sunne to view;
    His bare thin cheekes for want of better bits,°
    And empty sides deceived° of their dew,
    Could make a stony hart his hap to rew;°   *365*
    His rawbone armes, whose mighty brawned
      bowrs°

---

344 **deare** heartfelt. 346 **so fowle forlore** so foully lost.   351 **banefull** poisonous. 352 **bands** bonds. 353 **noyous** noxious. 354 **nicer** too nice or dainty. 359 **pined corse** body wasted away. 360 **ruefull** pitiful. 360 **drere** dreariness. 362 **unwonted** unaccustomed. 363 **bits** victuals. 364 **deceived** defrauded. 365 **his . . . rew** pity his misfortune. 366 **brawned bowrs** brawny muscles.

Were wont to rive° steele plates, and helmets
    hew,
Were cleane consum'd, and all his vitall powres
Decayd, and all his flesh shronk up like withered
    flowres.

42

370 Whom when his Lady saw, to him she ran
    With hasty joy: to see him made her glad,
    And sad to view his visage pale and wan,
    Who earst° in flowres of freshest youth was clad.
    Tho° when her well of teares she wasted had,°
375   She said, Ah dearest Lord, what evill starre
    On you hath fround, and pourd his influence°
    bad,
    That of your selfe ye thus berobbed arre,
And this misseeming hew° your manly looks doth
    marre?

43

But welcome now my Lord, in wele or woe,
380   Whose presence I have lackt too long a day;
    And fie on Fortune mine avowed foe,
    Whose wrathfull wreakes° them selves do now
    alay.
    And for these wrongs shall treble penaunce pay
    Of treble good: good growes of evils priefe.°
385   The chearelesse man, whom sorrow did dismay,
    Had no delight to treaten° of his griefe;
His long endured famine needed more reliefe.

44

Faire Lady, then said that victorious knight,
    The things, that grievous were to do, or beare,
390   Them to renew, I wote, breeds no delight;
    Best musicke breeds delight in loathing eare:

367 **rive** rend. 373 **earst** formerly. 374 **Tho** then. 374 **wasted
had** had spent. 376 **pourd his influence** astral influence by which
a substance flowing from the stars affected man's destiny. 378
misseeming hew unseemly appearance. 382 **wreakes** vengeance.
384 **evils priefe** the experience of evil. 386 **treaten** discourse.

But th'onely° good, that growes of passed feare,
Is to be wise, and ware° of like agein.
This dayes ensample hath this lesson deare
Deepe written in my heart with yron pen,   *395*
That blisse may not abide in state of mortall men.

45

Henceforth sir knight, take to you wonted° strength,
    And maister these mishaps with patient might;
    Loe where your foe lyes stretcht in monstrous
        length,
    And loe that wicked woman in your sight,   *400*
    The roote of all your care, and wretched plight,
    Now in your powre, to let her live, or dye.
    To do° her dye (quoth *Una*) were despight,°
    And shame t'avenge so weake an enemy;
But spoile° her of her scarlot robe, and let her fly.   *405*

46

So as she bad, that witch they disaraid,
    And robd of royall robes, and purple pall,
    And ornaments that richly were displaid;
    Ne spared they to strip her naked all.
    Then when they had despoild her tire and call,°   *410*
    Such as she was, their eyes might her behold,
    That her misshaped parts did them appall,
    A loathly,° wrinckled hag, ill favoured, old,
Whose secret filth good manners biddeth not be told.

47

Her craftie head was altogether bald,   *415*
    And as in hate of honorable eld,°
    Was overgrowne with scurfe° and filthy scald;°
    Her teeth out of her rotten gummes were feld,°
    And her sowre breath abhominably smeld;
    Her dried dugs, like bladders lacking wind,   *420*

392 **th'onely** the chief.   393 **ware** wary.   397 **wonted** accustomed.
403 **do** make.   403 **despight** malice.   405 **spoile** despoil.   410 **tire
and call** headdress.   413 **loathly** loathsome.   416 **eld** age.   417
scurfe scabs.   417 **scald** scall, a scabby disease of the scalp.   418
feld fallen.

Hong downe, and filthy matter from them weld;°
    Her wrizled° skin as rough, as maple rind,°
So scabby was, that would have loathd all woman-
    kind.°

48

Her neather° parts, the shame of all her kind,
    My chaster° Muse for shame doth blush to
425   write;
    But at her rompe° she growing had behind
A foxes taile, with dong all fowly dight;°
    And eke her feete most monstrous were in
    sight;°
    For one of them was like an Eagles claw,
430   With griping talaunts° armd to greedy fight,
The other like a Beares uneven° paw:
More ugly shape yet never living creature saw.

49

Which when the knights beheld, amazd they were,
    And wondred at so fowle deformed wight.
435   Such then (said *Una*) as she seemeth here,
    Such is the face of falshood, such the sight
    Of fowle *Duessa,* when her borrowed light
Is laid away, and counterfesaunce° knowne.
    Thus when they had the witch disrobed quight,
440   And all her filthy feature° open showne,
They let her goe at will, and wander wayes un-
    knowne.

50

She flying fast from heavens hated face,
    And from the world that her discovered wide,°
    Fled to the wastfull° wildernesse apace,
445   From living eyes her open shame to hide,

---

421 **weld** flowed.   422 **wrizled** wrinkled.   422 **rind** bark.   423
would ... womankind would have caused all women to loathe her.
424 **neather** lower.   425 **chaster** too chaste.   426 **rompe** rump.
427 **dight** adorned.   428 **in sight** to see.   430 **talaunts** talons.   431
uneven rugged.   438 **counterfesaunce** counterfeiting.   440 **feature**
form.   443 **wide** widely.   444 **wastfull** desolate.

And lurkt in rocks and caves long unespide.
But that faire crew° of knights, and *Una* faire
Did in that castle afterwards abide,
To rest them selves, and weary powres repaire,
Where store they found of all, that dainty was and
    rare.

       450

CANTO IX

His loves and lignage Arthur tells
   The knights knit friendly bands:
Sir Trevisan flies from Despayre,
   Whom Redcrosse knight withstands.

1

O Goodly golden chaine, wherewith yfere°
   The vertues linked are in lovely wize:°
   And noble minds of yore allyed were,
   In brave poursuit of chevalrous emprize,°
   That none did others safety despize,   *5*
   Nor aid envy° to him, in need that stands,
   But friendly each did others prayse devize,
   How to advaunce° with favourable hands,
As this good Prince redeemd the *Redcrosse* knight
    from bands.

2

Who when their powres empaird° through labour
   long,   *10*
   With dew repast they had recured° well,
   And that weake captive wight now wexed strong,
   Them list° no lenger there at leasure dwell,
   But forward fare, as their adventures fell,°

447 **crew** company. 1 **yfere** together. 2 **in lovely wize** in loving
manner. 4 **emprize** enterprise. 6 **envy** begrudge. 8 **advaunce** extol. 10 **empaird** impaired. 11 **recured** restored to health. 13
Them list It pleased them. 14 **fell** directed.

15 But ere they parted, *Una* faire besought
That straunger knight his name and nation tell;
Least so great good, as he for her had wrought,
Should die unknown, and buried be in thanklesse
     thought.

3

Faire virgin (said the Prince) ye me require°
20 A thing without the compas of my wit:°
For both the lignage and the certain Sire,
From which I sprong, from me are hidden yit.
For all so° soone as life did me admit
Into this world, and shewed heavens light,
25 From mothers pap I taken was unfit:°
And streight delivered to a Faery knight,°
To be upbrought in gentle thewes° and martiall
     might.

4

Unto old *Timon*° he me brought bylive,°
Old *Timon,* who in youthly yeares hath beene
30 In warlike feates th'expertest man alive,
And is the wisest now on earth I weene;
His dwelling is low in a valley greene,
Under the foot of *Rauran* mossy hore,°
From whence the river *Dee* as silver cleene°
35 His tombling billowes rolls with gentle rore:
There all my dayes he traind me up in vertuous lore.

5

Thither the great Magicien *Merlin* came,
As was his use, ofttimes to visit me:
For he had charge my discipline to frame,
40 And Tutours nouriture° to oversee.
Him oft and oft I askt in privitie,°

---

19 require request.   **20 without . . . wit** beyond my knowledge.   **23 all so** as.   **25 unfit** because not weaned.   **26 a Faery knight** i.e., Timon.   **27 thewes** discipline.   **28 Timon** Honor.   **28 bylive** forthwith.   **33 mossy hore** hoary with moss.   **34 cleene** pure.   **40 nouriture** nurture.   **41 in privitie** privately.

Of what loines and what lignage I did spring:
Whose aunswere bad me still assured bee,
That I was sonne and heire unto a king,
As time in her just terme° the truth to light should
 bring.   45

6

Well worthy impe,° said then the Lady gent,°
 And Pupill fit for such a Tutours hand.
 But what adventure, or what high intent
 Hath brought you hither into Faery land,
 Aread Prince *Arthur,* crowne of Martiall band?   50
 Full hard it is (quoth he) to read° aright
 The course of heavenly cause, or understand
 The secret meaning of th'eternall might,
That rules mens wayes, and rules the thoughts of
 living wight.

7

For whither he through fatall° deepe foresight   55
 Me hither sent, for cause to me unghest,
 Or that fresh bleeding wound, which day and
  night
 Whilome° doth rancle in my riven brest,
 With forced fury following his behest,°
 Me hither brought by wayes yet never found,   60
 You to have helpt I hold my selfe yet blest.
 Ah curteous knight (quoth she) what secret
  wound
Could ever find,° to grieve the gentlest hart on
 ground?°

8

Deare Dame (quoth he) you sleeping sparkes awake,
 Which troubled once, into huge flames will grow,   65
 Ne ever will their fervent fury slake

45 **in her just terme** in due course.   46 **impe** offspring.   46 **gent**
gentle.   51 **read** understand.   55 **fatall** ordained by fate.   58
Whilome ever.   59 **With . . . behest** With passion forces me to follow
love's command.   63 **find** be inclined.   63 **on ground** on earth.

Till living moysture into smoke do flow,°
And wasted life do lye in ashes low.
Yet sithens° silence lesseneth not my fire,
70   But told it flames, and hidden it does glow,
I will revele, what ye so much desire:
Ah Love, lay downe thy bow, the whiles I may respire.°

9

It was in freshest flowre of youthly° yeares,
When courage first does creepe in manly chest,
75   Then first the coale of kindly heat° appeares
To kindle love in every living brest;
But me had warnd° old *Timons* wise behest,
Those creeping flames by reason to subdew,
Before their rage grew to so great unrest,°
80   As miserable lovers use to rew,
Which still wex old in woe, whiles woe still wexeth new.

10

That idle name of love, and lovers life,
As losse of time, and vertues enimy
I ever scornd, and joyd to stirre up strife,
85   In middest of their mournfull Tragedy,
Ay wont° to laugh, when them I heard to cry,
And blow the fire, which them to ashes brent:°
Their God° himselfe, griev'd at my libertie,
Shot many a dart at me with fiers intent,
90   But I them warded all with wary government.°

11

But all in vaine: no fort can be so strong,
Ne fleshly brest can armed be so sound,
But will at last be wonne with battrie long,
Or unawares at disavantage found;

67 **Till . . . flow** Until he (or the world) is destroyed by fire.   69
sithens since.   72 **respire** take breath.   73 **youthly** youthful.   75
kindly heat natural passion.   77 **But me had warnd** But I had been
warned by.   79 **unrest** turmoil.   86 **Ay wont** ever used.   87 **brent**
burned.   88 **Their God** Cupid.   90 **government** governing.

Nothing is sure, that growes on earthly ground: *95*
  And who most trustes in arme of fleshly might,
  And boasts in beauties chaine not to be bound,
  Doth soonest fall in disaventrous° fight,
And yeeldes his caytive° neck to victours most
    despight.°

12

Ensample make of him° your haplesse joy,   *100*
  And of my selfe now mated,° as ye see;
  Whose prouder° vaunt that proud avenging boy°
  Did soone pluck downe, and curbd my libertie.
  For on a day prickt° forth with jollitie
  Of looser° life, and heat of hardiment,°   *105*
  Raunging the forest wide on courser free,°
  The fields, the floods,° the heavens with one
    consent°
Did seeme to laugh at me, and favour mine intent.°

13

For-wearied° with my sports, I did alight
  From loftie steed, and downe to sleepe me layd;   *110*
  The verdant gras my couch did goodly dight,°
  And pillow was my helmet faire displayd:
  Whiles every sence the humour sweet embayd,°
  And slombring soft my hart did steale away,
  Me seemed, by my side a royall Mayd   *115*
  Her daintie limbes full softly down did lay:
So faire a creature yet saw never sunny day.

14

Most goodly glee and lovely blandishment°
  She to me made, and bad me love her deare,

98 **disaventrous** unfortunate.   99 **caytive** captive.   99 **most despight** greatest outrage.   100 **him** i.e., the Red Cross Knight.   101 **mated** amated, cast down.   102 **prouder** too proud.   102 **that proud avenging boy** Cupid.   104 **prickt** incited.   105 **looser** too loose.   105 **hardiment** boldness.   106 **free** willing.   107 **floods** waters.   107 **consent** harmony.   108 **intent** frame of mind.   109 **For-wearied** utterly wearied.   111 **dight** prepare.   113 **Whiles . . . embayd** While the dew of sleep bathes every sense.   118 **lovely blandishment** loving flattery.

120 For dearely sure her love was to me bent,
As when just time expired should appeare.
But whether dreames delude, or true it were,
Was never hart so ravisht with delight,
Ne living man like words did ever heare,
125 As she to me delivered all that night;
And at her parting said, She Queene of Faeries hight.°

15

When I awoke, and found her place devoyd,°
And nought but pressed gras, where she had lyen,
I sorrowed all so much, as earst I joyd,
130 And washed all her place with watry eyen.
From that day forth I lov'd that face divine;
From that day forth I cast° in carefull° mind,
To seeke her out with labour, and long tyne,°
And never vow to rest,° till her I find,
Nine monethes I seeke in vaine yet ni'll° that vow
135 unbind.

16

Thus as he spake, his visage wexed pale,
And chaunge of hew great passion did bewray;°
Yet still he strove to cloke his inward bale,°
And hide the smoke, that did his fire display,
140 Till gentle *Una* thus to him gan say;
O happy Queene of Faeries, that hast found
Mongst many, one that with his prowesse may
Defend thine honour, and thy foes confound:
True Loves are often sown, but seldom grow on
ground.°

17

145 Thine, O then, said the gentle *Redcrosse* knight,
Next to that Ladies love, shalbe the place,
O fairest virgin, full of heavenly light,

126 **hight** was called.   127 **devoyd** empty.   132 **cast** resolved.   132
carefull sorrowful.   133 **tyne** teen, suffering.   134 **never . . . rest**
vowed never to rest.   135 **ni'll** will not.   137 **bewray** reveal.   138
bale torment.   144 **on ground** on earth, but with reference to
Arthur's vision on the grass.

Whose wondrous faith, exceeding earthly race,
Was firmest fixt in mine extremest case.°
And you, my Lord, the Patrone° of my life,   150
Of that great Queene may well gaine worthy
    grace:
For onely worthy you through prowes priefe°
Yf living man mote worthy be, to be her liefe.°

18

So° diversly discoursing of their loves,
    The golden Sunne his glistring head gan shew,   155
And sad remembraunce now the Prince amoves,
With fresh desire his voyage to pursew:
Als° Una earnd° her traveill to renew.
Then those two knights, fast friendship for to
    bynd,
    And love establish each to other trew,   160
Gave goodly gifts, the signes of gratefull mynd,
And eke as pledges firme, right hands together joynd.

19

Prince *Arthur* gave a boxe of Diamond sure,°
    Embowd° with gold and gorgeous ornament,
Wherein were closd° few drops of liquor pure,   165
Of wondrous worth, and vertue° excellent,
That any wound could heale incontinent:°
Which to requite, the *Redcrosse* knight him gave
    A booke, wherein his Saveours testament
Was writ with golden letters rich and brave;°   170
A worke of wondrous grace, and able soules to save.

20

Thus beene they parted, *Arthur* on his way
    To seeke his love, and th'other for to fight
With *Unaes* foe, that all her realme did pray.°

149 **case** plight.   150 **Patrone** protector.   152 **For . . . priefe** For
only you are worthy through proof of valor.   153 **liefe** beloved.
154 **So** as they were.   158 **Als** also.   158 **earnd** yearned.   163 **sure**
sound.   164 **Embowd** surrounded.   165 **closd** enclosed.   166 **vertue** power.   167 **incontinent** straightway.   170 **brave** splendid.
174 **pray** prey upon.

175　　But she now weighing the decayed plight,
　　　　And shrunken synewes of her chosen knight,
　　　　Would not a while her forward course pursew,
　　　　Ne bring him forth in face of dreadfull fight,
　　　　Till he recovered had his former hew:
180　For him to be yet weake and wearie well she knew.

21

So as they traveild, lo they gan espy
　　　　An armed knight towards them gallop fast,
　　　　That seemed from some feared foe to fly,
　　　　Or other griesly° thing, that him agast.°
185　　Still as he fled, his eye was backward cast,
　　　　As if his feare° still followed him behind;
　　　　Als flew his steed, as° he his bands had brast,°
　　　　And with his winged heeles did tread the wind,
As he had beene a fole of *Pegasus* his kind.°

22

190　Nigh as he drew, they might perceive his head
　　　　To be unarmd, and curld uncombed heares
　　　　Upstaring° stiffe, dismayd with uncouth dread;
　　　　Nor drop of bloud in all his face appeares
　　　　Nor life in limbe: and to increase his feares,
195　　In fowle reproch of knighthoods faire degree,
　　　　About his neck an hempen rope he weares,

184 **griesly** horrible.　184 **agast** horrified.　186 **his feare** what he feared.　187 **as** as if.　187 **brast** burst.　189 **a fole . . . kind** a foal bred of Pegasus, the winged horse.　192 **Upstaring** standing up.

That with his glistring armes does ill agree;
But he of rope or armes has now no memoree.

23

The *Redcrosse* knight toward him crossed fast,
 To weet, what mister wight° was so dismayd: 200
There him he finds all sencelesse and aghast,
That of him selfe he seemd to be afrayd;
Whom hardly he from flying forward stayd,
Till he these wordes to him deliver might;
Sir knight, aread° who hath ye thus arayd, 205
And eke from whom make ye this hasty flight:
For never knight I saw in such misseeming° plight.

24

He answerd nought at all, but adding new
 Feare to his first amazment, staring wide
With stony° eyes, and hartlesse hollow hew,° 210
Astonisht stood, as one that had aspide
Infernall furies, with their chaines untide.
Him yet againe, and yet againe bespake
The gentle knight; who nought to him replide,
But trembling every joynt did inly° quake, 215
And foltring tongue at last these words seemd forth
 to shake.

25

For Gods deare love, Sir knight, do me not stay;
 For loe he comes, he comes fast after mee.
Eft° looking backe would faine have runne
 away;
But he him forst to stay, and tellen free 220
The secret cause of his perplexitie:
Yet nathemore° by his bold hartie° speach,
Could his bloud-frosen hart emboldned bee,

---

200 **what mister wight** what kind of creature.   205 **aread** tell.   207
misseeming unseemly.   210 **stony** fixed.   210 **hartlesse hollow hew**
disheartened sunken countenance.   215 **inly** inwardly.   219 **Eft**
again.   222 **nathemore** never the more.   222 **hartie** heartening.

But through his boldnesse rather feare did
        reach,°
Yet forst, at last he made through silence suddein
225   breach.

26

And am I now in safetie sure (quoth he)
        From him, that would have forced me to dye?
        And is the point of death now turnd fro mee,
        That I may tell this haplesse history?
        Feare nought: (quoth he) no daunger now is
230   nye.
        Then shall I you recount a ruefull cace,
        (Said he) the which with this unlucky eye
        I late beheld, and had not greater° grace
Me reft from it, had bene partaker of the place.°

27

235 I lately chaunst (Would I had never chaunst)
        With a faire knight to keepen companee,
        Sir *Terwin* hight, that well himselfe advaunst
        In all affaires, and was both bold and free,
        But not so happie as mote happie bee:
240   He lov'd, as was his lot, a Ladie gent,
        That him againe lov'd in the least degree:°
        For she was proud, and of too high intent,
And joyd to see her lover languish and lament.

28

From whom returning sad and comfortlesse,
245   As on the way together we did fare,°
        We met that villen (God from him me blesse)°
        That cursed wight, from whom I scapt
        whyleare,°
        A man of hell, that cals himselfe *Despaire*:

224 **rather . . . reach** instead gave fear.   233 **greater** i.e., greater
than his companion enjoyed.   234 **had . . . place** i.e., I would have
shared his pitiful plight.   241 **in . . . degree** not at all.   242 **intent**
aim.   245 **fare** go.   246 **God . . . blesse** may God guard me from
him.   247 **scapt whyleare** escaped lately.

Who first us greets, and after faire areedes°
    Of tydings strange, and of adventures rare: *250*
    So creeping close, as Snake in hidden weedes,°
Inquireth of our states, and of our knightly deedes.

29

Which when he knew, and felt our feeble harts
    Embost with bale,° and bitter byting griefe,
    Which love had launched with his deadly darts,   *255*
    With wounding words and termes of foule
        repriefe,°
    He pluckt from us all hope of due reliefe,
    That earst us held in love of lingring life;
    Then hopelesse hartlesse,° gan the cunning
        thiefe
    Perswade us die, to stint all further strife: *260*
To me he lent this rope, to him a rustie knife.

30

With which sad° instrument of hastie death,
    That wofull lover, loathing lenger light,
    A wide way made to let forth living breath.
    But I more fearefull, or more luckie wight,   *265*
    Dismayd with that deformed° dismall sight,
    Fled fast away, halfe dead with dying feare:°
    Ne yet assur'd of life by you, Sir knight,
    Whose like infirmitie like chaunce may beare:
But God you never let° his charmed speeches heare.   *270*

31

How may a man (said he) with idle° speach
    Be wonne, to spoyle° the Castle of his health?
    I wote (quoth he) whom triall late did teach,
    That like would not° for all this worldes wealth:

---

249 **after faire areedes** and afterward tells us gently.   251 **as . . .
weedes** as a snake hidden in weeds.   254 **Embost with bale** exhausted with sorrow.   256 **repriefe** reproach.   259 **hartlesse** disheartened.   262 **sad** lamentable.   266 **deformed** i.e., the sight of
one disfigured.   267 **dying feare** fear of dying.   270 **But . . . let**
may God never let you.   271 **idle** vain.   272 **spoyle** despoil.   274
That . . . not that would not desire the like.

His subtill tongue, like dropping honny, mealt'th°
Into the hart, and searcheth every vaine,
That ere one be aware, by secret stealth
His powre is reft,° and weaknesse doth remaine.
O never Sir desire to try his guilefull traine.°

32

Certes° (said he) hence° shall I never rest,
    Till I that treachours° art have heard and tride;
    And you Sir knight, whose name mote° I request,
    Of grace do me unto his cabin guide.
    I that hight *Trevisan* (quoth he) will ride
    Against my liking backe, to doe you grace:
    But nor for gold nor glee° will I abide
    By you, when ye arrive in that same place;
For lever had I° die, then see his deadly face.

33

Ere long they come, where that same wicked wight
    His dwelling has, low in an hollow cave,
    Farre underneath a craggie clift ypight,°
    Darke, dolefull, drearie, like a greedie grave,
    That still for carrion° carcases doth crave:
    On top whereof aye° dwelt the ghastly Owle,
    Shrieking his balefull° note, which ever drave°
    Farre from that haunt all other chearefull fowle;
And all about it wandring ghostes did waile and howle.

34

And all about old stockes,° and stubs of trees,
    Whereon nor fruit, nor leafe was ever seene,

275 **mealt'th** melteth.   278 **reft** taken away.   279 **traine** wiles.   280 **Certes** assuredly.   280 **hence** henceforth.   281 **treachours** traitor's.   282 **mote** might.   286 **nor for gold nor glee** i.e., neither for love nor money.   288 **lever had I** I would rather.   291 **ypight** placed.   293 **carrion** rotten.   294 **aye** ever.   295 **balefull** deadly.   295 **drave** drove.   298 **stockes** stumps.

Did hang upon the ragged rocky knees;°   300
On which had many wretches hanged beene,
Whose carcases were scattered on the greene,
And throwne about the cliffs. Arrived there,
That bare-head knight for dread and dolefull
    teene,°
Would faine have fled, ne durst approchen
    neare,   305
But th'other forst him stay, and comforted in feare.

35

That darkesome° cave they enter, where they find
    That cursed man, low sitting on the ground,
    Musing full sadly in his sullein mind;
    His griesie° lockes, long growen, and unbound, 310
    Disordred hong about his shoulders round,°
    And hid his face; through which his hollow eyne
    Lookt deadly dull, and stared as astound;°
    His raw-bone cheekes through penurie and pine,
Were shronke into his jawes, as° he did never dine. 315

36

His garment nought but many ragged clouts,°
    With thornes together pind and patched was,
    The which his naked sides he wrapt abouts;
    And him beside there lay upon the gras
    A drearie° corse, whose life away did pas,   320
    All wallowd° in his owne yet luke-warme blood,
    That from his wound yet welled fresh alas;
    In which a rustie° knife fast fixed stood,
And made an open passage for the gushing flood.

37

Which piteous spectacle, approving° trew   325
    The wofull tale that *Trevisan* had told,
    When as the gentle *Redcrosse* knight did vew,

300 **ragged** rugged.   300 **knees** cliffs.   304 **teene** grief.   307 **darke-some** dark.   310 **griesie** grizzled.   311 **round** around.   313 **astound** astonished.   315 **as** as if.   316 **clouts** patches.   320 **drearie** sad. 321 **wallowd** lying prostrate.   323 **rustie** bloody.   325 **approving** proving.

With firie zeale he burnt in courage bold,
    Him to avenge, before his° bloud were cold,
330   And to the villein said, Thou damned wight,
    The author of this fact,° we here behold,
    What justice can but° judge against thee right,
With thine owne bloud to price° his bloud, here shed
    in sight.

38

What franticke fit (quoth he) hath thus distraught
335   Thee, foolish man, so rash a doome° to give?
    What justice ever other judgement taught,
    But he should die, who merites not to live?
    None else to death this man despayring drive,
    But his owne guiltie mind deserving death.
340   Is° then unjust to each his due to give?
    Or let him die, that loatheth living breath?
Or let him die at ease,° that liveth here uneath?°

39

Who travels by the wearie wandring way,
    To come unto his wished home in haste,
345   And meetes a flood,° that doth his passage stay,
    Is° not great grace to helpe him over past,
    Or free his feet, that in the myre sticke fast?
    Most envious man, that grieves at neighbours
        good,
    And fond,° that joyest in the woe thou hast,
350   Why wilt not let him passe, that long hath stood
Upon the banke, yet wilt thy selfe not passe the
    flood?

40

He there does now enjoy eternall rest
    And happie ease, which thou doest want and
        crave,

329 **his** i.e., Terwin's. 331 **fact** evil deed. 332 **What . . . but**
What justice is there that could do anything except. 333 **price** pay
for. 335 **doome** judgment. 340 **Is** is it. 342 **at ease** and be at
ease. 342 **uneath** only with difficulty. 345 **flood** body of water.
346 **Is** is it. 346 **over past** pass over. 349 **fond** foolish.

And further from it daily wanderest:
What if some litle paine the passage have,   355
That makes fraile flesh to feare the bitter wave?
Is not short paine well borne, that brings long
    ease,
And layes the soule to sleepe in quiet grave?
Sleepe after toyle, port after stormie seas,
Ease after warre, death after life does greatly please.   360

41

The knight much wondred at his suddeine° wit,
    And said, The terme of life is limited,
    Ne may a man prolong, nor shorten it;
    The souldier may not move from watchfull
      sted,°
    Nor leave his stand, untill his Captaine bed.°   365
    Who° life did limit by almightie doome,
    (Quoth he°) knowes best the termes established;
    And he, that points the Centonell his roome,°
Doth license him depart° at sound of morning
    droome.°

42

Is not his deed, what ever thing is donne,   370
    In heaven and earth? did not he all create
    To die againe? all ends that was begonne.
    Their times in his eternall booke of fate
    Are written sure, and have their certaine date.°
    Who then can strive with strong necessitie,   375
    That holds the world in his still chaunging state,
    Or shunne the death ordaynd by destinie?
When houre of death is come, let none aske whence,
    nor why.

43

The lenger life, I wote the greater sin,

361 **suddeine** quick. 364 **watchful sted** position of watch. 365
bed bids. 366 **Who** he who. 367 **he** Despair. 368 **points . . .
roome** appoints the sentinel to his station. 369 **depart** to depart.
369 **droome** drum. 374 **certaine date** fixed term.

380 The greater sin, the greater punishment:
    All those great battels, which thou boasts to win,
    Through strife, and bloud-shed, and avenge-
        ment,
    Now praysd, hereafter deare thou shalt repent:
    For life must life, and bloud must bloud repay.
385 Is not enough thy evill life forespent?°
    For he, that once hath missed the right way,
The further he doth goe, the further he doth stray.

44

Then do no further goe, no further stray,
    But here lie downe, and to thy rest betake,°
390 Th'ill to prevent, that life ensewen may.°
    For what hath life, that may it loved make,
    And gives not rather cause it to forsake?
    Feare, sicknesse, age, losse, labour, sorrow,
        strife,
    Paine, hunger, cold, that makes the hart to
        quake;
395 And ever fickle fortune rageth rife,°
All which, and thousands mo° do make a loathsome
        life.

45

Thou wretched man, of death hast greatest need,
    If in true ballance thou wilt weigh thy state:
    For never° knight, that dared warlike deede,
400 More lucklesse disaventures did amate:°
    Witnesse the dongeon deepe, wherein of late
    Thy life shut up, for death so oft did call;
    And though good lucke prolonged hath thy date,
    Yet death then,° would the like mishaps
        forestall,°
405 Into the which hereafter thou maiest happen fall.

385 **Is . . . forespent** Is it not enough for repentance that already
you have spent an evil life? 389 **betake** commit yourself. 390 **that
. . . may** that may follow after in life. 395 **rife** uncontrolled. 396
mo more. 399 **never** never was there. 400 **More . . . amate** More
unlucky mishaps did cast down. 404 **then** i.e., when you called
"of late." 404 **forestall** have forestalled.

46

Why then doest thou, O man of sin, desire
    To draw thy dayes forth to their last degree?°
    Is not the measure of thy sinfull hire°
    High heaped up with huge iniquitie,
    Against the day of wrath, to burden thee?   *410*
    Is not enough, that to this Ladie milde
    Thou falsed° hast thy faith with perjurie,
    And sold thy selfe to serve *Duessa* vilde,°
With whom in all abuse thou hast thy selfe defilde?

47

Is not he just, that all this doth behold   *415*
    From highest heaven, and beares an equall°
       eye?
    Shall he thy sins up in his knowledge fold,°
    And guiltie be of thine impietie?
    Is not his law, let every sinner die:
    Die shall all flesh? what then must needs be
      donne,   *420*
    Is it not better to doe willinglie,
    Then linger, till the glasse° be all out ronne?
Death is the end of woes: die soone, O faeries sonne.

48

The knight was much enmoved° with his speach,
    That as a swords point through his hart did
      perse,°   *425*
    And in his conscience made a secret breach,
    Well knowing true all, that he did reherse,
    And to his fresh remembrance did reverse°
    The ugly vew of his deformed crimes,
    That all his manly powres it did disperse,   *430*
    As° he were charmed with inchaunted rimes,°
That oftentimes he quakt, and fainted oftentimes.

407 **to . . . degree** to their utmost measure.   408 **sinfull hire** service
to sin.   412 **falsed** betrayed.   413 **vilde** vile.   416 **equall** just.
417 **fold** shut.   422 **glasse** i.e., the hourglass.   424 **enmoved** moved.
425 **perse** pierce.   428 **reverse** bring back.   431 **As** as if.   431
inchaunted rimes magic verses.

49

In which amazement,° when the Miscreant
    Perceived him to waver weake and fraile,
435   Whiles trembling horror did his conscience dant,°
    And hellish anguish did his soule assaile,
    To drive him to despaire, and quite to quaile,°
    He shew'd him painted in a table° plaine,
    The damned ghosts, that doe in torments waile,
    And thousand feends that doe them endlesse
440   paine
With fire and brimstone, which for ever shall remaine.

50

The sight whereof so throughly° him dismaid,
    That nought but death before his eyes he saw,
    And ever burning wrath before him laid,
445   By righteous sentence of th'Almighties law:
    Then gan the villein him to overcraw,°
    And brought unto him swords, ropes, poison,
      fire,
    And all that might him to perdition draw;
    And bad him choose, what death he would
      desire:
450 For death was due to him, that had provokt Gods ire.

51

But when as none of them he saw him take,
    He to him raught° a dagger sharpe and keene,
    And gave it him in hand: his hand did quake,
    And tremble like a leafe of Aspin greene,
    And troubled bloud through his pale face was
455   seene
    To come, and goe with tydings from the hart,
    As it a running messenger had beene.
    At last resolv'd to worke his finall smart,
He lifted up his hand, that backe againe did start.

---

433 **amazement** bewilderment.　435 **dant** daunt.　437 **quaile** lose
heart.　**438 table** picture.　442 **throughly** thoroughly.　446 **over-
craw** crow or triumph over.　452 **raught** held out.

52

Which when as *Una* saw, through every vaine   460
  The crudled° cold ran to her well of life,°
  As in a swowne: but soone reliv'd° againe,
  Out of his hand she snatcht the cursed knife,
  And threw it to the ground, enraged rife,°
  And to him said, Fie, fie, faint harted knight,   465
  What meanest thou by this reprochfull strife?°
  Is this the battell, which thou vauntst° to fight
With that fire-mouthed Dragon, horrible and bright?

53

Come, come away, fraile, feeble, fleshly wight,
  Ne let vaine words bewitch thy manly hart,   470
  Ne divelish thoughts dismay thy constant spright.
  In heavenly mercies hast thou not a part?
  Why shouldst thou then despeire, that chosen°
   art?
  Where justice growes, there grows eke greater
   grace,
  The which doth quench the brond of hellish
   smart,   475
  And that accurst hand-writing doth deface.°
Arise, Sir knight arise, and leave this cursed place.

54

So up he rose, and thence amounted streight.°
  Which when the carle° beheld, and saw his
   guest
  Would safe depart, for° all his subtill sleight,   480
  He chose an halter from among the rest,
  And with it hung himselfe, unbid unblest.°
  But death he could not worke himselfe thereby;

461 **crudled** congealing. 461 **well of life** heart. 462 **reliv'd** brought
to life. 464 **rife** greatly. 466 **reprochfull strife** strife in which you
reproach yourself. 467 **vauntst** boasts. 473 **chosen** i.e., one of
the Elect, being chosen by God for eternal life. 476 **that . . .
deface** "having blotted out the bond written in ordinances that
was against us" (Col. ii. 14). 478 **amounted streight** mounted his
horse straightway. 479 **carle** churl. 480 **for** in spite of. 482
unbid unblest not bidden to do so, as he bids the Knight; and not
blest, as the Knight is guarded by Una.

For thousand times he so himselfe had drest,°
485   Yet nathelesse° it could not doe him die,
Till he should die his last, that is eternally.

CANTO X

Her faithfull knight faire Una brings
    to house of Holinesse,
Where he is taught repentance, and
    *the way to heavenly blesse.**

1

What man is he, that° boasts of fleshly might,
    And vaine assurance of mortality,
    Which all so soone, as it doth come to fight,
    Against spirituall foes, yeelds by and by,°
5   Or from the field most cowardly doth fly?
    Ne let the man ascribe it to his skill,
    That thorough grace hath gained victory.
    If any strength we have, it is to ill,
But all the good is Gods, both power and eke will.

2

10 By that, which lately hapned, *Una* saw,
    That this her knight was feeble, and too faint;°
    And all his sinews woxen° weake and raw,°
    Through long enprisonment, and hard con-
        straint,°
    Which he endured in his late restraint,
15   That yet he was unfit for bloudie fight:
    Therefore to cherish him with diets daint,°

484 **drest** addressed, made ready. 485 **nathelesse** nevertheless.
Arg. **blesse** bliss. 1 **What . . . that** how foolish is that man who.
4 **by and by** immediately. 11 **faint** faint-hearted. 12 **woxen** grown.
12 **raw** painful, being raw-boned (viii. 41). 13 **Through . . . constraint** Through hard affliction of long confinement. 16 **daint**
dainty.

She cast° to bring him, where he chearen might,°
Till he recovered had° his late decayed plight.

3

There was an auntient house not farre away,
 Renowmd° throughout the world for sacred
  lore,°   20
 And pure unspotted life: so well they say
 It governd was, and guided evermore,
 Through wisedome of a matrone grave and
  hore;°
 Whose onely° joy was to relieve the needes
 Of wretched soules, and helpe the helpelesse
  pore: 25
 All night she spent in bidding of her bedes,°
And all the day in doing good and godly deedes.

4

Dame *Cælia*° men did her call, as thought
 From heaven to come, or thither to arise,
 The mother of three daughters, well upbrought 30
 In goodly thewes,° and godly exercise:
 The eldest two most sober, chast, and wise,
 Fidelia° and *Speranza*° virgins were,
 Though spousd, yet wanting wedlocks
  solemnize;°
 But faire *Charissa*° to a lovely fere° 35
Was lincked, and by him had many pledges° dere.

5

Arrived there, the dore they find fast lockt;
 For it was warely° watched night and day,
 For feare of many foes: but when they knockt,
 The Porter opened unto them streight way: 40

17 **cast** resolved. 17 **chearen might** might be cheered. 18 **recovered had** had recovered from. 20 **Renowmd** renowned. 20 **lore**
learning. 23 **hore** venerable. 24 **onely** chief. 26 **bidding of her
bedes** offering prayers. 28 **Cælia** Heavenly. 31 **thewes** discipline.
33 **Fidelia** Faith. 33 **Speranza** Hope. 34 **Though . . . solemnize**
Though betrothed, yet lacking the ceremonies of marriage. 35
Charissa Charity. 35 **lovely fere** loving mate. 36 **pledges** children
as tokens of their love. 38 **warely** warily.

He was an aged syre, all hory gray,
  With lookes full lowly cast, and gate full slow,
  Wont° on a staffe his feeble steps to stay,°
  Hight *Humiltá*.° They passe in stouping low;
For streight and narrow was the way, which he did
45   show.

6

Each goodly thing is hardest to begin,
  But entred in a spacious court they see,
  Both plaine, and pleasant to be walked in,
  Where them does meete a francklin° faire and
    free,°
50   And entertaines with comely courteous glee,
  His name was *Zele,* that him right well became,
  For in his speeches and behaviour hee
  Did labour lively to expresse the same,
And gladly did them guide, till to the Hall they came.

7

55 There fairely° them receives a gentle Squire,
  Of milde demeanure, and rare courtesie,
  Right cleanly clad in comely sad° attire;
  In word and deede that shew'd great modestie,
  And knew his good to all of each degree,°
60   Hight *Reverence.* He them with speeches meet°
  Does faire entreat; no courting nicetie,°
  But simple true, and eke unfained sweet,
As might become a Squire so great persons to greet.

8

And afterwards them to his Dame he leades,
65   That aged Dame, the Ladie of the place:
  Who all this while was busie at her beades:

---

43 **Wont** accustomed.   43 **stay** support.   44 **Hight Humiltá** called
Humility.   49 **francklin** a freeman, below the level of the gentry.
49 **free** open.   55 **fairely** becomingly.   57 **sad** sober.   59 **And . . .
degree** And knew how to behave with proper reverence or respect
toward all orders of society.   60 **meet** fitting.   61 **courting nicetie**
courtly affectation.

Which doen,° she up arose with seemely grace,
And toward them full matronely did pace.
Where when that fairest *Una* she beheld,
Whom well she knew to spring from heavenly
    race,   70
Her hart with joy unwonted° inly sweld,
As feeling wondrous comfort in her weaker eld.°

9

And her embracing said, O happie earth,
Whereon thy innocent feet doe ever tread,
Most vertuous virgin borne of heavenly berth,   75
That to redeeme thy woefull parents head,°
From tyrans rage, and ever-dying dread,°
Hast wandred through the world now long a
    day;°
Yet ceasest not thy wearie soles° to lead,
What grace hath thee now hither brought this
    way?   80
Or doen thy feeble feet unweeting° hither stray?

10

Strange thing it is an errant° knight to see
Here in this place, or any other wight,
That hither turnes his steps. So few there bee,
That chose the narrow path, or seeke the right: 85
All keepe the broad high way, and take delight
With many rather for to go astray,
And be partakers of their evill plight,
Then with a few to walke the rightest way;°
O foolish men, why haste ye to your owne decay?   90

11

Thy selfe to see, and tyred limbs to rest,
O matrone sage (quoth she) I hither came,

67 **Which doen** when her prayers were done.   71 **unwonted** unaccustomed.   72 **weaker eld** too weak age.   76 **parents head** parents.
77 **ever-dying dread** continual fear of death.   78 **long a day** many
a day.   79 **soles** with a pun on "souls" as Una is the Church Mili-
tant.   81 **unweeting** unwittingly.   82 **errant** wandering.   89 **the
rightest way** the only right way.

And this good knight his way with me addrest,°
Led with thy prayses and broad-blazed fame,
That up to heaven is blowne. The auncient
95   Dame
Him goodly greeted in her modest guise,
And entertaynd them both, as best became,°
With all the court'sies, that she could devise,
Ne wanted ought, to shew her bounteous or wise.

12

100 Thus as they gan of sundry things devise,°
Loe two most goodly virgins came in place,°
Ylinked arme in arme in lovely wise,°
With countenance demure, and modest grace,
They numbred even steps and equall pace:
105   Of which the eldest, that *Fidelia* hight,
Like° sunny beames threw from her Christall°
face,
That could have dazd the rash beholders sight,
And round about her head did shine like heavens
light.

13

She was araied all in lilly white,
110   And in her right hand bore a cup of gold,
With wine and water fild up to the hight,
In which a Serpent did himselfe enfold,
That horrour made to all, that did behold;
But she no whit did chaunge her constant
mood:
115   And in her other hand she fast did hold
A booke,° that was both signd and seald with
blood,
Wherein darke things were writ, hard to be under-
stood.

94 **addrest** directed,   97 **as best became** as was most suitable.   100
devise converse.   100 **in place** there   102 **wise** manner.   106 **Like**
what seemed like.   106 **Christall** clear, shining.   116 **A booke** the
Bible.

14

Her younger sister, that *Speranza* hight,
    Was clad in blew, that her beseemed well;
    Not all so chearefull seemed she of sight,°   120
    As was her sister; whether dread did dwell,
    Or anguish in her hart, is hard to tell:
    Upon her arme a silver anchor lay,
    Whereon she leaned ever, as befell:°
    And ever up to heaven, as she did pray,   125
Her stedfast eyes were bent, ne swarved other way.

15

They seeing *Una,* towards her gan wend,
    Who them encounters° with like courtesie;
    Many kind speeches they betwene them spend,
    And greatly joy each other well to see: 130
    Then to the knight with shamefast modestie
    They turne themselves, at *Unaes* meeke request,
    And him salute with well beseeming glee;
    Who faire them quites,° as him beseemed best,
And goodly gan discourse of many a noble gest.°   135

16

Then *Una* thus; But she your sister deare,
    The deare *Charissa* where is she become?°
    Or wants she health, or busie is elsewhere?
    Ah no, said they, but forth she may not come:
    For she of late is lightned of her wombe,   140
    And hath encreast the world with one sonne
        more,
    That her to see should be but troublesome.
    Indeede (quoth she) that should her trouble
        sore,
But thankt be God, and her encrease° so evermore.

<hr />

120 **of sight** in appearance.   124 **as befell** as was fitting.   128 **encounters** goes to meet.   134 **quites** requites, i.e., returns their greeting.   135 **noble gest** notable deed.   137 **where ... become** where is
she gone.   144 **her encrease** may God increase her.

17

145 Then said the aged *Cælia,* Deare dame,
        And you good Sir, I wote that of your toyle,
        And labours long, through which ye hither came,
        Ye both forwearied° be: therefore a whyle
        I read° you rest, and to your bowres recoyle.°
150   Then called she a Groome,° that forth him led
        Into a goodly lodge, and gan despoile°
        Of puissant armes, and laid in easie bed;
His name was meeke *Obedience* rightfully ared.°

18

Now when their wearie limbes with kindly° rest,
155   And bodies were refresht with due repast,
        Faire *Una* gan *Fidelia* faire request,
        To have her knight into her schoolehouse plaste,
        That of her heavenly learning he might taste,
        And heare the wisedome of her words divine.
160   She graunted, and that knight so much agraste,°
        That she him taught celestiall discipline,
    And opened his dull eyes, that light mote in them
        shine.

19

And that her sacred Booke, with bloud° ywrit,
        That none could read, except she did them teach,
165   She unto him disclosed every whit,
        And heavenly documents° thereout did preach,
        That weaker° wit of man could never reach,
        Of God, of grace, of justice, of free will,
        That wonder was to heare her goodly speach:
170   For she was able, with her words to kill,
    And raise againe to life the hart, that she did thrill.°

148 **forwearied** utterly wearied.   149 **read** advise.   149 **recoyle** retire.   150 **Groome** servant.   151 **despoile** undress.   153 **ared** inter-
preted.   154 **kindly** natural.   160 **so much agraste** showed so much
favor to.   163 **bloud** i.e., the blood of Christ.   166 **documents**
teaching.   167 **weaker** too weak.   171 **thrill** pierce.

20

And when she list° poure out her larger spright,°
    She would commaund the hastie Sunne to stay,
    Or backward turne his course from heavens
      hight;
    Sometimes great hostes of men she could dis-
      may,   175
    Dry-shod to passe,° she parts the flouds in tway;
    And eke huge mountaines from their native seat
    She would commaund, themselves to beare
      away,
    And throw° in raging sea with roaring threat.
Almightie God her gave such powre, and puissance
    great.   180

21

The faithfull° knight now grew in litle space,
    By hearing her, and by her sisters lore,
    To such perfection of all heavenly grace,
    That wretched world he gan for to abhore,
    And mortall life gan loath, as thing forlore,°   185
    Greev'd with remembrance of his wicked wayes,
    And prickt with anguish of his sinnes so sore,
    That he desirde to end his wretched dayes:
So much the dart of sinfull guilt the soule dismayes.

22

But wise *Speranza* gave him comfort sweet,   190
    And taught him how to take assured° hold
    Upon her silver anchor, as was meet;°
    Else had his sinnes so great, and manifold
    Made him forget all that *Fidelia* told.
    In this distressed doubtfull agonie,   195
    When him his dearest *Una* did behold,

---

172 **list** wished to.   172 **larger spright** higher power.   176 **to passe**
that men may pass. This line confusing in its syntax, was added in
the 1609 edition.   179 **throw** themselves to throw.   181 **faithfull**
full of faith.   185 **forlore** that he had abandoned.   191 **assured**
secure.   192 **meet** fitting.

Disdeining life, desiring leave to die,
She found her selfe assayld with great perplexitie.

23

And came to *Cælia* to declare her smart,
200   Who well acquainted with that commune° plight,
Which sinfull horror° workes in wounded hart,
Her wisely comforted all that she might,
With goodly counsell and advisement right;°
And streightway sent with carefull diligence,
205   To fetch a Leach,° the which had great insight
In that disease of grieved conscience,
And well could cure the same; His name was *Patience*.

24

Who comming to that soule-diseased knight,
Could hardly him intreat,° to tell his griefe:
Which knowne, and all that noyd° his heavie
210   spright
Well searcht, eftsoones° he gan apply reliefe
Of salves and med'cines, which had passing
priefe,°
And thereto added words of wondrous might:
By which to ease he him recured briefe,
215   And much asswag'd the passion of his plight,°
That he his paine endur'd, as seeming now more
light.

25

But yet the cause and root of all his ill,
Inward corruption, and infected sin,
Not purg'd nor heald, behind remained still,
220   And festring sore did rankle yet within,
Close creeping twixt the marrow and the skin.

---

200 **commune** common.   201 **sinfull horror** horror of sin.   203 **advisement** right proper advice.   205 **Leach** surgeon.   209 **Could . . . intreat** could hardly persuade him.   **210 noyd** troubled.   211 **eftsoones** immediately.   212 **passing priefe** surpassing goodness.   215 **the passion of his plight** his state of suffering.

Which to extirpe,° he laid him privily
Downe in a darkesome lowly place farre in,
Whereas° he meant his corrosives to apply,
And with streight° diet tame his stubborne malady.   225

26

In ashes and sackcloth he did array
    His daintie corse,° proud humors° to abate,
    And dieted with fasting every day,
    The swelling of his wounds to mitigate,
    And made him pray both earely and eke late: 230
    And ever as superfluous flesh did rot
    Amendment readie still at hand did wayt,
    To pluck it out with pincers firie whot,
That soone in him was left no one° corrupted jot.

27

And bitter *Penance* with an yron whip,   235
    Was wont him once to disple every day:°
    And sharpe *Remorse* his hart did pricke and nip,
    That drops of bloud thence like a well did play;°
    And sad *Repentance* used to embay°
    His bodie in salt water smarting sore,   240
    The filthy blots of sinne to wash away.
So in short space they did to health restore
The man that would not° live, but earst lay at deathes
    dore.

28

In which his torment often was so great,
    That like a Lyon he would cry and rore,   245
    And rend his flesh, and his owne synewes eat.
    His owne deare *Una* hearing evermore
    His ruefull shriekes and gronings, often tore
    Her guiltlesse garments, and her golden heare,
    For pitty of his paine and anguish sore;   250

222 **extirpe** extirpate, root out. 224 **Whereas** where. 225 **streight** strict (1609 edition). 227 **daintie corse** handsome body. 227 **humors** temperament. 234 **no one** not one. 236 **Was . . . day** Used to discipline him once every day. 238 **play** flow. 239 **embay** bathe. 243 **would not** did not wish to.

Yet all with patience wisely she did beare;
For well she wist, his crime could else be never
    cleare.°

29

Whom thus recover'd by wise Patience,
    And trew *Repentance* they to *Una* brought:
255 Who joyous of his cured conscience,
    Him dearely kist, and fairely eke besought
    Himselfe to chearish, and consuming thought
    To put away out of his carefull brest.
    By this *Charissa,* late in child-bed brought,
260 Was woxen strong, and left her fruitfull nest;
To her faire *Una* brought this unacquainted° guest.

30

She was a woman in her freshest age,
    Of wondrous beauty, and of bountie° rare,
    With goodly grace and comely personage,°
265 That was on earth not easie to compare;°
    Full of great love, but *Cupids* wanton snare
    As hell she hated, chast in worke and will;
    Her necke and breasts were ever open bare,
    That ay thereof her babes might sucke their fill;
270 The rest was all in yellow robes arayed still.

31

A multitude of babes about her hong,
    Playing their sports, that joyd her° to behold,
    Whom still she fed, whiles they were weake and
        young,
    But thrust them forth still, as they wexed old:
275 And on her head she wore a tyre° of gold,
    Adornd with gemmes and owches° wondrous
        faire,
    Whose passing price uneath was to be told;°

252 **cleare** acquitted from the charge of the crime. **261 un-acquainted** unfamiliar.   263 **bountie** goodness.   264 **personage** body.   265 **compare** rival.   272 **joyd her** it joyed her.   275 **tyre** head dress.   276 **owches** jewels.   277 **Whose . . . told** whose surpassing price it was difficult to reckon.

And by her side there sate a gentle paire
Of turtle doves, she sitting in an yvorie chaire.

32

The knight and *Una* entring, faire her greet,   *280*
    And bid her joy of that her happie brood;
    Who them requites with court'sies seeming
       meet,°
    And entertaines° with friendly chearefull mood.
    Then *Una* her besought, to be so good,
    As in her vertuous rules to schoole her knight,   *285*
    Now after all his torment well withstood,
    In that sad house of *Penaunce,* where his spright
Had past° the paines of hell, and long enduring night.

33

She was right joyous of her just request,
    And taking by the hand that Faeries sonne,   *290*
    Gan him instruct in every good behest,
    Of love, and righteousnesse, and well to donne,°
    And wrath, and hatred warely to shonne,
    That drew on men Gods hatred, and his wrath,
    And many soules in dolours° had fordonne:°   *295*
    In which when him she well instructed hath,
From thence to heaven she teacheth him the ready
       path.

34

Wherein his weaker° wandring steps to guide,
    An auncient matrone she to her does call,
    Whose sober lookes her wisedome well de-
       scride:°   *300*
    Her name was *Mercie,* well knowne over all,
    To be both gratious, and eke liberall:
    To whom the carefull charge of him she gave,
    To lead aright, that he should never fall

282 **Who . . . meet** She returns their greeting with proper courtesies.
283 **entertaines** receives.   288 **past** endured.   292 **well to donne**
well-doing.   295 **dolours** sorrows.   295 **fordonne** overcome.   298
weaker too weak.   300 **descride** revealed.

305   In all his wayes through this wide worldes wave,
That Mercy in the end his righteous soule might save.

35

The godly Matrone by the hand him beares
    Forth from her presence, by a narrow way,
    Scattred with bushy thornes, and ragged
        breares,°
310 Which still before him she remov'd away,
    That nothing might his ready passage stay:
    And ever when his feet encombred° were,
    Or gan to shrinke,° or from the right to stray,
    She held him fast, and firmely did upbeare,
As carefull Nourse her child from falling oft does
315   reare.

36

Eftsoones unto an holy Hospitall,
    That was fore by° the way, she did him bring,
    In which seven Bead-men° that had vowed all
    Their life to service of high heavens king
320 Did spend their dayes in doing godly thing:
    Their gates to all were open evermore,
    That by the wearie way were traveiling,
    And one sate wayting° ever them before,
To call in commers-by,° that needy were and pore.

37

325 The first of them that eldest was, and best,°
    Of all the house had charge and governement,°
    As Guardian and Steward of the rest:
    His office° was to give entertainement°
    And lodging, unto all that came, and went:
330 Not unto such, as could him feast againe,°
    And double quite,° for that he on them spent,

309 **breares** briers.   312 **encombred** hampered.   313 **shrinke** withdraw.   317 **fore by** hard by.   318 **Bead-men** men of prayer.   323 **wayting** watching.   324 **commers-by** passers-by.   325 **best** chiefest.
326 **government** management.   328 **office** duty.   328 **entertainement** hospitality.   330 **againe** in return.   331 **double quite** requite him doubly.

But such, as want of harbour did constraine:°
Those for Gods sake his dewty was to entertaine.

38

The second was as Almner° of the place,
    His office was, the hungry for to feed,   *335*
    And thristy give to drinke, a worke of grace:
    He feard not once him selfe to be in need,
    Ne car'd to hoord for those, whom he did
        breede:°
    The grace of God he layd up still in store,
    Which as a stocke° he left unto his seede;   *340*
    He had enough, what need him care for more?
And had he lesse, yet some he would give to the pore.

39

The third had of their wardrobe custodie,
    In which were not rich tyres, nor garments gay,
    The plumes of pride, and wings of vanitie,   *345*
    But clothes meet to keepe keene could away,
    And naked nature seemely to aray;
    With which bare wretched wights he dayly clad,
    The images of God in earthly clay;
    And if that no spare cloths to give he had,   *350*
His owne coate he would cut, and it distribute glad.

40

The fourth appointed by his office was,
    Poore prisoners to relieve with gratious ayd,
    And captives to redeeme with price of bras,°
    From Turkes and Sarazins,° which them had
        stayd;°   *355*
    And though they faultie were, yet well he wayd,°
    That God to us forgiveth every howre
    Much more then that, why they in bands were
        layd,°

332 **as . . . constraine** as were afflicted by lack of shelter. 334
Almner distributor of charity.   338 **breede** take charge of.   340
stocke fund.   354 **bras** money.   335 **Sarazins** Saracens.   335 **stayd**
caused to stay.   356 **wayd** weighed.   358 **why . . . layd** when mankind lay in bondage.

And he that harrowd hell° with heavie stowre,°
The faultie soules from thence brought to his heavenly
360   bowre.

41

The fift had charge sicke persons to attend,
        And comfort those, in point of death which lay;
        For them most needeth comfort in the end,
        When sin, and hell, and death do most dismay
365   The feeble soule departing hence away.
        All is but lost, that living we bestow,°
        If not well ended at our dying day.
        O man have mind of that last bitter throw;°
For as the tree does fall, so lyes it ever low.

42

370   The sixt had charge of them now being dead,
        In seemely sort their corses to engrave,°
        And deck with dainty flowres their bridall bed,
        That to their heavenly spouse both sweet and
            brave°
        They might appeare, when° he their soules shall
            save.
        The wondrous workemanship of Gods owne
375   mould,°
        Whose face he made, all beasts to feare, and gave
        All in his hand, even dead we honour should.
Ah dearest God me graunt, I dead be not defould.°

43

The seventh now after death and buriall done,
380   Had charge the tender Orphans of the dead
        And widowes ayd,° least they should be undone:
        In face of° judgement he their right would
            plead,

---

359 **he . . . hell** Christ who descended into hell to rob it of its cap-
tives.   359 **heavie stowre** laborious conflict.   366 **bestow** stow away.
368 **throw** throe.   371 **engrave** place in the grave.   373 **brave** handsome.   374 **when** i.e., at the Resurrection.   375 **mould** image.
378 **defould** despoiled.   381 **ayd** to aid.   382 **In face of** before.

Ne ought the powre of mighty men did dread
In their defence, nor would for gold or fee
Be wonne° their rightfull causes downe to tread: 385
And when they stood in most necessitee,
He did supply their want, and gave them ever free.°

44

There when the Elfin knight arrived was,
    The first and chiefest of the seven, whose care
    Was guests to welcome, towardes him did pas:°   390
    Where seeing *Mercie,* that his steps up bare,°
    And alwayes led, to her with reverence rare
    He humbly louted° in meeke lowlinesse,
    And seemely welcome for her did prepare:
    For of their order she was Patronesse,   395
Albe° *Charissa* were their chiefest founderesse.

45

There she awhile him stayes, him selfe to rest,
    That to the rest more able he might bee:
    During which time, in every good behest
    And godly worke of Almes and charitee   400
    She him instructed with great industree;
    Shortly therein so perfect he became,
    That from the first unto the last degree,
    His mortall life he learned had to frame
In holy righteousnesse, without rebuke or blame.   405

46

Thence forward by that painfull way they pas,
    Forth to an hill, that was both steepe and hy;
    On top whereof a sacred chappell was,
    And eke a litle Hermitage thereby,
    Wherein an aged holy man did lye,   410
    That day and night said his devotion,
    Ne other worldly business did apply;°

385 **wonne** prevailed upon.   387 **free** freely.   390 **pas** go.   391 **up bare** bore up.   393 **louted** bowed.   396 **Albe** although.   412 **Ne . . . apply** No worldly concern did he devote himself to.

His name was heavenly *Contemplation;*
Of God and goodnesse was his meditation.

47

415 Great grace that old man to him given had;
    For God he often saw from heavens hight,
    All° were his earthly eyen both blunt° and bad,
    And through great age had lost their kindly°
        sight,
    Yet wondrous quick and persant° was his spright,
420   As Eagles eye, that can behold the Sunne:
    That hill they scale with all their powre and
        might,
    That his frayle thighes nigh wearie and for-
        donne°
Gan faile, but by her helpe the top at last he wonne.

48

There they do finde that godly aged Sire,
425   With snowy lockes adowne his shoulders shed,
    As hoarie frost with spangles° doth attire
    The mossy branches of an Oke halfe ded.
    Each bone might through his body well be red,°
    And every sinew seene through° his long fast:
430   For nought he car'd his carcas long unfed;°
    His mind was full of spirituall repast,
And pyn'd° his flesh, to keepe his body low° and
    chast.

49

Who when these two approching he aspide,
    At their first presence° grew agrieved sore,
435   That forst him lay his heavenly thoughts aside;
    And had he not that Dame respected more,
    Whom highly he did reverence and adore,

417 **All** although.   417 **blunt** dull.   418 **kindly** natural.   419 **per-
sant** piercing.   422 **fordonne** exhausted.   426 **spangles** glittering
points of light.   428 **red** seen.   429 **through** because of.   430 **For
. . . unfed** For he did not take care of his body even though he had
not fed for a long time.   432 **And pyn'd** and he starved.   432 **low**
weak.   434 **At . . . presence** at their presence first.

He would not once have moved for the knight.
　　They him saluted standing far afore;°
　　Who well them greeting, humbly did requight,°   440
And asked, to what end they clomb that tedious
　　　height.

50

What end (quoth she) should cause us take such
　　　paine,
　　But that same end, which every living wight
　　Should make his marke, high heaven to attaine?
　　Is not from hence the way, that leadeth right   445
　　To that most glorious house, that glistreth bright
　　With burning starres, and everliving fire,
　　Whereof the keyes are to thy hand behight°
　　By wise *Fidelia?* she doth thee require,
To shew it to this knight, according° his desire.   450

51

Thrise happy man,° said then the father grave,
　　Whose staggering steps thy steady hand doth
　　　lead,
　　And shewes the way, his sinfull soule to save.
　　Who better can the way to heaven aread,°
　　Then thou thy selfe, that was both borne and
　　　bred   455
　　In heavenly throne, where thousand Angels
　　　shine?
　　Thou doest the prayers of the righteous sead°
　　Present before the majestie divine,
And his avenging wrath to clemencie incline.

52

Yet since thou bidst, thy pleasure shalbe donne.   460
　　Then come thou man of earth,° and see the way,
　　That never yet was seene of Faeries sonne,

439 **afore** before.   440 **did requight** returned the salutation.   448
behight delivered.   450 **according** consenting to.   451 **happy man**
happy is the man.   454 **aread** teach.   457 **sead** progeny.   461 **thou
man of earth** See stanza 66.

That never leads the traveiler astray,
But after labours long, and sad delay,
Brings them to joyous rest and endlesse blis.
But first thou must a season° fast and pray,
Till from her bands the spright assoiled° is,
And have her strength recur'd° from fraile infirmitis.

53

That done, he leads him to the highest Mount;°
Such one, as that same mighty man of God,°
That bloud-red billowes° like a walled front
On either side disparted with his rod,
Till that his army dry-foot through them yod,°
Dwelt fortie dayes upon; where writ in stone
With bloudy letters by the hand of God,
The bitter doome of death and balefull mone°
He did receive, whiles flashing fire about him shone.

54

Or like that sacred hill,° whose head full hie,
Adornd with fruitfull Olives all arownd,
Is, as it were for endlesse memory
Of that deare Lord, who oft thereon was fownd,
For ever with a flowring girlond crownd:
Or like that pleasaunt Mount,° that is for ay
Through famous Poets verse each where° renownd,
On which the thrise three learned Ladies° play
Their heavenly notes, and make full many a lovely lay.

55

From thence, far off he unto him did shew
A litle path, that was both steepe and long,

---

466 **a season** for some time.   467 **assoiled** set free.   468 **recur'd** recovered.   469 **highest Mount** crest of the mountain.   470 **that . . . God** Moses.   471 **bloud-red billowes** the waters of the Red Sea. 473 **yod** went.   476 **balefull mone** sorrowful grief.   478 **that sacred hill** the Mount of Olives.   483 **that pleasaunt Mount** Parnassus. 484 **each where** everywhere.   485 **the . . . Ladies** the nine Muses.

Which to a goodly Citie° led his vew;
Whose wals and towres were builded high and
    strong   490
Of perle and precious stone, that earthly tong
Cannot describe, nor wit of man can tell;
Too high a ditty° for my simple song;
The Citie of the great king hight it well,°
Wherein eternall peace and happinesse doth dwell.   495

56

As he thereon stood gazing, he might see
    The blessed Angels to and fro descend
    From highest heaven, in gladsome° companee,
    And with great joy into that Citie wend,
    As commonly° as friend does with his frend.   500
    Whereat he wondred much, and gan enquere,
    What stately building durst° so high extend
    Her loftie towres unto the starry sphere,
And what unknowen nation there empeopled were.°

57

Faire knight (quoth he) *Hierusalem* that is,   505
    The new *Hierusalem,* that God has built
    For those to dwell in, that are chosen his,
    His chosen people purg'd from sinfull guilt,
    With pretious bloud, which cruelly was spilt
    On cursed tree,° of that unspotted lam,°   510
    That for the sinnes of all the world was kilt:
    Now are they Saints all in that Citie sam,°
More deare unto their God, then younglings to their
    dam.

58

Till now, said then the knight, I weened well,
    That great *Cleopolis,* where I have beene,   515

489 **a goodly Citie** the heavenly city of Rev. xxi. 10.   493 **ditty** subject.   494 **hight it well** it is well called.   498 **gladsome** cheerful.
500 **commonly** mutually.   502 **durst** dare.   504 **empeopled were**
were established as the population.   510 **cursed tree** the Cross.   510
lam, etc. "Behold the Lamb of God, which taketh away the sin
of the world!" (John i. 29.)   512 **sam** together.

In which the fairest *Faerie Queene* doth dwell,
The fairest Citie was, that might be seene;
And that bright towre all built of christall
    cleene,°
Panthea, seemd the brightest thing, that was:
520 But now by proofe all otherwise I weene;
For this great Citie that does far surpas,
And this bright Angels towre quite dims that towre of
    glas.

59

Most trew, then said the holy aged man;
    Yet is *Cleopolis* for earthly frame,°
525 The fairest peece,° that eye beholden can:
And well beseemes all knights of noble name,
That covet in th'immortall booke of fame
To be eternized, that same to haunt,°
And doen their service to that soveraigne
    Dame,°
530 That glorie does to them for guerdon graunt:
For she is heavenly borne, and heaven may justly
    vaunt.°

60

And thou faire ymp, sprong out from English race,
    How ever now accompted° Elfins sonne,
Well worthy doest thy service for her grace,
535 To aide a virgin desolate foredonne.°
But when thou famous victorie hast wonne,
And high emongst all knights hast hong thy
    shield,
Thenceforth the suit° of earthly conquest shonne,
And wash thy hands from guilt of bloudy field:

---

518 **cleene** pure.   524 **for earthly frame** compared to structures on
earth.   525 **peece** work of construction.   528 **haunt** frequent.   529
that soveraigne Dame Queen Elizabeth.   531 **heaven may justly
vaunt** may justly boast of her heavenly descent.   533 **How . . .
accompted** although now accounted.   535 **foredonne** abandoned.
538 **suit** pursuit.

For bloud can nought but sin, and wars but sorrowes
  yield.   540

61

Then seeke this path, that I to thee presage,°
  Which after all° to heaven shall thee send;
  Then peaceably thy painefull pilgrimage
  To yonder same *Hierusalem* do bend,
  Where is for thee ordaind a blessed end: 545
  For thou emongst those Saints, whom thou doest
    see,
  Shalt be a Saint, and thine owne nations frend
  And Patrone: thou Saint *George* shalt called bee,
Saint *George* of mery England, the signe of victoree.

62

Unworthy wretch (quoth he) of so great grace,   550
  How dare I thinke such glory to attaine?
  These that have it attaind, were in like cace
  (Quoth he) as wretched, and liv'd in like paine.
  But deeds of armes must I at last be faine,°
  And Ladies love to leave so dearely bought?   555
  What need of armes, where peace doth ay re-
    maine,
  (Said he) and battailes none are to be fought?
As for loose loves are vaine,° and vanish into nought.

63

O let me not (quoth he) then turne againe
  Backe to the world, whose joyes so fruitlesse are; 560
  But let me here for aye in peace remaine,
  Or streight way on that last long voyage fare,
  That nothing may my present hope empare.°
  That may not be (said he) ne maist thou yit
  Forgo that royall maides bequeathed care,°   565

---

541 **presage** make known. 542 **after all** when all his service has
been done. 554 **faine** willing. 558 **are vaine** they are vaine (1590).
563 **may . . . empare** may injure my present promise. 565 **bequeathed care** the charge committed to you.

Who did her cause into thy hand commit,
Till from her cursed foe thou have her freely quit.°

64

Then shall I soone, (quoth he) so God me grace,
     Abet° that virgins cause disconsolate,
And shortly backe returne unto this place,
To walke this way in Pilgrims poore estate.
But now aread,° old father, why of late
Didst thou behight° me borne of English blood,
     Whom all a Faeries sonne doen nominate?
     That word shall I (said he) avouchen good,
Sith to thee is unknowne the cradle of thy brood.°

65

For well I wote, thou springst from ancient race
     Of *Saxon* kings, that have with mightie hand
And many bloudie battailes fought in place
High reard their royall throne in *Britane* land,
And vanquisht them, unable to withstand:
From thence a Faerie thee unweeting reft,
     There as thou slepst in tender° swadling band,
And her base Elfin brood there for thee left.
Such men do Chaungelings call, so chaungd by
          Faeries theft.

66

Thence she thee brought into this Faerie lond,
     And in an heaped furrow did thee hyde,
Where thee a Ploughman all unweeting fond,
As he his toylesome teme that way did guyde,
And brought thee up in ploughmans state to
          byde,°
Whereof° *Georgos*° he thee gave to name;
     Till prickt with courage, and thy forces pryde,°
To Faery court thou cam'st to seeke for fame,

567 **freely quit** made free.   569 **Abet** maintain.   572 **aread** tell.
573 **behight** name.   576 **the cradle of thy brood** the place from
which your race derives.   583 **tender** infant.   590 **byde** remain.
591 **Whereof** from which.   591 **Georgos** ploughman.   592 **forces**
pryde natural powers in their prime.

And prove thy puissaunt armes, as seemes thee best
    became.°

      67

O holy Sire (quoth he) how shall I quight°   595
    The many favours I with thee have found,
    That hast my name and nation red° aright,
    And taught the way that does to heaven bound?°
    This said, adowne he looked to the ground,
    To have returnd, but dazed° were his eyne,   600
    Through passing° brightnesse, which did quite
      confound
    His feeble sence, and too exceeding shyne.°
So darke are earthly things compard to things divine.

      68

At last whenas himselfe he gan to find,°
    To *Una* back he cast° him to retire;   605
    Who him awaited still with pensive mind.
    Great thankes and goodly meed to that good syre,
    He thence departing gave for his paines hyre.°
    So came to *Una,* who him joyd to see,
    And after litle rest, gan him desire,   610
    Of her adventure mindfull for to bee.
So leave they take of *Cælia,* and her daughters three.

---

594 **as ... became** as it seems it best suited you.   595 **quight** repay.
597 **red** declared.   598 **bound** go.   600 **dazed** dazzled.   601 **pass-ing** surpassing.   602 **shyne** brilliance.   604 **find** recover.   605 **cast** resolved.   608 **for his paines hyre** as payment for his trouble.

CANTO XI

The knight with that old Dragon° fights
two dayes incessantly:
The third him overthrowes, and gayns
most glorious victory.

1

High time now gan it wex for *Una* faire,
　　To thinke of those her captive Parents° deare,
　　And their forwasted° kingdome to repaire:
　　Whereto whenas they now approched neare,
　　With hartie words her knight she gan to cheare,
　　And in her modest manner thus bespake;
　　Deare knight, as deare, as ever knight was deare,
　　That all these sorrowes suffer for my sake,
High heaven behold the tedious toyle, ye for me take.

2

Now are we come unto my native soyle,
　　And to the place, where all our perils dwell;
　　Here haunts° that feend, and does his dayly
　　　　spoyle,
　　Therefore henceforth be at your keeping well,°
　　And ever ready for your foeman fell.
　　The sparke of noble courage now awake,
　　And strive your excellent selfe to excell;
　　That shall ye evermore renowmed make,
Above all knights on earth, that batteill undertake.

3

And pointing forth, lo yonder is (said she)
　　The brasen towre in which my parents deare
　　For dread of that huge feend emprisond be,

Arg. **that old Dragon** See Rev. xx. 2–7.　**2 Parents** Adam and Eve.
3 forwasted entirely laid waste.　**12 haunts** frequents.　**13 be . . .**
well be well on your guard.

Whom I from far, see on the walles appeare,
Whose sight my feeble soule doth greatly cheare:
And on the top of all I do espye
The watchman wayting tydings glad to heare,   25
That O my parents might I happily
Unto you bring, to ease you of your misery.

4

With that they heard a roaring hideous sound,
That all the ayre with terrour filled wide,
And seemed uneath° to shake the stedfast
    ground.   30
Eftsoones that dreadfull Dragon they espide,
Where stretcht he lay upon the sunny side
Of a great hill, himselfe like a great hill.
But all so soone, as he from far descride°
Those glistring armes, that heaven with light
    did fill,   35
He rousd himselfe full blith,° and hastned them
    untill.°

5

Then bad the knight his Lady yede aloofe,°
And to an hill her selfe with draw aside,
From whence she might behold that battailles
    proof°
And eke be safe from daunger far descryde:°   40
She him obayd, and turnd a little wyde.°
Now O thou sacred Muse,° most learned Dame,
Faire ympe of *Phœbus,* and his aged bride,
The Nourse of time, and everlasting fame,
That warlike hands ennoblest with immortall name;   45

6

O gently come into my feeble brest,
    Come gently, but not with that mighty rage,

30 **uneath** almost.   34 **descride** espied.   36 **blith** joyfully.   36 **them
untill** to them.   37 **yede aloofe** go aside.   39 **proof** trial.   40 **far
descryde** seen from afar.   41 **wyde** apart.   42 **thou sacred Muse**
Clio, muse of history, offspring ("ympe") of Phoebus and Mne-
mosyne (Memory).

Wherewith the martiall troupes thou doest infest,°
And harts of great Heroës doest enrage,
50 That nought their kindled courage may aswage,
Soone as thy dreadfull trompe begins to sownd;
The God of warre with his fiers equipage°
Thou doest awake, sleepe never he so sownd,
And scared nations doest with horrour sterne
          astownd.°

7

55 Faire Goddesse lay that furious fit° aside,
Till I of warres and bloudy *Mars* do sing,
And Briton fields with Sarazin bloud bedyde,
Twixt that great faery Queene and Paynim°
          king,
That with their horrour heaven and earth did
          ring,
60 A worke of labour long, and endlesse prayse:
But now a while let downe that haughtie° string,
And to my tunes thy second tenor° rayse,
That I this man of God his° godly armes may blaze.°

8

By this the dreadfull Beast drew nigh to hand,
65 Halfe flying, and halfe footing in his hast,
That with his largenesse measured much land,
And made wide shadow under his huge wast;°
As mountaine doth the valley overcast.
Approching nigh, he reared high afore°
70 His body monstrous, horrible, and vast,
Which to increase his wondrous greatnesse more,
Was swolne with wrath, and poyson, and with bloudy
          gore.

9

And over, all° with brasen scales was armd,

48 **infest** assault. 52 **equipage** equipment. 54 **astownd** astonish.
55 **fit** mood. 58 **Paynim** pagan. 61 **haughtie** aspiring, high. 62
second tenor lower strain. 63 **man of God his** man of God's.
63 **blaze** proclaim. 67 **wast** body. 69 **afore** in front. 73 **over, all**
everywhere.

Like plated coate of steele, so couched neare,°
That nought mote perce,° ne might his corse be
   harmd   75
With dint° of sword, nor push of pointed speare;
Which as an Eagle, seeing pray appeare,
His aery plumes doth rouze,° full rudely dight,°
So shaked he, that horrour was to heare,
For as the clashing of an Armour bright,   80
Such noyse his rouzed° scales did send unto the
   knight.

10

His flaggy° wings when forth he did display,
   Were like two sayles, in which the hollow wynd
   Is gathered full, and worketh speedy way:
   And eke the pennes, that did his pineons bynd,°   85
   Were like mayne-yards, with flying canvas lynd,
   With which whenas him list° the ayre to beat,
   And there by force unwonted passage find,
   The cloudes before him fled for terrour great,
And all the heavens stood still amazed with his
   threat.°   90

11

His huge long tayle wound up in hundred foldes,
   Does overspred his long bras-scaly backe,
   Whose wreathed boughts° when ever he unfoldes,
   And thicke entangled knots adown does slacke,
   Bespotted as with shields° of red and blacke,   95
   It sweepeth all the land behind him farre,
   And of three furlongs does but litle lacke;
   And at the point two stings in-fixed arre,
Both deadly sharpe, that sharpest steele exceeden
   farre.

---

74 **so couched neare** laid so closely.   73 **nought mote perce** nothing
might pierce.   76 **dint** blow.   78 **rouze** shake.   78 **rudely dight**
ruggedly arrayed.   81 **rouzed** ruffled.   82 **flaggy** drooping.   85 **And
. . . bynd** And also the feathers that covered his wings.   87 **whenas
him list** when he desired.   90 **threat** thrust.   93 **boughts** coils.   95
shields scales.

12

100 But stings and sharpest steele did far exceed°
       The sharpnesse of his cruell rending clawes;
       Dead was it sure, as sure as death in deed,
       What ever thing does touch his ravenous pawes,
       Or what within his reach he ever drawes.
105   But his most hideous head my toung to tell
       Does tremble: for his deepe devouring jawes
       Wide gaped, like the griesly° mouth of hell,
Through which into his darke abisse all ravin° fell.

13

And that° more wondrous was, in either jaw
110   Three ranckes of yron teeth enraunged were,
       In which yet trickling bloud and gobbets° raw
       Of late devoured bodies did appeare,
       That sight thereof bred cold congealed° feare:
       Which to increase, and all atonce° to kill,
       A cloud of smoothering smoke and sulphur
115   seare°
       Out of his stinking gorge° forth steemed still,°
That all the ayre about with smoke and stench did fill.

14

His blazing eyes, like two bright shining shields,
       Did burne with wrath, and sparkled living fyre;
120   As two broad Beacons, set in open fields,
       Send forth their flames farre off to every shyre,
       And warning give, that enemies conspyre,
       With fire and sword the region to invade;
       So flam'd his eyne with rage and rancorous yre:
125   But farre within, as in a hollow glade,
Those glaring lampes were set, that made a dreadfull
           shade.

---

100 **did far exceed** were far exceeded by. 107 **griesly** horrible. 108 **ravin** plunder. 109 **that** that which. 111 **gobbets** lumps of flesh. 113 **congealed** freezing. 114 **atonce** at once. 115 **seare** burning. 116 **gorge** throat. 116 **still** always.

15

So dreadfully he towards him did pas,°
    Forelifting up aloft his speckled brest,
    And often bounding on the brused gras,
    As for great joyance° of his newcome guest.   *130*
    Eftsoones he gan advance his haughtie crest,
    As chauffed° Bore his bristles doth upreare,
    And shoke his scales to battell readie drest;
    That made the *Redcrosse* knight nigh quake for
      feare,
As bidding bold defiance to his foeman neare.   *135*

16

The knight gan fairely couch° his steadie speare,
    And fiercely ran at him with rigorous might:
    The pointed steele arriving rudely° theare,
    His harder° hide would neither perce, nor bight,°
    But glauncing by forth passed forward right;   *140*
    Yet sore amoved° with so puissant push,
    The wrathfull beast about him turned light,
    And him so rudely passing by, did brush
With his long tayle, that horse and man to ground
    did rush.

17

Both horse and man up lightly rose againe,   *145*
    And fresh encounter towards him addrest:°
    But th'idle° stroke yet backe recoyld in vaine,
    And found no place his deadly point to rest.
    Exceeding rage enflam'd the furious beast,
    To be avenged of so great despight;°   *150*
    For never felt his imperceable brest
    So wondrous force, from hand of living wight;
Yet had he prov'd the powre of many a puissant
    knight.

---

127 **pas** pace.   130 **joyance** joy.   132 **chauffed** chafed.   136 **couch** place in its rest for charging.   138 **rudely** violently.   139 **harder** too hard.   139 **bight** bite.   141 **amoved** moved.   146 **addrest** prepared.   147 **th'idle** the useless.   150 **despight** outrage.

18

Then with his waving wings displayed wyde,
155   Himselfe up high he lifted from the ground,
    And with strong flight did forcibly divide
    The yielding aire, which nigh too feeble found
    Her flitting partes, and element unsound,
    To beare so great a weight: he cutting way
160   With his broad sayles, about him soared round:
    At last low stouping° with unweldie sway,
Snatcht up both horse and man, to beare them quite
    away.

19

Long he them bore above the subject plaine,°
    So farre as Ewghen° bow a shaft may send,
165   Till° struggling strong did him at last constraine,
    To let them downe before his flightes end:
    As hagard° hauke presuming to contend
    With hardie fowle, above his hable might,°
    His wearie pounces° all in vaine doth spend,
170   To trusse° the pray too heavie for his flight;
Which comming downe to ground, does free it selfe
    by fight.

20

He so disseized of his gryping grosse,°
    The knight his thrillant° speare againe assayd
    In his bras-plated body to embosse,°
175   And three mens strength unto the stroke he layd;
    Wherewith the stiffe beame quaked, as affrayd,
    And glauncing from his scaly necke, did glyde
    Close under his left wing, then broad displayd.
    The percing steele there wrought a wound full
    wyde,

---

161 **stouping** swooping down.   163 **the subject plaine** the plain lying
below.   164 **Ewghen** of yew.   165 **Till** until they.   167 **hagard**
wild.   168 **hable might** proper strength.   169 **pounces** claws.   170
trusse seize and carry off.   172 **He . . . grosse** When he (the dragon)
was dispossessed of his heavy grip.   173 **thrillant** piercing.   174 **embosse** plunge.

That with the uncouth smart the Monster lowdly
    cryde. 180

21

He cryde, as raging seas are wont to rore,
    When wintry storme his wrathfull wreck° does
        threat,
    The rolling billowes beat the ragged° shore,
    As they the earth would shoulder° from her seat,
    And greedie gulfe does gape, as he would eat 185
    His neighbour element° in his revenge:
    Then gin the blustring brethren° boldly threat,
    To move the world from off his stedfast henge,°
And boystrous battell make, each other to avenge.

22

The steely head stucke fast still in his flesh, 190
    Till with his cruell clawes he snatcht the wood,
    And quite a sunder broke. Forth flowed fresh
    A gushing river of blacke goarie blood,
    That drowned all the land, whereon he stood;
    The streame thereof would drive a water-mill. 195
    Trebly augmented was his furious mood
    With bitter sense° of his deepe rooted ill,
That flames of fire he threw forth from his large
    nosethrill.°

23

His hideous tayle then hurled he about,
    And therewith all enwrapt the nimble thyes 200
    Of his froth-fomy steed, whose courage stout
    Striving to loose the knot, that fast him tyes,
    Himselfe in streighter bandes too rash implyes,°
    That to the ground he is perforce constraynd°
    To throw his rider: who can° quickly ryse 205

---

182 **wreck** ruin. 183 **ragged** jagged. 184 **shoulder** push. 186
His neighbour element the earth. 187 **the blustring brethren** the
winds. 188 **henge** axis. 197 **sense** feeling. 198 **nosethrill** nostril.
203 **too rash implyes** too quickly entangles. 204 **perforce constraynd** forced of necessity. 205 **can** did.

From off the earth, with durty bloud distaynd,°
For that reprochfull fall right fowly he disdaynd.

24

And fiercely tooke his trenchand° blade in hand,
    With which he stroke so furious and so fell,
    That nothing seemd° the puissance could with-
210   stand:
    Upon his crest the hardned yron fell,
    But his more hardned crest was armd so well,
    That deeper° dint therein it would not make;
    Yet so extremely did the buffe° him quell,°
215   That from thenceforth he shund the like to take,
But when he saw them come, he did them still°
        forsake.

25

The knight was wrath to see his stroke beguyld,°
    And smote againe with more outrageous might;
    But backe againe the sparckling steele recoyld,
220   And left not any marke, where it did light;
    As if in Adamant° rocke it had bene pight.°
    The beast impatient of his smarting wound,
    And of so fierce and forcible despight,°
    Thought with his wings to stye° above the
        ground;
225 But his late wounded wing unserviceable found.

26

Then full of griefe and anguish vehement,
    He lowdly brayd, that like was never heard,
    And from his wide devouring oven sent
    A flake° of fire, that flashing in his beard,
230   Him all amazd, and almost made affeard:
    The scorching flame sore swinged° all his face,

206 **distaynd** stained.   208 **trenchand** cutting.   210 **That ... seemed**
that it seemed that nothing.   213 **deeper** very deep.   214 **buffe** blow.
214 **quell** daunt.   216 **still** always.   217 **beguyld** foiled.   221 **Ada-**
mant diamond.   221 **pight** thrust.   223 **forcible despight** powerful
defiance.   224 **stye** rise.   229 **flake** flash.   231 **swinged** singed.

And through his armour all his bodie seard,
That he could not endure so cruell cace,
But thought his armes to leave, and helmet to unlace.

27

Not that great Champion° of the antique° world,   235
   Whom famous Poetes verse so much doth vaunt,
   And hath for twelve huge labours high extold,
   So many furies and sharpe fits did haunt,
   When him° the poysoned garment did enchaunt°
   With° *Centaures* bloud, and bloudie verses
     charm'd,   240
   As did this knight twelve thousand dolours°
     daunt,
   Whom fyrie steele now burnt, that earst° him
     arm'd,
That erst him goodly arm'd, now most of all him
   harm'd.

28

Faint, wearie, sore, emboyled,° grieved, brent°
   With heat, toyle, wounds, armes, smart, and in-
     ward fire°   245
   That never man such mischiefes did torment;
   Death better were, death did he oft desire,
   But death will never come, when needes require.
   Whom so dismayd when that his foe beheld,
   He cast to suffer him no more respire,°   250
   But gan his sturdie sterne° about to weld,°
And him so strongly stroke, that to the ground him
   feld.

---

235 **that great Champion** Hercules.   235 **antique** ancient.   239
When him, etc. When Hercules put on the tunic soaked in the poisonous blood of Nessus, his flesh burned in great agony.   239 **did
enchaunt** exerted its magical influence upon him.   240 **With the**
garment with.   241 **dolours** sufferings.   242 **earst** before.   244 **emboyled** heated.   244 **brent** burned.   244–245 **Faint . fire** faint
with heat, weary with toil, etc.   250 **He . . . respire** He resolved to
allow him to live no longer.   251 **sterne** tail.   251 **weld** wield.

29

It fortuned (as faire° it then befell)
    Behind his backe unweeting, where he stood,
255   Of auncient time there was a springing well,
    From which fast trickled forth a silver flood,
    Full of great vertues,° and for med'cine good.
    Whylome,° before that cursed Dragon got
    That happie land, and all with innocent blood
260   Defyld those sacred waves, it rightly hot°
The well of life, ne yet his vertues had forgot.

30

For unto life the dead it could restore,
    And guilt of sinfull crimes cleane wash away,
    Those that with sicknesse were infected sore,
265   It could recure, and aged long decay
    Renew, as one were borne that very day.
    Both *Silo* this, and *Jordan* did excell,
    And th'English *Bath,* and eke the german *Spau,*
    Ne can *Cephise,* nor *Hebrus*° match this well:
270 Into the same the knight backe overthrowen, fell.

31

Now gan the golden *Phœbus* for to steepe
    His fierie face in billowes of the west,
    And his faint steedes watred in Ocean deepe,
    Whiles from their journall° labours they did rest,
275   When that infernall Monster, having kest°
    His wearie foe into that living well,
    Can high advance his broad discoloured brest,
    Above his wonted pitch, with countenance fell,
And clapt his yron° wings, as° victor he did dwell.°

32

280 Which when his pensive Ladie saw from farre,
    Great woe and sorrow did her soule assay,°

---

253 **faire** favorably. 257 **vertues** powers. 258 **Whylome** once.
260 **hot** was called. 267–269 **Silo . . . Hebrus** rivers famous for their
healing powers or their purity. 274 **journall** daily. 275 **kest** cast.
279 **yron** strong. 279 **as** as if. 279 **dwell** remain. 281 **assay** assail.

As weening that° the sad end of the warre,
And gan to highest God entirely pray,
That feared chance from her to turne away;
With folded hands and knees full lowly bent   285
All night she watcht, ne once adowne would lay
Her daintie limbs in her sad dreriment,°
But praying still did wake, and waking did lament.

33

The morrow next gan early to appeare,
That *Titan*° rose to runne his daily race;   290
But early ere the morrow next gan reare
Out of the sea faire *Titans* deawy face,
Up rose the gentle virgin from her place,
And looked all about, if she might spy
Her loved knight to move his manly pace: 295
For she had great doubt of his safety,
Since late she saw him fall before his enemy.

34

At last she saw, where he upstarted brave
Out of the well, wherein he drenched lay;
As Eagle° fresh out of the Ocean wave,   300
Where he hath left his plumes all hoary gray,
And deckt himselfe with feathers youthly gay,
Like Eyas hauke° up mounts unto the skies,
His newly budded pineons to assay,
And marveiles at himselfe, still as he flies: 305
So new this new-borne knight to battell new did rise.

35

Whom when the damned feend so fresh did spy,
No wonder if he wondred at the sight,
And doubted, whether his late enemy
It were, or other new supplied knight.   310
He, now to prove his late renewed might,

282 **that** that to be. 287 **dreriment** grief. 290 **That Titan** when
the sun. 300 **As Eagle,** etc. according to the legend that the eagle
renews his youth every ten years by plunging into the ocean. 303
Eyas hauke a young hawk reared from the nest and allowed to fly
only when grown.

High brandishing his bright deaw-burning° blade,
Upon his crested scalpe so sore did smite,
That to the scull a yawning wound it made:
315 The deadly dint his dulled senses all dismaid.

36

I wote° not, whether the revenging steele
   Were hardned with that holy water dew,
   Wherein he fell, or sharper edge did feele,
   Or his baptized hands° now greater° grew;
320   Or other secret vertue did ensew;
   Else never could the force of fleshly arme,
   Ne molten° mettall in his bloud embrew:°
For till that stownd° could never wight him harme,
By subtilty, nor slight,° nor might, nor mighty charme.

37

325 The cruell wound enraged him so sore,
   That loud he yelded for exceeding paine;
   As hundred ramping Lyons seem'd to rore,
   Whom ravenous hunger did thereto constraine:
   Then gan he tosse aloft his stretched traine,
330   And therewith scourge the buxome° aire so sore,
   That to his force to yeelden it was faine;
   Ne ought° his sturdie strokes might stand afore,°
That high trees overthrew, and rocks in peeces tore.

38

The same advancing high above his head,
335   With sharpe intended° sting so rude him smot,
   That to the earth him drove, as stricken dead,
   Ne living wight would have him life behot:°

---

312 **deaw-burning** shining with "that holy water dew." 316 **wote** know. 319 **baptized hands** baptized in the well of life. 319 **greater** stronger. 322 **molten** forged. 322 **embrew** steep. 323 **stownd** time. 324 **slight** trickery. 330 **buxome** unresisting. 332 **Ne ought** nothing. 332 **afore** before. 335 **intended** extended. 337 **Ne . . . behot** No living person would have promised him life.

The mortall sting his angry needle shot
   Quite through his shield, and in his shoulder
     seasd,
   Where fast it stucke, ne would there out be got: *340*
   The griefe thereof him wondrous sore diseasd,
Ne might his ranckling paine with patience be
     appeasd.

39

But yet more mindfull of his honour deare,
   Then of the grievous smart, which him did
     wring,°
   From loathed soile he can him lightly reare,°   *345*
   And strove to loose the farre infixed sting:
   Which when in vaine he tryde with struggeling,
   Inflam'd with wrath, his raging blade he heft,°
   And strooke so strongly, that the knotty string
   Of his huge taile he quite a sunder cleft,   *350*
Five joynts thereof he hewd, and but the stump him
     left.

40

Hart cannot thinke, what outrage, and what cryes,
   With foule enfouldred° smoake and flashing fire,
   The hell-bred beast threw forth unto the skyes,
   That all was covered with darknesse dire: *355*
   Then fraught with rancour, and engorged° ire,
   He cast at once him to avenge for all,
   And gathering up himselfe out of the mire,
   With his uneven wings did fiercely fall
Upon his sunne-bright shield, and gript it fast
     withall.°   *360*

41

Much was the man encombred with his hold,
   In feare to lose his weapon in his paw,
   Ne wist yet, how his talants° to unfold;

---

334 wring vex.   **345 he . . . reare** he reared himself quickly.   **348 heft** lifted.   **353 enfouldred** black as a thunder cloud.   **356 engorged** congested.   **360 withall** as well.   **363 talants** talons.

For harder was from *Cerberus*° greedie jaw
365 To plucke a bone, then from his cruell claw
To reave° by strength, the griped° gage away:
Thrise he assayd it from his foot to draw,
And thrise in vaine to draw it did assay,
It booted nought to thinke, to robbe him of his pray.

42

370 Tho° when he saw no power might prevaile,
His trustie sword he cald to his last aid,
Wherewith he fiercely did his foe assaile,
And double blowes about him stoutly laid,
That glauncing fire out of the yron plaid;
375 As sparckles from the Andvile° use to fly,
When heavie hammers on the wedge are swaid;°
Therewith at last he forst him to unty°
One of his grasping feete, him to defend thereby.

43

The other foot, fast fixed on his shield,
Whenas no strength, nor stroks mote him con-
380   straine
To loose, ne yet the warlike pledge° to yield,
He smot thereat with all his might and maine,
That nought so wondrous puissance might
    sustaine;
Upon the joynt the lucky steele did light,
And made such way, that hewd it quite in
385   twaine;
The paw yet missed not his minisht° might,
But hong still on the shield, as it at first was pight.°

44

For griefe thereof, and divelish despight,
From his infernall fournace° forth he threw
390 Huge flames, that dimmed all the heavens light,

364 **Cerberus** the ravenous dog that guards the entrance to hell.
366 **reave** take away.   366 **griped** grasped.   370 **Tho** then.   375
Andvile anvil.   376 **swaid** swung.   377 **unty** loosen.   381 **the warlike pledge** the gage of battle.   386 **minisht** diminished.   387 **pight**
placed.   389 **fournace** maw.

Enrold° in duskish° smoke and brimstone blew;°
As burning *Aetna* from his boyling stew°
Doth belch out flames, and rockes in peeces
    broke,
And ragged ribs of mountaines molten new,
Enwrapt in coleblacke clouds and filthy smoke,   *395*
That all the land with stench, and heaven with horror
    choke.

45

The heate whereof, and harmfull pestilence
    So sore him noyd,° that° forst him to retire
    A little backward for his best defence,
    To save his bodie from the scorching fire,   *400*
    Which he from hellish entrailes did expire.°
    It chaunst (eternall God that chaunce did guide)
    As he recoyled backward, in the mire
    His nigh forwearied° feeble feet did slide,
And downe he fell, with dread of shame sore terrifide.   *405*

46

There grew a goodly tree him faire beside,°
    Loaden with fruit and apples rosie red,
    As they in pure vermilion had beene dide,
    Whereof great vertues over all were red:°
    For happie life to all, which thereon fed,   *410*
    And life eke everlasting did befall:
    Great God it planted in that blessed sted°
    With his almightie hand, and did it call
The tree of life, the crime of our first fathers fall.°

47

In all the world like was not to be found,   *415*

391 **Enrold** wrapped up.   391 **duskish** dusky.   391 **blew** livid.   392
stew caldron.   398 **noyd** troubled.   398 **that** that it.   401 **expire**
breathe out.   404 **nigh forwearied** almost utterly wearied.   406 **faire
beside** close by.   409 **over all were red** everywhere were known.
412 **sted** place.   414 **the crime . . . fall** the cause of reproach made
against Adam for his fall. Adam was expelled from Eden for fear
that he would eat of the Tree of Life.

Save in that soile,° where all good things did
    grow,
And freely sprong out of the fruitfull ground,
As incorrupted° Nature did them sow,
Till that dread Dragon all did overthrow.
420 Another like faire tree° eke grew thereby,
Whereof who so did eat, eftsoones did know
Both good and ill: O mornefull memory:
That tree through one mans fault hath doen us
    to dy.

48

From that first tree forth flowd, as from a well,
425 A trickling streame of Balme, most soveraine
And daintie deare,° which on the ground still°
    fell,
And overflowed all the fertill plaine,
As it had deawed° bene with timely raine:
Life and long health that gratious ointment gave,
And deadly woundes could heale, and reare
430   againe
The senselesse corse appointed° for the grave,
Into that same he fell: which did from death him
    save.

49

For nigh thereto the ever damned beast
Durst not approch, for he was deadly made,°
435 And all that life preserved, did detest:
Yet he it oft adventur'd to invade.
By this the drouping day-light gan to fade,
And yeeld his roome to sad succeeding night,
Who with her sable mantle gan to shade
440 The face of earth, and wayes of living wight,
And high her burning torch set up in heaven bright.

---

416 **that soile** Eden.   418 **incorrupted** free from corruption.   420
Another like faire tree the Tree of Knowledge of Good and Evil.
426 **daintie deare** most precious.   426 **still** continually.   428 **deawed**
moistened.   431 **appointed** made ready.   434 **was deadly made** belonged to death.

50

When gentle *Una* saw the second fall
    Of her deare knight, who wearie of long fight,
    And faint through losse of bloud, mov'd not
      at all,
    But lay as in a dreame of deepe delight,   *445*
    Besmeard with pretious Balme, whose vertuous
      might
    Did heale his wounds, and scorching heat alay,
    Againe she stricken was with sore affright,
    And for his safetie gan devoutly pray;
And watch the noyous° night, and wait for joyous
    day.   *450*

51

The joyous day gan early to appeare,
    And faire *Aurora* from the deawy bed
    Of aged *Tithone* gan her selfe to reare,
    With rosie cheekes, for shame as blushing red;
    Her golden lockes for haste were loosely shed   *455*
    About her eares, when *Una* her did marke
    Clymbe to her charet, all with flowers spred,
    From heaven high to chase the chearelesse
      darke;
With merry note her loud salutes the mounting larke.

52

Then freshly up arose the doughtie knight,   *460*
    All healed of his hurts and woundes wide,
    And did himselfe to battell readie dight;
    Whose early foe awaiting him beside
    To have devourd, so soone as day he spyde,
    When now he saw himselfe so freshly reare,   *465*
    As if late fight had nought him damnifyde,°
    He woxe dismayd, and gan his fate to feare;
Nathlesse° with wonted rage he him advaunced neare.

450 **noyous** harmful.   466 **damnifyde** injured.   468 **Nathlesse** nevertheless.

53

And in his first encounter, gaping wide,
470 He thought attonce him to have swallowd quight,
  And rusht upon him with outragious pride;
  Who him r'encountring° fierce, as hauke in flight,
  Perforce rebutted backe.° The weapon bright
  Taking advantage of his open jaw,
475 Ran through his mouth with so importune°
   might,
  That deepe emperst° his darksome hollow maw,
And back retyrd,° his life bloud forth with all°
  did draw.

54

So downe he fell, and forth his life did breath,
  That vanisht into smoke and cloudes swift;
480 So downe he fell, that th'earth him underneath
  Did grone, as feeble so great load to lift;
  So downe he fell, as an huge rockie clift,
  Whose false foundation° waves have washt away,
  With dreadfull poyse° is from the mayneland rift,
485 And rolling downe, great *Neptune* doth dismay;
So downe he fell, and like an heaped mountaine lay.

55

The knight himselfe even trembled at his fall,
  So huge and horrible a masse it seem'd;
  And his deare Ladie, that beheld it all,
  Durst not approch for dread, which she
490   misdeem'd,°
  But yet at last, when as the direfull feend
  She saw not stirre, off-shaking vaine affright,
  She nigher drew, and saw that joyous end:
  Then God she praysd, and thankt her faithfull
   knight,
495 That had atchiev'd so great a conquest by his might.

472 **r'encountring** engaging in fight. 473 **rebutted backe** drove back.
475 **importune** violent. 476 **emperst** pierced. 477 **back retyrd**
drawn back. 477 **with all** with all life. 483 **false foundation** foundation having been made treacherous by the waves. 484 **poyse** impact. 490 **misdeem'd** misjudged in fearing for her knight's safety.

CANTO XII

Faire Una to the Redcrosse knight
betrouthed is with joy:
Though false Duessa it to barre
her false sleights doe imploy.

1

Behold I see the haven nigh at hand,
    To which I meane my wearie course to bend;
    Vere° the maine shete, and beare up with° the
      land,
    The which afore is fairely to be kend,°
    And seemeth safe from stormes, that may of-
      fend;°   5
    There this faire virgin wearie of her way
    Must landed be, now at her journeyes end:
    There eke my feeble barke a while may stay,
Till merry° wind and weather call her thence away.

2

Scarsely had *Phœbus* in the glooming East   10
    Yet harnessed his firie-footed teeme,
    Ne reard above the earth his flaming creast,
    When the last deadly smoke aloft did steeme,
    That signe of last outbreathed life did seeme
    Unto the watchman on the castle wall;   15
    Who thereby dead that balefull Beast did deeme,
    And to his Lord and Ladie lowd gan call,
To tell, how he had seene the Dragons fatall fall.

3

Uprose with hastie joy, and feeble speed
    That aged Sire, the Lord of all that land,   20

---

3 **Vere** turn. 3 **beare up with** sail toward. 4 **The . . . kend** Which
ahead is clearly to be seen. 5 **offend** harm the ship. 9 **merry** favorable.

281

And looked forth, to weet, if true indeede
Those tydings were, as he did understand,
Which whenas true by tryall he out fond,°
He bad to open wyde his brazen gate,
Which long time had bene shut, and out of hond°
Proclaymed joy and peace through all his state;
For dead now was their foe, which them forrayed°
    late.

4

Then gan triumphant Trompets sound on hie,
That sent to heaven the ecchoed report
Of their new joy, and happie victorie
Gainst him, that had them long opprest with tort,°
And fast imprisoned in sieged° fort.
Then all the people, as in solemne feast,
To him assembled with one full consort,°
Rejoycing at the fall of that great beast,
From whose eternall bondage now they were releast.

5

Forth came that auncient Lord and aged Queene,
Arayd in antique robes downe to the ground,
And sad habiliments right well beseene;°
A noble crew° about them waited round
Of sage and sober Peres, all gravely gownd;°
Whom farre before did march a goodly band
Of tall young men, all hable armes to sownd,°
But now they laurell braunches bore in hand;
Glad signe of victorie and peace in all their land.

6

Unto that doughtie Conquerour they came,
And him before themselves prostrating low,
Their Lord and Patrone loud did him proclame,
And at his feet their laurell boughes did throw.

23 **out found** found out.   25 **out of hond** straight off.   27 **forrayed**
ravaged.   31 **tort** wrong.   32 **sieged** besieged.   34 **consort** company.   39 **And . . . beseene** And sober attire appropriate to their
state.   40 **crew** company.   41 **gownd** dressed.   43 **all . . . sownd** all
able to strike arms in battle.

Soone after them all dauncing on a row   50
   The comely virgins came, with girlands dight,
   As fresh as flowres in medow greene do grow,
   When morning deaw upon their leaves doth
      light:
And in their hands sweet Timbrels° all upheld on
    hight.°

7

And them before, the fry° of children young   55
   Their wanton sports and childish mirth did play,
   And to the Maydens sounding tymbrels sung
   In well attuned notes, a joyous lay,
   And made delightfull musicke all the way,
   Untill they came, where that faire virgin stood;   60
   As faire *Diana* in fresh sommers day
   Beholds her Nymphes, enraung'd in shadie wood,
Some wrestle, some do run, some bathe in christall
    flood.

8

So she beheld those maydens meriment
   With chearefull vew; who when to her they
    came,   65
   Themselves to ground with gratious humblesse°
    bent,
   And her ador'd by honorable name,
   Lifting to heaven her everlasting fame:
   Then on her head they set a girland greene,
   And crowned her twixt earnest and twixt game;   70
   Who in her selfe-resemblance° well beseene,
Did seeme such, as she was, a goodly maiden Queene.

9

And after, all the raskall many° ran,
   Heaped together in rude rablement,°

---

54 **Timbrels** tambourines.   54 **hight** high.   55 **fry** crowd.   66 **humblesse** humility.   71 **her selfe-resemblance** i.e., resembling her true self.   73 **the raskall many** the rabble.   74 **rablement** tumult.

75 To see the face of that victorious man:
　　Whom all admired, as from heaven sent,
　　And gazd upon with gaping wonderment.
　　But when they came, where that dead Dragon
　　　lay,
　　Stretcht on the ground in monstrous large extent,
80 　　The sight with idle° feare did them dismay,
Ne durst approch him nigh, to touch, or once assay.°

10

Some feard, and fled; some feard and well it faynd;°
　　One that would wiser seeme, then all the rest,
　　Warnd him not touch, for yet perhaps remaynd
85 　　Some lingring life within his hollow brest,
　　Or in his wombe might lurke some hidden nest
　　Of many Dragonets, his fruitfull seed;
　　Another said, that in his eyes did rest
　　Yet sparckling fire, and bad thereof take heed;
90 Another said, he saw him move his eyes indeed.

11

One mother, when as her foolehardie chyld
　　Did come too neare, and with his talants° play,
　　Halfe dead through feare, her litle babe revyld,
　　And to her gossips° gan in counsell° say;
95 　　How can I tell, but that his talants may
　　Yet scratch my sonne, or rend his tender hand?
　　So diversly themselves in vaine they fray;°
　　Whiles some more bold, to measure him nigh
　　　stand,
To prove how many acres he did spread of land.

12

100 Thus flocked all the folke him round about,
　　The whiles that hoarie° king, with all his traine,
　　Being arrived, where that champion stout

---

80 **idle** groundless.　81 **once assay** even try.　82 **faynd** disguised.
92 **talants** talons.　94 **gossips** women friends.　94 **in counsell** in
private.　97 **fray** frighten.　101 **hoarie** gray-haired.

After his foes defeasance° did remaine,
 Him goodly greetes, and faire does entertaine,°
 With princely gifts of yvorie and gold,   *105*
 And thousand thankes him yeelds for all his
   paine.
 Then when his daughter deare he does behold,
Her dearely doth imbrace, and kisseth manifold.°

13

And after to his Pallace he them brings,
 With shaumes,° and trompets, and with Clarions
   sweet;   *110*
 And all the way the joyous people sings,
 And with their garments strowes the paved street:
 Whence mounting up, they find purveyance
   meet°
 Of all, that royall Princes court became,
 And all the floore was underneath their feet   *115*
 Bespred with costly scarlot of great name,°
On which they lowly sit, and fitting purpose° frame.

14

What needs me tell their feast and goodly guize,°
 In which was nothing riotous nor vaine?
 What needs of daintie dishes to devize,°   *120*
 Of comely services, or courtly trayne?°
 My narrow leaves cannot in them containe
 The large discourse of royall Princes state.
 Yet was their manner then but bare and plaine:
 For th'antique world excesse and pride did hate;   *125*
Such proud luxurious pompe is swollen up but late.

15

Then when with meates and drinkes of every kinde
 Their fervent appetites they quenched had,
 That auncient Lord gan fit occasion finde,

103 defeasance overthrow. **104 entertaine** receive. **108 manifold**
many times. **110 shaumes** a kind of oboe. **113 purveyance meet**
suitable provision. **116 name** value. **117 fitting purpose** seemly
discourse. **118 guize** behavior. **120 devize** tell. **121 trayne**
retinue.

130 Of straunge adventures, and of perils sad,
         Which in his travell him befallen had,
         For to demaund of his renowmed guest:
         Who then with utt'rance grave, and count'nance
            sad,
         From point to point, as is before exprest,
135 Discourst° his voyage long, according° his request.

16

Great pleasure mixt with pittifull regard,
         That godly King and Queene did passionate,°
         Whiles they his pittifull adventures heard,
         That oft they did lament his lucklesse state,
140 And often blame the too importune° fate,
         That heapd on him so many wrathfull wreakes:°
         For never gentle knight, as he of late,
         So tossed was in fortunes cruell freakes;°
And all the while salt teares bedeawd the hearers
            cheaks.

17

145 Then said the royall Pere in sober wise;
         Deare Sonne, great beene the evils, which ye bore
         From first to last in your late enterprise,
         That I note,° whether prayse, or pitty more:
         For never living man, I weene, so sore
150 In sea of deadly daungers was distrest;
         But since now safe ye seised° have the shore,
         And well arrived are, (high God be blest)
Let us devize of ease and everlasting rest.

18

Ah dearest Lord, said then that doughty knight,
155 Of ease or rest I may not yet devize;
         For by the faith, which I to armes have plight,
         I bounden am streight after this emprize,°

135 **Discourst** told. 135 **according** according to. 137 **passionate**
express with passion. 140 **importune** grievous. 141 **wreakes** injuries. 143 **freakes** changes. 148 **note** know not. 151 **seised**
reached. 157 **emprize** enterprise.

As that your daughter can ye well advize,
Backe to returne to that great Faerie Queene,
And her to serve six yeares in warlike wize,
Gainst that proud Paynim king, that workes her
    teene:°   *160*
Therefore I ought crave pardon, till I there have
    beene.

19

Unhappie falles that hard necessitie,
    (Quoth he) the troubler of my happie peace,
    And vowed foe of my felicitie;
    Ne I against the same can justly preace:°   *165*
    But since that band° ye cannot now release,
    Nor doen undo;° (for vowes may not be vaine)
    Soone as the terme of those six yeares shall
      cease,
    Ye then shall hither backe returne againe,
The marriage to accomplish vowd betwixt you twain.   *170*

20

Which for my part I covet to performe,
    In sort as° through the world I did proclame,
    That who so kild that monster most deforme,
    And him in hardy battaile overcame,   *175*
    Should have mine onely daughter to his Dame,°
    And of my kingdome heire apparaunt bee:
    Therefore since now to thee perteines the same,
    By dew desert of noble chevalree,
Both daughter and eke kingdome, lo I yield to thee.   *180*

21

Then forth he called that his daughter faire,
    The fairest *Un'* his onely daughter deare,
    His onely daughter, and his onely heyre;
    Who forth proceeding with sad sober cheare,°
    As bright as doth the morning starre appeare   *185*

161 **teene** sorrow.   166 **preace** contend.   167 **band** bond.   168 **doen
undo** undo.   173 **In sort as** according as.   176 **to his Dame** as his
wife.   184 **cheare** countenance.

Out of the East, with flaming lockes bedight,
To tell that dawning day is drawing neare,
And to the world does bring long wished light;
So faire and fresh that Lady shewd her selfe in sight.

22

190 So faire and fresh, as freshest flowre in May;
For she had layd her mournefull stole aside,
And widow-like sad wimple throwne away,
Wherewith her heavenly beautie she did hide,
195 Whiles on her wearie journey she did ride;
And on her now a garment she did weare,
All lilly white, withoutten spot, or pride,°
That seemd like silke and silver woven neare,°
But neither silke nor silver therein did appeare.

23

The blazing brightnesse of her beauties beame,
200 And glorious light of her sunshyny face
To tell, were as to strive against the streame.
My ragged° rimes are all too rude and bace,
Her heavenly lineaments for to enchace.°
Ne wonder; for her owne deare loved knight,
205 All° were she dayly with himselfe in place,
Did wonder much at her celestiall sight:
Oft had he seene her faire, but never so faire dight.°

24

So fairely dight, when she in presence came,
She to her Sire made humble reverence,
210 And bowed low, that her right well became,
And added grace unto her excellence:
Who with great wisedome, and grave eloquence
Thus gan to say. But eare he thus had said,
With flying speede, and seeming great pretence,
215 Came running in, much like a man dismaid,
A Messenger with letters, which his message said.

---

196 **spot, or pride** blemish, or ostentatious ornament. 197 **neare** closely. 202 **ragged** rugged. 203 **enchace** serve as a setting for 205 **All** although. 207 **dight** adorned.

25

All in the open hall amazed stood,
    At suddeinnesse of that unwarie° sight,
    And wondred at his breathlesse hastie mood.
    But he for nought would stay his passage right,°   220
    Till fast° before the king he did alight;
    Where falling flat, great humblesse° he did make,
    And kist the ground, whereon his foot was
        pight;°
    Then to his hands that writ° he did betake,°
Which he disclosing,° red thus, as the paper spake.   225

26

To thee, most mighty king of *Eden* faire,
    Her greeting sends in these sad lines addrest,
    The wofull daughter, and forsaken heire
    Of that great Emperour of all the West;
    And bids thee be advized for the best,   230
    Ere thou thy daughter linck in holy band
    Of wedlocke to that new unknowen guest:
    For he already plighted his right hand
Unto another love, and to another land.

27

To me sad mayd, or rather widow sad,   235
    He was affiaunced long time before,
    And sacred pledges he both gave, and had,
    False erraunt knight, infamous, and forswore:°
    Witnesse the burning Altars, which he swore,
    And guiltie heavens of° his bold perjury,   240
    Which though he hath polluted oft of yore,
    Yet I to them for judgement just do fly,
And them conjure° t'avenge this shamefull injury.

28

Therefore since mine he is, or free or bond,°

218 **unwarie** unexpected.   220 **right** straight.   221 **fast** close.   222
humblesse humbleness.   223 **pight** placed.   224 **writ** writing.   224
betake deliver.   225 **disclosing** opening up.   238 **forswore** for-
sworn.   240 **guiltie heavens of** heaven made guilty by.   243
conjure implore.   244 **bond** bound.

245
 Or false or trew, or living or else dead,
  Withhold, O soveraine Prince, your hasty hond
  From knitting league with him, I you aread;
  Ne weene my right with strength adowne to
   tread,
  Through weakenesse of my widowhed, or woe:
250
  For truth is strong, her rightfull cause to plead,
  And shall find friends, if need requireth soe,
So bids thee well to fare,° Thy neither friend, nor
   foe,

          Fidessa.

29

When he these bitter byting words had red,
  The tydings straunge did him abashed make,
255
  That still he sate long time astonished
  As in great muse, ne word to creature spake.
  At last his solemne silence thus he brake,
  With doubtfull eyes fast fixed on his guest;
  Redoubted knight, that for mine onely sake°
260
  Thy life and honour late adventurest,
Let nought be hid from me, that ought to be exprest.

30

What meane these bloudy vowes, and idle threats,
  Throwne out from womanish impatient mind?
  What heavens? what altars? what enraged heates
265
  Here heaped up with termes of love unkind,
  My conscience cleare with guilty bands would
   bind?
  High God be witnesse, that I guiltlesse ame.
  But if your selfe, Sir knight, ye faultie find,
  Or wrapped be in loves of former Dame,
270
With crime do not it cover, but disclose the same.

31

To whom the *Redcrosse* knight this answere sent,
  My Lord, my King, be nought hereat dismayd,

252 **well to fare** farewell. 259 **mine onely sake** my sake alone.

Till well ye wote by grave intendiment,°
What woman, and wherefore doth me upbrayd
With breach of love, and loyalty betrayd.   275
It was in my mishaps, as hitherward
I lately traveild, that unwares I strayd
Out of my way, through perils straunge and
    hard;
That day should faile me, ere I had them all declard.

32

There did I find, or rather I was found   280
    Of this false woman, that *Fidessa* hight,
    Fidessa hight the falsest Dame on ground,°
    Most false *Duessa,* royall richly dight,
    That easie was t'invegle weaker° sight:
    Who by her wicked arts, and wylie skill,   285
    Too false and strong for earthly skill or might,
    Unwares me wrought unto her wicked will,
And to my foe betrayd, when least I feared ill.

33

Then stepped forth the goodly royall Mayd,
    And on the ground her selfe prostrating low,
    With sober countenaunce thus to him sayd;   290
    O pardon me, my soveraigne Lord, to show
    The secret treasons, which of late I know
    To have bene wroght by that false sorceresse.
    She onely she it is, that earst did throw   295
    This gentle knight into so great distresse,
That death him did awaite in dayly wretchednesse.

34

And now it seemes, that she suborned hath
    This craftie messenger with letters vaine,
    To worke new woe and improvided scath,°   300
    By breaking of the band betwixt us twaine;

---

273 **intendiment** attention.   281 **on ground** on earth.   283 **royall
richly dight** adorned as richly as royalty.   284 **weaker** too weak.
300 **improvided scath** unforeseen harm.

Wherein she used hath the practicke paine°
Of this false footman, clokt with simplenesse,
Whom if ye please for to discover plaine,
305   Ye shall him *Archimago* find, I ghesse,
The falsest man alive; who tries shall find no lesse.

35

The king was greatly moved at her speach,
And all with suddein indignation fraight,°
Bad on that Messenger rude hands to reach.
310   Eftsoones the Gard, which on his state did wait,
Attacht° that faitor° false, and bound him strait:
Who seeming sorely chauffed° at his band,°
As chained Beare, whom cruell dogs do bait,
With idle force did faine them to withstand,
315   And often semblaunce made to scape out of their
      hand.

36

But they him layd full low in dungeon deepe,
And bound him hand and foote with yron chains.
And with continuall watch did warely keepe;
Who then would thinke, that by his subtile trains
320   He could escape fowle death or deadly paines?
Thus when that Princes wrath was pacifide,
He gan renew the late forbidden banes,°
And to the knight his daughter deare he tyde,
With sacred rites and vowes for ever to abyde.

37

325 His owne two hands the holy knots did knit,
That none but death for ever can devide;
His owne two hands, for such a turne° most fit,
The housling° fire did kindle and provide,
And holy water thereon sprinckled wide;
330   At which the bushy Teade° a groome did light,

302 **practicke paine** cunning pains.   308 **fraight** filled.   311 **Attacht** seized.   311 **faitor** impostor.   312 **chauffed** chafed.   312 **band** bonds.   322 **banes** banns.   327 **turne** task.   328 **housling** sacramental.   330 **Teade** the nuptial torch.

And sacred lampe in secret chamber hide,
Where it should not be quenched day nor night,
For feare of evill fates, but burnen ever bright.

38

Then gan they sprinckle all the posts with wine,
And made great feast to solemnize that day;   *335*
They all perfumde with frankencense divine,
And precious odours fetcht from far away,
That all the house did sweat with great aray:
And all the while sweete Musicke did apply
Her curious° skill, the warbling notes to play,   *340*
To drive away the dull Melancholy;
The whiles one sung a song of love and jollity.

39

During the which there was an heavenly noise°
Heard sound through all the Pallace pleasantly,
Like as it had bene many an Angels voice,   *345*
Singing before th'eternall majesty,
In their trinall triplicities° on hye;
Yet wist no creature, whence that heavenly
    sweet°
Proceeded, yet eachone felt secretly
Himselfe thereby reft of his sences meet,°   *350*
And ravished with rare impression in his sprite.

40

Great joy was made that day of young and old,
And solemne feast proclaimd throughout the
    land,
That their exceeding merth may not be told:
Suffice it heare by signes to understand   *355*
The usuall joyes at knitting of loves band.
Thrise happy man the knight himselfe did hold,
Possessed of his Ladies hart and hand,

---

340 **curious** elaborate. 343 **noise** music. 347 **trinall triplicities**
the three orders of angels, each with three degrees. 348 **sweet**
sweetness. 350 **meet** proper.

And ever, when his eye did her behold,
360 His heart did seeme to melt in pleasures manifold.

41

Her joyous presence and sweet company
    In full content he there did long enjoy,
    Ne wicked envie, ne vile gealosy
    His deare delights were able to annoy:
365   Yet swimming in that sea of blisfull joy,
    He nought forgot, how he whilome had sworne,
    In case he could that monstrous beast destroy,
    Unto his Farie Queene backe to returne:
The which he shortly did, and *Una* left to mourne.

42

370 Now strike your sailes ye jolly Mariners,
    For we be come unto a quiet rode,°
    Where we must land some of our passengers,
    And light this wearie vessell of her lode.
    Here she a while may make her safe abode,
375   Till she repaired have her tackles spent,°
    And wants supplide. And then againe abroad
    On the long voyage whereto she is bent:
Well may she speede and fairely finish her intent.

371 **rode** roadstead, place of anchorage.   375 **spent** worn out.

The Second Booke

OF THE FAERIE QUEENE

Contayning,

THE LEGEND OF SIR GUYON

OR

Of Temperaunce.

1

Right well I wote most mighty Soveraine,
    That all this famous antique° history,
    Of some th'aboundance of an idle braine
    Will judged be, and painted forgery,
    Rather then matter of just° memory,   5
    Sith none, that breatheth living aire, does know,
    Where is that happy land of Faery,
    Which I so much do vaunt,° yet no where
        show,
But vouch antiquities, which no body can know.

2 antique ancient.   5 just well-founded.   8 vaunt praise.

2

10 But let that man with better sence advize,°
      That of the world least part to us is red:°
      And dayly how through hardy enterprize,
      Many great Regions are discovered,
      Which to late° age were never mentioned.
15   Who ever heard of th'Indian *Peru?*
      Or who in venturous vessell measured
      The *Amazons* huge river now found trew?
  Or fruitfullest *Virginia* who did ever vew?

3

  Yet all these were, when no man did them know;
20   Yet have from wisest ages hidden beene:
      And later times things more unknowne shall
        show.
      Why then should witlesse man so much mis-
        weene°
      That nothing is, but that which he hath seene?
      What if within the Moones faire shining
        spheare?
25   What if in every other starre unseene
      Of other worldes he happily° should heare?
  He wonder would much more: yet such to some ap-
    peare.

4

  Of Faerie lond yet if he more inquire,
      By certaine signes here set in sundry place°
30   He may it find; ne let him then admire,°
      But yield his sence to be too blunt and bace,
      That no'te° without an hound fine footing°
        trace.
      And thou, O fairest Princesse under sky,
      In this faire mirrhour maist behold thy face,

10 **advize** consider. 11 **red** known. 14 **late** recent. 22 **misweene**
misjudge. 26 **happily** by hap, chance. 29 **in sundry place** in
different places. 30 **admire** marvel at his skill. 32 **no'te** might not.
32 **footing** footprints.

And thine owne realmes in lond of Faery,   35
And in this antique Image thy great auncestry.

5
The which O pardon me thus to enfold
    In covert vele, and wrap in shadowes light,
    That feeble eyes your glory may behold,
    Which else could not endure those beames
        bright,   40
    But would be dazled with exceeding light.
    O pardon, and vouchsafe with patient eare
    The brave adventures of this Faery knight
    The good Sir *Guyon,* gratiously to heare,
In whom great rule of Temp'raunce goodly doth ap-
    peare.   45

from CANTO I: THE OPENING EPISODE

1
That cunning Architect° of cancred° guile,
    Whom Princes late displeasure left in bands,
    For falsed letters and suborned wile,
    Soone as the *Redcrosse* knight he understands
    To beene departed out of *Eden* lands,   5
    To serve againe his soveraine Elfin Queene,
    His artes he moves,° and out of caytives hands°
    Himselfe he frees by secret meanes unseene;
His shackles emptie left, him selfe escaped cleene.

2
And forth he fares full of malicious mind,   10
    To worken mischiefe and avenging woe,
    Where ever he that godly knight may find,
    His onely hart sore, and his onely° foe,

---

1 **That cunning Architect** Archimago.   1 **cancred** malignant.   7
moves applies.   7 **caytives hands** the hands of those who held him
captive.   13 **onely** chief.

Sith *Una* now he algates° must forgoe,
15   Whom his victorious hands did earst restore
   To native crowne and kingdome late ygoe:°
   Where she enjoyes sure peace for evermore,
As weather-beaten ship arriv'd on happie shore.

3

Him therefore now the object of his spight
20   And deadly food° he makes: him to offend°
   By forged treason, or by open fight
   He seekes, of all his drift° the aymed end:
   Thereto his subtile engins° he does bend,
   His practick° wit, and his faire filed° tong,
25   With thousand other sleights: for well he kend,
   His credit now in doubtfull ballaunce hong;
For hardly could be° hurt, who was already stong.

4

Still as he went, he craftie stales° did lay,
   With cunning traines° him to entrap unwares,°
30   And privie spials° plast in all his way,
   To weete what course he takes, and how he
      fares;
   To ketch him at a vantage in his snares.
   But now so wise and warie was the knight
   By triall of his former harmes and cares,
35   That he describe,° and shonned still his slight:
The fish that once was caught, new bait will hardly
      bite.

5

Nath'lesse° th'Enchaunter would not spare his paine,
   In hope to win occasion to his will;
   Which when he long awaited had in vaine,
40   He chaungd his minde from one to other ill:

14 **algates** wholly.   16 **late ygoe** lately.   20 **food** feud.   20 **offend** injure.   22 **drift** purpose.   23 **engins** wiles.   24 **practick** cunning. 24 **faire filed** smooth.   27 **be** he be.   28 **stales** traps.   29 **traines** stratagems.   29 **unwares** suddenly.   30 **privie spials** secret spies. 35 **describe** caught sight of   37 **Nath'lesse** nevertheless.

For to all good he enimy was still.
Upon the way him fortuned to meet,
Faire marching underneath a shady hill,
A goodly knight, all armd in harnesse meete,°
That from his head no place appeared to his feete.   45

6

His carriage was full comely and upright,
His countenaunce demure and temperate,
But yet so sterne and terrible in sight,
That cheard his friends, and did his foes amate:°
He was an Elfin borne of noble state,   50
And mickle worship° in his native land;
Well could he tourney and in lists debate,°
And knighthood tooke of good Sir *Huons*° hand,
When with king *Oberon*° he came to Faerie land.

7

Him als° accompanyd upon the way   55
A comely Palmer, clad in blacke attire,
Of ripest yeares, and haires all hoarie gray,
That with a staffe his feeble steps did stire,°
Least his long way his aged limbes should tire:
And if by lookes one may the mind aread,°   60
He seemd to be a sage and sober sire,
And ever with slow pace the knight did lead,
Who taught his trampling steed with equall steps to
    tread.

8

Such whenas *Archimago* them did view,
He weened° well to worke some uncouth° wile,   65
Eftsoones° untwisting his deceiptfull clew,°
He gan to weave a web of wicked guile,
And with faire countenance and flattring stile,
To them approching, thus the knight bespake:

44 **harnesse meete** proper armor.   49 **amate** dismay.   51 **mickle
worship** much honor.   52 **debate** fight.   53 **Sir Huons** Sir Huon of
Bordeaux's.   54 **Oberon** a fairy king.   55 **als** also.   58 **stire** steer.
60 **aread** discover.   65 **weened** expected.   65 **uncouth** unknown.
66 **eftsoones** immediately.   66 **clew** ball of thread.

Faire sonne of *Mars,* that seeke with warlike
70   spoile,
And great atchiev'ments great your selfe to
        make,
Vouchsafe to stay your steed for humble misers° sake.

9

He stayd his steed for humble misers sake,
    And bad tell on the tenor of his plaint;°
75   Who feigning then in every limbe to quake,
    Through inward feare, and seeming pale and
        faint
    With piteous mone his percing° speach gan
        paint;°
    Deare Lady how shall I declare thy cace,
    Whom late I left in langourous° constraint?
80   Would God thy selfe now present were in place,
To tell this ruefull° tale; thy sight could win thee
        grace.

10

Or rather would, O would it so had chaunst,
    That you, most noble Sir, had present beene,
    When that lewd ribauld° with vile lust advaunst°
85   Layd first his filthy hands on virgin cleene,°
    To spoile her daintie corse so faire and sheene,°
    As on the earth, great mother of us all,
    With living eye more faire was never seene,
    Of chastitie and honour virginall:
Witnesse ye heavens, whom she in vaine to helpe did
90   call.

11

How may it be, (said then the knight halfe wroth,)
    That knight should knighthood ever so have
        shent?°

---

72 **misers** wretch's.   74 **plaint** complaint.   77 **percing** piercing.
77 **gan paint** gave false coloring to.   79 **langourous** distressful.
81 **ruefull** grievous.   84 **ribauld** rascal.   84 **advaunst** moved.   85
cleene pure.   86 **sheene** bright.   92 **shent** disgraced.

None but that saw (quoth he) would weene for
   troth,
How shamefully that Maid he did torment.
Her looser° golden lockes he rudely rent,   *95*
And drew her on the ground, and his sharpe
   sword
Against her snowy brest he fiercely bent,
And threatned death with many a bloudie word;
Toung hates to tell the rest, that eye to see abhord.

12

Therewith amoved° from his sober mood,   *100*
   And lives he yet (said he) that wrought this act,
   And doen the heavens afford him vitall food?
   He lives, (quoth he) and boasteth of the fact,
   Ne yet hath any knight his courage crackt.
   Where may that treachour° then (said he) be
     found,   *105*
   Or by what meanes may I his footing tract?°
   That shall I shew (said he) as sure, as hound
The stricken Deare doth chalenge° by the bleeding
   wound.

13

He staid not lenger talke,° but with fierce ire
   And zealous hast away is quickly gone   *110*
   To seeke that knight, where him that craftie
     Squire
   Supposd to be. They do arrive anone,
   Where sate a gentle Lady all alone,
   With garments rent, and haire discheveled,
   Wringing her hands, and making piteous mone; *115*
   Her swollen eyes were much disfigured,
And her faire face with teares was fowly blubbered.°

14

The knight approching nigh, thus to her said,

95 **looser** loose. 100 **amoved** moved. 105 **treachour** traitor. 106
tract track. 108 **chalenge** track (?) 109 **talke** to talk. 117
blubbered disfigured.

Faire Ladie, through foule sorrow ill bedight,°
120 Great pittie is to see you thus dismaid,
And marre the blossome of your beautie bright:
For thy° appease your griefe and heavie plight,
And tell the cause of your conceived paine.
For if he live, that hath you doen despight,°
125 He shall you doe due recompence againe,
Or else his wrong with greater puissance maintaine.

15

Which when she heard, as in despightfull wise,°
She wilfully her sorrow did augment,
And offred hope of comfort did despise:
130 Her golden lockes most cruelly she rent,
And scratcht her face with ghastly dreriment,°
Ne would she speake, ne see, ne yet be seene,
But hid her visage, and her head downe bent,
Either for grievous shame, or for great teene,°
135 As if her hart with sorrow had transfixed beene.

16

Till her that Squire bespake, Madame my liefe,°
For Gods deare love be not so wilfull bent,
But doe vouchsafe now to receive reliefe,
The which good fortune doth to you present.
140 For what bootes it to weepe and to wayment,°
When ill is chaunst, but doth the ill increase,
And the weake mind with double woe torment?
When she her Squire heard speake, she gan appease
Her voluntarie° paine, and feele some secret ease.

145 ### 17

Eftsoone she said, Ah gentle trustie Squire,
What comfort can I wofull wretch conceave,
Or why should ever I henceforth desire

---

119 **bedight** arrayed.   122 **For thy** therefore.   124 **despight** outrage.   127 **despightfull wise** spiteful manner.   131 **dreriment** sorrow.   134 **teene** sorrow.   136 **liefe** dear.   140 **wayment** lament.   144 **voluntarie** self-willed.

To see faire heavens face, and life not leave,
Sith that false Traytour did my honour reave?°
False traytour certes (said the Faerie knight)   150
I read° the man, that ever would deceave
A gentle Ladie, or her wrong through might:
Death were too little paine for such a foule despight.

18

But now, faire Ladie, comfort to you make,
And read,° who hath ye wrought this shamefull
plight,
That short° revenge the man may overtake,   155
Where so he be, and soone upon him light.
Certes (said she) I wote not how he hight,
But under him a gray steede did he wield,°
Whose sides with dapled circles weren dight;   160
Upright he rode, and in his silver shield
He bore a bloudie Crosse, that quartred all the field.°

19

Now by my head (said *Guyon*) much I muse,°
How that same knight should do so foule amis,
Or ever gentle Damzell so abuse: 165
For may I boldly say, he surely is
A right good knight, and true of word ywis:°
I present was, and can it witnesse well,
When armes he swore,° and streight did enter-
pris°
Th'adventure of the *Errant damozell*,°   170
In which he hath great glorie wonne, as I heare tell.

20

Nathlesse he shortly shall againe be tryde,
And fairely quite him° of th'imputed blame,

149 reave take away. 151 read consider. 155 read tell. 156 short
speedy. 159 wield control. 162 quartred all the field divided the
shield into quarters. 163 muse wonder. 167 ywis I know. 169
When armes he swore i.e., "taking on him knighthood" (*Letter to
Raleigh*). 169 enterpris take in hand. 170 the Errant damozell
Una. 173 fairely quite him fully prove himself innocent.

Else be ye sure he dearely shall abyde,°
Or make you good amendment for the same:
All wrongs have mends, but no amends of
   shame.
Now therefore Ladie, rise out of your paine,
And see the salving° of your blotted° name.
Full loth she seemd thereto, but yet did faine;
For she was inly glad her purpose so to gaine.

21

Her purpose was not such, as she did faine,
Ne yet her person such, as it was seene,
But under simple shew and semblant° plaine
Lurckt false *Duessa* secretly unseene,
As a chast Virgin, that had wronged beene:
So had false *Archimago* her disguisd,
To cloke her guile with sorrow and sad teene;
And eke himselfe had craftily devisd
To be her Squire, and do her service well aguisd.°

22

Her late forlorne and naked he had found,
Where she did wander in waste wildernesse,
Lurking in rockes and caves farre under ground,
And with greene mosse cov'ring her nakednesse,
To hide her shame and loathly filthinesse;
Sith her Prince *Arthur* of proud ornaments
And borrow'd beautie spoyld.° Her nathelesse
Th'enchaunter finding fit for his intents,
Did thus revest,° and deckt with due habiliments.°

23

For all he did, was to deceive good knights,
And draw them from pursuit of praise and fame,
To slug° in slouth and sensuall delights,
And end their daies with irrenowmed° shame.

174 **abyde** abye, pay the penalty. 178 **salving** clearing up. 178
blotted disgraced. 183 **semblant** outward appearance. 189 **aguisd**
arrayed. 196 **spoyld** despoiled. 198 **revest** dress again. 178 **due**
habiliments proper attire. 201 **slug** live idly. 202 **irrenowmed** un-
renowned.

And now exceeding griefe him overcame,
To see the *Redcrosse* thus advaunced hye;°
Therefore this craftie engine° he did frame,   205
Against his praise to stirre up enmitye
Of such, as vertues like mote unto him allye.°

24

So now he *Guyon* guides an uncouth way
    Through woods and mountaines, till they came
        at last
    Into a pleasant dale, that lowly lay   210
    Betwixt two hils, whose high heads overplast,
    The valley did with coole shade overcast;
    Through midst thereof a little river rold,
    By which there sate a knight with helme° unlast,
    Himselfe refreshing with the liquid cold,   215
After his travell long, and labours manifold.

25

Loe yonder he, cryde *Archimage* alowd,
    That wrought the shamefull fact,° which I did
        shew;
    And now he doth himselfe in secret shrowd,
    To flie the vengeance for his outrage dew;   220
    But vaine: for ye shall dearely do him rew,°
    So God ye speed, and send you good successe;
    Which we farre off will here abide to vew.
    So they him left, inflam'd with wrathfulnesse,
That streight against that knight his speare he did ad-
        dresse.°   225

26

Who seeing him from farre so fierce to pricke,°
    His warlike armes about him gan embrace,°
    And in the rest° his readie speare did sticke;

---

204 **advaunced hye** highly extolled.   205 **engine** trick.   207 **as . . .
allye** being like virtuous might ally themselves with him.   214 **helme**
helmet.   218 **fact** evil deed.   221 **do him rew** make him repent.
225 **addresse** aim.   226 **pricke** spur.   227 **gan embrace** put on.
228 **rest** a support for the butt-end of the spear.

Tho° when as still he saw him towards pace,°
230   He gan rencounter° him in equall race.°
They bene ymet, both readie to affrap,°
When suddenly that warriour gan abace°
His threatned° speare, as if some new mishap
Had him betidde,° or hidden daunger did entrap.

27

235   And cryde, Mercie Sir knight, and mercie Lord,
For mine offence and heedlesse hardiment,°
That had almost committed crime abhord,
And with reprochfull shame mine honour shent,°
Whiles cursed steele against that badge I bent,
240   The sacred badge of my Redeemers death,
Which on your shield is set for ornament:
But his fierce foe his steede could stay uneath,°
Who prickt with courage kene, did cruell battell
    breath.

28

But when he heard him speake, streight way he knew
245   His error, and himselfe inclyning sayd;
Ah deare Sir *Guyon,* well becommeth you,
But me behoveth rather to upbrayd,°
Whose hastie hand so farre from reason strayd,
That almost it did haynous violence
250   On that faire image of that heavenly Mayd,°
That decks and armes your shield with faire de-
    fence:
Your court'sie takes on you anothers due offence.°

29

So bene they both attone,° and doen upreare°

229 **Tho** then.   229 **him towards pace** come toward him.   230 **rencounter** encounter.   230 **race** rapid riding.   231 **They . . . affrap**
They met, both ready to strike.   232 **abace** lower.   233 **threatned**
threatening.   234 **betidde** happened.   236 **hardiment** boldness.
238 **shent** disgraced.   242 **uneath** with difficulty.   247 **But . . . upbrayd** But it is fitting rather for me to be reproached.   250 **that
heavenly Mayd** the Faery Queen.   252 **Your . . . offence** In your
courtesy you take upon yourself blame that belongs to another   253
attone reconciled.   253 **doen upreare** raise up.

Their bevers° bright, each other for to greete;
    Goodly comportance° each to other beare,   255
    And entertaine themselves with court'sies meet.
    Then said the *Redcrosse* knight, Now mote I
        weet,°
    Sir *Guyon,* why with so fierce saliaunce,°
    And fell intent ye did at earst me meet;
    For sith I know your goodly governaunce,°   260
Great cause, I weene, you guided, or some uncouth
        chaunce.

30

Certes (said he) well mote I shame to tell
    The fond encheason,° that me hither led.
    A false infamous faitour° late befell
    Me for to meet, that seemed ill bested,°   265
    And playnd° of grievous outrage, which he red°
    A knight had wrought against a Ladie gent;
    Which to avenge, he to this place me led,
    Where you he made the marke of his intent,
And now is fled; foule shame him follow, where he
        went.   270

31

So can° he turne his earnest° unto game,
    Through goodly handling and wise temperance.
    By this his aged guide in presence came;
    Who soone as on that knight his eye did glance,
    Eft soones of him had perfect cognizance,   275
    Sith him in Faerie court he late avizd;°
    And said, Faire sonne, God give you happie°
        chance,
    And that deare Crosse upon your shield devizd,°
Wherewith above all knights ye goodly seeme aguizd.°

---

254 **bevers** face guards. 255 **comportance** bearing. 257 **mote I
weet** may I know. 258 **saliaunce** sally, rush. 260 **goodly govern-
aunce** wise self-control. 263 **fond encheason** foolish occasion.
264 **faitour** impostor. 265 **ill bested** in a bad fix. 266 **playnd** complained. 266 **red** said. 271 **can** did. 271 **earnest** seriousness.
276 **avizd** saw. 277 **happie** fortunate. 278 **devizd** marked. 279
aguizd arrayed.

32

280 Joy may you have, and everlasting fame,
Of late most hard atchiev'ment by you donne,
For which enrolled is your glorious name
In heavenly Registers above the Sunne,
Where you a Saint with Saints your seat have
wonne:
285 But wretched we, where ye have left your marke,
Must now anew begin, like race to runne;
God guide thee, *Guyon,* well to end thy warke,
And to the wished haven bring thy weary barke.

33

Palmer, (him answered the *Redcrosse* knight)
290 His be the praise, that this atchiev'ment wrought,
Who made my hand the organ of his might;
More then goodwill to me attribute nought:
For all I did, I did but as I ought.
But you, faire Sir, whose pageant° next ensewes,
Well mote yee thee,° as well can wish your
295 thought,°
That home ye may report thrise happie newes;
For well ye worthie bene for worth and gentle
thewes.°

34

So courteous conge° both did give and take,
With right hands plighted, pledges of good will.
300 Then *Guyon* forward gan his voyage make,
With his blacke Palmer, that him guided still.
Still he him guided over dale and hill,
And with his steedie staffe did point his way:
His race° with reason, and with words his will,
305 From foule intemperance he oft did stay,
And suffred not in wrath his hastie steps to stray.

After leaving the Red Cross Knight, Guyon determines

294 **pageant** adventure.   295 **thee** thrive.   295 **as . . . thought** as
well as your thought can wish.   297 **thewes** discipline.   298 **conge**
farewell.   304 **race** course of life.

*to avenge a bloody-handed babe whose parents have been
slain through the enchantments of a wicked temptress,
Acrasia. In succeeding episodes he demonstrates the
capacities and limitations of the virtue of Temperance by
subduing, though not destroying, the intemperate foes,
Pyrochles and Cymochles. At the midpoint of his journey,
he confronts his greatest temptation in the figure of
Mammon. He has been deprived of the Palmer's guidance
by yielding to the immodest mirth of the Lady Phaedria
in her Idle Lake.*

CANTO VII

*Guyon findes Mammon in a delve,°
    Sunning his treasure hore.°
Is by him tempted, and led downe,
    To see his secret store.*

1

As Pilot well expert in perilous wave,
        That to a stedfast starre his course hath bent,
        When foggy mistes, or cloudy tempests have
        The faithfull light of that faire lampe yblent,°
        And cover'd heaven with hideous dreriment,°   5
        Upon his card° and compas firmes° his eye,
        The maisters of his long experiment,°
        And to them does the steddy helme apply,
Bidding his winged vessell fairely forward fly.

2

So *Guyon* having lost his trusty guide,   10
        Late left beyond that *Ydle lake,* proceedes
        Yet on his way, of none accompanide;
        And evermore himselfe with comfort feedes,

Arg. **delve** cave.   Arg. **hore** hoar, mouldy; perhaps, old.   4 **yblent**
obscured.   5 **dreriment** darkness.   6. **card** map.   6 **firmes** fixes.
7 **experiment** experience.

15   Of his owne vertues, and prayse-worthy deedes.
       So long he yode,° yet no adventure found,
       Which fame of her shrill trompet worthy reedes:°
       For still he traveild through wide wastfull°
         ground,
That nought but desert wildernesse shew'd all around.

       3
At last he came unto a gloomy glade,
       Cover'd with boughes and shrubs from heavens
20   light,
       Whereas he sitting found in secret shade
       An uncouth, salvage,° and uncivile wight,
       Of griesly hew, and fowle ill favour'd sight;°
       His face with smoke was tand, and eyes were
         bleard,
25   His head and beard with sout were ill bedight,
       His cole-blacke hands did seeme to have beene
         seard
In smithes fire-spitting forge, and nayles like clawes
         appeard.

       4
His yron coate all overgrowne with rust,
       Was underneath enveloped with gold,
30   Whose glistring glosse darkned with filthy dust,
       Well it appeared, to have beene of old
       A worke of rich entayle,° and curious° mould,
       Woven with antickes° and wild Imagery:
       And in his lap a masse of coyne he told,°
35   And turned upsidowne, to feede his eye
And covetous desire with his huge threasury.

       5
And round about him lay on every side
       Great heapes of gold, that never could be spent:

15 **yode** went. 16 **reedes** declares. 17 **wastfull** desolate. 22 **sal-vage** savage. 23 **sight** appearance. 32 **entayle** carving. 32 **curi-ous** elaborate. 33 **antickes** fantastic representations. 34 **told** counted.

Of which some were rude owre, not purifide
Of *Mulcibers* devouring element;°   *40*
Some others were new driven,° and distent°
Into great Ingoes,° and to wedges square;
Some in round plates withouten moniment;°
But most were stampt, and in their metall bare
The antique shapes of kings and kesars° straunge and
    rare.   *45*

6

Soone as he *Guyon* saw, in great affright
    And hast he rose, for to remove aside
    Those pretious hils from straungers envious sight,
    And downe them poured through an hole full
      wide,
    Into the hollow earth, them there to hide.   *50*
    But *Guyon* lightly to him leaping, stayd
    His hand, that trembled, as one terrifyde;
    And though him selfe were at the sight dismayd,
Yet him perforce° restraynd, and to him doubtfull°
    sayd.

7

What art thou man, (if man at all thou art)   *55*
    That here in desert hast thine habitaunce,°
    And these rich heapes of wealth doest hide
      apart
    From the worldes eye, and from her right
      usaunce?°
    Thereat° with staring eyes fixed askaunce,°
    In great disdaine, he answerd; Hardy Elfe,°   *60*
    That darest vew my direfull countenaunce,
    I read° thee rash, and heedlesse of thy selfe,

---

40 **Mulcibers . . . element** fire, as belonging to Vulcan by Mulciber, the god of fire. 41 **driven** beaten out. 41 **distent** extended. 42 **Ingoes** ingots. 43 **moniment** inscription. 45 **kesars** kaisers. 54 **perforce** forcibly. 54 **to him doubtfull** i.e., to the fearful Mammon. 56 **habitaunce** habitation. 58 **right usuance** proper use. 59 **Thereat** because of that. 59 **askaunce** sideways. 60 **Elfe** knight. 62 **read** consider.

To trouble my still seate, and heapes of pretious
  pelfe.

8

God of the world and worldlings I me call,
65 Great *Mammon,* greatest god below the skye,
  That of my plenty poure out unto all,
  And unto none my graces do envye:°
  Riches, renowme, and principality,
  Honour, estate, and all this worldes good,
70 For which men swinck° and sweat incessantly,
  Fro me do flow into an ample flood,
And in the hollow earth have their eternall brood.°

9

Wherefore if me thou deigne to serve and sew,°
  At thy commaund lo all these mountaines bee;
75 Or if to thy great mind, or greedy° vew
  All these may not suffise, there shall to thee
  Ten times so much be numbred° francke and
    free.
  Mammon (said he) thy godheades vaunt° is
    vaine,
  And idle offers of thy golden fee;°
80 To them, that covet such eye-glutting gaine,
Proffer° thy giftes, and fitter servaunts entertaine.°

10

Me ill besits, that in der-doing armes,°
  And honours suit° my vowed dayes do spend,°
  Unto thy bounteous baytes,° and pleasing
    charmes,
  With which weake men thou witchest,° to at-
85   tend:

67 **envye** begrudge. 70 **swinck** labor. 72 **brood** breeding place.
73 **sew** follow. 75 **greedy** eager. 77 **numbred** counted out. 78
godheades vaunt boast of godhead. 79 **fee** bribes. 81 **Proffer** offer. 81 **entertaine** receive. 82 **Me . . . armes** It ill suits me who in
arms doing daring deeds. 83 **suit** pursuit. 83 **my . . . spend** have
vowed to spend my days. 84 **bounteous baytes** baits of bounty. 85
witchest bewitch.

Regard of worldly mucke doth fowly blend,°
And low abase the high heroicke spright,°
That joyes for crownes and kingdomes to con-
    tend;
Faire shields, gay steedes, bright armes be my
    delight:
Those be the riches fit for an advent'rous knight.   90

11

Vaine glorious° Elfe (said he) doest not thou weet,°
    That money can thy wantes at will supply?
    Sheilds, steeds, and armes, and all things for thee
        meet
    It can purvay° in twinckling of an eye;
    And crownes and kingdomes to thee multiply.   95
    Do not I kings create, and throw the crowne
    Sometimes to him, that low in dust doth ly?
    And him that raignd, into his rowme° thrust
        downe,
And whom I lust,° do heape with glory and renowne?

12

All otherwise (said he) I riches read,   100
    And deeme them roote of all disquietnesse;
    First got with guile, and then preserv'd with
        dread,
    And after spent with pride and lavishnesse,
    Leaving behind them griefe and heavinesse.
    Infinite mischiefes of them do arize,   105
    Strife, and debate, bloudshed, and bitternesse,
    Outrageous wrong, and hellish covetize,°
That noble heart as great dishonour doth despize.

13

Ne thine be kingdomes, ne° the scepters thine;

86 **blend** pollute.   87 **spright** spirit.   91 **Vaine glorious** vain glorious.   91 **weet** know.   94 **purvay** provide.   98 **rowme** place.   99
lust desire.   107 **covetize** covetousness.   109 **Ne . . . ne** neither . . .
nor.

But realmes and rulers thou doest both con-
110   found,°
And loyall truth to treason doest incline;
Witnesse the guiltlesse bloud pourd oft on
            ground,
The crowned often slaine, the slayer cround,
The sacred Diademe in peeces rent,
115   And purple robe gored with many a wound;
Castles surprizd, great cities sackt and brent:°
So mak'st thou kings, and gaynest wrongfull governe-
            ment.

            14

Long were to tell the troublous° stormes, that tosse
The private state, and make the life unsweet:
120 Who° swelling sayles in Caspian sea doth crosse,
And in frayle wood in *Adrian°* gulfe doth fleet,°
Doth not, I weene, so many evils meet.
Then *Mammon* wexing wroth, And why then,
            said,
Are mortall men so fond° and undiscreet,
125   So evill thing to seeke unto their ayd,
And having not complaine, and having it upbraid?°

            15

Indeede (quoth he) through fowle intemperaunce,
Frayle men are oft captiv'd to covetise:
But would they thinke, with how small allow-
            aunce
130   Untroubled Nature doth her selfe suffise,
Such superfluities they would despise,
Which with sad cares empeach° our native°
            joyes:
At the well head the purest streames arise:
But mucky filth his braunching armes annoyes,
135 And with uncomely weedes the gentle wave accloyes.°

---

110 **confound** defeat. 116 **brent** burned. 118 **troublous** troublesome. 120 **Who** who with. 121 **Adrian** Adriatic. 121 **fleet** float.
124 **fond** foolish. 126 **upbraid** to be reproached. 132 **empeach**
hinder. 132 **native** natural. 135 **accloyes** clogs.

16

The antique° world, in his first flowring youth,
    Found no defect in his Creatours grace,
    But with glad thankes, and unreproved° truth,
    The gifts of soveraigne bountie did embrace:
    Like Angels life was then mens happy cace;°   *140*
    But later ages pride, like corn-fed steed,
    Abusd her plenty, and fat swolne encreace
    To all licentious lust, and gan exceed
The measure of her meane,° and naturall first need.

17

Then gan a cursed hand the quiet wombe   *145*
    Of his great Grandmother with steele to wound,
    And the hid treasures in her sacred tombe,
    With Sacriledge to dig. Therein he found
    Fountaines of gold and silver to abound,
    Of which the matter of his huge desire   *150*
    And pompous pride eftsoones he did compound;
    Then avarice gan through his veines inspire
His greedy flames, and kindled life-devouring fire.

18

Sonne (said he then) let be° thy bitter scorne,
    And leave the rudenesse of that antique age   *155*
    To them, that liv'd therein in state forlorne;
    Thou that doest live in later times, must wage°
    Thy workes for wealth, and life for gold engage.
    If then thee list my offred grace to use,
    Take what thou please of all this surplusage;°   *160*
    If thee list not, leave have thou to refuse:
But thing refused, do not afterward accuse.

19

Me list not (said the Elfin knight) receave
    Thing offred, till I know it well be got,

---

136 **antique** ancient.   138 **unreproved** without reproof, blameless.
140 **cace** state.   144 **measure of her meane** the limits of her moderation.   154 **let be** cease.   157 **wage** pledge.   160 **surplusage** excess.

165   Ne wote I, but° thou didst these goods bereave
         From rightfull owner by unrighteous lot,°
         Or that bloud guiltnesse or guile them blot.
         Perdy° (quoth he) yet never eye did vew,
         Ne toung did tell, ne hand these handled not,
170   But safe I have them kept in secret mew,°
    From heavens sight, and powre of all which them
              pursew.

              20
    What secret place (quoth he) can safely hold
         So huge a masse, and hide from heavens eye?
         Or where hast thou thy wonne,° that so much
              gold
175   Thou canst preserve from wrong and robbery?
         Come thou (quoth he) and see. So by and by°
         Through that thicke covert he him led, and
              found
         A darkesome way, which no man could descry,°
         That deepe descended through the hollow
              ground,
180 And was with dread and horrour compassed around.

              21
    At length they came into a larger space,
         That stretcht it selfe into an ample plaine,
         Through which a beaten broad high way did
              trace,
         That streight did lead to *Plutoes* griesly raine:°
185   By that wayes side, there sate infernall Payne,
         And fast beside him sat tumultuous Strife:
         The one in hand an yron whip did straine,°
         The other brandished a bloudy knife,
    And both did gnash their teeth, and both did threaten
         life.

---

165 **Ne . . . but** I do not know but that.   166 **lot** chance.   168 **Perdy**
assuredly.   170 **mew** den.   174 **wonne** dwelling.   176 **by and by**
immediately.   178 **descry** espy.   184 **Plutoes griesly raine** the grim
kingdom of Pluto, god of the infernal regions.   187 **straine** wield.

22

On thother side in one consort° there sate,   *190*
   Cruell Revenge, and rancorous Despight,
   Disloyall Treason, and hart-burning Hate,
   But gnawing Gealosie out of their sight
   Sitting alone, his bitter lips did bight,
   And trembling Feare still to and fro did fly,   *195*
   And found no place, where safe he shroud him
      might,
   Lamenting Sorrow did in darknesse lye,
And Shame his ugly face did hide from living eye.

23

And over them sad horrour with grim hew,°
   Did alwayes sore, beating his yron° wings;   *200*
   And after him Owles and Night-ravens flew,
   The hatefull messengers of heavy things,
   Of death and dolour° telling sad tidings;
   Whiles sad *Celeno,*° sitting on a clift,
   A song of bale° and bitter sorrow sings,   *205*
   That hart of flint a sunder could have rift:°
Which having ended, after him she flyeth swift.

24

All these before the gates of *Pluto* lay,
   By whom they passing, spake unto them nought.
   But th'Elfin knight with wonder all the way   *210*
   Did feed his eyes, and fild his inner thought.
   At last him to a litle dore he brought,
   That to the gate of Hell, which gaped wide,
   Was next adjoyning, ne them parted ought:°
   Betwixt them both was but a litle stride,   *215*
That did the house of Richesse from hell-mouth di-
      vide.

25

Before the dore sat selfe-consuming Care,

190 **consort** fellowship.   199 **hew** countenance.   200 **yron** strong.
203 **dolour** grief.   204 **Celeno** a Harpy.   205 **bale** woe.   206 **rift**
rent.   214 **ne . . . ought** nothing separated them.

Day and night keeping wary watch and ward,°
For feare least Force or Fraud should unaware
220   Breake in, and spoile the treasure there in gard:°
Ne would he suffer Sleepe once thither-ward
Approch, albe° his drowsie den were next;
For next to death is Sleepe to be compard:
Therefore his house is unto his annext;
Here Sleep, there Richesse, and Hel-gate them both
225   betwext.

26

So soone as *Mammon* there arriv'd, the dore
To him did open, and affoorded way;
Him followed eke Sir *Guyon* evermore,
Ne darkenesse him, ne daunger might dismay.
230   Soone as he entred was, the dore streight way
Did shut, and from behind it forth there lept
An ugly feend, more fowle then dismall day,°
The which with monstrous stalke behind him
         stept,
And ever as he went, dew° watch upon him kept.

27

235 Well hoped he, ere long that hardy guest,
If ever covetous hand, or lustfull eye,
Or lips he layd on thing, that likt him best,°
Or ever sleepe his eye-strings did untye,
Should be his pray. And therefore still on hye
240   He over him did hold his cruell clawes,
Threatning with greedy gripe to do him dye°
And rend in peeces with his ravenous pawes,
If ever he transgrest the fatall *Stygian* lawes.°

28

That houses forme within was rude and strong,

218 **watch and ward** lookout.   220 **in gard** under guard.   222 **albe**
although.   232 **dismall day** day of doom or death.   234 **dew** proper.
237 **that . . . best** that best he liked.   241 **do him dye** make him die.
243 **Stygian lawes** the laws of the infernal kingdom.

Like an huge cave, hewne out of rocky clift,°   245
From whose rough vaut° the ragged breaches°
     hong,
Embost with massy gold of glorious gift,°
And with rich metall loaded every rift,
That heavy ruine they did seeme to threat;
And over them *Arachne*° high did lift   250
Her cunning web, and spred her subtile° net,
Enwrapped in fowle smoke and clouds more blacke
     then Jet.

29

Both roofe, and floore, and wals were all of gold,
     But overgrowne with dust and old decay,
     And hid in darkenesse, that none could behold   255
The hew thereof: for vew of chearefull day
Did never in that house it selfe display,
But a faint shadow of uncertain light;
Such as a lamp, whose life does fade away:
Or as the Moone cloathed with clowdy night,   260
Does shew to him, that walkes in feare and sad
     affright.

30

In all that rowme was nothing to be seene,
     But huge great yron chests and coffers strong,
     All bard with double bends,° that none could
          weene
Them to efforce° by violence or wrong;   265
On every side they placed were along.
But all the ground with sculs was scattered,
And dead mens bones, which round about were
     flong,°
Whose lives, it seemed, whilome there were shed,
And their vile carcases now left unburied.   270

---

245 **clift** cliff.   246 **vaut** vault.   246 **breaches** fissures.   247 **Embost
. . . gift** Covered with solid gold of brilliant quality.   250 **Arachne**
the spider.   251 **subtile** delicate.   264 **bends** bands.   265 **efforce**
force open.   268 **flong** flung.

31

They forward passe, ne *Guyon* yet spoke word,
  Till that they came unto an yron dore,
  Which to them opened of his owne accord,
  And shewd of richesse such exceeding store,
275 As eye of man did never see before;
  Ne ever could within one place be found,
  Though all the wealth, which is, or was of yore,
  Could gathered be through all the world around,
And that above were added to that under ground.

32

280 The charge thereof unto a covetous Spright
  Commaunded was,° who thereby did attend,
  And warily awaited day and night,
  From other covetous feends it to defend,
  Who it to rob and ransacke did intend.
285 Then *Mammon* turning to that warriour, said;
  Loe here the worldes blis, loe here the end,
  To which all men do ayme, rich to be made:
Such grace now to be happy, is before thee laid.

33

Certes (sayd he) I n'ill° thine offred grace,
290 Ne to be made so happy° do intend:
  Another blis before mine eyes I place,
  Another happinesse, another end.
  To them, that list, these base regardes° I lend:
  But I in armes, and in atchievements brave,
295 Do rather choose my flitting° houres to spend,
  And to be Lord of those, that riches have,
Then them to have my selfe, and be their servile
    sclave.°

34

Thereat the feend his gnashing teeth did grate,

---

281 **Commaunded was** was enjoined.   289 **n'ill** will not have.   290
happy blessed.   293 **regardes** considerations.   295 **flitting** fleeting.
297 **sclave** slave.

And griev'd, so long to lacke his greedy pray;°
For well he weened, that so glorious bayte   *300*
Would tempt his guest, to take thereof assay:°
Had he so doen, he had him snatcht away,
More light then Culver° in the Faulcons fist.
Eternall God thee save from such decay.°
But whenas *Mammon* saw his purpose mist,   *305*
Him to entrap unwares another way he wist.°

35

Thence forward he him led, and shortly brought
    Unto another rowme, whose dore forthright,
    To him did open, as it had beene taught:
    Therein an hundred raunges weren pight,°   *310*
    And hundred fornaces all burning bright;
    By every fornace many feends did bide,
    Deformed creatures, horrible in sight,
    And every feend his busie paines applide,
To melt the golden metall, ready to be tride.°   *315*

36

One with great bellowes gathered filling aire,
    And with forst wind the fewell did inflame;
    Another did the dying bronds° repaire
    With yron toungs,° and sprinckled oft the same
    With liquid waves, fiers *Vulcans* rage to tame, *320*
    Who maistring° them, renewd his former heat;
    Some scumd the drosse, that from the metall came;
    Some stird the molten owre with ladles great;
And every one did swincke, and every one did sweat.

37

But when an earthly wight they present saw,   *325*
    Glistring in armes and battailous° aray,

---

299 **his greedy pray** the prey which he eagerly desires.   301 **assay** trial.   303 **Culver** dove.   304 **decay** ruin.   306 **wist** knew.   310 **pight** placed.   315 **tride** purified.   318 **the dying bronds** embers. 319 **toungs** tongs.   321 **maistring** subduing.   326 **battailous** warlike.

From their whot worke they did themselves with-
draw
To wonder at the sight; for till that day,
They never creature saw, that came that way.
Their staring eyes sparckling with fervent° fire,
And ugly shapes did nigh the man dismay,
That were it not for shame, he would retire,
Till that him thus bespake their soveraigne Lord and
sire.

38

Behold, thou Faeries sonne, with mortall eye,
That living eye before did never see:
The thing, that thou didst crave so earnestly,
To weet, whence all the wealth late shewd by
mee,
Proceeded, lo now is reveald to thee.
Here is the fountaine° of the worldes good:
Now therefore, if thou wilt enriched bee,
Avise thee° well, and chaunge thy wilfull mood,
Least thou perhaps hereafter wish, and be withstood.

39

Suffise it then, thou Money God (quoth hee)
That all thine idle° offers I refuse.
All that I need I have; what needeth mee
To covet more, then I have cause to use?
With such vaine shewes thy worldlings vile abuse:
But give me leave to follow mine emprise.°
Mammon was much displeasd, yet no'te he
chuse,°
But beare the rigour° of his bold mesprise,°
And thence him forward led, him further to entise.

40

He brought him through a darksome° narrow strait,
To a broad gate, all built of beaten gold:

330 **fervent** hot.   339 **fountaine** source.   341 **Avise thee** consider.
344 **idle** vain.   348 **emprise** enterprise.   349 **no'te he chuse** he
could not choose.   350 **rigour** harshness.   350 **mesprise** misprision,
scorn.   352 **darksome** dark.

The gate was open, but therein did wait
    A sturdy villein, striding stiffe and bold,   355
    As if that highest God defie he would;
    In his right hand an yron club he held,
    But he himselfe was all of golden mould,
    Yet had both life and sence, and well could weld
That cursed weapon, when his cruell foes he queld.°   360

41

Disdayne he called was, and did disdaine
    To be so cald, and who so did him call:
    Sterne was his looke, and full of stomacke° vaine,
    His portaunce° terrible, and stature tall,
    Far passing th'hight of men terrestriall;   365
    Like an huge Gyant of the *Titans* race,
    That made him scorne all creatures great and small,
    And with his pride all others powre deface:
More fit amongst blacke fiendes, then men to have his place.

42

Soone as those glitterand° armes he did espye,   370
    That with their brightnesse made that darknesse light,
    His harmefull club he gan to hurtle° hye,
    And threaten batteill to the Faery knight;
    Who likewise gan himselfe to batteill dight,°
    Till *Mammon* did his hasty hand withhold,   375
    And counseld him abstaine from perilous fight:
    For nothing might abash° the villein bold,
Ne mortall steele emperce° his miscreated° mould.

43

So having him with reason pacifide,
    And the fiers Carle° commaunding to forbeare,   380

360 **when ... queld** when cruelly he subdued his foes.   363 **stomacke**
haughtiness.   364 **portaunce** bearing.   370 **glitterand** shining.   372
hurtle brandish.   374 **dight** prepare.   377 **abash** disconcert.   378
emperce pierce through.   378 **miscreated** unnaturally created, being
made of gold.   280 **Carle** churl.

He brought him in. The rowme was large and
    wide,
As it some Gyeld° or solemne Temple weare:
Many great golden pillours did upbeare
The massy° roofe, and riches huge sustayne,
385 And every pillour decked was full deare°
With crownes and Diademes, and titles vaine,
Which mortall Princes wore, whiles they on earth did
    rayne.

44

A route° of people there assembled were,
    Of every sort and nation under skye,
390 Which with great uprore preaced° to draw nere
To th'upper part, where was advaunced hye
A stately siege° of soveraigne majestye;
And thereon sat a woman gorgeous gay,
And richly clad in robes of royaltye,
395 That never earthly Prince in such aray
His glory did enhaunce, and pompous pride display.

45

Her face right wondrous faire did seeme to bee,
    That her broad beauties beam great brightnes
      threw
Through the dim shade, that all men might it see:
400 Yet was not that same her owne native hew,
But wrought by art and counterfetted shew,
Thereby more lovers unto her to call;
Nath'lesse most heavenly faire in deed and vew
She by creation was, till she did fall;
Thenceforth she sought for helps, to cloke her crime
405   withall.°

46

There, as in glistring glory she did sit,
She held a great gold chaine ylincked well,

---

382 **Gyeld** guild hall.   384 **massy** massive.   385 **deare** costly.   388
route crowd.   390 **preaced** pressed.   392 **siege** throne.   405 **withall**
as well.

Whose upper end to highest heaven was knit,
And lower part did reach to lowest Hell;
And all that preace° did round about her swell,   410
To catchen hold of that long chaine, thereby
To clime aloft, and others to excell:
That was *Ambition,* rash desire to sty,°
And every lincke thereof a step of dignity.

47

Some thought to raise themselves to high degree,   415
By riches and unrighteous reward,
Some by close shouldring, some by flatteree;
Others through friends, others for base regard;°
And all by wrong wayes for themselves prepard.
Those that were up themselves, kept others low,   420
Those that were low themselves, held others
hard,
Ne suffred them to rise or greater grow,
But every one did strive his fellow downe to throw.

48

Which whenas *Guyon* saw, he gan inquire,
What meant that preace about that Ladies
throne,   425
And what she was that did so high aspire.
Him *Mammon* answered; That goodly one,
Whom all that folke with such contention,
Do flocke about, my deare, my daughter is;
Honour and dignitie from her alone   430
Derived are, and all this worldes blis
For which ye men doe strive: few get, but many mis.

49

And faire *Philotime*° she rightly hight.
The fairest wight that wonneth° under skye,
But that this darksome neather world her light   435
Doth dim with horrour and deformitie,

Worthy of heaven and hye felicitie,
From whence the gods have her for envy thrust:
But sith thou hast found favour in mine eye,
440   Thy spouse I will her make, if that thou lust,°
That she may thee advance for workes and merites
    just.

50

Gramercy° *Mammon* (said the gentle knight)
For so great grace and offred high estate;
But I, that am fraile flesh and earthly wight,
445   Unworthy match for such immortall mate
My selfe well wote, and mine unequall fate;
And were I not, yet is my trouth yplight,°
And love avowd to other Lady late,
That to remove the same I have no might:
To chaunge love causelesse is reproch to warlike
450   knight.

51

Mammon emmoved° was with inward wrath;
Yet forcing it to faine, him forth thence led,
Through griesly° shadowes by a beaten path,
Into a gardin goodly garnished
With hearbs and fruits, whose kinds mote not be
455   red:°
Not such, as earth out of her fruitfull woomb
Throwes forth to men, sweet and well savoured,
But direfull deadly blacke both leafe and bloom,
Fit to adorne the dead, and decke the drery toombe.

52

460 There mournfull *Cypresse*° grew in greatest store,
And trees of bitter *Gall,*° and *Heben*° sad,

440 **lust** desire.   442 **Gramercy** thanks.   447 **trouth yplight** troth
pledged.   451 **emmoved** moved.   453 **griesly** horrible.   455 **red** declared.   460 **mournfull Cypresse** cf. "the Cypresse funerall" (I.i.8).
461 **bitter Gall** the oak that produces bitter excrescences.   461
Heben ebony.

Dead sleeping *Poppy,* and black *Hellebore,*
Cold *Coloquintida,*° and *Tetra* mad,°
Mortall *Samnitis,* and *Cicuta*° bad,
With which th'unjust *Atheniens* made to dy   465
Wise *Socrates,* who thereof quaffing glad
Pourd out his life, and last Philosophy
To the faire *Critias*° his dearest Belamy.°

53

The *Gardin* of *Proserpina* this hight;°
And in the midst thereof a silver seat,   470
With a thicke Arber goodly over dight,°
In which she often usd from open heat
Her selfe to shroud, and pleasures to entreat.°
Next thereunto did grow a goodly tree,
With braunches broad dispred° and body great,   475
Clothed with leaves, that none the wood mote see
And loaden all with fruit as thicke as it might bee.

54

Their fruit were golden apples glistring bright,
That goodly was their glory to behold,
On earth like never grew, ne living wight   480
Like ever saw, but they from hence were sold;°
For those,° which *Hercules* with conquest bold
Got from great *Atlas* daughters, hence began,
And planted there, did bring forth fruit of gold:
And those with which th'*Eubœan* young man°
wan   485
Swift *Atalanta,* when through craft he her out ran.

55

Here also sprong that goodly golden fruit,
 With which *Acontius*° got his lover trew,
 Whom he had long time sought with fruitlesse
  suit:
490 Here eke that famous golden Apple° grew
 The which emongst the gods false *Ate* threw;
 For which th'*Idæan* Ladies disagreed,
 Till partiall° *Paris* dempt° it *Venus* dew,
495 And had of her, faire *Helen* for his meed,
That many noble *Greekes* and *Trojans* made to bleed.

56

The warlike Elfe much wondred at this tree,
 So faire and great, that shadowed all the ground,
 And his broad braunches, laden with rich fee,°
 Did stretch themselves without° the utmost
  bound
500 Of this great gardin, compast° with a mound,
 Which over-hanging, they themselves did steepe,
 In a blacke flood which flow'd about it round;
 That is the river of *Cocytus*° deepe,
In which full many soules do endlesse waile and
 weepe.

57

505 Which to behold, he clomb up to the banke,
 And looking downe, saw many damned wights,
 In those sad waves, which direfull deadly stanke,
 Plonged continually of° cruell Sprights,
 That with their pitteous cryes, and yelling
  shrights,°

488 **Acontius** the lover of Cydippe tricked her into repeating a vow
written on the rind of golden fruit that she would marry him.   490
that famous Golden Apple the apple of discord inscribed "To the
fairest," for the right to which Venus, Minerva, and Juno quarreled.
Paris was appointed judge to resolve their quarrel. On Mount Ida he
awarded the apple to Venus. By gaining Helena from the Greeks as
his reward, he provoked the Trojan War.   493 **partiall** biased.   493
dempt deemed.   498 **fee** reward.   499 **without** beyond.   500 **com-
past** encircled.   503 **Cocytus** a river in hell.   508 **of** by.   509
shrights shrieks.

They made the further shore resounden wide:°   510
Emongst the rest of those same ruefull sights,
One cursed creature he by chaunce espide,
That drenched lay full deepe, under the Garden side.

58

Deepe was he drenched to the upmost chin,
Yet gaped still, as coveting to drinke
Of the cold liquor, which he waded in,   515
And stretching forth his hand, did often thinke
To reach the fruit, which grew upon the brincke:
But both the fruit from hand, and floud from
        mouth
Did flie abacke, and made him vainely swinke: 520
The whiles he sterv'd° with hunger and with
        drouth°
He daily dyde, yet never throughly dyen couth.°

59

The knight him seeing labour so in vaine,
Askt who he was, and what he ment thereby:°
Who groning deepe, thus answerd him againe;°   525
Most cursed of all creatures under skye,
Lo _Tantalus,_ I here tormented lye:
Of whom high _Jove_ wont whylome feasted bee,°
Lo here I now for want of food doe dye:
But if that thou be such, as I thee see,   530
Of grace° I pray thee, give to eat and drinke to mee.

60

Nay, nay, thou greedie _Tantalus_ (quoth he)
Abide the fortune of thy present fate,
And unto all that live in high degree,
Ensample° be of mind intemperate,   535

---

510 **wide** over a wide area.   521 **sterv'd** died.   521 **drouth** drought,
thirst.   522 **yet . . . couth** yet never could die thoroughly.   524 **ment
thereby** signified by that action.   525 **againe** in reply.   528 **Of . . .
bee** With whom high Jove at one time used to feast. (Tantalus is
being punished for inviting the gods to a banquet of his son's flesh.)
531 **grace** favor.   535 **Ensample** example.

To teach them how to use their present state.
Then gan the cursed wretch aloud to cry,
Accusing highest *Jove* and gods ingrate,°
And eke blaspheming heaven bitterly,
540 As authour of unjustice,° there to let him dye.

61

He lookt a little further, and espyde
    Another wretch, whose carkasse deepe was
      drent°
    Within the river, which the same did hyde:
    But both his hands most filthy feculent,°
545   Above the water were on high extent,°
    And faynd° to wash themselves incessantly;
    Yet nothing cleaner were for such intent,
    But rather fowler seemed to the eye;
So lost his labour vaine and idle industry.

62

550 The knight him calling, asked who he was,
    Who lifting up his head, him answerd thus:
    I *Pilate* am the falsest Judge, alas,
    And most unjust, that by unrighteous
    And wicked doome,° to Jewes despiteous°
555   Delivered up the Lord of life to die,
    And did acquite a murdrer felonous;°
    The whiles my hands I washt in puritie,°
The whiles my soule was soyld with foule iniquitie.

63

Infinite moe,° tormented in like paine
560   He there beheld, too long here to be told:°
    Ne *Mammon* would there let him long remaine,
    For terrour of the tortures manifold,
    In which the damned soules he did behold,
    But roughly him bespake. Thou fearefull foole,

538 ingrate not grateful. **540 unjustice** unjustness. **542 drent**
544 feculent covered with filth. **545 extent** extended. **546 faynd**
desired. **554 doome** judgment. **554 despiteous** merciless. **556
felonous** wicked. **557 in puritie** to purify from blame. **559 moe**
more. **560 told** counted.

Why takest not of that same fruit of gold,   565
    Ne sittest downe on that same silver stoole,
To rest thy wearie person, in the shadow coole.

64

All which he did, to doe° him deadly fall
    In frayle intemperance through sinfull bayt;
    To which if he inclined had at all,   570
    That dreadfull feend, which did behind him
        wayt,
    Would him have rent in thousand peeces strayt:°
    But he was warie wise in all his way,
    And well perceived his deceiptfull sleight,
    Ne suffred lust his safetie to betray;   575
So goodly did beguile the Guyler° of the pray.

65

And now he has so long remained there,
    That vitall powres gan wexe both weake and
        wan,
    For want of food, and sleepe, which two
        upbeare,
    Like mightie pillours, this fraile life of man,   580
    That none without the same enduren can.
    For now three dayes of men were full out-
        wrought,°
    Since he this hardie enterprize began:
    For thy° great *Mammon* fairely° he besought,
Into the world to guide him backe, as he him brought. 585

66

The God, though loth, yet was constraind° t'obay,
    For lenger time, then that, no living wight
    Below the earth, might suffred be to stay:
    So backe againe, him brought to living light.
    But all so soone as his enfeebled spright°   590
    Gan sucke this vitall aire into his brest,

568 **doe** cause.   572 **strayt** straightway.   576 **Guyler** beguiler.   582
full outwrought fully passed.   584 **For thy** therefore.   584 **fairely**
gently.   586 **constraind** obliged.   590 **spright** spirit.

As overcome with too exceeding might,
The life did flit away out of her nest,
And all his senses were with deadly fit opprest.

CANTO VIII

Sir Guyon laid in swowne is by
*   Acrates sonnes despoyld,*
Whom Arthur soone hath reskewed
*   And Paynim brethren foyld.*

1

And is there care in heaven? and is there love
    In heavenly spirits to these creatures bace,
    That may compassion of their evils move?
    There is: else much more wretched were the
        cace
Of men, then beasts. But O th'exceeding grace
    Of highest God, that loves his creatures so,
    And all his workes with mercy doth embrace,
    That blessed Angels, he sends to and fro,
To serve to wicked man, to serve his wicked foe.

2

How oft do they, their silver bowers leave,
    To come to succour us, that succour want?
    How oft do they with golden pineons, cleave
    The flitting° skyes, like flying Pursuivant,°
    Against foule feends to aide us millitant?°
    They for us fight, they watch and dewly ward,°
    And their bright Squadrons round about us plant,
    And all for love, and nothing for reward:
O why should heavenly God to men have such regard?

13 **flitting** yielding.   13 **Pursuivant** royal messenger.   14 **millitant**
by engaging in warfare.   15 **dewly ward** properly guard.

3

During the while, that *Guyon* did abide
   In *Mammons* house, the Palmer, whom
     whyleare°   20
   That wanton Mayd° of passage had denide,
   By further search had passage found elsewhere,
   And being on his way, approched neare,
   Where *Guyon* lay in traunce, when suddenly
   He heard a voice, that called loud and cleare,   25
   Come hither, come hither, O come hastily;
That all the fields resounded with the ruefull cry.

4

The Palmer lent his eare unto the noyce,
   To weet,° who called so importunely:°
   Againe he heard a more efforced° voyce,   30
   That bad him come in haste. He by and by°
   His feeble feet directed to the cry;
   Which to that shadie delve° him brought at last,
   Where *Mammon* earst° did sunne his threasury:°
   There the good *Guyon* he found slumbring fast   35
In senselesse° dreame; which sight at first him sore
     aghast.

5

Beside his head there sate a faire young man,
   Of wondrous beautie, and of freshest yeares,
   Whose tender bud to blossome new began,
   And flourish faire above his equall peares;°   40
   His snowy front curled with golden heares,
   Like *Phœbus* face adornd with sunny rayes,
   Divinely shone, and two sharpe winged sheares,°
   Decked with diverse plumes, like painted Jayes,°
Were fixed at his backe, to cut his ayerie° wayes.   45

---

20 **whyleare** erewhile, some time ago. 21 **That wanton Mayd** Phaedria of the Idle Lake, as related in Canto VI. 29 **weet** learn. 29
importunely urgently. 30 **more efforced** uttered with more effort.
31 **by and by** immediately. 33 **delve** cave. 34 **earst** earlier. 34
threasury treasures. 36 **senselesse** unconscious. 40 **equal peares**
companions of the same age. 43 **sheares** wings. 44 **painted Jayes**
the jay's brightly colored feathers. 45 **ayerie** airy.

6

Like as *Cupido* on *Idæan* hill,°
    When having laid his cruell bow away,
    And mortall arrowes, wherewith he doth fill
    The world with murdrous spoiles and bloudie
        pray,
50   With his faire mother he him dights° to play,
    And with his goodly sisters, *Graces* three;°
    The Goddesse pleased with his wanton play,
    Suffers her selfe through sleepe beguild to bee,
The whiles° the other Ladies mind their merry glee.

7

55 Whom when the Palmer saw, abasht he was
    Through feare and wonder, that he nought could
        say,
    Till him the child bespoke, Long lackt, alas,
    Hath bene thy faithfull aide in hard assay,
    Whiles deadly fit thy pupill doth dismay;°
60   Behold this heavie sight, thou reverend Sire,
    But dread of death and dolour doe away;
    For life ere long shall to her home retire,
And he that breathlesse seemes, shal corage bold
    respire.°

8

The charge, which God doth unto me arret,°
65   Of his deare safetie, I to thee commend;°
    Yet will I not forgoe, ne yet forget
    The care thereof my selfe unto the end,
    But evermore him succour, and defend
    Against his foe and mine: watch thou I pray;
70   For evill is at hand him to offend.°
    So having said, eftsoones he gan display°
His painted nimble wings, and vanisht quite away.

---

46 **Cupido . . . hill** Cupid on Mount Ida.   50 **him dights** prepares
himself.   51 **Graces three** see VI.x.15.   54 **The whiles** meanwhile.
59 **dismay** defeat.   63 **corage bold respire** again breathe brave spirit.
64 **arret** entrust.   65 **commend** commit.   70 **offend** harm.   71 **display** spread out.

9

The Palmer seeing his left empty place,
　　And his slow eyes beguiled of their sight,
　　Woxe sore affraid, and standing still a space, 　　　75
　　Gaz'd after him, as fowle escapt by flight;
　　At last him turning to his charge behight,°
　　With trembling hand his troubled pulse gan try;
　　Where finding life not yet dislodged quight,
　　He much rejoyst, and courd it° tenderly, 　　　80
As chicken newly hatcht, from dreaded destiny.

10

At last he spide, where towards him did pace
　　Two Paynim° knights, all armd as bright as skie,
　　And them beside an aged Sire° did trace,°
　　And farre before a light-foot Page° did flie, 　　　85
　　That breathed strife and troublous enmitie;
　　Those were the two sonnes of *Acrates* old,
　　Who meeting earst with *Archimago* slie,
　　Foreby that idle strond,° of him were told,
That he, which earst them combatted, was *Guyon*
　　　bold. 　　　90

11

Which to avenge on him they dearely vowd,
　　Where ever that on ground° they mote him fynd;
　　False *Archimage* provokt their courage prowd,
　　And stryfull° *Atin* in their stubborne mynd
　　Coles of contention and whot vengeance tynd.° 　　　95
　　Now bene° they come, whereas the Palmer sate,
　　Keeping that slombred corse to him assynd;
　　Well knew they both his person, sith of late
With him in bloudie armes they rashly did debate.°

12

Whom when *Pyrochles* saw, inflam'd with rage, 　　　100

77 **his charge behight** the charge entrusted to him.　80 **courd it** bent
over the knight's body.　83 **Paynim** pagan.　84 **an aged Sire** Archimago.　84 **trace** walk.　85 **Page** Atin.　89 **Foreby ... strond** close
by the shore of the Idle Lake.　92 **ground** earth.　94 **stryfull** strife-
ful.　95 **tynd** kindled.　96 **bene** are.　99 **debate** fight.

That sire he foule bespake, Thou dotard vile,
That with thy brutenesse° shendst° thy comely
    age,
Abandone soone, I read,° the caitive° spoile
Of that same outcast carkasse, that erewhile
105   Made it selfe famous through false trechery,
And crownd his coward crest° with knightly
    stile;°
Loe where he now inglorious doth lye,
To prove he lived ill, that did thus foully dye.

13

To whom the Palmer fearelesse answered;
110   Certes, Sir knight, ye bene too much to blame,
Thus for to blot° the honour of the dead,
And with foule cowardize his carkasse shame,
Whose living hands immortalizd his name.
Vile is the vengeance on the ashes cold,
115   And envie base, to barke at sleeping fame:°
Was never° wight, that treason of him told;
Your selfe his prowesse prov'd and found him fiers
    and bold.

14

Then said *Cymochles;* Palmer, thou doest dote,
Ne canst of prowesse, ne of knighthood deeme,°
120   Save as thou seest or hearst. But well I wote,
That of his puissance tryall made extreeme;
Yet gold all is not, that doth golden seeme,
Ne all good knights, that shake° well speare and
    shield:
The worth of all men by their end esteeme,
125   And then due praise, or due reproch them yield;
Bad therefore I him deeme, that thus lies dead on
    field.

---

102 **brutenesse** brutishness, stupidity. 102 **shendst** disgrace. 103 **read** advise. 103 **caitive** captive. 106 **crest** a device worn on the helmet. 106 **stile** title. 111 **blot** blemish. 115 **sleeping fame** the fame of a knight who is sleeping. 116 **Was never** There was never. 119 **deeme** judge. 123 **shake** brandish.

15

Good or bad (gan his brother fierce reply)
    What doe I recke, sith that he dyde entire?°
    Or what doth his bad death now satisfy
    The greedy hunger of revenging ire,   130
    Sith wrathfull hand wrought not her owne desire?
    Yet since no way is left to wreake my spight,
    I will him reave° of armes, the victors hire,°
    And of that shield, more worthy of good knight;
For why should a dead dog be deckt in armour
    bright?   135

16

Faire Sir, said then the Palmer suppliaunt,°
    For knighthoods love, do not so foule a deed,
    Ne blame° your honour with so shamefull vaunt
    Of vile revenge. To spoile° the dead of weed
    Is sacrilege, and doth all sinnes exceed;   140
    But leave these relicks of his living might,°
    To decke his herce, and trap his tomb-blacke
        steed.°
    What herce or steed (said he) should he have
        dight,°
But be entombed in the raven or the kight?°

17

With that, rude hand upon his shield he laid,   145
    And th'other brother gan his helme unlace,
    Both fiercely bent to have him disaraid;
    Till that they spide, where towards them did
        pace
    An armed knight, of bold and bounteous grace,
    Whose squire bore after him an heben° launce,   150

128 **dyde entire** (1) died rather than being killed; or (2) died in perfect state, without being wounded.   133 **reave** despoil.   133 **hire** reward.   136 **suppliaunt** supplicating.   138 **blame** bring blame upon.   139 **spoile** despoil.   141 **living might** his strength while he was alive.   142 **trap . . . steed** adorn the black trappings for the horse that carries his body to the tomb.   143 **should . . . dight** should be dressed for him.   144 **kight** kite.   150 **heben** ebony.

And coverd shield. Well kend him so farre
        space°
Th'enchaunter by his armes and amenaunce,°
When under him he saw his Lybian steed° to praunce.

18

And to those brethren said, Rise rise by live,°
155   And unto battell doe your selves addresse;
        For yonder comes the prowest° knight alive,
        Prince *Arthur,* flowre of grace and nobilesse,°
        That hath to Paynim knights wrought great dis-
        tresse,
        And thousand Sar'zins° foully donne° to dye.
160   That word so deepe did in their harts impresse,
        That both eftsoones upstarted furiously,
And gan themselves prepare to battell greedily.

19

But fierce *Pyrochles,* lacking his owne sword,
        The want thereof now greatly gan to plaine,°
165   And *Archimage* besought, him that afford,°
        Which he had brought for *Braggadocchio* vaine.
        So would I (said th'enchaunter) glad and faine°
        Beteeme° to you this sword, you to defend,
        Or ought that else your honour might maintaine.
170   But that this weapons powre I well have kend,°
To be contrarie to the worke, which ye intend.

20

For that same knights owne sword this is of yore,
        Which *Merlin* made° by his almightie art
        For that his noursling, when he knighthood
        swore,°

151 **kend . . . space** knew him at such a distance.   152 **amenaunce**
bearing.   153 **Lybian steed** Arabian horse.   154 **by live** immediately.   156 **prowest** bravest.   157 **nobilesse** nobility.   159 **Sar'zins**
Saracens.   159 **donne** caused.   164 **plaine** complain.   165 **him that
afford** to give him that sword.   167 **faine** eager.   168 **Beteeme**
grant.   170 **kend** learned.   173 **Which Merlin made** See I.vii.36.
174 **when . . . swore** took the oath of knighthood.

Therewith to doen his foes eternall smart. 175
The metall first he mixt with *Medæwart,*°
That no enchauntment from his dint° might
 save;
Then it in flames of *Aetna* wrought apart,°
And seven times dipped in the bitter wave
Of hellish *Styx,* which hidden vertue° to it gave. 180

21

The vertue is, that neither steele, nor stone
 The stroke thereof from entrance may defend;
 Ne ever may be used by his fone,°
 Ne forst his rightfull owner to offend,°
 Ne ever will it breake, ne ever bend. 185
 Wherefore *Morddure*° it rightfully is hight.
 In vaine therefore, *Pyrochles,* should I lend
 The same to thee, against his lord to fight,
For sure it would deceive thy labour, and thy might.

22

Foolish old man, said then the Pagan wroth, 190
 That weenest words or charmes may force with-
  stond:
 Soone shalt thou see, and then beleeve for troth,
 That I can carve with this inchaunted brond°
 His Lords owne flesh. Therewith out of his hond
 That vertuous° steele he rudely snatcht away, 195
 And *Guyons* shield about his wrest he bond;°
 So readie dight, fierce battaile to assay,
And match his brother proud in battailous array.

23

By this that straunger knight in presence came,
 And goodly salved° them; who nought againe 200
 Him answered, as courtesie became,°

---

176 **Medæwart** meadwort on meadow-sweet. 177 **dint** blow. 178
apart separately. 180 **vertue** power. 183 **fone** foes. 184 **offend**
injure. 186 **Morddure** hard biter. 193 **brond** sword. 195 **vertuous** powerful. 196 **bond** bound. 200 **goodly salved** courteously
saluted. 201 **as courtesie became** as befitting courtesy.

But with sterne lookes, and stomachous° dis-
    daine,
Gave signes of grudge° and discontentment vaine:
Then turning to the Palmer, he gan spy
Where at his feete, with sorrowfull demaine°
And deadly hew, an armed corse did lye,
In whose dead face he red° great magnanimity.

24

Said he then to the Palmer, Reverend syre,
    What great misfortune hath betidd° this knight?
Or° did his life her fatall date° expyre,
Or did he fall by treason, or by fight?
How ever, sure I rew° his pitteous plight.
Not one, nor other, (said the Palmer grave)
Hath him befalne, but cloudes of deadly night
A while his heavie eylids cover'd have,
And all his senses drowned in deepe senselesse wave.

25

Which, those his cruell foes, that stand hereby,
    Making advantage, to revenge their spight,
Would him disarme, and treaten shamefully,
Unworthy usage of redoubted knight.
But you, faire Sir, whose honorable sight°
Doth promise hope of helpe, and timely grace,
Mote I beseech to succour his sad plight,
And by your powre protect his feeble cace.°
First praise of knighthood is, foule outrage to de-
    face.°

26

Palmer, (said he) no knight so rude, I weene,
    As to doen outrage to a sleeping ghost:°
Ne was there ever noble courage seene,

---

202 **stomachous** resentful. 203 **grudge** ill-will. 205 **demaine** demeanor. 207 **red** perceived. 209 **betidd** befallen. 210 **Or** whether
he. 210 **fatefall date** term of life ordained by destiny. 212 **rew**
pity. 221 **whose honorable sight** the sight of one who is honorable.
224 **cace** condition. 225 **deface** destroy. 227 **ghost** spirit.

That in advauntage would his puissance bost:
Honour is least, where oddes appeareth most.° 230
May be, that better reason will asswage
The rash revengers heat. Words well dispost°
Have secret powre, t'appease inflamed rage:
If not, leave unto me thy knights last patronage.°

27

Tho° turning to those brethren, thus bespoke, 235
Ye warlike payre, whose valorous great might
It seemes, just wrongs to vengeance doe pro-
voke,
To wreake your wrath on this dead seeming
knight,
Mote ought allay the storme of your despight,°
And settle patience in so furious heat? 240
Not to debate the chalenge° of your right,
But for this carkasse pardon I entreat,
Whom fortune hath alreadie laid in lowest seat.

28

To whom *Cymochles* said; For what art thou,
That mak'st thy selfe his dayes-man,° to prolong 245
The vengeance prest?° Or who shall let° me now,
On this vile bodie from to wreake° my wrong,
And make his carkasse as the outcast dong?
Why should not that dead carrion satisfie
The guilt, which if he lived had thus long, 250
His life for due revenge should deare abie?°
The trespasse still doth live, albe° the person die.

29

Indeed (then said the Prince) the evill donne
Dyes not, when breath the bodie first doth leave,
But from the grandsyre to the Nephewes° sonne, 255

<hr>

230 **most** most in one's favor. 232 **dispost** arranged. 234 **patronage** defense. 235 **Tho** then. 239 **despight** anger. 241 **debate the
chalenge** contest the claim. 245 **dayes-man** arbitrator. 246 **prest**
at hand. 246 **let** hinder. 247 **from to wreake** from wreaking. 251
abie pay. 252 **albe** although. 255 **Nephewes** grandson's.

And all his seed the curse doth often cleave,°
Till vengeance utterly the guilt bereave:
So streightly° God doth judge. But gentle knight,
That doth against the dead his hand upreare°
260 His honour staines with rancour and despight,
And great disparagment makes to his former might.

30

Pyrochles gan reply the second time,
And to him said, Now felon sure I read,°
How that° thou art partaker of his crime:
265 Therefore by *Termagaunt*° thou shalt be dead.
With that his hand, more sad° then lomp of lead,
Uplifting high, he weened with *Morddure,*
His owne good sword *Morddure,* to cleave his
head.
The faithfull steele such treason no'uld° endure,
But swarving from the marke, his Lords life did as-
270 sure.

31

Yet was the force so furious and so fell,°
That horse and man it made to reele aside;
Nath'lesse the Prince would not forsake his sell.°
For well of yore he learned had to ride,
275 But full of anger fiercely to him cride;
False traitour miscreant,° thou broken hast
The law of armes, to strike foe undefide.°
But thou thy treasons fruit, I hope, shalt taste
Right sowre, and feele the law, the which thou hast
defast.°

32

280 With that his balefull° speare he fiercely bent

256 **cleave** stick fast. 258 **streightly** strictly. 259 **upreare** raise.
263 **read** call. 264 **How** that because. 265 **Termagaunt** a god sup-
posedly worshiped by Saracens. 266 **sad** heavy. 269 **no'uld** would
not. 271 **fell** fierce. 273 **forsake his sell** leave his saddle. 276
miscreant wretch. 277 **undefide** who has not been challenged to
combat. 279 **defast** broken. 280 **balefull** harmful.

Against the Pagans brest, and therewith thought
His cursed life out of her lodge have rent:°
But ere the point arrived, where it ought,
That seven-fold shield, which he from *Guyon*
    brought
He cast betwene to ward the bitter stound:°   285
Through all those foldes the steelehead passage
    wrought
And through his shoulder pierst; wherwith to
    ground
He groveling fell, all gored in his gushing wound.

33

Which when his brother saw, fraught with great griefe
    And wrath, he to him leaped furiously,   290
    And fowly said, By *Mahoune,*° cursed thiefe,
    That direfull stroke thou dearely shalt aby.°
    Then hurling up his harmefull blade on hye,
    Smote him so hugely on his haughtie crest,
    That from his saddle forced him to fly: 295
    Else mote it needes downe to his manly brest
Have cleft his head in twaine, and life thence dispos-
    sest.

34

Now was the Prince in daungerous distresse,
    Wanting his sword, when he on foot should
        fight:°
    His single speare° could doe him small redresse,   300
    Against two foes of so exceeding might,
    The least of which was match for any knight.
    And now the other, whom he earst did daunt,
    Had reard himselfe againe to cruell fight,
    Three times more furious, and more puissant,   305
Unmindfull of his wound, of his fate ignoraunt.

---

282 **have rent** to have torn.   285 **stound** attack.   291 **Mahoune** Mu-
hammead.   292 **aby** pay for.   299 **fight** the knight uses his spear on
horseback, and his sword on foot.   300 **single speare** speare alone.

35

So both attonce° him charge on either side,
    With hideous strokes, and importable° powre,
    That forced him his ground to traverse wide,°
310   And wisely watch to ward that deadly stowre:°
    For in° his shield, as thicke as stormie showre,
    Their strokes did raine, yet did he never quaile,
    Ne backward shrinke, but as a stedfast towre,
    Whom foe with double battry doth assaile,
Them on her bulwarke beares, and bids them nought
315   availe.

36

So stoutly he withstood their strong assay,°
    Till that at last, when he advantage spyde,
    His poinant° speare he thrust with puissant
       sway°
    At proud *Cymochles,* whiles his shield was
       wyde,°
    That through his thigh the mortall steele did
320   gryde:°
    He swarving with the force, within his flesh
    Did breake the launce, and let the head abyde:
    Out of the wound the red blood flowed fresh,
That underneath his feet soone made a purple plesh.°

37

325 Horribly then he gan to rage, and rayle,
    Cursing his Gods, and himselfe damning deepe:
    Als° when his brother saw the red bloud rayle°
    Adowne so fast, and all his armour steepe,
    For very felnesse° lowd he gan to weepe,
330   And said, Caytive, cursse on thy cruell hond,
    That twise hath sped;° yet shall it not thee keepe
    From the third brunt of this my fatall brond:

307 **attonce** at once.   308 **importable** unendurable.   309 **traverse
wide** dodge repeatedly.   310 **stowre** encounter.   311 **in** on.   316
assay assault.   318 **poinant** piercing.   318 **sway** force.   319 **wyde**
turned away.   320 **gryde** pierce.   324 **plesh** pool.   327 **Als** also.
327 **rayle** flow.   329 **felnesse** fury.   331 **sped** succeeded.

Loe where the dreadfull Death behind thy backe doth
　　　stond.

　　　38

With that he strooke,° and th'other strooke withall,°
　　　That nothing seem'd mote beare so monstrous
　　　　　might: 335
　　　The one° upon his covered shield did fall,
　　　And glauncing downe would not his owner byte:
　　　But th'other did upon his troncheon° smyte,
　　　Which hewing quite a sunder, further way
　　　It made, and on his hacqueton° did lyte,   340
　　　The which dividing with importune° sway,
It seizd° in his right side, and there the dint° did stay.

　　　39

Wyde was the wound, and a large lukewarme flood,
　　　Red as the Rose, thence gushed grievously;
　　　That when the Paynim spyde the streaming
　　　　　blood,
　　　Gave him great hart, and hope of victory.   345
　　　On th'other side, in huge perplexity,
　　　The Prince now stood, having his weapon broke;
　　　Nought could he hurt, but still at ward did ly:
　　　Yet with his troncheon he so rudely stroke   350
Cymochles twise, that twise him forst his foot re-
　　　voke.°

　　　40

Whom when the Palmer saw in such distresse,
　　　Sir Guyons sword he lightly to him raught,°
　　　And said; Faire Son, great God thy right hand
　　　　blesse,
　　　To use that sword so wisely as it° ought.   355

334 **strooke** struck.   334 **withall** as well, that is, at the same time.
336 **The one** Morddure.   338 **his troncheon** the shaft of his spear.
340 **hacqueton** a jacket plated with mail.   341 **importune** heavy.
342 **seizd** fixed.   342 **dint** blow.   351 **revoke** withdraw.   353 **lightly
... raught** quickly handed to him.   355 **it** the right hand.

Glad was the knight, and with fresh courage
    fraught,
When as againe he armed felt his hond;
Then like a Lion, which hath long time saught
His robbed° whelpes, and at the last them fond
Emongst the shepheard swaynes, then wexeth wood
360   and yond.°

41

So fierce he laid about him, and dealt blowes
    On either side, that neither mayle could hold,
Ne shield defend the thunder of his throwes:°
Now to *Pyrochles* many strokes he told;°
365 Eft° to *Cymochles* twise so many fold:°
Then backe againe turning his busie hond,
Them both attonce compeld with courage bold,
To yield wide way to his hart-thrilling brond;°
And though they both stood stiffe, yet could not both
    withstond.

42

370 As salvage Bull, whom two fierce mastives bayt,
    When rancour doth with rage him once engore,°
Forgets with warie ward them to awayt,
But with his dreadfull hornes them drives afore,
Or flings aloft, or treads downe in the flore,
375 Breathing out wrath, and bellowing disdaine,
That all the forrest quakes to heare him rore:
So rag'd Prince *Arthur* twixt his foemen twaine,
That neither could his mightie puissance sustaine.

43

But ever at *Pyrochles* when he smit,
380   Who *Guyons* shield cast ever him before,
Whereon the Faery Queenes pourtract was writ,°
His hand relented, and the stroke forbore,

359 **robbed** stolen.   360 **wexeth . . . yond** grows mad and fierce.
363 **throwes** thrusts.   364 **told** counted.   365 **Eft** afterward.   365
twise . . . fold twice as many.   368 **hart-thrilling brond** heart-pierc-
ing sword.   371 **engore** goad.   381 **pourtract was writ** picture was
painted.

And his deare hart the picture gan adore,
Which oft the Paynim sav'd from deadly stowre.°
But him henceforth the same can save no more;   385
For now arrived is his fatall howre,
That no'te° avoyded be by earthly skill or powre.

44

For when *Cymochles* saw the fowle reproch,
Which them appeached,° prickt with guilty shame,
And inward griefe, he fiercely gan approch,   390
Resolv'd to put away that loathly blame,
Or dye with honour and desert of fame;
And on the hauberk° stroke the Prince so sore,
That quite disparted° all the linked frame,°
And pierced to the skin, but bit no more,   395
Yet made him twise to reele, that never moov'd afore.

45

Whereat renfierst° with wrath and sharpe regret,
He stroke so hugely° with his borrowd blade,
That it empierst the Pagans burganet,°
And cleaving the hard steele, did deepe invade   400
Into his head, and cruell passage made
Quite through his braine. He tombling downe on
    ground,
Breathd out his ghost, which to th'infernall
    shade°
Fast flying, there eternall torment found,
For all the sinnes, wherewith his lewd life did
    abound.   405

46

Which when his german° saw, the stony feare
Ran to his hart, and all his sence dismayd,
Ne thenceforth life ne courage did appeare,
But as a man, whom hellish feends have frayd,°

384 **stowre** peril.   387 **no'te** might not.   389 **appeached** disparaged.
393 **hauberk** coat of mail.   394 **disparted** parted asunder.   394
linked frame chain mail.   397 **renfierst** strengthened.   398 **hugely**
violently.   399 **burganet** helmet.   403 **shade** darkness.   406 **german**
a full brother.   409 **frayd** frightened.

410 Long trembling still he stood: at last thus sayd;
     Traytour what hast thou doen? how ever may°
     Thy cursed hand so cruelly have swayd°
     Against that knight: Harrow and well away,°
After so wicked deed why liv'st thou lenger day?°

     47
415 With that all desperate as loathing light,
     And with revenge desiring soone to dye,
     Assembling all his force and utmost might,
     With his owne° sword he fierce at him did flye,
     And strooke, and foynd,° and lasht outrageously,
420 Withouten reason or regard. Well knew
     The Prince, with patience and sufferaunce sly°
     So hasty heat soone cooled to subdew:
Tho when this° breathlesse woxe, that° batteil gan
     renew.

     48
As when a windy tempest bloweth hye,
425 That nothing may withstand his stormy stowre,°
     The cloudes, as things affrayd, before him flye;
     But all so soone as his outrageous powre
     Is layd,° they fiercely then begin to shoure,
     And as in scorne of his spent stormy spight,
430 Now all attonce their malice forth do poure;
     So did Prince *Arthur* beare himselfe in fight,
And suffred rash *Pyrochles* wast his idle might.

     49
At last when as the Sarazin perceiv'd,
     How that straunge° sword refusd, to serve his
          need,
435 But when he stroke most strong, the dint
          deceiv'd,°

---

411 **how ever may** how could. 412 **swayd** wielded. 413 **Harrow**
. . . **away** a cry of distress. 414 **day** life. 418 **his owne** Arthur's.
419 **foynd** thrust. 421 **sly** wise. 423 **this** Pyrochles. 423 **that** Arthur. 425 **stowre** tumult. 428 **layd** subsided. 434 **straunge** borrowed. 435 **the dint deceiv'd** the blow failed him.

He flong it from him, and devoyd of dreed,°
Upon him lightly leaping without heed,
Twixt his two mighty armes engrasped fast,
Thinking to overthrow and downe him tred:
But him in strength and skill the Prince surpast,   440
And through his nimble sleight° did under him down
    cast.

50

Nought booted it° the Paynim then to strive;
    For as a Bittur° in the Eagles claw,
    That may not hope by flight to scape alive,
    Still waites for death with dread and trembling
        aw;°   445
    So he now subject to the victours law,
    Did not once move, nor upward cast his eye,
    For vile disdaine and rancour, which did gnaw
    His hart in twaine with sad melancholy,
As one that loathed life, and yet despisd to dye.   450

51

But full of Princely bounty° and great mind,°
    The Conquerour nought cared him to slay,
    But casting wrongs and all revenge behind,
    More glory thought to give life, then decay,°
    And said, Paynim, this is thy dismall day;°   455
    Yet if thou wilt renounce thy miscreaunce,°
    And my trew liegeman yield thy selfe for ay,°
    Life will I graunt thee for thy valiaunce,
And all thy wrongs will wipe out of my sovenaunce.°

52

Foole (said the Pagan) I thy gift defye,   460
    But use thy fortune, as it doth befall,
    And say, that I not overcome do dye,
    But in despight of life, for death do call.

436 **devoyd of dreed** without fear.   441 **sleight** skill.   442 **Nought
booted it** nothing availed.   443 **Bittur** bittern.   445 **aw** terror.   451
bounty goodness.   451 **great mind** magnanimity.   454 **decay** death.
455 **dismall day** day of death.   456 **miscreance** false faith.   457 **ay**
ever.   459 **sovenaunce** memory.

Wroth was the Prince, and sory yet withall,
465   That he so wilfully refused grace;
Yet sith his fate so cruelly did fall,
His shining Helmet he gan soone unlace,
And left his headlesse body bleeding all the place.

53

By this Sir *Guyon* from his traunce awakt,
470   Life having maistered her sencelesse foe;°
And looking up, when as his shield he lakt,°
And sword saw not, he wexed wondrous woe:°
But when the Palmer, whom he long ygoe
Had lost, he by him spide, right glad he grew,
475   And said, Deare sir, whom wandring to and fro
I long have lackt, I joy thy face to vew;
Firme is thy faith, whom daunger never fro° me drew.

54

But read° what wicked hand hath robbed mee
Of my good sword and shield? The Palmer glad,
480   With so fresh hew uprising him to see,
Him answered; Faire sonne, be no whit sad
For want of weapons, they shall soone be had.
So gan he to discourse the whole debate,°
Which that straunge knight for him sustained
    had,
485   And those two Sarazins confounded late,
Whose carcases on ground were horribly prostrate.

55

Which when he heard, and saw the tokens trew,
His hart with great affection was embayd,°
And to the Prince bowing with reverence dew,
490   As to the Patrone of his life, thus sayd;
My Lord, my liege, by whose most gratious ayd
I live this day, and see my foes subdewd,

---

470 **her sencelesse foe** the swoon, the enemy that made him sense-
less. 471 **lakt** wanted. 472 **wexed . . . woe** grew wonderfully sad.
477 **fro** from. 478 **read** tell me. 483 **discourse . . . debate** tell him
the whole battle. 488 **embayd** suffused.

What may suffise, to be for meede repayd
    Of so great graces, as ye have me shewd,
But to be ever bound

495

56

To whom the Infant° thus, Faire Sir, what need
    Good turnes be counted, as a servile bond,
    To bind their doers, to receive their meede?
    Are not all knights by oath bound, to withstond
    Oppressours powre by armes and puissant hond?   500
    Suffise, that I have done my dew in place.°
    So goodly purpose° they together fond,°
    Of kindnesse and of curteous aggrace;°
The whiles false *Archimage* and *Atin* fled apace.°

CANTO IX

*The house of Temperance, in which
    doth sober Alma dwell,
Besiegd of many foes, whom straunger
    knightes to flight compell.*

1

Of all Gods workes, which do this world adorne,
    There is no one more faire and excellent,
    Then is mans body both for powre and forme,
    Whiles it is kept in sober government;
    But none then it, more fowle and indecent,°   5
    Distempred° through misrule and passions
        bace:°
    It growes a Monster, and incontinent°
    Doth loose his dignitie and native grace.
Behold, who list, both one° and other° in this place.

496 **Infant** Prince.   501 **my . . . place** my duty here.   502 **purpose**
conversation.   502 **fond** devised.   503 **aggrace** favor.   504 **apace**
quickly.

5 **indecent** unseemly.   6 **Distempred** disordered.   6 **bace** lowe.   7
incontinent immediately.   9 **one** the House of Alma.   9 **other**
Maleger, described in Canto XI.

2

10 After the Paynim brethren conquer'd were,
      The *Briton* Prince recov'ring his stolne sword,
      And *Guyon* his lost shield, they both yfere°
      Forth passed on their way in faire accord,
      Till him the Prince with gentle court did bord;°
15   Sir knight, mote I of you this curt'sie read,°
      To weet° why on your shield so goodly scord
      Beare ye the picture of that Ladies head?
Full lively° is the semblaunt,° though the substance
      dead.

3

Faire Sir (sayd he) if in that picture dead
20   Such life ye read,° and vertue° in vaine shew,
      What mote ye weene, if the trew lively-head°
      Of that most glorious visage ye did vew?
      But if the beautie of her mind ye knew,
      That is her bountie, and imperiall powre,
25   Thousand times fairer then her mortall hew,°
      O how great wonder would your thoughts
      devoure,
And infinite desire into your spirite poure!

4

She is the mighty Queene of *Faerie,*
      Whose faire retrait° I in my shield do beare;
30   She is the flowre of grace and chastitie,
      Throughout the world renowmed° far and neare,
      My liefe,° my liege, my Soveraigne, my deare,
      Whose glory shineth as the morning starre,
      And with her light the earth enlumines° cleare;
35   Far reach her mercies, and her prayses farre,
As well in state of peace, as puissaunce° in warre.

12 **yfere** together.   14 **with ... bord** accosted with courteous address.   15 **mote ... read** may I ask this courtesy of your.   16 **weet** know.   18 **lively** lifelike.   18 **semblaunt** resemblance.   20 **read** perceive.   20 **vertue** natural power.   21 **What ... head** What would you think if the true living form.   25 **hew** shape.   29 **retrait** portrait.   31 **renowmed** renowned.   32 **liefe** love.   34 **enlumines** illuminates.   36 **puissaunce** power.

5

Thrise happy man, (said then the *Briton* knight)
    Whom gracious lot, and thy great valiaunce
    Have made thee souldier of that Princesse bright,
    Which with her bounty and glad countenance   40
    Doth blesse her servaunts, and them high
        advaunce.
    How may straunge knight hope ever to aspire,
    By faithfull service, and meete amenance,°
    Unto such blisse? sufficient were that hire°
For losse of thousand lives, to dye at her desire.   45

6

Said *Guyon,* Noble Lord, what meed so great,
    Or grace of earthly Prince so soveraine,
    But by your wondrous worth and warlike feat
    Ye well may hope, and easely attaine?
    But were your will, her sold to entertaine,°   50
    And numbred be mongst knights of *Maydenhed,*
    Great guerdon, well I wote, should you° remaine,
    And in her favour high be reckoned,
As *Arthegall,*° and *Sophy*° now beene honored.

7

Certes (then said the Prince) I God avow,   55
    That sith I armes and knighthood first did plight,
    My whole desire hath beene, and yet is now,
    To serve that Queene with all my powre and
        might.
    Now hath the Sunne with his lamp-burning light,
    Walkt° round about the world, and I no lesse,°   60
    Sith of that Goddesse I have sought the sight,
    Yet no where can her find: such happinesse
Heaven doth to me envy,° and fortune favourlesse.°

43 **meete amenance** fitting conduct. 44 **hire** reward. 50 **her . . .
entertaine** to receive her pay, and so become her servant. 52 **you** to
you. 54 **Arthegall** the patron of Justice in Book V. 54 **Sophy** pre-
sumably the hero of a projected Book. 60. **Walkt** gone. 60 **no
lesse** i.e., no less distance. 63 **envy** begrudge. 63 **favourlesse** is un-
favorable.

8

Fortune, the foe of famous chevisaunce°
65   Seldome (said *Guyon*) yields to vertue aide,
      But in her way throwes mischiefe° and
          mischaunce,
      Whereby her course is stopt, and passage staid.
      But you, faire Sir, be not herewith dismaid,
      But constant keepe the way, in which ye stand;
70   Which were it not, that I am else delaid
      With hard adventure, which I have in hand,
I labour would to guide you through all Faery land.

9

Gramercy° Sir (said he) but mote I weete,
      What straunge adventure do ye now pursew?
75   Perhaps my succour, or advizement meete
      Mote stead° you much your purpose to subdew.
      Then gan Sir *Guyon* all the story shew
      Of false *Acrasia,* and her wicked wiles,
      Which to avenge, the Palmer him forth drew
80   From Faery court. So talked they, the whiles
They wasted had much way, and measurd many miles.

10

And now faire *Phœbus* gan decline in hast
      His weary wagon to the Westerne vale,
      Whenas they spide a goodly castle, plast
85   Foreby° a river in a pleasaunt dale,
      Which choosing for that evenings hospitale,°
      They thither marcht: but when they came in
          sight,
      And from their sweaty Coursers did avale,°
      They found the gates fast barred long ere night,
90   And every loup° fast lockt, as° fearing foes despight.

11

Which when they saw, they weened fowle reproch

64 **chevisaunce** enterprise.   66 **mischiefe** misfortune.   73 **Gramercy**
thanks.   76 **stead** help.   85 **Foreby** close by.   86 **hospitale** place of
rest.   88 **avale** dismount.   90 **loup** fastening.   90 **as** as if.

Was to them doen, their entrance to forstall,°
Till that the Squire gan nigher to approch;
And wind° his horne under the castle wall,
That with the noise it shooke, as it would fall: 95
Eftsoones forth looked from the highest spire
The watch, and lowd unto the knights did call,
To weete, what they so rudely did require.°
Who gently answered, They entrance did desire.

12

Fly fly, good knights, (said he) fly fast away   100
    If that your lives ye love, as meete ye should;
Fly fast, and save your selves from neare decay,°
Here may ye not have entraunce, though we
    would:°
We would and would againe, if that we could;
But thousand enemies about us rave,°   105
And with long siege us in this castle hould:
Seven yeares this wize° they us besieged have,
And many good knights slaine, that have us sought
    to save.

13

Thus as he spoke, loe with outragious cry
    A thousand villeins round about them swarmd   110
Out of the rockes and caves adjoyning nye,
Vile caytive° wretches, ragged, rude, deformd,
All threatning death, all in straunge manner
    armd,
Some with unweldy clubs, some with long
    speares,
Some rusty knives, some staves in fire warmd.°   115
Sterne was their looke, like wild amazed steares,
Staring with hollow eyes, and stiffe upstanding heares.

---

92 **forstall** prevent.   94 **wind** blow.   98 **require** request.   102 **neare decay** approaching destruction.   103 **would** would be willing to admit you.   105 **rave** rage.   107 **Seven . . . wize** seven years in this manner (referring to the seven ages of the world or the seven ages of man).   112 **caytive** villainous.   115 **warmd** hardened.

14

Fiersly at first those knights they did assaile,
  And drove° them to recoile: but when againe
120 They gave fresh charge, their forces gan to faile,
  Unhable their encounter to sustaine;
  For with such puissaunce and impetuous maine°
  Those Champions broke on them, that forst them fly,
  Like scattered Sheepe, whenas the Shepheards swaine
125   A Lyon and a Tigre doth espye,
With greedy pace forth rushing from the forest nye.

15

A while they fled, but soone returnd againe
  With greater fury, then before was found;
  And evermore their cruell Captaine°
130 Sought with his raskall routs° t'enclose them round,
  And overrun to tread them to the ground.
  But soone the knights with their bright-burning blades
  Broke their rude troupes, and orders° did confound,
  Hewing and slashing at their idle° shades;
For though they bodies seeme, yet substance from
135   them fades.°

16

As when a swarme of Gnats at eventide
  Out of the fennes of Allan° do arise,
  Their murmuring small trompets sounden wide,
  Whiles in the aire their clustring army flies,
140 That as a cloud doth seeme to dim the skies;
  Ne man nor beast may rest, or take repast,
  For their sharpe wounds, and noyous° injuries,

119 **drove** forced.   122 **maine** force.   129 **Captaine** Maleger.   130
raskall routs rabble companies.   133 **orders** ranks.   134 **idle** empty.
135 **fades** vanishes.   137 **the fennes of Allan** a great Irish bog west
of Dublin.   142 **noyous** annoying.

Till the fierce Northerne wind with blustring
    blast
Doth blow them quite away, and in the *Ocean* cast.

17

Thus when they had that troublous rout disperst,   *145*
    Unto the castle gate they come againe,
    And entraunce crav'd, which was denied erst.°
    Now when report of that their perilous paine,
    And combrous° conflict, which they did sus-
        taine,
    Came to the Ladies eare, which there did dwell,   *150*
    She forth issewed with a goodly traine
    Of Squires and Ladies equipaged° well,
And entertained° them right fairely, as befell.°

18

Alma° she called was, a virgin bright;
    That had not yet felt *Cupides* wanton rage,   *155*
    Yet was she woo'd of many a gentle knight,
    And many a Lord of noble parentage,
    That sought with her to lincke in marriage:
    For she was faire, as faire mote ever bee,
    And in the flowre now of her freshest age;   *160*
    Yet full of grace and goodly modestee,
That even heaven rejoyced her sweete face to see.

19

In robe of lilly white she was arayd,
    That from her shoulder to her heele downe
        raught,°
    The traine whereof loose° far behind her
        strayd,   *165*
    Braunched° with gold and pearle, most richly
        wrought,

---

147 **erst** formerly. 149 **combrous** harassing. 152 **equipaged** ar-
rayed. 153 **entertained** received. 153 **befell** was fitting. 154
Alma the soul. 164 **raught** reached. 165 **loose** being loose. 166
Braunched embroidered.

And borne of two faire Damsels, which were
    taught
That service well. Her yellow golden heare
Was trimly woven, and in tresses wrought,
170   Ne other tyre° she on her head did weare,
But crowned with a garland of sweete Rosiere.°

20

Goodly she entertaind those noble knights,
    And brought them up into her castle hall;
    Where gentle court° and gracious delight
175   She to them made, with mildnesse virginall,°
    Shewing her selfe both wise and liberall:
    There when they rested had a season dew,°
    They her besought of favour speciall,
    Of that faire Castle to affoord them vew;
She graunted, and them leading forth, the same did
180   shew.

21

First she them led up to the Castle wall,
    That was so high, as foe might not it clime,
    And all so faire, and fensible° withall,
    Not built of bricke, ne yet of stone and lime,
185   But of thing like to that *Ægyptian* slime,°
  Whereof king *Nine*° whilome built *Babell* towre;
    But O great pitty, that no lenger° time
    So goodly workemanship should not endure:
Soone it must turne to earth; no earthly thing is sure.

22

190 The frame thereof° seemd partly circulare,

170 **tyre** headdress.   171 **Rosiere** rose bush.   174 **court** attention.
175 **mildnesse virginall** graciousness befitting a virgin.   177 **season
dew** proper time.   183 **fensible** capable of being defended.   185
that Ægyptian slime alluding to the Assyrian bitumen which was
used to build the walls of Babylon.   186 **Nine** Ninus, founder of
Nineveh; or, according to Scripture, Nimrod.   187 **lenger** longer.
190 **The frame thereof**, etc. This stanza demands more commentary
than is possible in a short note. The simplest explanation is that the
circle refers to the head, the quadrate to the trunk of the body, and
the triangle to the open legs. The circle has always been recognized

And part triangulare, O worke divine;
   Those two the first and last proportions are,
   The one imperfect, mortall, fœminine;
   Th'other immortall, perfect, masculine,
   And twixt them both a quadrate was the base,   *195*
   Proportioned equally by seven and nine;
   Nine was the circle set in heavens place,
All which compacted made a goodly diapase.

23

Therein two gates were placed seemly well:
   The one before,° by which all in did pas,   *200*
   Did th'other far in workmanship excell;
   For not of wood, nor of enduring bras,
   But of more worthy substance fram'd it was;
   Doubly disparted, it did locke and close,
   That when it locked, none might thorough pas,   *205*
   And when it opened, no man might it close,
Still open to their friends, and closed to their foes.

24

Of hewen stone the porch° was fairely wrought,
   Stone more of valew, and more smooth and fine,
   Then Jet or Marble far from Ireland brought;   *210*
   Over the which was cast a wandring vine,°
   Enchaced° with a wanton yvie twine.

---

as the primary figure, and hence "immortall, perfect, masculine"
while the triangle being less simple and unstable is "imperfect,
mortall, fœminine." Or the circle and the triangle may refer to the
soul and body of man, and the quadrate to the four humors that
connect the soul and body. Seven is the number of the body, from
the seven members of the body, and man's seven ages ruled by the
seven planets; nine is the number of the mind or soul, from the nine
spheres in the Ptolemaic system, and the nine orders of angels. Their
product, the number "Proportioned equally by seven and nine" is 63,
the climacteric year of man's life. Or the quadrate, 4, is connected
with 7 and 9 because its square is their sum. The "circle set in heavens
place" is the ninth sphere of fixed stars that encloses the universe.
Though body and soul are opposed, they are kept in harmony in the
temperate body, even as the octave, 8, is the arithmetic mean between 7 and 9; being so joined, or "compacted" there is a "goodly
diapase" or complete harmony.   200 **The one before** the mouth.
208 **porch** lips.   211 **vine** beard and mustache.   212 **Enchaced**
adorned.

And over it a faire Portcullis° hong,
   Which to the gate directly did incline,
   With comely compasse,° and compacture°
215   strong,
Neither unseemely short, nor yet exceeding long.

25

Within the Barbican° a Porter° sate,
   Day and night duely keeping watch and ward,
   Nor wight, nor word mote passe out of the gate,
220   But in good order, and with dew regard;
   Utterers of secrets he from thence debard,
   Bablers of folly, and blazers° of crime.
   His larumbell° might lowd and wide be hard,
   When cause requird, but never out of time;
225 Early and late it rong, at evening and at prime.°

26

And round about the porch on every side
   Twise sixteen warders° sat, all armed bright
   In glistring steele, and strongly fortifide:
   Tall yeomen seemed they, and of great might,
230   And were enraunged° ready, still for fight.°
   By them as *Alma* passed with her guestes,
   They did obeysaunce,° as beseemed right,
   And then againe returned to their restes:
The Porter eke to her did lout with humble gestes.°

27

235 Thence she them brought into a stately Hall,°
   Wherein were many tables faire dispred,°
   And ready dight with drapets° festivall,

---

213 **Portcullis** a grating to close the gateway of a castle; here, the nose.   215 **compasse** proportion.   215 **compacture** compact structure.   217 **the Barbican** a castle's outer defenses; here, the mouth. 217 **a Porter** the tongue.   222 **blazers** proclaimers.   223 **larumbell** alarm bell.   225 **prime** morning.   227 **warders** the teeth.   230 **enraunged** arranged.   230 **still for fight** always for fighting.   232 **did obeysaunce** made respectful salutation.   234 **did . . . gestes** bowed with humble gestures.   235 **a stately Hall** the mouth and throat. 236 **dispred** spread out.   237 **drapets** coverings.

    Against the viaundes should be ministred.°
    At th'upper end there sate, yclad in red
    Downe to the ground, a comely personage,   *240*
    That in his hand a white rod menaged,°
    He Steward was hight *Diet;* rype of age,
And in demeanure° sober, and in counsell sage.

28

And through the Hall there walked to and fro
    A jolly yeoman, Marshall of the same,   *245*
    Whose name was *Appetite;* he did bestow°
    Both guestes and meate, when ever in they came,
    And knew them how to order without blame,
    As him the Steward bad. They both attone°
    Did dewty to their Lady, as became;   *250*
    Who passing by, forth led her guestes anone°
Into the kitchin rowme, ne spard for nicenesse none.°

29

It was a vaut° ybuilt for great dispence,°
    With many raunges reard along the wall;
    And one great chimney, whose long tonnell
       thence   *255*
    The smoke forth threw. And in the midst of all
    There placed was a caudron° wide and tall,
    Upon a mighty furnace, burning whot,
    More whot, then *Aetn',* or flaming *Mongiball:*°
    For day and night it brent, ne ceased not,   *260*
So long as any thing it in the caudron got.

30

But to delay° the heat, least by mischaunce
    It might breake out, and set the whole on fire,
    There added was by goodly ordinaunce,°

---

238 **Against . . . ministred** When the food should be administered.
241 **menaged** wielded. 243 **demeanure** behavior. 246 **bestow**
place. 249 **attone** together. 251 **anone** immediately. 252 **ne . . .
none** nothing was restrained for the sake of fastidiousness. 253
vaut vault, the stomach. 253 **dispence** dispensing. 257 **caudron**
caldron, the digestive processes. 259 **Mongiball** the Arabic name
for Aetna. 262 **delay** allay. 264 **ordinaunce** arrangement.

An huge great paire of bellowes,° which did styre°
265   Continually, and cooling breath inspyre.°
About the Caudron many Cookes accoyld,°
With hookes and ladles, as need did require;
The whiles the viandes in the vessell boyld
They did about their businesse sweat, and sorely
270   toyld.

31

The maister Cooke was cald *Concoction*,°
A carefull man, and full of comely guise:
The kitchin Clerke, that hight *Digestion*,
Did order all th'Achates° in seemely wise,
275   And set them forth, as well he could devise.
The rest had severall offices° assind,
Some to remove the scum, as it did rise;
Others to beare the same away did mind;
And others it to use according to his kind.

32

280 But all the liquour, which was fowle and wast,
Not good nor serviceable else for ought,°
They in another great round vessell plast,
Till by a conduit pipe it thence were brought:
And all the rest, that noyous was, and nought,°
285   By secret wayes, that none might it espy,
Was close convaid, and to the back-gate brought,
That cleped° was *Port Esquiline*,° whereby
It was avoided° quite, and throwne out privily.

33

Which goodly order, and great workmans skill
290   Whenas those knights beheld, with rare delight,

---

265 **bellowes** the lungs.   265 **styre** move.   266 **inspyre** breathe in.
267 **accoyld** collected.   271 **Concoction** the digestive processes.
274 **Achates** provisions.   276 **offices** duties.   281 **ought** anything.
284 **noyous . . . nought** noxious was, and of no value.   287 **cleped**
named.   287 **Port Esquiline** the gate in ancient Rome that led to the
cemetery for the poor, and refuse dump.   288 **avoided** voided.

And gazing wonder they their minds did fill;
For never had they seene so straunge a sight.
Thence backe againe faire *Alma* led them right,
And soone into a goodly Parlour° brought,
That was with royall arras richly dight,   *295*
In which was nothing pourtrahed, nor wrought,
Not wrought, nor pourtrahed, but easie to be
    thought.°

34

And in the midst thereof upon the floure,
A lovely bevy° of faire Ladies° sate,
Courted of° many a jolly Paramoure,   *300*
The which them did in modest wise amate,°
And eachone sought his Lady to aggrate:°
And eke emongst them litle *Cupid* playd
His wanton sports, being returned late
From his fierce warres, and having from him
    layd   *305*
His cruell bow, wherewith he thousands hath dis-
    mayd.

35

Diverse delights they found them selves to please;
Some song in sweet consort,° some laught for
    joy,
Some plaid with strawes,° some idly sat at ease;
But other some° could not abide to toy,°   *310*
All pleasaunce° was to them griefe and annoy:°
This frownd, that faund, the third for shame did
    blush,
Another seemed envious, or coy,
Another in her teeth did gnaw a rush:°
But at these straungers presence every one did hush.   *315*

294 **Parlour** the heart.   297 **but . . . thought** which was not easy to
be understood.   299 **bevy** company.   299 **Ladies** the affections.
300 **of** by.   301 **amate** be a mate to.   302 **aggrate** gratify.   308
consort harmony.   309 **plaid with strawes** spent their time on matters of little value.   310 **other some** some others.   310 **toy** play.
311 **pleasaunce** pleasantries.   311 **annoy** annoyance.   314 **did . . .
rush** the emblem of anger, the rush signifying a thing of no impor-
tance.

36

Soone as the gracious *Alma* came in place,°
    They all attonce out of their seates arose,
    And to her homage made, with humble grace:
    Whom when the knights beheld, they gan dispose
    Themselves to court,° and each a Damsell
320   chose:
    The Prince by chaunce did on a Lady light,
    That was right faire and fresh as morning rose,
    But somwhat sad, and solemne eke in sight,°
As if some pensive thought constraind° her gentle
      spright.

37

325 In a long purple pall,° whose skirt with gold
    Was fretted° all about, she was arayd;
    And in her hand a Poplar braunch° did hold:
    To whom the Prince in curteous manner said;
    Gentle Madame, why beene° ye thus dismaid,
330   And your faire beautie do with sadnesse spill?°
    Lives any, that you hath thus ill apaid?°
    Or doen you love, or doen you lacke your will?
What ever be the cause, it sure beseemes you ill.

38

Faire Sir, (said she halfe in disdainefull wise,)
335   How is it, that this mood in me ye blame,
    And in your selfe do not the same advise?°
    Him ill beseemes, anothers fault to name,
    That may unwares be blotted with the same:
    Pensive I yeeld I am, and sad in mind,
340   Through great desire of glory and of fame;
    Ne ought I weene are ye therein behind,
That have twelve moneths sought one,° yet no where
      can her find.

316 **in place** there.   319–20 **they gan . . . court** they made themselves
ready to pay courteous attention to the ladies.   323 **in sight** in her
appearance.   324 **constraind** oppressed.   325 **pall** garment.   326
fretted adorned.   327 a **Poplar braunch** the crown for victors.
329 **beene** are.   330 **spill** spoil.   331 **apaid** treated.   336 **advise**
notice.   324 **one** the Faery Queen.

39

The Prince was inly° moved at her speach,
 Well weeting° trew, what she had rashly° told;
 Yet with faire semblaunt° sought to hide the
  breach,   *345*
 Which chaunge of colour did perforce unfold,°
 Now seeming flaming whot, now stony cold.
 Tho turning soft aside, he did inquire,
 What wight° she was, that Poplar braunch did
  hold:
 It answered was, her name was *Prays-desire*,° *350*
That by well doing sought to honour to aspire.

40

The whiles, the *Faerie* knight did entertaine
 Another Damsell of that gentle crew,°
 That was right faire, and modest of demaine,°
 But that too oft she chaung'd her native hew:° *355*
 Straunge was her tyre, and all her garment blew,
 Close round about her tuckt with many a
  plight:°
 Upon her fist the bird,° which shonneth vew,
 And keepes in coverts° close° from living wight,
Did sit, as yet ashamd, how rude *Pan* did her dight.° *360*

41

So long as *Guyon* with her commoned,°
 Unto the ground she cast her modest eye,
 And ever and anone with rosie red
 The bashfull bloud her snowy cheekes did dye,
 That her became,° as polisht yvory, *365*
 Which cunning° Craftesman hand hath overlayd
 With faire vermilion or pure Castory.°

343 **inly** inwardly. 344 **weeting** knowing. 344 **rashly** hastily.
345 **semblaunt** countenance.   346 **perforce unfold** of necessity reveal. 349 **wight** creature. 350 **Prays-desire** desire of praise. 353
crew company. 354 **demaine** demeanor. 355 **native hew** natural
color. 357 **plight** pleat. 358 **the bird** the owl. 359 **coverts** hiding
places. 359 **close** hidden. 360 **how . . . dight** how rude Pan violated her. The myth seems to be Spenser's. 361 **commoned** con-
versed. 365 **her became** was becoming to her. 366 **cunning** skillful. 367 **Castory** the color red.

Great wonder had the knight, to see the mayd
So straungely passioned,° and to her gently sayd,

42

370 Faire Damzell, seemeth,° by your troubled cheare,°
That either me too bold ye weene, this wise
You to molest, or other ill to feare
That in the secret of your hart close lyes,
From whence it doth, as cloud from sea arise.
375 If it be I, of pardon I you pray;
But if ought else that I mote not devise,
I will, if please you it discure,° assay,
To ease you of that ill, so wisely as I may.

43

She answerd nought, but more abasht for shame,
380 Held downe her head, the whiles her lovely face
The flashing bloud with blushing did inflame,
And the strong passion° mard her modest grace,
That *Guyon* mervayld at her uncouth cace:°
Till *Alma* him bespake, Why wonder yee
385 Faire Sir at that, which ye so much embrace?°
She is the fountaine of your modestee;
You shamefast are, but *Shamefastnesse*° it selfe is
    shee.

44

Thereat the Elfe did blush in privitee,°
And turnd his face away; but she the same
390 Dissembled faire, and faynd to oversee.°
Thus they awhile with court and goodly game,
Themselves did solace each one with his Dame,
Till that great Ladie thence away them sought,°
To vew her castles other wondrous frame.

---

369 **passioned** affected by passion. 370 **seemeth** it seemeth. 370
cheare face. 377 **discure** discover, reveal. 382 **passion** affection.
383 **uncouth cace** strange condition. 385 **embrace** include. 387
Shamefastnesse Modesty. 388 **privitee** privacy. 390 **faynd to oversee** pretended to overlook. 393 **sought** requested.

    Up to a stately Turret° she them brought,   *395*
Ascending by ten steps of Alablaster° wrought.

45

That Turrets frame most admirable was,
    Like highest heaven compassed around,
    And lifted high above this earthly masse,
    Which it survew'd,° as hils doen lower ground; *400*
    But not on ground mote like to this be found,
    Not that, which antique *Cadmus*° whylome built
    In *Thebes,* which *Alexander* did confound;
    Nor that proud towre of *Troy,* though richly
        guilt,°
From which young *Hectors* bloud° by cruell *Greekes*
    was spilt.   *405*

46

The roofe hereof was arched over head,
    And deckt with flowers and herbars° daintily;
    Two goodly Beacons,° set in watches stead,°
    Therein gave light, and flam'd continually:
    For they of living fire most subtilly   *410*
    Were made, and set in silver sockets bright,
    Cover'd with lids deviz'd of substance sly,°
    That readily they shut and open might.
O who can tell the prayses of that makers might!

47

Ne can I tell, ne° can I stay to tell   *415*
    This parts great workmanship, and wondrous
        powre,
    That all this other worlds worke doth excell,

---

395 **a stately Turret** the head. 396 **Alablaster** alabaster, referring to
the neck. 400 **survew'd** surveyed. 402 **which antique Cadmus,** etc.
the acropolis of Thebes built by Cadmus and overthrown by Alexander in 335 B.C. 404 **guilt** gilded. 405 **young Hectors blood,** etc.
Astyanax, Hector's son, was hurled from the tower when the Greeks
captured the city. 407 **herbars** plants, i.e., the hair. 408 **Beacons**
the eyes. 408 **in watches stead** in place of watchmen. 412 **sly** skillfully made. 415 **Ne ... ne** neither ... nor.

And likest is unto that heavenly towre,
That God hath built for his owne blessed bowre.
420 Therein were diverse roomes, and diverse stages,
But three the chiefest, and of greatest powre,
In which there dwelt three honorable sages,
The wisest men, I weene, that lived in their ages.

48

Not he,° whom *Greece,* the Nourse of all good arts,
425 By *Phœbus* doome,° the wisest thought alive,
Might be compar'd to these by many parts:°
Nor that sage *Pylian* syre,° which did survive
Three ages,° such as mortall men contrive,°
By whose advise old *Priams* cittie fell,
430 With these in praise of pollicies° mote strive.
These three in these three roomes did sundry°
    dwell,
And counselled faire *Alma,* how to governe well.

49

The first° of them could things to come foresee:
The next° could of things present best advize;
435 The third° things past could keepe in memoree,
So that no time, nor reason could arize,
But that the same could one of these comprize.°
For thy° the first did in the forepart sit,
That nought mote hinder his quicke prejudize:°
440 He had a sharpe foresight, and working wit,
That never idle was, ne once could rest a whit.

50
His chamber was dispainted° all within,

424 **Not he,** etc. Socrates, whom Apollo's oracle declared to be the wisest man alive. 425 **doome** judgment. 426 **parts** times. 427 **Nor that sage Pylian syre** Nestor, king of Pylos, who ruled over three generations of men, was renowned for his wisdom. Largely through his counsel, Troy fell. 428 **ages** generations. 428 **contrive** spend time. 430 **praise of pollicies** whatever is praiseworthy in political wisdom. 431 **sundry** separately. 433 **The first** Imagination or Phantastes. 434 **The next** Judgment. 435 **The third** Memory. 437 **comprize** comprehend. 438 **For thy** therefore. 439 **prejudize** prejudgment. 422 **dispainted** diversely painted.

With sundry colours, in the which were writ
Infinite shapes of things dispersed thin;
Some such as in the world were never yit,   445
Ne can devized be of mortall wit;
Some daily seene, and knowen by their names,
Such as in idle fantasies doe flit:
  Infernall Hags, *Centaurs,* feendes, *Hippodames,*°
Apes, Lions, Ægles, Owles, fooles, lovers, children,
      Dames.   450

51

And all the chamber filled was with flyes,
Which buzzed all about, and made such sound,
That they encombred all mens eares and eyes,
Like many swarmes of Bees assembled round,
After their hives with honny do abound: 455
All those were idle thoughts and fantasies,
Devices, dreames, opinions unsound,
  Shewes, visions, sooth-sayes,° and prophesies;
And all that fained is, as leasings,° tales, and lies.

52

Emongst them all sate he, which wonned° there,   460
That hight *Phantastes* by his nature trew;
A man of yeares yet fresh, as mote appere,
Of swarth° complexion, and of crabbed hew,°
That him full of melancholy did shew;
Bent hollow beetle browes,° sharpe staring eyes,   465
That mad or foolish seemd: one by his vew
  Mote deeme him borne with ill disposed skyes,°
When oblique° *Saturne*° sate in the house° of agonyes.°

449 **Hippodames** seahorses.   458 **sooth-sayes** predictions.   459 **leasings** falsehoods.   460 **wonned** dwelled.   463 **swarth** dark.   463
hew countenance.   465 **hollow beetle browes** indented shaggy eye-
brows.   467 **with ... skyes** under unlucky stars.   468 **oblique** in the
ascendant.   468 **When oblique Saturne,** etc. The unlucky influence
of Saturn on the imaginative man is at its worst when the planet rises
in the sign of the Lion.   468 **house** the region or division of the sky
in which a planet rises.   468 **agonyes** struggles, afflictions.

53

Whom *Alma* having shewed to her guestes,
    Thence brought them to the second roome,
      whose wals
    Were painted faire with memorable gestes,°
    Of famous Wisards, and with picturals°
    Of Magistrates, of courts, of tribunals,
    Of commen wealthes, of states, of pollicy,
    Of lawes, of judgements, and of decretals;°
    All artes, all science, all Philosophy,
And all that in the world was aye thought wittily.°

54

Of those that roome was full, and them among
    There sate a man of ripe and perfect age,
    Who did them meditate all his life long,
    That through continuall practise and usage,
    He now was growne right wise, and wondrous
      sage.
    Great pleasure had those stranger knights, to see
    His goodly reason, and grave personage,
    That his disciples both desir'd to bee;
But *Alma* thence them led to th'hindmost roome of
    three.

55

That chamber seemed ruinous and old,
    And therefore was removed farre behind,
    Yet were the wals, that did the same uphold,
    Right firme and strong, though somewhat they
      declind;°
    And therein sate an old oldman, halfe blind,
    And all decrepit in his feeble corse,°
    Yet lively vigour rested in his mind,
    And recompenst him with a better scorse:°
Weake body well is chang'd for minds redoubled
    forse.

471 **gestes** deeds.   472 **picturals** pictures.   475 **decretals** decrees.
477 **aye thought wittily** ever wisely thought.   490 **declind** inclined.
493 **corse** body.   494 **scorse** exchange.

56

This man of infinite remembrance was,
    And things foregone° through many ages held,
    Which he recorded still, as they did pas,
    Ne suffred them to perish through long eld,°
    As all things else, the which this world doth
        weld,°
    But laid them up in his immortall scrine,°   500
    Where they for ever incorrupted dweld:
    The warres he well remembred of king *Nine*,°
Of old *Assaracus*,° and *Inachus* divine.°

57

The yeares of *Nestor*° nothing were to his,   505
    Ne yet *Mathusalem*,° though longest liv'd;
    For he remembred both their infancies:
    Ne wonder then, if that he were depriv'd
    Of native strength now, that he them surviv'd.
    His chamber all was hangd about with rolles,   510
    And old records from auncient times deriv'd,
    Some made in books, some in long parchment
        scrolles,
That were all worme-eaten, and full of canker holes.

58

Amidst them all he in a chaire was set,
    Tossing and turning them withouten end;   515
    But for° he was unhable them to fet,°
    A litle boy did on him still attend,
    To reach, when ever he for ought did send;
    And oft when things were lost, or laid amis,
    That boy them sought, and unto him did lend.°   520
    Therefore he *Anamnestes*° cleped is,
And that old man *Eumnestes*,° by their propertis.

497 **foregone** gone by. 499 **eld** age. 500 **weld** wield. 501 **scrine**
chest. 503 **Nine** Ninus of Babylon. 504 **Assaracus** king of Troy,
son of the founder of Troy and great-grandfather of Aeneas. 504
Inachus divine the first king of Argos, son of Oceanus and Tethys.
505 **Nestor** See note to line 427. 506 **Mathusalem** "and all the days
of Methusaleh were nine hundred and sixty and nine years" (Gen.
v. 27). 516 **But for** because. 516 **fet** fetch. 520 **lend** give.
521 **Anamnestes** the reminder. 522 **Eumnestes** of good memory.

59

The knights there entring, did him reverence dew
 And wondred at his endlesse exercise,
525 Then as they gan his Librarie to vew,
 And antique Registers for to avise,°
 There chaunced to the Princes hand to rize,°
 An auncient booke, hight *Briton moniments,*°
 That of this lands first conquest did devize,°
530 And old division into Regiments,°
Till it reduced was to one mans governments.°

60

Sir *Guyon* chaunst eke on another booke,
 That hight *Antiquitie*° of *Faerie* lond.
 In which when as he greedily° did looke,
535 Th'off-spring° of Elves and Faries there he fond,
 As it delivered was from hond to hond:
 Whereat they burning both with fervent fire,
 Their countries auncestry to understond,
 Crav'd leave of *Alma* and that aged sire,
To read those bookes; who gladly graunted their de-
540 sire.

After the chronicles of the Briton kings and Elfin emperors are related, Arthur destroys Maleger whose forces besiege the Castle of Alma while Guyon travels to Acrasia's Bower of Bliss. Through the Palmer's governance, he succeeds in passing through many perils until he arrives at the Bower.

---

526 **avise** examine.   527 **rize** come (?).   528 **Briton moniments** records or chronicles of Britain, referring to Geoffrey of Monmouth's *Monumenta Britannica.*   529 **devize** recount.   530 **Regiments** separate governments.   531 **governments** government. The "one man" is Arthur.   533 **Antiquitie** ancient records.   534 **greedily** eagerly.   535 **off-spring** origin.

from CANTO XII: THE BOWER OF BLISS

42

Thence passing forth, they shortly do arrive,
    Whereas the Bowre of *Blisse* was situate;°
    A place pickt out by choice of best alive,
    That natures worke by art can imitate:
    In which what ever in this worldly state   5
    Is sweet, and pleasing unto living sense,
    Or that may dayntiest fantasie aggrate,°
    Was poured forth with plentifull dispence,°
And made there to abound with lavish affluence.

43

Goodly it was enclosed round about,   10
    Aswell their entred guestes to keepe within,
    As those unruly beasts to hold without;
    Yet was the fence thereof but weake and thin;
    Nought feard their force, that fortilage to win,°
    But wisedomes powre, and temperaunces might,   15
    By which the mightiest things efforced bin:°
    And eke the gate was wrought of substaunce light,
Rather for pleasure, then for battery or fight.

44

Yt framed was of precious yvory,
    That seemd a worke of admirable wit;   20
    And therein all the famous history°

2 **situate** situated.   7 **may . . . aggrate** may gratify the most fastidious fancy.   8 **dispence** liberality.   14 **Nought . . . win** It was feared
not at all that the force of the beasts could win that fortress.   16
efforced bin are enforced.   21 **the famous history,** etc. Jason sailed
in the *Argo*, together with the choice Grecian warriors to Colchis in
order to obtain the Golden Fleece, which belonged to King Aeëtes.
The King's daughter, Medea, aided him with her magical powers; and
after obtaining the fleece, he married her. They escaped from her
(*Footnotes continued on page 374*)

Of *Jason* and *Medæa* was ywrit;
  Her mighty charmes, her furious loving fit,
  His goodly conquest of the golden fleece,
25 His falsed faith, and love too lightly flit,°
  The wondred° *Argo,* which in venturous peece°
First through the *Euxine* seas° bore all the flowr of
      Greece.

45

Ye might have seene the frothy billowes fry°
  Under the ship, as thorough them she went,
30 That seemd the waves were into yvory,
  Or yvory into the waves were sent;
  And other where° the snowy substaunce sprent°
  With vermell,° like the boyes bloud therein shed,
  A piteous spectacle did represent,
35 And otherwhiles° with gold besprinkeled;
Yt seemd th'enchaunted flame, which did *Creüsa* wed.

46

All this, and more might in that goodly gate
  Be red;° that ever open stood to all,
  Which thither came: but in the Porch there sate
40 A comely personage of stature tall,
  And semblaunce° pleasing, more then naturall,
  That travellers to him seemd to entize;
  His looser° garment to the ground did fall,
  And flew about his heeles in wanton wize,°
45 Not fit for speedy pace, or manly exercize.

47

They in that place him *Genius* did call:

father when she cut up her brother's body and threw the pieces
into the sea. Later he left her for Creusa. In revenge, she killed
her children by Jason, and sent Creusa a poisoned garment which
burned her to death.   25 **flit** departed.   26 **wondred** wonderful.
26 **venturous peece** adventurous ship.   27 **the Euxine seas** the Black
Sea.   28 **fry** foam.   32 **other where** elsewhere.   32 **sprent** sprinkled.
33 **vermell** vermilion.   35 **otherwhiles** elsewhere.   38 **red** seen.   41
semblaunce appearance.   43 **looser** too loose.   44 **wize** manner.

Not that celestiall powre,° to whom the care
Of life, and generation of all
That lives, pertaines in charge particulare,
Who wondrous things concerning our welfare,   *50*
And straunge phantomes doth let us oft forsee,
And oft of secret ill bids us beware:
That is our Selfe, whom though we do not see,
Yet each doth in him selfe it well perceive to bee.

48

Therefore a God him sage Antiquity   *55*
Did wisely make, and good *Agdistes*° call:
But this same was to that quite contrary,
The foe of life, that good envyes° to all,
That secretly doth us procure to fall,
Through guilefull semblaunts,° which he makes
    us see.   *60*
He of this Gardin had the governall,°
And Pleasures porter was devizd to bee,
Holding a staffe in hand for more formalitee.

49

With diverse flowres he daintily was deckt,
And strowed round about, and by his side   *65*
A mighty Mazer bowle° of wine was set,
As if it had to him bene sacrifide;°
Wherewith all new-come guests he gratifide:
So did he eke Sir *Guyon* passing by:
But he his idle curtesie defide,   *70*
And overthrew his bowle disdainfully;
And broke his staffe, with which he charmed sem-
    blants sly.°

---

47 **Not that celestiall powre,** etc. the true and false geniuses that
govern man's life: his better self ("our Selfe" or conscience) and his
worse self, or Bad Angel, who leads him astray.   56 **Agdistes** a god
of Nature.   58 **envyes** begrudges.   60 **semblants** deceiving appear-
ances.   61 **governall** governing.   66 **Mazer bowle** drinking cup.
67 **sacrifide** sacrificed.   72 **charmed semblants sly** i.e., called up the
"guilefull semblaunts, which he makes us see."

50

Thus being entred, they behold around
    A large and spacious plaine, on every side
    Strowed with pleasauns,° whose faire grassy
        ground
    Mantled with greene, and goodly beautifide
    With all the ornaments of *Floraes* pride,°
    Wherewith her mother Art, as halfe in scorne
    Of niggard Nature, like a pompous bride
    Did decke her, and too lavishly adorne,
When forth from virgin bowre she comes in th'early
        morne.

51

Thereto° the Heavens alwayes Joviall,°
    Lookt on them lovely,° still in stedfast state,
    Ne suffred storme nor frost on them to fall,
    Their tender buds or leaves to violate,
    Nor scorching heat, nor cold intemperate
    T'afflict the creatures, which therein did dwell,
    But the milde aire with season moderate
    Gently attempred, and disposd so well,
That still it breathed forth sweet spirit° and holesome
        smell.

52

More sweet and holesome, then the pleasaunt hill
    Of *Rhodope,* on which the Nimphe,° that bore
    A gyaunt babe, her selfe for griefe did kill;
    Or the Thessalian *Tempe,*° where of yore
    Faire *Daphne Phœbus* hart with love did gore;°
    Or *Ida,*° where the Gods lov'd to repaire,°
    When ever they their heavenly bowres forlore;°

75 pleasauns pleasure grounds.   **77 Floraes pride** Flora, the goddess
of flowers, in her most flourishing state.   **82 Thereto** to that place.
82 Joviall joyful and happy, being under the influence of the planet
Jupiter.   **83 lovely** lovingly.   **90 spirit** breath.   **92 the Nimphe**
Rhodope had a giant-babe, Athos, by Neptune; later she was transformed into the mountain in Thrace that bears her name.   **94
Tempe,** etc. the Thessalian mountain where Phoebus pursued
Daphne.   **95 gore** pierce.   **96 Ida** a mountain in Phrygia.   **96 re-
paire** resort.   **97 forlore** forsake.

Or sweet *Parnasse,*° the haunt of Muses faire;
Or *Eden* selfe if ought with *Eden* mote compaire.°

53

Much wondred *Guyon* at the faire aspect   *100*
  Of that sweet place, yet suffred no delight
  To sincke into his sence, nor mind affect,
  But passed forth, and lookt still forward right,°
  Bridling his will, and maistering his might:
  Till that he came unto another gate,   *105*
  No gate, but like one, being goodly dight
  With boughes and braunches, which did broad
    dilate°
Their clasping armes, in wanton wreathings intricate.

54

So fashioned a Porch with rare device,
  Archt over head with an embracing vine,   *110*
  Whose bounches hanging downe, seemed to en-
    tice
  All passers by, to tast their lushious wine,
  And did themselves into their hands incline,
  As freely offering to be gathered:
  Some deepe empurpled as the *Hyacint,*°   *115*
  Some as the Rubine,° laughing sweetly red,
Some like faire Emeraudes,° not yet well ripened.°

55

And them amongst, some were of burnisht gold,
  So made by art, to beautifie the rest,
  Which did themselves emongst the leaves enfold,   *120*
  As lurking from the vew of covetous guest,
  That the weake bowes,° with so rich load op-
    prest,
  Did bow adowne, as over-burdened.
  Under that Porch a comely dame did rest,

---

98 **Parnasse** Parnassus, sacred to the Muses.   99 **mote compaire**
might be compared.   103 **forward right** straight ahead.   107 **dilate**
spread out.   115 **Hyacint** Hyacinth or jacinth, a sapphire-colored
stone.   116 **Rubine** ruby.   117 **Emeraudes** emeralds.   117 **ripened**
brought to perfection by polishing (?).   122 **bowes** boughs.

125 Clad in faire weedes,° but fowle disordered,
And garments loose, that seemd unmeet° for
    womanhed.

56

In her left hand a Cup of gold she held,
    And with her right the riper° fruit did reach,
    Whose sappy liquor, that with fulnesse sweld,
130   Into her cup she scruzd,° with daintie breach°
    Of her fine° fingers, without fowle empeach,°
    That so faire wine-presse made the wine more
        sweet:
    Thereof she usd to give to drinke to each,
    Whom passing by she happened to meet:
135 It was her guise,° all Straungers goodly so to greet.

57

So she to *Guyon* offred it to tast;
    Who taking it out of her tender hond,
    The cup to ground did violently cast,
    That all in peeces it was broken fond,°
140   And with the liquor stained all the lond:
    Whereat° *Excesse* exceedingly was wroth,
    Yet no'te° the same amend, ne yet withstond,
    But suffered him to passe, all° were she loth;
Who not regarding her displeasure forward goth.

58

145 There the most daintie Paradise on ground,
    It selfe doth offer to his sober eye,
    In which all pleasures plenteously abound,
    And none does others happinesse envye:
    The painted flowres, the trees upshooting hye,
    The dales for shade, the hilles for breathing
150   space,
    The trembling groves, the Christall° running by;

125 **weedes** clothes.   126 **unmeet** not fitting.   128 **riper** overripe.
130 **scruzd** squeezed.   130 **breach** breaking.   131 **fine** delicate.
131 **empeach** injury.   135 **guise** manner.   139 **fond** found.   141
Whereat at which.   142 **no'te** might not.   143 **all** although.   151
Christall the crystal streams.

And that, which all faire workes doth most ag-
    grace,°
The art, which all that wrought, appeared in no place.

59

One would have thought, (so cunningly,° the rude,
    And scorned° parts were mingled with the fine,)   *155*
    That nature had for wantonesse ensude°
    Art, and that Art at nature did repine;°
    So striving each th'other to undermine,
    Each did the others worke more beautifie;
    So diff'ring both in willes, agreed in fine:°   *160*
    So all agreed through sweete diversitie,
This Gardin to adorne with all varietie.

60

And in the midst of all, a fountaine stood,
    Of richest substaunce, that on earth might bee,
    So pure and shiny, that the silver flood°   *165*
    Through every channell running one might see;
    Most goodly it with curious imageree
    Was over-wrought, and shapes of naked boyes,
    Of which some seemd with lively jollitee,
    To fly about, playing their wanton toyes,°   *170*
Whilest others did them selves embay° in liquid joyes.

61

And over all, of purest gold was spred,
    A trayle of yvie in his native hew:
    For the rich mettall was so coloured,
    That wight, who did not well avis'd° it vew,   *175*
    Would surely deeme it to be yvie trew:
    Low his lascivious armes adown did creepe,
    That themselves dipping in the silver dew,
    Their fleecy flowres they tenderly did steepe,

---

152 **aggrace** give grace to.　154 **cunningly** skillfully.　155 **scorned**
deserving to be scorned.　156 **ensude** imitated.　157 **did repine** was
dissatisfied.　160 **in fine** in the end.　165 **flood** water.　170 **toyes**
amorous sports.　171 **embay** bathe.　175 **well avis'd** warily.

Which° drops of Christall seemd for wantones to
weepe.

62

Infinit streames continually did well°
    Out of this fountaine, sweet and faire to see,
    The which into an ample laver° fell,
    And shortly grew to so great quantitie,
    That like a little lake it seemd to bee;
    Whose depth exceeded not three cubits° hight,
    That through the waves one might the bottom
      see,
    All pav'd beneath with Jaspar shining bright,
That seemd the fountaine in that sea did sayle up-
    right.

63

And all the margent° round about was set,
    With shady Laurell trees, thence to defend°
    The sunny beames, which on the billowes bet,°
    And those which therein bathed, mote offend.
    As *Guyon* hapned by the same to wend,°
    Two naked Damzelles he therein espyde,
    Which therein bathing, seemed to contend,
    And wrestle wantonly, ne car'd to hyde,
Their dainty parts from vew of any, which them eyde.

64

Sometimes the one would lift the other quight
    Above the waters, and then downe againe
    Her plong, as over maistered by might,
    Where both awhile would covered remaine,
    And each the other from to rise restraine;
    The whiles their snowy limbes, as through a
      vele,°
    So through the Christall waves appeared plaine:

---

180 **Which** on which. 181 **well** flow. 183 **laver** basin of the fountain. 186 **three cubits** about five feet. 190 **margent** margin. 191
defend keep off. 192 **bet** beat. 194 **wend** go. 204 **vele** veil.

    Then suddeinly both would themselves unhele,°
And th'amarous sweet spoiles to greedy eyes revele.

65

As that faire Starre,° the messenger of morne,
    His deawy face out of the sea doth reare:
    Or as the *Cyprian* goddesse,° newly borne   210
    Of th'Oceans fruitfull froth, did first appeare:
    Such seemed they, and so their yellow heare
    Christalline humour° dropped downe apace.°
    Whom such when *Guyon* saw, he drew him neare,
    And somewhat gan relent° his earnest pace,   215
His stubborne brest gan secret pleasaunce° to embrace.

66

The wanton Maidens him espying, stood
    Gazing a while at his unwonted guise;°
    Then th'one her selfe low ducked in the flood,
    Abasht, that her a straunger did a vise:°   220
    But th'other rather higher did arise,
    And her two lilly paps aloft displayd,
    And all, that might his melting hart entise
    To her delights,° she unto him bewrayd:°
The rest hid underneath, him more desirous made.   225

67

With that, the other likewise up arose,
    And her faire lockes, which formerly° were bownd
    Up in one knot, she low adowne did lose:°
    Which flowing long and thick, her cloth'd arownd,

---

206 **unhele** uncover.   208 **that faire Starre** Venus, the morning star.
210 **the Cyprian goddesse** Venus, born of the sea-foam.   213 **Christalline humour** clear moisture.   213 **apace** swiftly.   215 **relent** slacken.   216 **pleasaunce** pleasure.   218 **unwonted guise** unaccustomed behavior.   222 **a vise** look at.   224 **her delights** the pleasures that she could give.   224 **bewrayd** revealed.   227 **formerly** just before.   228 **lose** loosen.

230   And th'yvorie in golden mantle gownd:°
      So that faire spectacle from him was reft,°
      Yet that, which reft it, no lesse faire was fownd:
      So hid in lockes and waves from lookers theft,
Nought but her lovely face she for his looking left.

68

235 Withall she laughed, and she blusht withall,°
      That blushing to her laughter gave more grace,
      And laughter to her blushing, as did fall:°
      Now when they spide the knight to slacke his
          pace,
      Them to behold, and in his sparkling face
240   The secret signes of kindled lust appeare,
      Their wanton meriments they did encreace,
      And to him beckned, to approch more neare,
And shewd him many sights, that courage° cold
          could reare.°

69

On which when gazing him the Palmer saw,
245   He much rebukt those wandring eyes of his,
      And counseld well, him forward thence did
          draw.
      Now are they come nigh to the *Bowre of blis*
      Of her fond favorites so nam'd amis:
      When thus the Palmer; Now Sir, well avise;°
250   For here the end of all our travell° is:
      Here wonnes° *Acrasia,* whom we must surprise,
Else she will slip away, and all our drift° despise.°

70

Eftsoones they heard a most melodious sound,
      Of all that mote delight a daintie eare,
255   Such as attonce° might not on living ground,°

230 **And ... gownd** And covered her ivory skin with a golden cloak.
231 **reft** taken away.   235 **Withall** at the same time.   237 **as did fall**
as it happened.   243 **courage** sexual vigor.   243 **reare** rouse.   249
well avise consider well.   250 **travell** (1) journey; (2) travail.   251
wonnes lives.   252 **drift** purpose.   252 **despise** set at nought.   255
attonce at once.   255 **on living ground** on earth.

Save in this Paradise, be heard elswhere:
Right hard it was, for wight,° which did it heare,
To read, what manner musicke that mote bee:°
For all that pleasing is to living eare,
Was there consorted° in one harmonee, 260
Birdes, voyces, instruments, windes, waters, all agree.

71

The joyous birdes shrouded in chearefull shade,
Their notes unto the voyce attempred° sweet;
Th'Angelicall soft trembling voyces made
To th'instruments divine respondence meet:° 265
The silver sounding instruments did meet°
With the base° murmure of the waters fall:
The waters fall with difference discreet,°
Now soft, now loud, unto the wind did call:
The gentle warbling wind low answered to all. 270

72

There, whence that Musick seemed heard to bee,
Was the faire Witch° her selfe now solacing,
With a new Lover, whom through sorceree
And witchcraft, she from farre did thither bring:
There she had him now layd a slombering, 275
In secret shade, after long wanton joyes:
Whilst round about them pleasauntly did sing
Many faire Ladies, and lascivious boyes,
That ever mixt their song with light licentious toyes.

73

And all that while, right over him she hong, 280
With her false° eyes fast fixed in his sight,°
As seeking medicine, whence° she was stong,
Or greedily depasturing° delight:
And oft inclining downe with kisses light,

257 **wight** creature. 258 **To . . . bee** To tell what kind of music it
could be. 260 **consorted** united. 263 **attempred** attuned. 265 **respondence meet** fitting response. 266 **did meet** blended. 267 **base**
low. 268 **difference discreet** distinct variation. 272 **the faire Witch**
Acrasia. 281 **false** deceitful. 281 **sight** eyes. 282 **whence** from
which. 283 **depasturing** feeding on.

285   For feare of waking him, his lips bedewd,
      And through his humid eyes did sucke his
         spright,
      Quite molten into lust and pleasure lewd;
  Wherewith she sighed soft, as if his case she rewd.°

74

  The whiles some one did chaunt this lovely lay;
290   Ah see, who so faire thing doest faine° to see,
      In springing flowre the image of thy day;°
      Ah see the Virgin Rose, how sweetly shee
      Doth first peepe forth with bashfull modestee,
      That fairer seemes, the lesse ye see her may;
295   Lo see soone after, how more bold and free
      Her bared bosome she doth broad display;
  Loe see soone after, how she fades, and falles away.

75

  So passeth, in the passing of a day,
      Of mortall life the leafe, the bud, the flowre,
300   Ne more doth flourish after first decay,
      That earst° was sought to decke both bed and
         bowre,
      Of many a Ladie, and many a Paramowre:°
      Gather therefore the Rose, whilest yet is prime,°
      For soone comes age, that will her pride°
         deflowre:
305   Gather the Rose of love, whilest yet is time,
  Whilest loving thou mayst loved be with equall
      crime.°

76

  He ceast, and then gan all the quire of birdes
      Their diverse notes t'attune unto his lay,
      As in approvance° of his pleasing words.
310   The constant paire heard all, that he did say,

---

288 **rewd** pitied.   290 **doest faine** delights.   291 **day** life.   301 **That earst** that which before.   302 **Paramowre** lover.   303 **prime** the "springtime" of human life.   304 **pride** flourishing state.   306 **crime** sin.   309 **approvance** approval.

Yet swarved not, but kept their forward way,
Through many covert groves, and thickets close,
In which they creeping did at last display°
That wanton Ladie, with her lover lose,°
Whose sleepie head she in her lap did soft dispose.°   *315*

77

Upon a bed of Roses she was layd,
As faint through heat, or dight to° pleasant sin,
And was arayd, or rather disarayd,
All in a vele of silke and silver thin,
That hid no whit her alablaster° skin,   *320*
But rather shewd more white, if more might bee:
More subtile° web *Arachne*° can not spin,
Nor the fine nets,° which oft we woven see
Of scorched deaw, do not in th'aire more lightly flee.

78

Her snowy brest was bare to readie spoyle   *325*
Of hungry eies, which n'ote° therewith be fild,
And yet through languour of her late sweet toyle,
Few drops, more cleare than Nectar, forth distild,
That like pure Orient perles adowne it trild,°
And her faire eyes sweet smyling in delight,   *330*
Moystened their fierie beames, with which she
    thrild°
Fraile harts, yet quenched not; like starry light
Which sparckling on the silent waves, does seeme
    more bright.

79

The young man sleeping by her, seemd to bee
Some goodly swayne of honorable place,°   *335*
That certes° it great pittie was to see
Him his nobilitie so foule deface;°

313 **display** discover.   314 **lose** loose.   315 **did soft dispose** gently
placed.   317 **dight to** prepared for.   320 **alablaster** alabaster.   322
subtile delicate.   322 **Arachne** the spider.   323 **the fine nets** gossa-
mer on which the dew has dried ("scorched deaw").   326 **no'te**
might not.   329 **trild** rolled.   331 **thrild** pierced.   335 **place** rank.
336 **certes** surely.   337 **deface** disgrace.

A sweet regard, and amiable grace,
   Mixed with manly sternnesse did appeare
340   Yet sleeping,° in his well proportiond face,
   And on his tender lips the downy heare
Did now but freshly spring, and silken blossomes
      beare.

80

His warlike armes, the idle instruments
   Of sleeping praise, were hong upon a tree,
345   And his brave shield, full of old moniments,°
   Was fowly ra'st,° that none the signes might see;
   Ne for them, ne for honour cared hee,
   Ne ought, that did to his advauncement tend,
   But in lewd loves, and wastfull luxuree,
350   His dayes, his goods, his bodie he did spend:
O horrible enchantment, that him so did blend.°

81

The noble Elfe,° and carefull Palmer drew
   So nigh them, minding nought, but lustfull game,
   That suddein forth they on them rusht, and threw
355   A subtile net, which onely for the same°
   The skilfull Palmer formally° did frame.
   So held them under fast, the whiles the rest
   Fled all away for feare of fowler° shame.
   The fair Enchauntresse, so unwares° opprest,°
360   Tryde all her arts, and all her sleights, thence out to
      wrest.°

82

And eke her lover strove: but all in vaine;
   For that same net so cunningly was wound,
   That neither guile, nor force might it distraine.°

340 **Yet sleeping** even as he slept.   345 **moniments** records or marks
of heroic deeds.   346 **ra'st** razed, erased.   351 **did blend** blinded.
352 **Elfe** knight.   355 **A . . . same** A fine net which especially for that
purpose.   356 **formally** in good form, skillfully.   358 **fowler** (1)
fouler; (2) also with reference to the fowler's net.   359 **unwares** suddenly.   359 **opprest** taken by surprise.   360 **out to wrest** to force
a way out.   363 **distraine** rend.

They tooke them both, and both them strongly
    bound
In captive bandes, which there they readie
    found: 365
But her in chaines of adamant° he tyde;
For nothing else might keepe her safe and sound;
But *Verdant* (so he hight) he soone untyde,
And counsell sage in steed thereof to him applyde.

83

But all those pleasant bowres and Pallace brave,° 370
    Guyon broke downe, with rigour pittilesse;
Ne ought° their goodly workmanship might save
Them from the tempest of his wrathfulnesse,
But that their blisse he turn'd to balefulnesse:°
Their groves he feld, their gardins did deface, 375
Their arbers spoyld, their Cabinets° suppresse,
Their banket° houses burne, their buildings
    race,°
And of the fairest late, now made the fowlest place.

84

Then led they her away, and eke that knight
    They with them led, both sorrowfull and sad: 380
The way they came, the same retourn'd they
    right,
Till they arrived, where they lately had
Charm'd those wild-beasts, that rag'd with furie
    mad.
Which now awaking, fierce at them gan fly,
As in their mistresse reskew, whom they lad;° 385
But them the Palmer soone did pacify.
Then *Guyon* askt, what meant those beastes, which
    there did ly.

85

Said he, these seeming beasts are men indeed,

366 **of adamant** of impregnable hardness. 370 **brave** splendid. 372
Ne ought not at all. 374 **balefulnesse** distress. 376 **Cabinets** sum-
mer houses. 377 **banket** banquet. 377 **race** raze. 385 **lad** led.

Whom this Enchauntresse hath transformed thus,
390 Whylome her lovers, which her lusts did feed,
Now turned into figures hideous,
According to their mindes like monstruous.°
Sad end (quoth he) of life intemperate,
And mournefull meed of joyes delicious:
395 But Palmer, if it mote thee so aggrate,°
Let them returned be unto their former state.

86

Streight way he with his vertuous° staffe them strooke,
And streight of beasts they comely men became;
Yet being men they did unmanly looke,
400 And stared ghastly, some for inward shame,
And some for wrath, to see their captive Dame:
But one above the rest in speciall,°
That had an hog beene late, hight *Grille* by
name,
Repined greatly, and did him miscall,°
405 That had from hoggish forme him brought to
naturall.

87

Said *Guyon,* See the mind of beastly man,
That hath so soone forgot the excellence
Of his creation, when he life began,
That now he chooseth, with vile difference,°
410 To be a beast, and lacke intelligence.
To whom the Palmer thus, The donghill kind
Delights in filth and foule incontinence:
Let *Grill*° be *Grill,* and have his hoggish mind,
But let us hence depart, whilest wether serves and
wind.

392 According . . . monstruous Even as their minds which were simi-
larly monstrous.   395 aggrate please.   397 vertuous powerful.   402
in speciall specially.   404 miscall revile.   409 difference change.
413 Grill a companion of Ulysses whom Circe transformed into a
swine, and who refused to be restored to human form.

The Third Booke

OF THE FAERIE QUEENE.

Contayning,

THE LEGEND OF

BRITOMARTIS,

OR

Of Chastitie.

1

It falles° me here to write of Chastity,
   That fairest vertue, farre above the rest;
   For which what needs me fetch° from *Faery*
   Forreine ensamples,° it to have exprest?
   Sith it is shrined in my Soveraines brest,   5
   And form'd so lively° in each perfect part,
   That to all Ladies, which have it profest,
   Need but behold the pourtraict° of her hart,
If pourtrayd it might be by any living art.

1 **falles** befalls.   3 **what . . . fetch** what need is there for me to fetch.
4 **ensamples** examples.   6 **lively** lifelike.   8 **pourtraict** image.

2

10 But living art may not least part expresse,
      Nor life-resembling pencill° it can paint:
      All° were it *Zeuxis*° or *Praxiteles*:°
      His dædale° hand would faile, and greatly faint,
      And her perfections with his error taint:
15   Ne Poets wit, that passeth Painter farre
      In picturing the parts of beautie daint,°
      So hard a workmanship adventure darre,°
For feare through want of words her excellence to
            marre.

3

How then shall I, Apprentice of the skill,
20   That whylome° in divinest wits did raine,
      Presume so high to stretch mine humble quill?
      Yet now my lucklesse lot doth me constraine
      Hereto perforce.° But O dred Soveraine
      Thus farre forth pardon, sith° that choicest wit
25   Cannot your glorious pourtraict figure plaine
      That I in colourd showes may shadow it,
And antique° praises unto present persons fit.

4

But if in living colours, and right hew,
      Your selfe you covet to see pictured,
30   Who can it doe more lively, or more trew,
      Then that sweete verse, with *Nectar* sprinckeled,
      In which a gracious servant° pictured
      His *Cynthia,* his heavens fairest light?
      That with his melting sweetnesse ravished,
35   And with the wonder of her beames bright,
My senses lulled are in slomber of delight.

11 **life-resembling pencill** the artist's brush that creates "living art."
12 **All** although.   12 **Zeuxis** a famous Greek painter.   12 **Praxiteles**
a famous Greek sculptor.   13 **dædale** cunning.   16 **daint** fine, exquisite.   17 **darre** dare.   20 **whylome** formerly.   23 **Hereto perforce** to this subject by necessity.   24 **sith** since.   27 **antique** ancient.   32 **a gracious servant** Sir Walter Raleigh, in his *Book of the
Ocean to Cynthia.*

5

But let that same delitious° Poet lend
 A little leave unto a rusticke Muse
 To sing his mistresse prayse, and let him mend,
 If ought amis her liking may abuse:°   *40*
 Ne let his fairest *Cynthia* refuse,
 In mirrours more then one her selfe to see,
 But either *Gloriana*° let her chuse,
 Or in *Belphœbe* fashioned to bee:
In th'one her rule, in th'other her rare chastitee. *45*

from CANTO I: THE OPENING EPISODE

1

The famous Briton Prince° and Faerie knight,
 After long wayes and perilous paines endured,
 Having their wearie limbes to perfect plight°
 Restord, and sory° wounds right well recured,°
 Of the faire *Alma* greatly were procured,° *5*
 To make there lenger sojourne and abode;
 But when thereto they might not be allured,
 From seeking praise, and deeds of armes abrode,
They courteous conge° tooke, and forth together
 yode.°

2

But the captiv'd *Acrasia* he sent,   *10*
 Because of travell long, a nigher way,
 With a strong gard, all reskew to prevent,
 And her to Faerie court safe to convay,
 That her for witnesse of his hard assay,°
 Unto his *Faerie* Queene he might present: *15*
 But he himselfe betooke another way,

37 **delitious** pleasing. 40 **abuse** impair. 43 **either Gloriana, etc.**
See the *Letter to Raleigh.* 1 **The famous Briton Prince** Arthur. 3
plight condition. 4 **sory** sore. 4 **recured** healed. 5 **procured** entreated. 9 **conge** farewell. 9 **yode** went. 14 **assay** endeavor.

To make more triall of his hardiment,°
And seeke adventures, as he with Prince *Arthur*
    went.

3

Long so they travelled through wastefull° wayes,
    Where daungers dwelt, and perils most did
20   wonne,°
    To hunt for glorie and renowmed° praise;
    Full many Countries they did overronne,
    From the uprising to the setting Sunne,
    And many hard adventures did atchieve;°
25 Of all the which they honour ever wonne,
    Seeking the weake oppressed to relieve,
And to recover right for such, as wrong did grieve.

4

At last as through an open plaine they yode,
    They spide a knight, that towards pricked faire,°
30 And him beside an aged Squire there rode,
    That seem'd to couch under his shield three-
        square,°
    As if that age bad him that burden spare,
    And yield it those, that stouter could it wield:
    He them espying, gan himselfe prepare,
35 And on his arme addresse° his goodly shield
That bore a Lion passant in a golden field.°

5

Which seeing good Sir *Guyon*, deare besought
    The Prince of grace, to let him runne that turne.
    He graunted: then the Faery quickly raught°
40 His poinant° speare, and sharpely gan to spurne°
    His fomy steed, whose fierie feete did burne
    The verdant grasse, as he thereon did tread;

---

17 **hardiment** courage.   19 **wastefull** desolate.   20 **wonne** dwell.
21 **renowmed** renowned.   24 **atchieve** finish successfully.   29 **that
. . . faire** that toward them rode well.   31 **shield three-square** triangular shield.   35 **addresse** put on.   36 **a Lion . . . field** heraldic description of a lion walking, against a golden background.   39
raught took.   40 **poinant** piercing.   40 **spurne** spur.

Ne did the other backe his foot returne,
But fiercely forward came withouten dread,
And bent° his dreadfull speare against the others head. 45

6

They bene ymet, and both their points arrived,°
But *Guyon* drove so furious and fell,°
That seem'd both shield and plate it would have
rived;°
Nathelesse° it bore his foe not from his sell,° 50
But made him stagger, as he were not well:
But *Guyon* selfe, ere well he was aware,
Nigh a speares length behind his crouper° fell,
Yet in his fall so well him selfe he bare,
That mischievous mischance his life and limbes
did spare.

7

Great shame and sorrow of that fall he tooke; 55
For never yet, sith warlike armes he bore,
And shivering° speare in bloudie field first
shooke,
He found himselfe dishonored so sore.
Ah gentlest knight, that ever armour bore,
Let not thee grieve dismounted to have beene, 60
And brought to ground, that never wast before;
For not thy fault, but secret powre unseene,
That speare enchaunted was, which layd thee on the
greene.

8

But weenedst thou° what wight thee overthrew,
Much greater griefe and shamefuller regret 65
For thy hard fortune then thou wouldst renew,
That of a single damzell° thou wert met
On equall plaine, and there so hard beset;

45 **bent** aimed.   46 **They ... arrived** They met and both spears made
contact.   47 **fell** fiercely.   48 **rived** pierced.   49 **Nathelesse** nevertheless.   49 **sell** saddle.   52 **crouper** crupper, the back of his saddle.
57 **shivering** capable of splitting.   64 **But weenedst thou** if you knew.
67 **a single damzell** a damsel alone.

    Even the famous *Britomart* it was,
70   Whom straunge adventure did from *Britaine* fet,°
    To seeke her lover (love farre sought alas,)
Whose image° she had seene in *Venus* looking glas.

9

Full of disdainefull wrath, he fierce uprose,
    For to revenge that foule reprochfull shame,
75   And snatching his bright sword began to close
    With her on foot, and stoutly forward came;
    Die rather would he, then endure that same.
    Which when his Palmer saw, he gan to feare
    His toward° perill and untoward blame,°
80   Which by that new rencounter° he should reare:°
For death sate on the point of that enchaunted speare.

10

And hasting towards him gan faire perswade,
    Not to provoke misfortune, nor to weene
    His speares default to mend with cruell blade;
85   For by his mightie Science° he had seene
    The secret vertue° of that weapon keene,
    That mortall puissance mote not withstond:
    Nothing on earth mote alwaies happie° beene.
    Great hazard were it, and adventure fond,°
90 To loose long gotten honour with one evill hond.°

11

By such good meanes he him discounselled,°
    From prosecuting his revenging rage;
    And eke the Prince like treaty handeled,°
    His wrathfull will with reason to asswage,
95   And laid the blame, not to his carriage,
    But to his starting steed, that swarv'd asyde,

---

70 **fet** fetch.　72 **Whose image,** etc. the episode is related in Canto ii.
79 **toward** imminent.　79 **untoward blame** unlucky injury.　80 **rencounter** encounter.　80 **reare** cause.　85 **Science** knowledge.　86 **vertue** power.　88 **happie** fortunate.　89 **fond** foolish.　90 **hond** action.　91 **discounselled** advised against.　93 **like treaty handeled** made the same entreaty.

And to the ill purveyance° of his page,
That had his furnitures° not firmely tyde:
So is his angry courage fairely pacifyde.

12

Thus reconcilement was betweene them knit,   100
   Through goodly temperance, and affection
      chaste,
   And either vowd with all their power and wit,°
   To let not others honour be defaste,°
   Of friend or foe, who ever it embaste,°
   Ne armes to beare against the others syde: 105
   In which accord the Prince was also plaste,
   And with that golden chaine of concord tyde.
So goodly all agreed, they forth yfere° did ryde.

13

O goodly usage of those antique times,
   In which the sword was servant unto right;   110
   When not for malice and contentious crimes,
   But all for praise, and proofe of manly might,
   The martiall brood° accustomed to fight:
   Then honour was the meed of victorie,
   And yet the vanquished had no despight: 115
   Let later age that noble use° envie,°
Vile rancour to avoid, and cruell surquedrie.°

14

Long they thus travelled in friendly wise,°
   Through countries waste,° and eke well edifyde,°
   Seeking adventures hard, to exercise   120
   Their puissance, whylome full dernely tryde:°
   At length they came into a forrest wyde,
   Whose hideous horror and sad trembling sound
   Full griesly° seem'd: Therein they long did ryde,

97 **purveyance** managing. 98 **furnitures** harness. 102 **wit** understanding. 103 **defaste** disgraced. 104 **embaste** degraded. 108
yfere together. 113 **brood** race. 116 **use** custom 116 **envie** seek
to rival. 117 **surquedrie** arrogance. 118 **wise** manner. 119 **waste**
desolate. 119 **edifyde** built up. 121 **whylome . . . tryde** at times
very grievously proven. 124 **griesly** horrible.

125   Yet tract° of living creatures none they found,
Save Beares, Lions, and Buls, which romed them
        around.

15

All suddenly out of the thickest brush,
        Upon a milk-white Palfrey° all alone,
        A goodly Ladie° did foreby them rush,
        Whose face did seeme as cleare as Christall
130   stone,
        And eke through feare as white as whales bone:
        Her garments all were wrought of beaten gold,
        And all her steed with tinsell trappings shone,
        Which fled so fast, that nothing mote him hold,
135 And scarse them leasure gave, her passing to behold.

16

Still as she fled, her eye she backward threw,
        As fearing evill, that pursewd her fast;
        And her faire yellow locks behind her flew,
        Loosely disperst with puffe of every blast:
140   All as a blazing starre° doth farre outcast
        His hearie° beames, and flaming lockes dispred,°
        At sight whereof the people stand aghast:
        But the sage wisard telles, as he has red,°
That it importunes death and dolefull drerihed.°

17

145 So as they gazed after her a while,
        Lo where a griesly Foster° forth did rush,
        Breathing out beastly lust her to defile:
        His tyreling° jade he fiercely forth did push,
        Through thicke and thin, both over banke and
        bush
150   In hope her to attaine by hooke or crooke,
        That from his gorie sides the bloud did gush:

125 **tract** track.   128 **Palfrey** a small saddle-horse.   129 **A goodly
Ladie** Florimell.   140 **a blazing starre** a comet, according to its ety-
mology, a long-haired star.   141 **hearie** hairy.   141 **dispred** spread
out.   143 **red** predicted.   144 **drerihed** sorrow.   146 **Foster** forester.   148 **tyreling** tired.

Large were his limbes, and terrible his looke,
And in his clownish° hand a sharp bore speare he
    shooke.

18

Which outrage when those gentle knights did see,
    Full of great envie° and fell gealosy,°   155
    They stayd not to avise,° who first should bee,
    But all spurd after fast, as they mote fly,
    To reskew her from shamefull villany.
    The Prince and *Guyon* equally bylive°
    Her selfe pursewd, in hope to win thereby   160
    Most goodly meede, the fairest Dame alive:
But after the foule foster *Timias* did strive.

19

The whiles faire *Britomart*, whose constant mind,
    Would not so lightly follow beauties chace,
    Ne reckt of° Ladies Love, did stay behind,   165
    And them awayted there a certaine space,
    To weet if they would turne backe to that place:
    But when she saw them gone, she forward went,
    As lay her journey, through that perlous Pace,°
    With stedfast courage and stout hardiment;   170
Ne evill thing she fear'd, ne evill thing she ment.

*In his pursuit of the foster, the wounded Timias is suc-
cored by the virgin, Belphoebe. At this point Spenser in-
terrupts his narrative to describe her birth and that of her
twin sister, Amoret. Belphoebe is raised by Diana "in
perfect Maydenhed" while Amoret is adopted by Venus
in place of Cupid and raised "in goodly womanhed" in
the Garden of Adonis.*

153 **clownish** rustic.   155 **envie** ill-will.   155 **gealosy** wrath.   156
avise consider.   159 **bylive** quickly.   165 **Ne reckt of** nor cared for.
169 **perlous Pace** perilous place.

from CANTO VI: THE GARDEN OF ADONIS

30

In that same Gardin all the goodly flowres,
    Wherewith dame Nature doth her beautifie,
    And decks the girlonds of her paramoures,°
    Are fetcht: there is the first seminarie°
5   Of all things, that are borne to live and die,
    According to their kindes.° Long worke it were,
    Here to account the endlesse progenie
    Of all the weedes, that bud and blossome there;
But so much as doth need, must needs be counted°
    here.

31

10 It sited was° in fruitfull soyle of old,
    And girt in with two walles on either side;
    The one of yron, the other of bright gold,
    That none might thorough breake, nor over-
        stride:
    And double gates it had, which opened wide,
15   By which both in and out men moten pas;
    Th'one faire and fresh, the other old and dride:
    Old *Genius*° the porter of them was,
Old *Genius,* the which a double nature has.

32

He letteth in, he letteth out to wend,
20   All that to come into the world desire;
    A thousand thousand naked babes attend
    About him day and night, which doe require,
    That he with fleshly weedes° would then attire:
    Such as him list, such as eternall fate
25   Ordained hath, he clothes with sinfull mire,°

3 **paramoures** lovers. 4 **seminarie** seed-plot. 6 **kindes** natures. 9
counted recounted. 10 **sited was** was situated. 17 **Old Genius** See
II. xii. 47. 23 **weedes** body. 25 **sinfull mire** i.e., the flesh.

And sendeth forth to live in mortall state,
Till they againe returne backe by the hinder gate.

33

After that they againe returned beene,°
    They in that Gardin planted be againe;
    And grow afresh, as they had never seene   *30*
    Fleshly corruption, nor mortall paine.
    Some thousand yeares so doen° they there re-
        maine;
    And then of him are clad with other hew,°
    Or sent into the chaungefull world againe,
    Till thither they returne, where first they grew: *35*
So like a wheele around they runne from old to new.

34

Ne needs there Gardiner to set, or sow,
    To plant or prune: for of their owne accord
    All things, as they created were, doe grow,
    And yet remember well the mightie word,   *40*
    Which first was spoken by th'Almightie lord,
    That bad them to increase and multiply:
    Ne doe they need with water of the ford,°
    Or of the clouds to moysten their roots dry;
For in themselves eternall moisture they imply.°   *45*

35

Infinite shapes of creatures there are bred,
    And uncouth° formes, which none yet ever
        knew,
    And every sort is in a sundry° bed
    Set by it selfe, and ranckt in comely rew:°
    Some fit for reasonable soules t'indew,°   *50*
    Some made for beasts, some made for birds to
        weare,
    And all the fruitfull spawne of fishes hew
    In endlesse rancks along enraunged were,

---

28 **beene** are. 32 **doen** do. 33 **hew** form. 43 **ford** stream. 45 **imply** contain. 47 **uncouth** strange. 48 **sundry** separate. 49 **rew** row. 50 **t'indew** to put on.

That seem'd the *Ocean* could not containe them
  there.

36

55 Daily they grow, and daily forth are sent
      Into the world, it to replenish more;
      Yet is the stocke not lessened, nor spent,
      But still remaines in everlasting store,
      As it at first created was of yore.
60   For in the wide wombe of the world there lyes,
      In hatefull darkenesse and in deepe horrore,
      An huge eternall *Chaos,* which supplyes
    The substances of natures fruitfull progenyes.

37

  All things from thence doe their first being fetch,
65   And borrow matter, whereof they are made,
      Which when as forme and feature it does ketch,°
      Becomes a bodie, and doth then invade
      The state of life, out of the griesly shade.
      That substance is eterne, and bideth° so,
70   Ne when the life decayes, and forme does fade,
      Doth it consume, and into nothing go,
    But chaunged is, and often altred to and fro.

38

  The substance is not chaunged, nor altered,
      But th'only° forme and outward fashion;°
75   For every substance is conditioned°
      To change her hew, and sundry formes to don,
      Meet for her temper and complexion:°
      For formes are variable and decay,
      By course of kind,° and by occasion;
80   And that faire flowre of beautie fades away,
    As doth the lilly fresh before the sunny ray.

66 **ketch** catch, assume.   69 **bideth** remains.   74 **th'only** only the.
74 **fashion** appearance.   75 **conditioned** bound.   77 **Meet . . . complexion** Fitting for her temperament and quality.   79 **By . . . kind**
in the course of nature.

39

Great enimy to it, and to all the rest,
    That in the *Gardin* of *Adonis* springs,
    Is wicked *Time,* who with his scyth addrest,°
    Does mow the flowring herbes and goodly things,   *85*
    And all their glory to the ground downe flings,
    Where they doe wither, and are fowly mard:
    He flyes about, and with his flaggy° wings
    Beates downe both leaves and buds without re-
        gard,
Ne ever pittie may relent° his malice hard.   *90*

40

Yet pittie often did the gods relent,
    To see so faire things mard, and spoyled quight:
    And their great mother *Venus* did lament
    The losse of her deare brood, her deare de-
        light;
    Her hart was pierst with pittie at the sight,   *95*
    When walking through the Gardin, them she
        spyde,
    Yet no'te° she find redresse for such despight.°
    For all that lives, is subject to that law:
All things decay in time, and to their end do draw.

41

But were it not, that *Time* their troubler is,   *100*
    All that in this delightfull Gardin growes,
    Should happie be, and have immortall blis:
    For here all plentie, and all pleasure flowes,
    And sweet love gentle fits° emongst them
        throwes,
    Without fell rancor, or fond gealosie;   *105*
    Franckly each paramour his leman° knowes,
    Each bird his mate, ne any does envie
Their goodly meriment, and gay felicitie.

---

84 **addrest** armed.   88 **flaggy** drooping.   90 **relent** soften.   97 **no'te**
could not.   97 **despight** injury.   104 **fits** attacks of passion.   106
leman beloved.

42

There is continuall spring, and harvest there
110   Continuall, both meeting at one time:
     For both the boughes doe laughing blossomes
        beare,
     And with fresh colours decke the wanton Prime,°
     And eke attonce the heavy trees they clime,
     Which seeme to labour under their fruits lode:
115   The whiles the joyous birdes make their pastime
     Emongst the shadie leaves, their sweet abode,
And their true loves without suspition tell abrode.

43

Right in the middest of that Paradise,
     There stood a stately Mount, on whose round top
120   A gloomy grove of mirtle trees did rise,
     Whose shadie boughes sharpe steele did never
        lop,
     Nor wicked beasts their tender buds did crop,
     But like a girlond compassed the hight,
     And from their fruitfull sides sweet gum did
        drop,
125   That all the ground with precious deaw bedight,
Threw forth most dainty odours, and most sweet de-
        light.

44

And in the thickest covert of that shade,
     There was a pleasant arbour, not by art,
     But of the trees owne inclination° made,
     Which knitting their rancke° braunches part to
130   part,
     With wanton yvie twyne entrayld° athwart,
     And Eglantine, and Caprifole° emong,
     Fashiond above within their inmost part,

---

112 **Prime** spring.   129 **owne inclination** bending themselves.   130
rancke dense.   131 **entrayld** entwined.   132 **Caprifole** honeysuckle.

That nether *Phœbus* beams could through them
  throng,
Nor *Aeolus*° sharp blast could worke them any wrong.   *135*

45

And all about grew every sort of flowre,
  To which sad lovers were transformd of yore;
  Fresh *Hyacinthus,*° *Phœbus* paramoure,
  And dearest love°
  Foolish *Narcisse,*° that likes the watry shore,   *140*
  Sad *Amaranthus,* made a flowre but late,
  Sad *Amaranthus,* in whose purple gore
Me seemes I see *Amintas* wretched fate,°
To whom sweet Poets verse hath given endlesse date.

46

There wont faire *Venus* often to enjoy   *145*
  Her deare *Adonis* joyous company,
  And reape sweet pleasure of the wanton boy;
  There yet, some say, in secret he does ly,
  Lapped in flowres and pretious spycery,
  By her hid from the world, and from the skill°   *150*
  Of *Stygian*° Gods, which doe her love envy;
  But she her selfe, when ever that she will,
Possesseth him, and of his sweetnesse takes her fill.

47

And sooth it seemes they say: for he may not°
  For ever die, and ever buried bee   *155*
  In balefull night, where all things are forgot;
  All be he° subject to mortalitie,

135 **Aeolus** god of the winds.   138 **Fresh Hyacinthus, etc.** When
Hyacinthus was slain by a discus, Phoebus, through grief for his lost
love, caused the hyacinth to spring from his blood.   139 This half
line was added in the 1609 ed.   140 **Foolish Narcisse** Narcissus who
died through love of his own reflection in the water.   143 **Amintas
wretched fate, etc.** the death of Sidney in 1586, marked by elegies of
most poets of the time including Spenser.   150 **skill** knowledge.
151 **Stygian** of hell; from Styx, a river of hell.   154 **And . . . not**
And it seems true what they say, for he cannot.   157 **All be he** although he is.

Yet is eterne° in mutabilitie,
And by succession made perpetuall,
160   Transformed oft, and chaunged diverslie:
For him the Father of all formes they call;
Therefore needs mote he live, that living gives to all.

48

There now he liveth in eternall blis,
Joying° his goddesse, and of her enjoyd:
165   Ne feareth he henceforth that foe of his,
Which with his cruell tuske him deadly cloyd:°
For that wilde Bore, the which him once an-
noyd,°
She firmely hath emprisoned for ay,
That her sweet love his malice mote avoyd,
170   In a strong rocky Cave, which is they say,
Hewen underneath that Mount, that none him losen°
may.

49

There now he lives in everlasting joy,
With many of the Gods in company,
Which thither haunt, and with the winged boy
175   Sporting himselfe in safe felicity:
Who when he hath with spoiles and cruelty
Ransackt the world, and in the wofull harts
Of many wretches set his triumphes hye,
Thither resorts, and laying his sad darts
180 Aside, with faire *Adonis* playes his wanton parts.

50

And his true love faire *Psyche*° with him playes,
Faire *Psyche* to him lately reconcyld,
After long troubles and unmeet upbrayes,°

---

158 **eterne** eternal.   164 **Joying** enjoying.   166 **cloyd** gored.   167
annoyd injured.   171 **losen** loosen.   182 **Faire Psyche,** etc. When
Psyche attempted to see her nightly lover, Cupid, she was abandoned
by him and punished by the jealous Venus who imposed severe trials
upon her. Later she was reunited with Cupid, and made immortal.
183 **unmeet upbrayes** unfitting reproaches.

With which his mother *Venus* her revyld,°
And eke himselfe her cruelly exyld: *185*
But now in stedfast love and happy state
She with him lives, and hath him borne a chyld,
Pleasure, that doth both gods and men aggrate,°
Pleasure, the daughter of *Cupid* and *Psyche* late.

51

Hither great *Venus* brought this infant faire,°   *190*
The younger daughter of *Chrysogonee,*
And unto *Psyche* with great trust and care
Committed her, yfostered to bee,
And trained up in true feminitee:°
Who no lesse carefully her tendered,°   *195*
Then her owne daughter *Pleasure,* to whom shee
Made her companion, and her lessoned°
In all the lore of love, and goodly womanhead.

52

In which when she to perfect ripenesse grew,
Of grace and beautie noble Paragone,   *200*
She brought her forth into the worldes vew,
To be th'ensample of true love alone,
And Lodestarre of all chaste affectione,
To all faire Ladies, that doe live on ground.
To Faery court she came, where many one   *205*
Admyrd her goodly haveour,° and found
His feeble hart wide launched with loves cruell
    wound.

53

But she to none of them her love did cast,
Save to the noble knight Sir *Scudamore,*
To whom her loving hart she linked fast   *210*
In faithfull love, t'abide for evermore,
And for his dearest sake endured sore,°

---

184 **revyld** assailed.   188 **aggrate** please.   190 **this infant faire** Amoret.   194 **feminitee** womanhood.   195 **tendered** cherished.   197 **lessoned** taught.   206 **haveour** behavior.   212 **sore** with great grief.

Sore trouble of an hainous enimy;
Who her would forced have to have forlore°
215   Her former love, and stedfast loialty,
As ye may elsewhere read that ruefull history.

54

But well I weene, ye first desire to learne,
What end unto that fearefull Damozell,
Which fled so fast from that same foster° stearne,
220   Whom with his brethren *Timias* slew, befell:
That was to weet, the goodly *Florimell;*
Who wandring for to seeke her lover deare,
Her lover deare, her dearest *Marinell,*
Into misfortune fell, as ye did heare,
And from Prince *Arthur* fled with wings of idle°
225   feare.

*The fleeing Florimell remains for a time with a witch,
but then must flee from her lustful son. In revenge, the
witch sends after her a monster that feeds on woman's
flesh. Florimell escapes to a fisherman's boat, only to
arouse his lust. At the moment when she is thrown down
in the boat and her garments are covered with the scales
of fish, Proteus, the shepherd of the seas, rescues her.
Upon rejecting his love, she is imprisoned at the bottom
of the sea.*

*In her search for Artegall, Britomart meets the de-
spairing Scudamour who cannot pass through the fire
that guards the house of Busyrane where Amoret is held
captive. Through the power of her armor, Britomart
passes through the flames and enters the castle. There
she comes into a room covered with tapestries that portray the power of Cupid. She enters another room whose
door is also inscribed with the motto, "Be bold," and
waits by a closed iron door that bears the motto, "Be not
too bold."*

214 **forlore** abandoned.   219 **foster** forester.   225 **idle** being without cause.

CANTO XII

The maske of Cupid, and th'enchaunted
    Chamber are displayd,
Whence Britomart redeemes faire
    Amoret, through charmes decayd.°

1

Tho° when as chearelesse Night ycovered had
    Faire heaven with an universall cloud,
    That every wight dismayd with darknesse sad,°
    In silence and in sleepe themselves did shroud,
    She heard a shrilling Trompet sound aloud,   5
    Signe of nigh battell, or got victory;
    Nought therewith daunted was her courage
        proud,
    But rather stird to cruell enmity,
Expecting ever,° when some foe she might descry.°

2

With that, an hideous storme of winde arose,   10
    With dreadfull thunder and lightning atwixt,°
    And an earth-quake, as if it streight would lose°
    The worlds foundations from his centre fixt;
    A direfull stench of smoke and sulphure mixt
    Ensewd, whose noyance fild the fearefull sted,°   15
    From the fourth houre of night untill the sixt;
    Yet the bold *Britonesse* was nought ydred,°
Though much emmov'd,° but stedfast still persevered.

3

All suddenly a stormy whirlwind blew
    Throughout the house, that clapped every dore,   20

Arg. **decayd** wasted away. 1 **Tho** then. 3 **sad** heavy. 9 **Expecting ever** waiting for the time. 9 **descry** espy. 11 **atwixt** among it.
12 **lose** loosen. 15 **Ensewd . . . sted** Followed, the annoyance of
which filled the fearful place. 17 **ydred** terrified. 18 **emmov'd**
moved.

With° which that yron wicket° open flew,
    As it with mightie levers had bene tore:
    And forth issewd, as on the ready° flore
    Of some Theatre, a grave personage,
25   That in his hand a branch of laurell bore,
    With comely haveour and count'nance sage,
Yclad in costly garments, fit for tragicke Stage.

4

Proceeding to the midst, he still did stand,
    As if in mind he somewhat° had to say,
30   And to the vulgar° beckning with his hand,
    In signe of silence, as to heare a play,
    By lively actions he gan bewray°
    Some argument° of matter passioned;°
    Which doen, he backe retyred soft away,
35   And passing by, his name discovered,°
Ease, on his robe in golden letters cyphered.

5

The noble Mayd, still standing all this vewd,
    And merveild at his strange intendiment;°
    With that a joyous fellowship issewd
40   Of Minstrals, making goodly meriment,
    With wanton Bardes, and Rymers impudent,
    All which together sung full chearefully
    A lay of loves delight, with sweet consent:°
    After whom marcht a jolly company,
45 In manner of a maske, enranged orderly.

6

The whiles a most delitious harmony,
    In full straunge notes was sweetly heard to
      sound,

---

21 **With** at.   21 **that yron wicket** the door through which Britomart
entered the room.   23 **ready** prepared.   29 **somewhat** something.
30 **the vulgar** the common people.   32 **gan bewray** did reveal.   33
argument subject or theme of the play.   33 **passioned** expressed with
deep feeling.   35 **discovered** revealed.   38 **intendiment** intention.
43 **consent** harmony.

That the rare sweetnesse of the melody
The feeble senses wholly did confound,
And the fraile soule in deepe delight nigh
    dround: 50
And when it ceast, shrill trompets loud did
    bray,°
That their report did farre away rebound,
And when they ceast, it gan againe to play,
The whiles the maskers marched forth in trim° aray.

7

The first was *Fancy,* like a lovely boy,   55
Of rare aspect, and beautie without peare;°
Matchable either to that ympe of *Troy,*°
Whom *Jove* did love, and chose his cup to beare,
Or that same daintie lad,° which was so deare
To great *Alcides,* that when as he dyde,   60
He wailed womanlike with many a teare,
And every wood, and every valley wyde
He fild with *Hylas* name; the Nymphes eke *Hylas*
    cryde.

8

His garment neither was of silke nor say,°
But painted plumes, in goodly order dight,°   65
Like as the sunburnt *Indians*° do aray
Their tawney bodies, in their proudest plight:°
As those same plumes, so seemd he vaine and
    light,
That by his gate° might easily appeare;
For still he far'd° as dauncing in delight,   70
And in his hand a windy fan° did beare,
That in the idle° aire he mov'd still here and there.

---

51 **bray** resound.   54 **trim** fit, proper.   56 **peare** equal.   57 **that ympe of Troy** the child, Ganymede, whom Jove made his cupbearer. 59 **that same daintie lad** the handsome Hylas who was loved by Hercules. When he was carried off by the nymphs, Hercules called for him but heard only his own echo in reply.   64 **say** a kind of cloth. 65 **dight** adorned.   66 **the sunburnt Indians** Indians of North America.   67 **plight** attire.   69 **gate** gait.   70 **far'd** went.   71 **a windy fan** to produce wind.   72 **idle** still.

9

And him beside marcht amorous *Desyre*,
    Who seemd of riper yeares, then th'other Swaine,
75   Yet was that other swayne this elders syre,
    And gave him being, commune° to them twaine:
    His garment was disguised very vaine,°
    And his embrodered Bonet sat awry;
    Twixt both his hands few sparkes he close did
        straine,°
80   Which still he blew, and kindled busily,
That soone they life conceiv'd, and forth in flames
        did fly.

10

Next after him went *Doubt,* who was yclad
    In a discolour'd° cote, of straunge disguyse,°
    That at his backe a brode Capuccio° had,
85   And sleeves dependant *Albanese*-wyse:°
    He lookt askew with his mistrustfull eyes,
    And nicely° trode, as thornes lay in his way,
    Or that the flore to shrinke he did avyse,°
    And on a broken reed he still did stay°
His feeble steps, which shrunke, when hard theron
90   he lay.

11

With him went *Daunger,* cloth'd in ragged weed,°
    Made of Beares skin, that him more dreadfull
        made,
    Yet his owne face was dreadfull, ne did need
    Straunge° horrour, to deforme his griesly shade;°
95   A net in th'one hand, and a rustie° blade
    In th'other was, this Mischiefe, that Mishap;
    With th'one his foes he threatned to invade,

---

76 commune common. **77 disguised very vaine** colored fantasti-
cally. **79 close did straine** closely clasped. **83 discolour'd** differ-
ently colored. **83 disguyse** fashion. **84 Capuccio** the hood of a
cloak. **85 dependent Albanese-wyse** hanging in Albanian fashion.
87 nicely fastidiously. **88 avyse** perceive. **89 stay** support. **91
weed** dress. **94 Straunge** added from outside. **94 shade** form. **95
rustie** bloody.

With th'other he his friends ment to enwrap:
For whom he could not kill, he practizd° to entrap.

12

Next him was *Feare,* all arm'd from top to toe,   100
    Yet thought himselfe not safe enough thereby,
    But feard each shadow moving to and fro,
    And his owne armes when glittering he did spy,
    Or clashing heard, he fast away did fly,
    As ashes pale of hew, and wingyheeld;   105
    And evermore on daunger fixt his eye,
    Gainst whom he alwaies bent° a brasen shield,
Which his right hand unarmed fearefully did wield.

13

With him went *Hope* in rancke,° a handsome Mayd,
    Of chearefull looke and lovely to behold;   110
    In silken samite° she was light arayd,
    And her faire lockes were woven up in gold;
    She alway smyld, and in her hand did hold
    An holy water Sprinckle,° dipt in deowe,°
    With which she sprinckled favours manifold,   115
    On whom she list, and did great liking sheowe,
Great liking unto many, but true love to feowe.

14

And after them *Dissemblance,* and *Suspect*°
    Marcht in one rancke, yet an unequall paire:
    For she was gentle, and of milde aspect,   120
    Courteous to all, and seeming debonaire,°
    Goodly adorned, and exceeding faire:
    Yet was that all but painted, and purloynd,
    And her bright browes were deckt with bor-
        rowed haire:
    Her deedes were forged, and her words false
        coynd,   125

99 **practizd** plotted.   107 **bent** directed.   109 **rancke** together in a row.   111 **samite** a rich fabric.   114 **An holy water Sprinckle** an aspergill, a brush used to sprinkle holy water.   114 **deowe** dew.   118 **Dissemblance, and Suspect** Dissimulation and Suspicion.   121 **debonaire** gracious.

And alwaies in her hand two clewes° of silke she
        twynd.

15

But he was foule, ill favoured, and grim,
        Under his eyebrowes looking still askaunce;
        And ever as *Dissemblance* laught on him,
130   He lowrd° on her with daungerous eyeglaunce;
        Shewing his nature in his countenance;
        His rolling eyes did never rest in place,
        But walkt each where,° for feare of hid mis-
            chaunce,
        Holding a lattice still before his face,
Through which he still did peepe, as forward he did
135   pace.

16

Next him went *Griefe,* and *Fury* matcht yfere;°
        Griefe all in sable sorrowfully clad,
        Downe hanging his dull head, with heavy chere,°
        Yet inly being more, then seeming sad:°
140   A paire of Pincers in his hand he had,
        With which he pinched people to the hart,
        That from thenceforth a wretched life they lad,°
        In wilfull languor and consuming smart,
Dying each day with inward wounds of dolours dart.

17

145 But *Fury* was full ill appareiled
        In rags, that naked nigh she did appeare,
        With ghastly lookes and dreadfull drerihed;°
        For from her backe her garments she did teare,
        And from her head oft rent her snarled heare:
150   In her right hand a firebrand she did tosse
        About her head, still roming here and there;

126 **clewes** threads.   130 **lowrd** scowled.   133 **walkt each where**
moved everywhere.   136 **yfere** together.   138 **chere** mood.   139
Yet . . . sad Inwardly he was more sad than he appeared to be.
142 **lad** led.   147 **drerihed** grief.

As a dismayed Deare in chace embost,°
Forgetfull of his safety, hath his right way lost.

18

After them went *Displeasure* and *Pleasance,*
    He looking lompish° and full sullein sad,   155
    And hanging downe his heavy countenance;
    She chearefull fresh and full of joyance° glad,
    As if no sorrow she ne felt ne drad;°
    That evill matched paire they seemd to bee:
    An angry Waspe th'one in a viall had,   160
    Th'other in hers an hony-lady Bee;°
Thus marched these six couples forth in faire de-
    gree.°

19

After all these there marcht a most faire Dame,
    Led of two grysie villeins, th'one *Despight,*°
    The other cleped *Cruelty* by name: 165
    She dolefull Lady, like a dreary Spright,°
    Cald by strong charmes out of eternall night,
    Had deathes owne image figurd in her face,
    Full of sad signes, fearefull to living sight;
    Yet in that horror shewd a seemely° grace,   170
And with her feeble feet did move a comely pace.

20

Her brest all naked, as net° ivory,
    Without adorne of gold or silver bright,
    Wherewith the Craftesman wonts it beautify,°
    Of her dew honour° was despoyled quight,   175
    And a wide wound therein (O ruefull sight)
    Entrenched deepe with knife accursed keene,
    Yet freshly bleeding forth her fainting spright,

152 embost exhausted. **155 lompish** dejected. **157 joyance** enjoyment. **158 ne felt ne drad** neither felt nor feared. **161 hony-
lady Bee** honeybee; perhaps "honey-laden bee." **162 degree** order.
164 Led . . . Despight Led by two horrible villains, the one Despight
or Outrage. **166 Spright** spirit. **170 seemely** pleasing. **172 net**
pure. **174 wonts it beautify** is accustomed to beautify it. **175 Of
. . . honour** of the adornments due her.

(The worke of cruell hand) was to be seene,
180 That dyde in sanguine red her skin all snowy cleene.

21

At that wide orifice her trembling hart
　　　Was drawne forth, and in silver basin layd,
　　　Quite through transfixed with a deadly dart,
185　　And in her bloud yet steeming fresh embayd:°
　　　And those two villeins, which her steps upstayd,°
　　　When her weake feete could scarcely her sus-
　　　　　taine,
　　　And fading vitall powers gan to fade,
　　　Her forward still with torture did constraine,
And evermore encreased her consuming paine.

22

190 Next after her the winged God° himselfe
　　　Came riding on a Lion ravenous,
　　　Taught to obay the menage° of that Elfe,
　　　That man and beast with powre imperious
　　　Subdeweth to his kingdome tyrannous:
195　　His blindfold eyes he bad a while unbind,
　　　That his proud spoyle of that same dolorous
　　　Faire Dame he might behold in perfect kind;°
Which seene, he much rejoyced in his cruell mind.

23

Of which full proud, himselfe up rearing hye,
200　　He looked round about with sterne disdaine;
　　　And did survay his goodly company:
　　　And marshalling the evill ordered traine,
　　　With that the darts which his right hand did
　　　　　straine,°
　　　Full dreadfully he shooke that all did quake,
205　　And clapt on hie his coulourd winges twaine,

184 yet . . . embayd still steaming, was freshly steeped.   185 upstayd upheld.   190 the winged God Cupid.   192 menage manege,
horsemanship.   197 in perfect kind in perfect manner, i.e., clearly.
203 straine clasp.

That all his many° it affraide did make:
Tho blinding him againe, his way he forth did take.

24

Behinde him was *Reproch, Repentance, Shame;*
    Reproch the first, *Shame* next, *Repent* behind:
    Repentance feeble, sorrowfull, and lame: *210*
    Reproch despightfull, carelesse, and unkind;
    Shame most ill favour, bestiall, and blind:
    Shame lowrd,° *Repentance* sigh'd, *Reproch* did
        scould;
    Reproch sharpe stings, *Repentance* whips en-
        twind,
    Shame burning brond-yrons° in her hand did
        hold: *215*
All three to each unlike,° yet all made in one mould.

25

And after them a rude confused rout°
    Of persons flockt, whose names is hard to read:°
    Emongst them was sterne *Strife,* and *Anger* stout,
    Unquiet *Care,* and fond *Unthriftihead,*°   *220*
    Lewd° *Losse of Time,* and *Sorrow* seeming dead,
    Inconstant *Chaunge,* and false *Disloyaltie,*
    Consuming *Riotise,*° and guilty *Dread*
    Of heavenly vengeance, faint *Infirmitie,*
Vile *Povertie,* and lastly *Death* with infamie.   *225*

26

There were full many moe like° maladies,
    Whose names and natures I note° readen well;
    So many moe, as there be phantasies
    In wavering wemens wit,° that none can tell,°
    Or paines in love, or punishments in hell;   *230*

206 **many** meinie, company.   213 **lowrd** glowered.   215 **brond-
yrons** swords. 216 **to each unlike** unlike each other. 217 **rout**
company. 218 **read** distinguish. 220 **Unthriftihead** the state of
loose living, profligacy. 221 **Lewd** wicked. 223 **Riotise** Riotousness. 226 **moe like** more similar. 227 **note** know not how to. 229
wit mind. 229 **tell** count.

All which disguized marcht in masking wise,°
About the chamber with that Damozell,
And then returned, having marched thrise,
Into the inner roome, from whence they first did rise.°

27

235 So soone as they were in, the dore streight way
Fast locked, driven with that stormy blast,
Which first it opened; and bore all away.
Then the brave Maid, which all this while was plast
In secret shade, and saw both first and last,
240 Issewed forth, and went unto the dore,
To enter in, but found it locked fast:
It vaine she thought with rigorous uprore°
For to efforce, when charmes had closed it afore.°

28

Where force might not availe, there sleights and art
245 She cast° to use, both fit for hard emprize;°
For thy° from that same roome not to depart
Till morrow next, she did her selfe avize,
When that same Maske againe should forth arize.
The morrow next appeard with joyous cheare,
250 Calling men to their daily exercize,
Then she, as morrow fresh, her selfe did reare°
Out of her secret stand, that day for to out weare.°

29

All that day she outwore in wandering,
And gazing on that Chambers ornament,
255 Till that againe the second evening
Her covered with her sable vestiment,°
Wherewith the worlds faire beautie she hath blent:°

231 in masking wise in manner of a masque. 234 rise issue. 242 rigorous uprore strong force. 243 afore before. 245 cast resolved. 245 emprize enterprise. 246 For thy therefore. 251 reare rise. 252 out weare spend. 256 sable vestiment black garment, i.e., darkness. 257 blent obscured.

Then when the second watch° was almost past,
That brasen dore flew open, and in went
Bold *Britomart,* as she had late forecast,°   260
Neither of idle shewes, nor of false charmes aghast.

30

So soone as she was entred, round about
    She cast her eies, to see what was become
    Of all those persons, which she saw without:
    But lo, they streight were vanisht all and some,° 265
    Ne living wight she saw in all that roome,
    Save that same woefull Ladie, both whose hands
    Were bounden fast, that did her ill become,
    And her small wast girt round with yron bands,
Unto a brasen pillour, by the which she stands.   270

31

And her before the vile Enchaunter° sate,
    Figuring° straunge characters of his art,
    With living bloud he those characters wrate,
    Dreadfully dropping from her dying hart,
    Seeming transfixed with a cruell dart,   275
    And all perforce° to make her him to love.
    Ah who can love the worker of her smart?
    A thousand charmes he formerly did prove;°
Yet thousand charmes could not her stedfast heart
    remove.

32

Soone as that virgin knight he saw in place,°   280
    His wicked bookes in hast he overthrew,
    Not caring his long labours to deface,°
    And fiercely ronning to that Lady trew,
    A murdrous knife out of his pocket drew,

---

258 **the second watch** the second of the periods into which night is
divided, from 9 P.M. to 12 midnight.   260 **late forecast** resolved
earlier.   265 **all and some** every one.   271 **the vile Enchaunter**
Busyrane.   272 **Figuring** representing.   276 **perforce** by violence.
278 **prove** try.   280 **in place** there.   282 **Not . . . deface** Not caring
whether he destroyed his long labors.

285   The which he thought, for villeinous despight,°
        In her tormented bodie to embrew:°
        But the stout Damzell to him leaping light,
His cursed hand withheld, and maistered his might.

                33
From her, to whom his fury first he ment,°
290   The wicked weapon rashly he did wrest,°
        And turning to her selfe his fell intent,°
        Unwares it strooke into her snowie chest,
        That little drops empurpled her faire brest.
        Exceeding wroth therewith the virgin grew,
295   Albe° the wound were nothing deepe imprest,°
        And fiercely forth her mortall blade she drew,
To give him the reward for such vile outrage dew.

                34
So mightily she smote him, that to ground
        He fell halfe dead; next stroke him should have
            slaine,
300   Had not the Lady, which by him stood bound,
        Dernely° unto him called to abstaine,
        From doing° him to dy. For else her paine
        Should be remedilesse, sith none but hee,
        Which wrought it, could the same recure° againe.
305   Therewith she stayd her hand, loth stayd to bee;
For life she him envyde,° and long'd revenge to see.

                35
And to him said, Thou wicked man, whose meed
        For so huge mischiefe, and vile villany
        Is death, or if that ought do death exceed,
310   Be sure, that nought may save thee from to dy,°
        But if that° thou this Dame doe presently
        Restore unto her health, and former state;
        This doe and live, else die undoubtedly.

285 **despight** anger. 286 **embrew** plunge. 289 **ment** aimed. 290
rashly ... wrest quickly did he turn. 291 **fell intent** fierce intention.
295 **Albe** although. 295 **imprest** pressed in. 301 **Dernely** grievously. 302 **doing** causing. 304 **recure** cure. 306 **envyde** begrudged. 310 **to dy** dying. 311 **But if that** unless.

He glad of life, that lookt for death but late,
Did yield himselfe right willing to prolong his date.°   315

36

And rising up, gan streight to overlooke°
　　Those cursed leaves, his charmes backe to re-
　　　　verse;
　　Full dreadfull things out of that balefull booke
　　He red,° and measur'd° many a sad verse,
　　That horror gan the virgins hart to perse,°   320
　　And her faire lockes up stared stiffe° on end,
　　Hearing him those same bloudy lines reherse;°
　　And all the while he red, she did extend
Her sword high over him, if ought° he did offend.

37

Anon she gan perceive the house to quake,   325
　　And all the dores to rattle round about;
　　Yet all that did not her dismaied make,
　　Nor slacke her threatfull hand for daungers
　　　　dout,°
　　But still with stedfast eye and courage stout
　　Abode, to weet° what end would come of all.   330
　　At last that mightie chaine, which round about
　　Her tender waste was wound, adowne gan fall,
And that great brasen pillour broke in peeces small.

38

The cruell steele, which thrild° her dying hart,
　　Fell softly forth, as of his owne accord,   335
　　And the wyde wound, which lately did dispart°
　　Her bleeding brest, and riven bowels gor'd,°
　　Was closed up, as it had not bene bor'd,
　　And every part to safety° full sound,

---

315 **date** term of life.   316 **overlooke** examine.   319 **red** said.   319
measur'd spoke in meter.   320 **perse** pierce.   321 **up stared stiffe**
stood stiffly.   322 **reherse** recite.   324 **ought** at all.   328 **Nor . . .
dout** Nor slackened her threatening hand for fear of danger.   330
weet learn.   334 **thrild** pierced.   336 **dispart** cleave.   337 **riven
bowels gor'd** pierced her torn insides.   339 **safety** freedom from
injury.

340   As she were never hurt, was soone restor'd:
            Tho when she felt her selfe to be unbound,
And perfect hole, prostrate she fell unto the ground.

        39
Before faire *Britomart,* she fell prostrate,
            Saying, Ah noble knight, what worthy meed
345   Can wretched Lady, quit from wofull state,
            Yield you in lieu of this your gratious deed?
            Your vertue selfe° her owne reward shall breed,
            Even immortall praise, and glory wyde,
            Which I your vassall, by your prowesse freed,
350   Shall through the world make to be notifyde,
And goodly well advance,° that° goodly well was
            tryde.

        40
But *Britomart* uprearing her from ground,
            Said, Gentle Dame, reward enough I weene
            For many labours more, then I have found,
355   This,° that in safety now I have you seene,
            And meane° of your deliverance have beene:
            Henceforth faire Lady comfort to you take,
            And put away remembrance of late teene;°
            In stead thereof know, that your loving Make,°
360 Hath no lesse griefe endured for your gentle sake.

        41
She much was cheard to heare him mentiond,
            Whom of all living wights she loved best.
            Then laid the noble Championesse strong hond
            Upon th'enchaunter, which had her distrest
365   So sore, and with foule outrages opprest:
            With that great chaine, wherewith not long ygo°
            He bound that pitteous Lady prisoner, now re-
            lest,°

347 **Your vertue selfe** your virtuous self.   351 **advance** extol.   351
that that which.   355 **This** is this.   356 **meane** means.   358 **teene**
sorrow.   359 **Make** mate.   366 **ygo** ago.   367 **relest** released.

Himselfe she bound, more worthy to be so,
And captive with her led to wretchednesse and wo.

42

Returning backe, those goodly roomes, which erst   370
    She saw so rich and royally arayd,
    Now vanisht utterly, and cleane subverst°
    She found, and all their glory quite decayd,°
    That sight of such a chaunge her much dismayd.
    Thence forth descending to that perlous° Porch,   375
    Those dreadfull flames she also found delayd,°
    And quenched quite, like a consumed torch,
That erst all entrers wont° so cruelly to scorch.

43

More easie issew now, then entrance late
    She found: for now that fained° dreadfull
        flame,   380
    Which chokt the porch of that enchaunted gate,
    And passage bard to all, that thither came,
    Was vanisht quite, as it were not the same,
    And gave her leave at pleasure forth to passe.
    Th'Enchaunter selfe, which all that fraud did
        frame,   385
    To have efforst° the love of that faire lasse,
Seeing his worke now wasted deepe engrieved was.

44

But when the victoresse arrived there,
    Where late she left the pensife *Scudamore,*
    With her owne trusty Squire, both full of feare,   390
    Neither of them she found where she them lore:°
    Thereat her noble hart was stonisht sore;
    But most faire *Amoret,* whose gentle spright
    Now gan to feede on hope, which she before
    Conceived had, to see her owne deare knight,   395
Being thereof beguyld was fild with new affright.

372 **cleane subverst** entirely razed.   373 **decayd** destroyed.   375 **perlous** perilous.   376 **delayd** allayed.   378 **wont** used.   380 **fained**
counterfeit.   386 **efforst** enforced.   391 **lore** left.

45

But he sad man, when he had long in drede
    Awayted there for *Britomarts* returne,
    Yet saw her not nor signe of her good speed,°
    His expectation to despaire did turne,
    Misdeeming sure that her those flames did
        burne;
    And therefore gan advize° with her old Squire,
    Who her deare nourslings losse° no lesse did
        mourne,
    Thence to depart for further aide t'enquire:
Where let them wend° at will, whilest here I doe re-
        spire.°

400

405

399 **speed** fortune.   402 **advize** consult.   403 **nourslings losse** the loss of the child that she nursed.   405 **wend** go.   405 **respire** breathe.

The Fourth Booke

OF THE FAERIE QUEENE.

Containing,

THE LEGEND OF

CAMBEL AND TELAMOND,

OR

Of Friendship.

1

The rugged° forhead° that with grave foresight
    Welds° kingdomes causes, and affaires of state,
    My looser° rimes (I wote) doth sharply wite,°
    For praising love, as I have done of late,°
    And magnifying° lovers deare debate;   5
    By which fraile youth is oft to follie led,
    Through false allurement of that pleasing baite,

---

1 **rugged** frowning.   1 **forhead** The forehead is the dwelling place of
fantasy, the power that is linked with foresight in the Castle of Alma.
2 **Welds** wields.   3 **looser** too loose.   3 **wite** censure.   4 **of late** i.e.,
six years earlier, with the publication of the first three books of his
poem.   5 **magnifying** extolling.

That better were in vertues discipled,°
Then with vaine poemes weeds° to have their fancies
      fed.

2

10 Such ones ill judge of love, that cannot love,
      Ne° in their frosen hearts feele kindly flame:
      For thy° they ought not thing unknowne reprove,
      Ne naturall affection faultlesse° blame,
      For fault of few that have abusd the same.
15   For it of honor and all vertue is
      The roote, and brings forth glorious flowres of
            fame,
      That crowne true lovers with immortall blis,
The meed of them that love, and do not live amisse.

3

Which who so list° looke backe to former ages,
      And call to count the things that then were
20   donne,
      Shall find, that all the workes of those wise sages,
      And brave exploits which great Heroes wonne,
      In love were either ended or begunne:
      Witnesse the father of Philosophie,°
25   Which to his *Critias*,° shaded oft from sunne,
      Of love full manie lessons did apply,
The which these Stoicke censours cannot well deny.

4

To such therefore I do not sing at all,
      But to that sacred Saint my soveraigne Queene,
30   In whose chast breast all bountie° naturall,
      And treasures of true love enlocked beene,
      Bove° all her sexe that ever yet was seene;

---

8 **discipled** made subject to discipline; with a whip, as in I.x.27.
9 **weeds** outward adornment, the "historicall fiction," and "Allegoricall devises" referred to in the *Letter to Raleigh*.   11 **Ne** nor.   12
For thy therefore.   13 **fauntlesse** which is faultless.   19 **list** desires
to.   24 **the father of Philosophie** Socrates.   25 **Critias** according to
Spenser, a discipline of Socrates.   30 **bountie** goodness.   32 **Bove**
above.

To her I sing of love, that loveth best,
   And best is lov'd of all alive I weene:
   To her this song most fitly is addrest,   35
The Queene of love, and Prince of peace from heaven
      blest.

5

Which that she may the better deigne° to heare,
   Do thou dred infant,° *Venus* dearling° dove,
   From her high spirit chase imperious feare,°
   And use of awfull Majestie° remove: 40
   In sted thereof with drops of melting love,
   Deawd with ambrosiall kisses, by thee gotten
   From thy sweete smyling mother° from above,
   Sprinckle her heart, and haughtie° courage
      soften,
That she may hearke to love, and reade this lesson
      often.   45

*While the virtue of Friendship is illustrated by the in-
troduction of new characters, chiefly the book extends the
stories begun in Book III.*

*Later Amoret is raped by Lust but saved by Belphœbe.
She is wounded by Timias, and later aided by Arthur
who, apparently, restores her to Scudamour at the
moment when the discord among the various lovers is
brought to a final harmony. In Canto x, Scudamour relates how he first gained Amoret. The gathering of the
waters at the marriage of the Thames and Medway, related in Canto xi, becomes the occasion for Florimell's
restoration to Marinell.*

37 **deigne** condescend.   38 **thou dred infant** Cupid, whose powers
are dreaded by lovers.   38 **dearling** darling.   39 **imperious feare**
majesty that arouses fear in others.   40 **use . . . Majestie** the custom
of majesty to arouse awe.   43 **thy sweet smyling mother** Venus; see
IV.x.47.   44 **haughtie** high.

CANTO X

Scudamour doth his conquest tell,
   Of vertuous Amoret:
Great Venus Temple is describ'd,
   And lovers life forth set.

1

True he it said, what ever man it sayd,°
   That love with gall and hony doth abound,
   But if the one be with the other wayd,°
   For every dram of hony therein found,
5   A pound of gall doth over it redound.°
   That I° too true by triall have approved:°
   For since the day that first with deadly wound
   My heart was launcht,° and learned to have
      loved,
I never joyed howre, but still with care was moved.

2

10 And yet such grace is given them° from above,
   That all the cares and evill which they meet,
   May nought at all their setled mindes remove,°
   But seeme gainst common sence to them most
      sweet;
   As bosting in their martyrdome unmeet.°
15   So all that ever yet I have endured,
   I count as naught, and tread downe under feet,
   Since of my love at length I rest assured,
That to disloyalty she will not be allured.

3

Long were to tell the travell° and long toile,

1 **True . . . sayd** Whatever man he was, he told the truth when he
said.   3 **wayd** weighed.   5 **redound** be in excess.   6 **I** Scudamour.
6 **approved** proved.   8 **launcht** pierced.   10 **them** lovers.   12 **remove** change.   14 **As . . . unmeet** Making them glory in their unfitting martyrdom.   19 **travell** travail.

426

Through which this shield of love° I late have
    wonne,   20
And purchased° this peerelesse beauties spoile,°
That harder° may be ended, then begonne.
But since ye so desire, your will be donne.
Then hearke ye gentle knights and Ladies free,°
My hard mishaps, that ye may learne to shonne;   25
For though sweet love to conquer glorious bee,
Yet is the paine thereof much greater then the fee.°

4

What time the fame of this renowmed prise°
    Flew first abroad, and all mens eares possest,
I having armes then taken, gan avise°   30
To winne me honour by some noble gest,°
And purchase me some place amongst the best.
I boldly thought (so young mens thoughts are
    bold)
That this same brave emprize° for me did rest,°
And that both shield and she whom I behold,   35
Might be my lucky lot; sith all by lot° we hold.

5

So on that hard adventure forth I went,
    And to the place of perill shortly came.
That was a temple faire and auncient,
Which of great mother *Venus*° bare° the name,   40
And farre renowmed through exceeding fame;
Much more then that,° which was in *Paphos*
    built,
Or that in *Cyprus,* both long since° this same,

20 **this shield of love** He bears a shield with the picture of Cupid;
hence his name, Scud-amor.   21 **purchased** acquired.   21 **this peerelesse beauties spoile** Amoret, who seems to stand beside him; cf. line
35. She is the spoil or plunder that he acquired by his victory in the
Temple.   22 **harder** with greater difficulty.   24 **free** of gentle birth.
27 **fee** reward.   28 **What ... prise** At the time when the fame of this
renowned prize, Amoret.   30 **gan avise** considered how.   31 **gest**
action.   34 **emprize** enterprise.   34 **rest** remain to be accomplished.
36 **lot** chance or fortune.   40 **great mother Venus** "Venus genetrix."
40 **bare** bore.   42 **Much more then that,** etc. Both temples were dedicated to Venus.   43 **both long since** both built long after.

Though all the pillours of the one were guilt,°
45 And all the others pavement were with yvory spilt.

6

And it was seated in an Island strong,
　　Abounding all with delices° most rare,
　　And wall'd by nature gainst invaders wrong,
　　That none mote have accesse, nor inward fare,°
50　　But by one way, that passage did prepare.°
　　It was a bridge ybuilt in goodly wize,
　　With curious Corbes and pendants graven faire,°
　　And arched all with porches, did arize°
On stately pillours, fram'd after the Doricke guize.

7

55 And for defence thereof, on th'other end

　　There reared was a castle faire and strong,
　　That warded all which in or out did wend,
　　And flancked both the bridges sides along,
　　Gainst all that would it faine° to force or wrong.
60　　And therein wonned° twenty valiant Knights;
　　All twenty tride in warres experience long;
　　Whose office was, against all manner wights°
By all meanes to maintaine that castels ancient rights.

8

Before that Castle was an open plaine,
65　　And in the midst thereof a piller placed;
　　On which this shield, of many sought in vaine,
　　The shield of Love, whose guerdon° me hath
　　　　graced,
　　Was hangd on high with golden ribbands laced;
　　And in the marble stone was written this,
70　　With golden letters goodly well enchaced,°

44 guilt gilded.   47 delices delights.   49 fare passage.   50 prepare
provide.   52 With . . . faire With exquisitely fashioned projecting-
supports and beautifully engraven hanging ornaments.   53 did arize
that arose.   59 faine desire.   60 wonned dwelt.   62 all manner
wights all manner of persons.   67 whose guerdon the reward which.
70 enchaced engraved.

Blessed the man that well can use his blis:
Whose ever be the shield, faire Amoret be his.

9

Which when I red, my heart did inly earne,°
    And pant with hope of that adventures hap:°
    Ne stayed further newes thereof to learne,   75
    But with my speare upon the shield did rap,
    That all the castle ringed with the clap.
    Streight forth issewd a Knight all arm'd to
        proofe,°
    And bravely mounted to his most mishap:°
    Who staying nought to question from aloofe,°   80
    Ran fierce at me, that fire glaunst° from his
        horses hoofe.

10

Whom boldly I encountred (as I could)
    And by good fortune shortly him unseated.
    Eftsoones out sprung two more of equall mould;
    But I them both with equall hap defeated: 85
    So all the twenty I likewise entreated,°
    And left them groning there upon the plaine.
    Then preacing° to the pillour I repeated°
    The read thereof for guerdon of my paine,°
And taking downe the shield, with me did it retaine.   90

11

So forth without impediment I past,
    Till to the Bridges utter° gate I came:
    The which I found sure lockt and chained fast.
    I knockt, but no man aunswred me by name;
    I cald, but no man answerd to my clame.°   95
    Yet I persever'd still to knocke and call,

---

73 **inly earne** inwardly yearn.   74 **that adventures hap** the chance of that adventure.   78 **all arm'd to proofe** of proven power.   79 **to . . . mishap** as it turned out, for his greatest misfortune.   80 **from aloofe** from a distance.   81 **glaunst** flashed.   86 **entreated** treated. 88 **preacing** pressing.   88 **repeated** recited.   89 **The . . . paine** Its rede, or saying, concerning the reward for my labor.   92 **utter** outer. 95 **clame** call.

Till at the last I spide within the same,
Where one stood peeping through a crevis small,
To whom I cald aloud, halfe angry therewithall.°

12

100 That was to weet° the Porter of the place,
Unto whose trust the charge thereof was lent:°
His name was *Doubt,* that had a double face,
Th'one forward looking, th'other backeward bent,
105 Therein resembling *Janus*° auncient,
Which hath in charge the ingate° of the yeare:
And evermore his eyes about him went,
As if some proved perill he did feare,
Or did misdoubt some ill, whose cause did not
appeare.

13

On th'one side he, on th'other sate *Delay,*
110 Behinde the gate, that none her might espy;
Whose manner° was all passengers to stay,
And entertaine with her occasions° sly,
Through which some lost great hope unheedily,°
Which never they recover might againe;
115 And others quite excluded forth,° did ly
Long languishing there in unpittied paine,
And seeking often entraunce, afterwards in vaine.

14

Me when as he had privily espide,
Bearing the shield which I had conquerd late,
120 He kend° it streight, and to me opened wide.
So in I past, and streight° he closd the gate.
But being in, *Delay* in close awaite°
Caught hold on° me, and thought my steps to stay,

---

99 **therewithall** with that (i.e., the "peeping"). 100 **to weet** to wit, namely. 101 **lent** granted. 104 **Janus** the god with two faces to whom the month of January (Janus) is sacred. 105 **ingate** entrance, beginning. 111 **manner** custom. 112 **occasions** inducements. 113 **unheedily** heedlessly. 115 **forth** forward, i.e., being barred from going forward. 120 **kend** recognized. 121 **streight** immediately. 122 **awaite** watch. 123 **on** of.

Feigning full many a fond excuse to prate,
    And time to steale, the threasure of mans day,°   *125*
Whose smallest minute lost, no riches render may.°

15

But by no meanes my way I would forslow,°
    For ought that ever she could doe or say,
    But from my lofty steede dismounting low,
    Past forth on foote, beholding all the way   *130*
    The goodly workes, and stones of rich assay,°
    Cast into sundry shapes by wondrous skill,
    That like on earth no where I recken may:
    And underneath, the river rolling still
With murmure soft, that seem'd to serve° the work-
    mans will.   *135*

16

Thence forth I passed to the second gate,
    The *Gate of good desert,* whose goodly pride
    And costly frame, were long here to relate.
    The same to all stoode alwaies open wide:
    But in the Porch did evermore abide   *140*
    An hideous Giant, dreadfull to behold,
    That stopt the entraunce with his spacious stride,
    And with the terrour of his countenance bold
Full many did affray,° that else faine enter would.

17

His name was *Daunger* dreaded over all,   *145*
    Who day and night did watch and duely ward,°
    From fearefull cowards, entrance to forstall,°
    And faint-heart-fooles, whom shew of perill hard
    Could terrifie from Fortunes faire adward:°
    For oftentimes faint hearts at first espiall°   *150*
    Of his grim face, were from approaching scard;

---

125 **threasure of mans day** treasure of man's life.   126 **render may**
may restore.   127 **forslow** delay.   131 **assay** quality.   135 **serve**
obey.   144 **affray** frighten.   146 **duely ward** guard properly.   147
forstall obstruct.   149 **adward** award.   150 **espiall** sight.

Unworthy they of grace, whom one deniall
Excludes from fairest hope, withouten further triall.

18

Yet many doughty warriours, often tride°
155 In greater perils to be stout and bold,
  Durst not the sternnesse of his looke abide,
  But soone as they his countenance did behold,
  Began to faint, and feele their corage cold.°
  Againe some other, that in hard assaies°
160 Were cowards knowne, and litle count did hold,°
  Either through gifts, or guile, or such like waies,
Crept in by stouping low, or stealing of the kaies.°

19

But I though meanest man of many moe,°
  Yet much disdaining unto him to lout,°
165 Or creepe betweene his legs, so in to goe,
  Resolv'd him to assault with manhood stout,
  And either beat him in, or drive him out.
  Eftsoones advauncing that enchaunted shield,
  With all my might I gan to lay about:
  Which when he saw, the glaive° which he did
170   wield
He gan forthwith t'avale,° and way unto me yield.

20

So as I entred, I did backeward looke
  For feare of harme, that might lie hidden there;
  And loe his hindparts, whereof heed I tooke,
175 Much more deformed fearefull ugly were,
  Then all his former parts did earst appere.
  For hatred, murther, treason, and despight,°
  With many moe lay in ambushment there,
  Awayting to entrap the warelesse° wight,
180 Which did not them prevent with vigilant foresight.

---

154 **tride** proven. 158 **cold** become cold. 159 **assaies** endeavors.
160 **little . . . hold** were held in low esteem. 162 **kaies** keys. 163
moe more. 164 **lout** bow. 170 **glaive** sword. 171 **t'avale** to lower.
177 **despight** outrage. 179 **warelesse** unwary.

21

Thus having past all perill, I was come
    Within the compasse of that Islands space;
    The which did seeme unto my simple doome,°
    The onely° pleasant and delightfull place,
    That ever troden was of footings trace.°   185
    For all that nature by her mother wit°
    Could frame in earth, and forme of substance
        base,
    Was there, and all that nature did omit,
Art playing second natures part, supplyed it.

22

No tree, that is of count,° in greenewood growes,°   190
    From lowest Juniper to Ceder tall,
    No flowre in field, that daintie odour throwes,
    And deckes his branch with blossomes over all,
    But there was planted, or grew naturall:
    Nor sense of man so coy and curious nice,°   195
    But there mote find to please it selfe withall;
    Nor hart could wish for any queint° device,
But there it present was, and did fraile sense entice.

23

In such luxurious° plentie of all pleasure,
    It seem'd a second paradise to ghesse,°   200
    So lavishly enricht with natures threasure,
    That if the happie soules, which doe possesse
    Th'Elysian fields,° and live in lasting blesse,°
    Should happen this with living eye to see,
    They soone would loath their lesser happinesse,   205
    And wish to life return'd againe to bee,
That in this joyous place they mote have joyance free.

183 **doome** judgment.   184 **onely** most.   185 **footings trace** the
track of footprints; hence: "that ever had been walked on."   186
mother wit natural powers.   190 **count** estimation.   190 **growes**
groves.   195 **so . . . nice** however needing to be coaxed and fastidious.   197 **queint** ingenious.   199 **luxurious** excessive.   200 **to ghesse**
one may suppose.   203 **Th'Elysian fields** Elysium, "a place of pleasure like Paradise, where the happye soules doe rest in peace and
eternal happynesse" (E.K.'s note to *Shep. Cal.*, Nov. 179).   203
blesse bliss.

24

Fresh° shadowes, fit to shroud from sunny ray;
    Faire lawnds, to take the sunne in season dew;
    Sweet springs, in which a thousand Nymphs did
210   play;
    Soft rombling° brookes, that gentle slomber
      drew;
    High reared mounts,° the lands about to vew;
    Low looking dales, disloignd° from common
      gaze;
    Delightfull bowres, to solace lovers trew;
215   False Labyrinthes, fond runners eyes to daze;°
All which by nature made did nature self amaze.

25

And all without were walkes and alleyes dight
    With divers° trees, enrang'd in even rankes;
    And here and there were pleasant arbors pight,
220   And shadie seates, and sundry flowring bankes,
    To sit and rest the walkers wearie shankes,
    And therein thousand payres of lovers walkt,
    Praysing their god, and yeelding him great
      thankes,
    Ne ever ought° but of their true loves talkt,
225 Ne ever for rebuke or blame of any balkt.°

26

All these together by themselves did sport
    Their spotlesse° pleasures, and sweet loves
      content.
    But farre away from these, another sort°
    Of lovers lincked in true harts consent;
230   Which loved not as these, for like intent,
    But on chast vertue grounded their desire,
    Farre from all fraud, or fayned blandishment;
    Which° in their spirits kindling zealous fire,

208 **Fresh** refreshing.   211 **rombling** murmuring.   212 **mounts** hills.
213 **disloignd** removed.   215 **daze** dazzle.   218 **divers** different.
224 **ought** at all.   225 **Ne . . . balkt** Nor ever rebuked or blamed by
anyone.   227 **spotlesse** pure.   228 **sort** group.   233 **Which** i.e.,
their desire.

Brave thoughts and noble deedes did evermore
    aspire.°

27

Such were great *Hercules,* and *Hylas*° deare;   235
    Trew *Jonathan,* and *David* trustie° tryde;
    Stout *Theseus,* and *Pirithous*° his feare;°
    Pylades and *Orestes*° by his syde;
    Myld *Titus* and *Gesippus*° without pryde;
    Damon and *Pythias*° whom death could not
        sever: 240
    All these and all that ever had bene tyde
    In bands of friendship there did live for ever,
Whose lives although decay'd, yet loves decayed
    never.

28

Which when as I, that never tasted blis,
    Nor happie howre, beheld with gazefull° eye,   245
    I thought there was none other heaven then this;
    And gan their endlesse happinesse envye,
    That being free from feare and gealosye,
    Might frankely there their loves desire possesse;
    Whilest I through paines and perlous° jeopardie,   250
    Was forst to seeke my lifes deare patronesse:
Much dearer be the things, which come through hard
    distresse.

29

Yet all those sights, and all that else I saw,
    Might not my steps withhold, but that forthright°

234 **aspire** inspire.   235 **Hercules, and Hylas** See III. xii. 7.   236
trustie faithfully.   237 **Theseus, and Pirithous** At the wedding of
Pirithous, Theseus aided him in his battle against the Centaurs, and
later descended into hell to help him carry off Persephone.   237
feare companion.   238 **Pylades and Orestes** Pylades helped Orestes
murder his mother, Clytemnestra.   239 **Titus and Gesippus** Gesippus gave Titus his betrothed when he learned that his friend loved
her. Later when Gesippus was under penalty of death, Titus offered
his own life as substitute.   240 **Damon and Pythias** Each pleaded
to have his life substituted in place of his friend's.   245 **gazefull** in-
tently gazing.   250 **perlous** perilous.   254 **forthright** straightway.

255   Unto that purposd place° I did me draw,
        Where as° my love was lodged day and night:
        The temple of great *Venus,* that is hight
        The Queene of beautie, and of love the mother,
        There worshipped of every living wight;
260   Whose goodly workmanship farre past all other
  That ever were on earth, all were they° set together.

30

Not that same famous Temple of *Diane,*
        Whose hight all *Ephesus* did oversee,
        And which all *Asia* sought with vowes prophane,
265   One of the worlds seven wonders sayd to bee,
        Might match with this by many a degree:°
        Nor that, which that wise King of *Jurie*° framed,
        With endlesse cost,° to be th'Almighties see;°
        Nor all that else through all the world is named
270   To all° the heathen Gods, might like to this be
        clamed.°

31

I much admyring that so goodly frame,
        Unto the porch approcht, which open stood;
        But therein sate an amiable Dame,
        That seem'd to be of very sober mood,
        And in her semblant° shewed great woman-
275   hood:°
        Strange was her tyre;° for on her head a crowne
        She wore much like unto a Danisk° hood,
        Poudred° with pearle and stone, and all her
        gowne
  Enwoven was with gold, that raught° full low a
        downe.

225 **purposd place** place to which I was bound.   256 **Where as** where.   261 **all were they** although they were.   266 **by many a degree** by many stages of "goodly workmanship."   267 **that wise King of Jurie** Solomon.   268 **With endlesse cost** see I Kings 6.   268 **see** seat, dwelling place.   270 **all** any of.   270 **clamed** called.   275 **semblant** appearance.   275 **womanhood** womanliness.   276 **tyre** headdress.   277 **Danisk** Danish.   278 **Poudred** sprinkled.   279 **raught** reached.

32

On either side of her, two young men stood,   *280*
    Both strongly arm'd, as fearing one another;
    Yet were they brethren both of halfe the blood,°
    Begotten by two fathers of one mother,
    Though of contrarie natures each to other:
    The one of them hight *Love,* the other *Hate,*   *285*
    Hate was the elder, *Love* the younger brother;
    Yet was the younger stronger in his state
Then th'elder, and him maystred still° in all debate.

33

Nathlesse that Dame so well them tempred° both,
    That she them forced hand to joyne in hand,   *290*
    Albe that *Hatred* was thereto full loth,
    And turn'd his face away, as he did stand,
    Unwilling to behold that lovely band.°
    Yet she was of such grace and vertuous might,
    That her commaundment he could not withstand,   *295*
    But bit his lip for felonous despight,°
And gnasht his yron tuskes at that displeasing sight.

34

Concord she cleeped° was in common reed,°
    Mother of blessed *Peace,* and *Friendship* trew;
    They both her twins, both borne of heavenly
        seed,   *300*
    And she her selfe likewise divinely grew;
    The which right well her workes divine did shew:
    For strength, and wealth, and happinesse she
        lends,
    And strife, and warre, and anger does subdew:
    Of litle much,° of foes she maketh frends,   *305*
And to afflicted minds sweet rest and quiet sends.

282 **brethren . . . blood** both brothers by one parent only.   288 **still**
always.   289 **tempred** governed.   293 **lovely band** loving bond.
296 **felonous despight** fierce anger.   297 **yron tuskes** strong teeth.
298 **cleeped** named.   298 **reed** speech.   305 **Of litle much** of little
she makes much.

35

By her the heaven is in his course contained,°
    And all the world in state unmoved stands,
    As their Almightie maker first ordained,
310   And bound them with inviolable bands;
    Else would the waters overflow the lands,
    And fire devoure the ayre, and hell them quight,°
    But that she holds them with her blessed hands.
    She is the nourse of pleasure and delight,
315 And unto *Venus* grace° the gate doth open right.

36

By her I entring halfe dismayed was,
    But she in gentle wise° me entertayned,°
    And twixt her selfe and *Love* did let me pas;
    But *Hatred* would my entrance have restrayned,
320   And with his club me threatned to have brayned,
    Had not the Ladie with her powrefull speach
    Him from his wicked will uneath refrayned;°
    And th'other eke his malice did empeach,°
Till I was throughly past the perill of his reach.

37

325 Into the inmost Temple thus I came,
    Which fuming all with frankensence I found,
    And odours rising from the altars flame.
    Upon an hundred marble pillors round
    The roofe up high was reared from the ground,
    All deckt with crownes, and chaynes, and
330   girlands gay,
    And thousand pretious gifts worth many a pound,
    The which sad lovers for their vowes did pay;
And all the ground was strow'd with flowres, as fresh
    as May.

---

307 **contained** controlled. 312 **quight** retaliate, by overcoming the
waters and fire in turn. 315 **Venus grace** those to whom Venus
offers the grace of true love. 317 **wise** manner. 317 **entertayned**
received. 322 **uneath refraynd** with difficulty restrained. 323 **And
. . . empeach** And Love also prevented his malice.

38

An hundred Altars round about were set,
  All flaming with their sacrifices fire,°   *335*
  That with the steme° thereof the Temple swet,°
  Which rould in clouds to heaven did aspire,
  And in them bore true lovers vowes entire:°
  And eke an hundred brasen caudrons° bright,
  To bath in joy and amorous desire,   *340*
  Every of which was to a damzell hight;°
For all the Priests were damzels, in soft linnen dight.

39

Right in the midst the Goddesse selfe did stand
  Upon an altar of some costly masse,°
  Whose substance was uneath to understand: *345*
  For neither pretious stone, nor durefull° brasse,
  Nor shining gold, nor mouldring° clay it was;
  But much more rare and pretious to esteeme,°
  Pure in aspect, and like to christall glasse,
  Yet glasse was not, if one did rightly deeme,   *350*
But being faire and brickle,° likest glasse did seeme.

40

But it in shape and beautie did excell
  All other Idoles, which the heathen adore,
  Farre passing that, which by surpassing skill
  Phidias did make° in *Paphos* Isle° of yore,   *355*
  With which that wretched Greeke, that life
    forlore,°
  Did fall in love: yet this much fairer shined,
  But covered with a slender veile afore;°
  And both her feete and legs together twyned

335 **their sacrifices fire** the fire of their sacrifices.   336 **steme** fume.
336 **swet** sweated.   338 **vowes entire** unbroken vows.   339 **caudrons**
cauldrons, baths.   241 **hight** committed.   344 **masse** substance.
346 **durefull** enduring.   347 **mouldring** moulded.   348 **to esteeme**
to be valued.   351 **brickle** brittle.   355 **Phidias did make** Pliny relates that a youth fell in love with a statue of Venus, by Praxiteles.
355 **Paphos Isle** Cyprus.   356 **forlore** lost.   358 **afore** before.

Were with a snake, whose head and tail were fast
360   combyned.

41

The cause why she was covered with a vele,
    Was hard to know, for that her Priests the same
    From peoples knowledge labour'd to concele.
    But sooth it was not sure° for womanish shame,
365 Nor any blemish, which the worke mote blame;°
    But for,° they say, she hath both kinds° in one,
    Both male and female, both under one name:
    She syre and mother is her selfe alone,
Begets and eke conceives, ne needeth other none.

42

370 And all about her necke and shoulders flew
    A flocke of litle loves, and sports, and joyes,
    With nimble wings of gold and purple hew;
    Whose shapes seem'd not like to terrestriall
        boyes,
    But like to Angels playing heavenly toyes;°
375 The whilest their eldest brother was away,
    Cupid their eldest brother; he enjoyes
    The wide kingdome of love with Lordly sway,
And to his law compels all creatures to obay.

43

And all about her altar scattered lay
380   Great sorts of lovers piteously complayning,
    Some of their losse, some of their loves delay,
    Some of their pride, some paragons disdayning,°
    Some fearing fraud, some fraudulently fayning,
    As every one had cause of good or ill.
    Amongst the rest some one° through loves
385   constrayning,

364 **But ... sure** but in truth it was surely not.   365 **which ... blame**
for which the work might be blamed.   366 **But for** but because.
366 **kinds** sexes.   374 **toyes** games.   382 **Some ... disdayning** Some
complain of the pride of their mates, and some of their disdain.
385 **some one** one in particular.

Tormented sore, could not containe it still,
But thus brake forth, that all the temple it did fill.

44

Great *Venus,* Queene of beautie and of grace,
    The joy of Gods and men, that under skie°
    Doest fayrest shine, and most adorne thy place,   *390*
    That with thy smyling looke doest pacifie
    The raging seas, and makst the stormes to flie;
    Thee goddesse, thee the winds, the clouds doe
      feare,
    And when thou spredst thy mantle forth on hie,
    The waters play and pleasant lands appeare,   *395*
And heavens laugh, and al the world shews joyous
    cheare.

45

Then doth the dædale° earth throw forth to thee
    Out of her fruitfull lap aboundant flowres,
    And then all living wights, soone as they see
    The spring breake forth out of his lusty°
      bowres,   *400*
    They all doe learne to play the Paramours;
    First doe the merry birds, thy prety pages
    Privily pricked° with thy lustfull powres,
    Chirpe loud to thee out of their leavy cages,
And thee their mother call to coole their kindly
    rages.°   *405*

46

Then doe the salvage° beasts begin to play
    Their pleasant friskes, and loath their wonted
      food;
    The Lyons rore, the Tygres loudly bray,
    The raging Buls rebellow through the wood,

---

389 **under skie** in the lower sky, as the morning and evening star.
397 **dædale** fertile. 400 **lusty** joyful. 403 **Privily pricked** secretly
urged or driven. 405 **kindly rages** natural passions. 406 **salvage**
savage.

And breaking forth, dare tempt° the deepest
410   flood,
To come where thou doest draw them with
      desire:
So all things else, that nourish° vitall blood,
Soone as with fury thou doest them inspire,
In generation seeke to quench their inward fire.

47

415 So all the world by thee at first was made,
And dayly yet thou doest the same repayre:
Ne ought° on earth that merry is and glad,
Ne ought on earth that lovely is and fayre,
But thou the same for pleasure didst prepayre.
420   Thou art the root of all that joyous is,
Great God of men and women, queene of th'ayre,
Mother of laughter, and welspring of blisse,
O graunt that of my love at last I may not misse.

48

So did he say: but I with murmure soft,
425   That none might heare the sorrow of my hart,
Yet inly groning deepe and sighing oft,
Besought her to graunt ease unto my smart,
And to my wound her gratious help impart.
Whilest thus I spake, behold with happy eye
430   I spyde, where at the Idoles feet apart°
A bevie of fayre damzels close did lye,
Wayting when as the Antheme should be sung on
      hye.

49

The first of them did seeme of ryper yeares,
And graver countenance then all the rest;
435   Yet all the rest were eke her equall peares,
Yet unto her obayed all the best.

---

410 **tempt** attempt   412 **nourish** are nourished by.   417 **Ne ought**
nothing.   430 **apart** to one side.

Her name was *Womanhood,* that she exprest
By her sad semblant° and demeanure wyse:
For stedfast still her eyes did fixed rest,
Ne rov'd at randon° after gazers guyse,°   *440*
Whose luring baytes oftimes doe heedlesse harts
     entyse.

50

And next to her sate goodly *Shamefastnesse,*
    Ne ever durst her eyes from ground upreare,
    Ne ever once did looke up from her desse,°
    As if some blame of evill she did feare,   *445*
    That in her cheekes made roses oft appeare:
    And her against° sweet *Cherefulnesse* was
     placed,
    Whose eyes like twinkling stars in evening cleare,
    Were deckt with smyles, that all sad humors°
     chaced,
And darted forth delights, the which her goodly
     graced.   *450*

51

And next to her sate sober *Modestie,*
    Holding her hand upon her gentle hart;
    And her against sate comely *Curtesie,*
    That unto every person knew her part;°
    And her before was seated overthwart°   *455*
    Soft *Silence,* and submisse° *Obedience,*
    Both linckt together never to dispart,°
    Both gifts of God not gotten but from thence,
Both girlonds° of his Saints against their foes of-
     fence.°

---

438 **sad semblant** grave countenance.   440 **randon** random.   440
guyse manner.   444 **desse** dais, seat.   447 **her against** opposite her.
449 **humors** moods.   454 **That . . . part** She knew how to act properly to each person; as does Reverence, I. x. 7.   455 **overthwart** opposite.   456 **submisse** submissive.   457 **dispart** separate.   459 **girlonds** garlands, wreaths of honor.   459 **against their foes offence**
i.e., Silence and Obedience are woman's defense—and hence a token
of her victory—against the attack of foes.

52

460 Thus sate they all a round in seemely rate:°
 And in the midst of them a goodly mayd,
 Even in the lap of *Womanhood* there sate,
 The which was all in lilly white arayd,
 With silver streames amongst the linnen stray'd;
465 Like to the Morne, when first her shyning face
 Hath to the gloomy world it selfe bewray'd,°
 That same was fayrest *Amoret* in place,°
Shyning with beauties light, and heavenly vertues
  grace.

53

Whom soone as I beheld, my hart gan throb,
 And wade° in doubt, what best were to be
470   donne:
 For sacrilege me seem'd° the Church to rob,
 And folly seem'd to leave the thing undonne,
 Which with so strong attempt I had begonne.
 Tho shaking off all doubt and shamefast° feare,
475 Which Ladies love I heard had never wonne
 Mongst men of worth, I to her stepped neare,
And by the lilly hand her labour'd up to reare.

54

Thereat that formost matrone° me did blame,
 And sharpe rebuke, for being over bold;
480 Saying it was to Knight unseemely shame,
 Upon a recluse° Virgin to lay hold,
 That unto *Venus* services was sold.°
 To whom I thus, Nay but it fitteth best,
 For *Cupids* man with *Venus* mayd to hold,
485 For ill your goddesse services are drest°
By virgins, and her sacrifices let to rest.°

---

460 **Thus ... rate** There they sat in a circle in fitting manner. 466
bewray'd revealed. 467 **in place** there. 470 **wade** proceed. 471
me seem'd it seemed to me. 474 **shamefast** bashful. 478 **that for-most matrone** Womanhood. 481 **recluse** secluded from the world
in the service of Venus. 482 **sold** given. 485 **drest** performed.
486 **let to rest** allowed to cease.

55

With that my shield I forth to her did show,
    Which all that while I closely had conceld;
    On which when *Cupid* with his killing bow
    And cruell shafts emblazond she beheld,   *490*
    At sight thereof she was with terror queld,
    And said no more: but I which all that while
    The pledge of faith, her hand engaged held,
    Like warie° Hynd within the weedie soyle,
For no intreatie would forgoe so glorious spoyle.°   *495*

56

And evermore upon the Goddesse face
    Mine eye was fixt, for feare of her offence,°
    Whom when I saw with amiable grace
    To laugh at me, and favour my pretence,°
    I was emboldned with more confidence,   *500*
    And nought for nicenesse nor for envy sparing,°
    In presence of them all forth led her thence,
    All looking on, and like° astonisht staring,
Yet to lay hand on her, not one of all them daring.

57

She often prayd, and often me besought,   *505*
    Sometime with tender teares to let her goe,
    Sometime with witching smyles: but yet for
        nought,
    That ever she to me could say or doe,
    Could she her wished freedome fro° me wooe;
    But forth I led her through the Temple gate,   *510*
    By which I hardly past° with much adoe:
    But that same Ladie° which me friended late
In entrance, did me also friend in my retrate.

494 **warie** perhaps "wearie," as an early editor conjectured; hence:
her hand was held in mine as firmly as a weary hind is held in ground
that is overgrown with weeds. 495 **spoyle** the booty or plunder of
his victory. 497 **of her offence** of offending her. 499 **pretence**
claim. 501 **And . . . sparing** And sparing nothing neither for the
sake of modesty in Amoret nor for envy in others. 503 **like** all like.
509 **fro** from. 511 **hardly past** passed with hardship in his earlier
entrance. 512 **that same Ladie** Concord.

58

No lesse did *Daunger* threaten me with dread,
515   When as he saw me, maugre° all his powre,
       That glorious spoyle of beautie with me lead,
       Then *Cerberus,*° when *Orpheus* did recoure°
       His Leman° from the Stygian Princes boure.°
       But evermore my shield did me defend,
520   Against the storme of every dreadfull stoure:°
       Thus safely with my love I thence did wend.°
So ended he his tale, where I this Canto end.

CANTO XII

Marin for love of Florimell,
  In languor wastes his life:
The Nymph his mother getteth her,
  And gives to him for wife.

1

O what an endlesse worke° have I in hand,
       To count the seas abundant progeny,
       Whose fruitfull seede farre passeth those in land,
       And also those which wonne° in th'azure sky?
5   For much more eath to tell° the starres on hy,
       Albe they endlesse seeme in estimation,
       Then to recount the Seas posterity:
       So fertile be the flouds° in generation,

---

515 **maugre** in spite of.   517 **Cerberus** the monster guarding the
gates of hell who opposed Orpheus when he descended into hell to
recover Eurydice. Through the power of his music, Orpheus persuaded Persephone to allow him to return to the world with Eurydice, only to lose her when he disobeyed the injunction not to look
back to see if she was following him.   517 **recoure** recover.   518
Leman wife.   518 **the . . . boure** the dwelling of the Prince of hell,
named after Styx, the chief river of hell.   520 **stoure** peril.   521
wend go.
1 **O what an endlesse worke** referring to the catalog of the waters
that gathered at the marriage of the Thames and the Medway, related in the previous canto.   4 **wonne** live.   5 **eath to tell** easy is it
to count.   8 **flouds** waters.

So huge their numbers, and so numberlesse their
    nation.

2

Therefore the antique wisards° well invented,   *10*
    That *Venus* of the fomy sea° was bred;
    For that° the seas by her are most augmented.
    Witnesse th'exceeding fry, which there are fed,
    And wondrous sholes,° which may of none be
      red.°
    Then blame me not, if I have err'd in count   *15*
    Of Gods, of Nymphs, of rivers yet unred:
    For though their numbers do much more sur-
      mount,°
Yet all those same were there, which erst° I did re-
    count.

3

All those were there, and many other more,
    Whose names and nations° were too long to tell,   *20*
    That *Proteus* house they fild even to the dore;
    Yet were they all in order, as befell,
    According their degrees disposed well.
    Amongst the rest, was faire *Cymodoce,*
    The mother of unlucky *Marinell,*   *25*
    Who thither with her came, to learne and see
The manner of the Gods when they at banquet be.

4

But for° he was halfe mortall, being bred
    Of mortall sire, though of immortall wombe,°
    He might not with immortall food be fed,   *30*
    Ne° with th'eternall Gods to bancket come;
    But walkt abrode, and round about did rome,

---

10 **antique wisards** ancient sages. 11 **the fomy sea** the sea's foam.
12 **For that** because. 14 **sholes** schools of fish. 14 **of none be red**
by none be seen. 17 **surmount** surpass. 18 **erst** before. 20 **nations** kinds. 28 **But for** because. 29 **of immortall wombe** Cymodoce, or Cymoent, is a sea nymph. Marinell's father is "an
earthly peare,/The famous *Dumarin*" (III.iv.19). 31 **Ne** nor.

To view the building of that uncouth° place,
That seem'd unlike unto his earthly home:
35 Where, as he to and fro by chaunce did trace,
There unto him betid a disaventrous case.°

5

Under the hanging° of an hideous clieffe,
He heard the lamentable voice of one,
That piteously complaind her carefull grieffe,°
40 Which never she before disclosd to none,
But to her selfe her sorrow did bemone.
So feelingly her case she did complaine,
That ruth° it moved in the rocky stone,
And made it seeme to feele her grievous paine,
And oft to grone with billowes beating from the
45 maine.

6

Though vaine I see my sorrowes to unfold,
And count my cares, when none is nigh to heare,
Yet hoping griefe may lessen being told,
I will them tell though unto no man neare:
50 For heaven that unto all lends equall° eare,
Is farre from hearing of my heavy plight;
And lowest hell, to which I lie most neare,
Cares not what evils hap to wretched wight;
And greedy seas doe in the spoile° of life delight.

7

55 Yet loe the seas I see by often beating,
Doe pearce the rockes, and hardest marble
weares;
But his hard rocky hart for no entreating
Will yeeld, but when my piteous plaints he
heares,
Is hardned more with my aboundant teares.

---

33 **uncouth** strange. 36 **betid . . . case** befell an unfortunate plight.
37 **hanging** steep slope. 39 **carefull grieffe** full of grief. 43 **ruth**
pity. 50 **equall** impartial. 54 **spoile** plundering.

Yet though he never list° to me relent,   60
  But let me waste in woe my wretched yeares,
  Yet will I never of my love repent,
But joy that for his sake I suffer prisonment.

8

And when my weary ghost° with griefe outworne,
  By timely° death shall winne her wished rest,   65
  Let then this plaint unto his eares be borne,
  That blame it is to him, that armes profest,
  To let her die, whom he might have redrest.°
  There did she pause, inforced° to give place,
  Unto the passion, that her heart opprest,   70
  And after she had wept and wail'd a space,
She gan afresh thus to renew her wretched case.

9

Ye Gods of seas, if any Gods at all
  Have care of right, or ruth of wretches wrong,
  By one or other way me woefull thrall,   75
  Deliver hence out of this dungeon strong,
  In which I daily dying am° too long.
  And if ye deeme me death° for loving one,
  That loves not me, then doe it not prolong,
  But let me die and end my daies attone,°   80
And let him live unlov'd, or love him selfe alone.

10

But if that life ye unto me decree,
  Then let mee live, as lovers ought to do,
  And of my lifes deare love beloved be:
  And if he shall through pride your doome°
    undo,   85
  Do you by duresse him compell thereto,
  And in this prison put him here with me:
  One prison fittest is to hold us two:

---

60 **list** desired.   64 **ghost** spirit.   65 **timely** early.   68 **redrest** delivered from death.   69 **inforced** forced.   77 **am** have been.
78 **deeme me death** judge the penalty of death for me.   80 **attone** at
once.   85 **doome** judgment.

So° had I rather to be thrall, then free;
90 Such thraldome or such freedome let it surely be.

11

But O vaine judgement, and conditions vaine,
    The which° the prisoner points° unto the free,
    The whiles I him condemne, and deeme° his
        paine,°
    He where he list goes loose, and laughes at me.
95 So ever loose, so ever happy be.
    But where so loose or happy that thou art,
    Know *Marinell* that all this is for thee.
    With that she wept and wail'd, as if her hart
Would quite have burst through great abundance of
        her smart.

12

100 All which complaint when *Marinell* had heard,
    And understood the cause of all her care°
    To come of him, for using° her so hard,
    His stubborne heart, that never felt misfare°
    Was toucht with soft remorse and pitty rare;
105   That even for griefe of minde he oft did grone,
    And inly wish, that in his powre it weare
    Her to redresse: but since he meanes found none
He could no more but° her great misery bemone.

13

Thus whilst his stony heart with tender ruth
110   Was toucht, and mighty courage mollifide,°
    Dame *Venus* sonne° that tameth stubborne youth
    With iron bit, and maketh him abide,
    Till like a victor on his backe he ride,
    Into his mouth his maystring° bridle threw,
115   That made him stoupe, till he did him bestride:

89 **So** then. 92 **The which** are those which. 92 **points** appoints.
93 **deeme** decree. 93 **paine** punishment. 101 **care** grief. 102
using treating. 103 **misfare** misfortune. 108 **could . . . but** could
do no more than. 110 **courage mollifide** heart softened. 111 **Dame
Venus sonne** Cupid. 114 **maystring** taming.

Then gan° he make him tread his steps anew,
And learne to love, by learning lovers paines to rew.

14

Now gan he in his grieved minde devise,
    How from that dungeon he might her enlarge;
    Some while° he thought, by faire and humble
      wise   120
    To *Proteus* selfe to sue for her discharge:
    But then he fear'd his mothers former charge°
    Gainst womens love, long given him in vaine.
    Then gan he thinke, perforce with sword and
      targe°
    Her forth to fetch, and *Proteus* to constraine: 125
But soone he gan such folly to forthinke° againe.

15

Then did he cast° to steale her thence away,
    And with him beare, where none of her might
      know.
    But all in vaine: for why° he found no way
    To enter in, or issue forth below: 130
    For all about that rocke the sea did flow.
    And though unto his will she given were,
    Yet without ship or bote her thence to row,
    He wist not how her thence away to bere;
And daunger well he wist long to continue there. 135

16

At last when as no meanes he could invent,°
    Backe to him selfe, he gan returne the blame,
    That° was the author of her punishment;
    And with vile curses, and reprochfull shame
    To damne° him selfe by every evill name;   140
    And deeme unworthy or of love or° life,

116 **gan** did.   120 **Some while** at one time.   122 **his mothers former charge** Cymodoce "gave him warning every day,/The love of women not to entertaine" (III. iv. 26).   124 **targe** shield.   126 **forthinke** regret.   127 **cast** resolve.   129 **for why** because.   136 **invent** find.   138 **That** who.   140 **damne** condemn.   141 **or . . . or** either . . . or.

That had despisde so chast and faire a dame,
Which him had sought through trouble and long
         strife;
Yet had refusde a God that her had sought to wife.°

17

145 In this sad plight he walked here and there,
         And romed round about the rocke in vaine,
         As he had lost him selfe, he wist not where;
         Oft listening if he mote her heare againe;
         And still bemoning her unworthy paine.
150   Like as an Hynde whose calfe is falne unwares
         Into some pit, where she him heares complaine,
         An hundred times about the pit side fares,°
Right sorrowfully mourning her bereaved cares.°

18

And now by this the feast was throughly° ended,
155   And every one gan homeward to resort.
         Which seeing Marinell, was sore offended,
         That his departure thence should be so short,°
         And leave his love in that sea-walled fort.
         Yet durst he not his mother disobay,
160   But her attending in full seemly sort,°
         Did march amongst the many° all the way:
And all the way did inly mourne, like one astray.

19

Being returned to his mothers bowre,
         In solitary silence far from wight,°
165   He gan record the lamentable stowre,°
         In which his wretched love lay day and night,
         For his deare sake, that ill deserv'd that plight:
         The thought whereof empierst his hart so deepe,
         That of no worldly thing he tooke delight;

144 to wife for a wife.   152 fares goes.   153 her bereaved cares the
object of her cares from which she has been deprived.   154
throughly thoroughly.   157 short near at hand.   160 in full seemly
sort in entirely proper manner.   161 many meinie, company.   164
from wight from any human beings.   165 gan . . . stowre did recall
the lamentable peril.

Ne dayly food did take, ne nightly sleepe,   *170*
But pyn'd, and mourn'd, and languisht, and alone
   did weepe.

20

That in short space his wonted chearefull hew
   Gan fade, and lively spirits deaded quight:°
   His cheeke bones raw,° and eie-pits hollow grew,
   And brawney armes had lost their knowen
      might,°   *175*
   That nothing like himselfe he seem'd in sight.
   Ere long so weake of limbe, and sicke of love
   He woxe, that lenger he note stand upright,°
   But to his bed was brought, and layd above,°
Like ruefull ghost, unable once to stirre or move.   *180*

21

Which when his mother saw, she in her mind
   Was troubled sore, ne wist well what to weene,°
   Ne could by search nor any meanes out find
   The secret cause and nature of his teene,°
   Whereby she might apply some medicine;   *185*
   But weeping day and night, did him attend,
   And mourn'd to see her losse before her eyne,
   Which griev'd her more, that she it could not
      mend:
To see an helpelesse evill, double griefe doth lend.°

22

Nought could she read° the roote of his disease,   *190*
   Ne weene what mister° maladie it is,
   Whereby to seeke some meanes it to appease.
   Most did she thinke, but most she thought amis,
   That that same former fatall wound of his
   Whyleare° by *Tryphon* was not throughly healed,   *195*

---

173 **deaded quight** died entirely.   174 **raw** grew raw-boned, showing
through the skin.   175 **knowen might** strength familiar to all.
178 **He . . . upright** He grew, that longer he could not stand upright.
179 **above** on it.   182 **ne . . . weene** nor knew well what to think.
184 **teene** sorrow.   189 **lend** give.   190 **read** discover.   191 **what
mister** what kind of.   195 **Whyleare** a while before.

But closely rankled under th'orifis:
Least did she thinke, that which he most con-
    cealed,
That love it was, which in his hart lay unrevealed.

23

Therefore to *Tryphon* she againe doth hast,
And him doth chyde as false and fraudulent,
That fayld° the trust, which she in him had plast,
To cure her sonne, as he his faith had lent:
Who now was falne into new languishment
Of his old hurt, which was not throughly cured.
So backe he came unto her patient,
Where searching every part, her well assured,
That it was no old sore, which his new paine pro-
    cured.

24

But that it was some other maladie,
Or griefe unknowne, which he could not discerne:
So left he her withouten remedie.
Then gan her heart to faint, and quake, and
    earne,°
And inly troubled was, the truth to learne.
Unto himselfe she came, and him besought,
Now with faire speches, now with threatnings
    sterne,
If ought lay hidden in his grieved thought,
It to reveale: who still her answered, there was
    nought.

25

Nathlesse she rested not so satisfide,
But leaving watry gods, as booting nought,°
Unto the shinie heaven in haste she hide,°
And thence *Apollo* King of Leaches brought.
Apollo came; who soone as he had sought
Through his disease, did by and by° out find,

201 **fayld** disappointed.   211 **earne** yearn.   218 **as booting nought**
as availing nothing.   219 **hide** hied.   222 **by and by** at once.

That he did languish of some inward thought,
   The which afflicted his engrieved° mind;
Which love he red° to be, that leads each living kind.   225

26

Which when he had unto his mother told,
   She gan thereat to fret, and greatly grieve.
   And comming to her sonne, gan first to scold,
   And chyde at him, that made her misbelieve:
   But afterwards she gan him soft to shrieve,°   230
   And wooe with fair intreatie, to disclose,
   Which of the Nymphes his heart so sore did
      mieve.°
For sure she weend° it was some one of those,
Which he had lately seene, that for his love he chose.

27

Now lesse she feared that same fatall read,°   235
   That warned him of womens love beware:
   Which being ment of mortall creatures sead,
   For love of Nymphes she thought she need not
      care,
   But promist him, what ever wight° she weare,
   That she her love, to him would shortly gaine: 240
   So he her told: but soone as she did heare
   That *Florimell* it was, which wrought his paine,
She gan a fresh to chafe, and grieve in every vaine.

28

Yet since she saw the streight° extremitie,
   In which his life unluckily was layd,   245
   It was no time to scan the prophecie,
   Whether old *Proteus* true or false had sayd,
   That his decay should happen by a mayd.
   It's late in death of daunger to advize,°

224 **engrieved** grieving.   225 **red** perceived.   230 **shrieve** to hear his
confession.   232 **mieve** move.   233 **weend** knew.   235 **read** counsel.   239 **wight** creature; she uses the term in its original sense, "a
supernatural being," and hence a nymph, but he takes the term in its
extended sense of "a human being."   244 **streight** full.   249 **advize**
consider.

250 Or love forbid him, that is life denayd:°
But rather gan in troubled mind devize,
How she that Ladies libertie might enterprize.°

29

To *Proteus* selfe to sew° she thought it vaine,
Who was the root and worker of her woe;
255 Nor unto any meaner to complaine,
But unto great king *Neptune* selfe did goe,
And on her knee before him falling lowe,
Made humble suit unto his Majestie,
To graunt to her, her sonnes life, which his foe
260 A cruell Tyrant had presumpteouslie
By wicked doome condemn'd, a wretched death to
die.

30

To whom God *Neptune* softly smyling, thus;
Daughter me seemes of double wrong ye plaine,
Gainst one that hath both wronged you, and us:
265 For death t'adward I ween'd did appertaine°
To none, but to the seas sole Soveraine.
Read° therefore who it is, which this hath
wrought,
And for what cause; the truth discover plaine.
For never wight so evill did or thought,
270 But would some rightfull cause pretend, though
rightly nought.°

31

To whom she answerd, Then it is by name
Proteus, that hath ordayn'd my sonne to die;
For that a waift,° the which by fortune came
Upon your seas, he claym'd as propertie:
275 And yet nor his, nor his in equitie,
But yours the waift by high prerogative.

250 **denayd** denied. 252 **enterprize** attempt. 253 **sew** sue.
265 **For . . . appertaine** For death to award I believe did pertain.
266 **the seas sole Soveraine** i.e., to Neptune himself. 267 **Read** tell.
270 **though rightly nought** though nothing rightful. 273 **For . . .
waift** because a waif.

.Therefore I humbly crave your Majestie,
It to replevie,° and my sonne reprive:
So shall you by one gift save all us three alive.

32

He graunted it: and streight his warrant made,   280
Under the Sea-gods seale autenticall,°
Commaunding *Proteus* straight t'enlarge the
    mayd,
Which wandring on his seas imperiall,
He lately tooke, and sithence° kept as thrall.
Which she receiving with meete thankefulnesse,   285
Departed straight to *Proteus* therewithall:°
Who reading it with inward loathfulnesse,
Was grieved to restore the pledge, he did possesse.

33

Yet durst he not the warrant to withstand,
But unto her delivered *Florimell*.   290
Whom she receiving by the lilly hand,
Admyr'd her beautie much, as she mote well:°
For she all living creatures did excell;
And was right joyous, that she gotten had
So faire a wife for her sonne *Marinell*.   295
So home with her she streight the virgin lad,°
And shewed her to him, then being sore bestad.°

34

Who soone as he beheld that angels face
Adorn'd with all divine perfection,
His cheared heart eftsoones away gan chace   300
Sad death, revived with her sweet inspection,°
And feeble spirit inly felt refection;
As withered weed through cruell winters tine,°
That feeles the warmth of sunny beames reflec-
    tion,

278 **replevie** replevy, recover.   281 **autenticall** authentic.   284
sithence since.   286 **therewithall** with that.   292 **as . . . well** as well
she might.   296 **lad** led.   297 **bestad** beset.   301 **her sweet inspection** the sweet sight of her.   302 **refection** refreshment.   303 **tine**
affliction.

305   Liftes up his head, that did before decline
And gins to spread his leafe before the faire sunshine.

35

Right so° himselfe did *Marinell* upreare,
    When he in place his dearest love did spy;
    And though his limbs could not his bodie beare,
310   Ne former strength returne so suddenly,
    Yet chearefull signes he shewed outwardly.
    Ne lesse was she in secret hart affected,
    But that she masked it with modestie,
    For feare she should of lightnesse be detected:
315 Which to another place I leave to be perfected.

307 **Right so** even so.

The Fifth Booke

OF THE FAERIE QUEENE

Contayning,

THE LEGEND OF ARTEGALL

OR

Of Justice.

from CANTO I: THE OPENING STANZAS

1

Though vertue then were held in highest price,
    In those old times,° of which I doe intreat,°
    Yet then likewise the wicked seede of vice
    Began to spring which shortly grew full great,
    And with their boughes the gentle plants did
        beat.
    But evermore some of the vertuous race   5

---

2 **In those old times** in the Prologue to the book, Spenser explains
that he has fashioned his heroes according to the pattern of the
antique world; that is, the golden world before its degeneration into
the present stony one.   2 **intreat** treat.

Rose up, inspired with heroicke heat,
That cropt the branches of the sient° base,
And with strong hand their fruitfull rancknes did deface.°

2

Such first was *Bacchus*,° that with furious might
All th'East before untam'd did overronne,
And wrong repressed, and establisht right,
Which lawlesse men had formerly fordonne.°
There Justice first her princely rule begonne.
Next *Hercules*° his like ensample° shewed,
Who all the West with equall conquest wonne,
And monstrous tyrants with his club subdewed;
The club of Justice dread, with kingly powre endewed.°

3

And such was he, of whom I have to tell,
The Champion of true Justice *Artegall*,
Whom (as ye lately mote° remember well)
An hard adventure, which did then befall,
Into redoubted° perill forth did call;
That was to succour a distressed Dame,
Whom a strong tyrant did unjustly thrall,°
And from the heritage, which she did clame,
Did with strong hand withhold: *Grantorto*° was his name.

4

Wherefore the Lady, which *Eirena* hight,°
Did to the Faery Queene her way addresse,°

8 **sient** scion, offshoot. 9 **fruitfull rancknes** luxuriant growth.
9 **deface** destroy. 10 **Bacchus** the god of wine. Here he is honored
as the champion of Justice for his travels through the countries of
Asia, which he first civilized. 13 **fordonne** destroyed. 15 **Hercules**
In his travels through the western sea, Hercules killed the giant,
Eurytion; on his return journey, he founded cities in Spain and Gaul,
and established the rule of law in Italy. 15 **ensample** example.
18 **endewed** endowed. 21 **mote** may. 23 **redoubted** dreaded.
25 **thrall** enthrall, hold in thralldom. 27 **Grantorto** Great Wrong.
28 **hight** was called. 29 **addresse** direct.

To whom complayning her afflicted plight,   30
She her besought of gratious redresse.
That soveraine Queene, that mightie Emperesse,
Whose glorie is to aide all suppliants pore,
And of weake Princes to be Patronesse,
Chose *Artegall* to right her to restore;   35
For that° to her he seem'd best skild in righteous lore.

5

For *Artegall* in justice was upbrought
Even from the cradle of his infancie,
And all the depth of rightfull doome° was taught
By faire *Astræa*,° with great industrie,   40
Whilest here on earth she lived mortallie.°
For till the world from his perfection fell
Into all filth and foule iniquitie,
Astræa here mongst earthly men did dwell,
And in the rules of justice them instructed well.   45

6

Whiles through the world she walked in this sort,°
Upon a day she found this gentle childe,
Amongst his peres° playing his childish sport:
Whom seeing fit, and with no crime defilde,
She did allure with gifts and speaches milde,   50
To wend° with her. So thence him farre she
   brought
Into a cave from companie exilde,
In which she noursled him, till yeares he raught,°
And all the discipline of justice there him taught.

7

There she him taught to weigh both right and wrong   55
In equall ballance with due recompence,
And equitie to measure out along,°
According to the line° of conscience,

36 **For that** because.   39 **rightfull doome** judgment in conformity
with what is right.   40 **Astræa** the goddess of justice.   41 **mortallie**
as a mortal.   46 **sort** manner.   48 **peres** companions.   51 **wend** go.
53 **In . . . raught** In which she nursed him until he came to maturity.
57 **along** along with justice.   58 **line** rule.

When so it needs with rigour° to dispence.
Of all the which, for want there of mankind,
She caused him to make experience°
Upon wyld beasts, which she in woods did find,
With wrongfull powre oppressing others of their kind.

8

Thus she him trayned, and thus she him taught,
In all the skill of deeming° wrong and right,
Untill the ripenesse of mans yeares he raught;°
That even wilde beasts did feare his awfull
sight,°
And men admyr'd his overruling might;°
Ne any liv'd on ground, that durst withstand
His dreadfull heast,° much lesse him match in
fight,
Or bide° the horror of his wreakfull° hand,
When so he list in wrath lift up his steely brand.°

9

Which steely brand, to make him dreaded more,
She gave unto him, gotten by her slight°
And earnest search, where it was kept in store
In *Joves* eternall house, unwist of wight,°
Since he himselfe it us'd in that great fight
Against the *Titans,* that whylome° rebelled
Gainst highest heaven; *Chrysaor*° it was hight;
Chrysaor that all other swords excelled,
Well prov'd in that same day, when *Jove* those Gyants
quelled.

10

For of most perfect metall° it was made,

---

59 **rigour** the strict application of the letter of the law.   61 **to make
experience** to experiment.   65 **deeming** judging.   66 **raught** reached.
67 **his awfull sight** the sight of him, which aroused awe.   68 **his overruling might** his might which rules over others.   70 **heast** hest,
command.   71 **bide** endure.   71 **wreakfull** vengeful.   72 **his steely
brand** his sword.   74 **slight** skill.   76 **unwist of wight** not known to
anyone.   78 **whylome** once upon a time.   79 **Chrysaor** Golden
Sword.   82 **metall** steel.

Tempred with Adamant° amongst the same,
And garnisht all with gold upon the blade
In goodly wise, whereof it tooke his name,   85
And was of no lesse vertue,° then of fame.
For there no substance was so firme and hard,
But it would pierce or cleave, where so it came;
Ne any armour could his dint out ward,°
But wheresoever it did light, it throughly shard.°   90

11

Now when the world with sinne gan to abound,
   Astræa loathing lenger° here to space°
Mongst wicked men, in whom no truth she found,
Return'd to heaven, whence she deriv'd her
   race;°
Where she hath now an everlasting place,   95
Mongst those twelve signes,° which nightly we
   doe see
The heavens bright-shining baudricke° to en-
   chace;°
And is the *Virgin,* sixt in her degree,°
And next her selfe her righteous ballance° hanging
   bee.

12

But when she parted hence, she left her groome°   100
   An yron man, which did on her attend
Alwayes, to execute her stedfast doome,
And willed him with *Artegall* to wend,
And doe what ever thing he did intend.
His name was *Talus,* made of yron mould,°   105
   Immoveable, resistlesse, without end.
Who in his hand an yron flaile did hould,

83 **Adamant** a substance of fabulous hardness. 86 **vertue** power.
89 **dint out ward** blow turn aside. 90 **throughly shard** cut right
through. 92 **lenger** longer. 92 **space** walk. 94 **her race** she is the
daughter of Zeus and Themis. 96 **signes** signs of the Zodiac. 97
baudricke baldric, a gem-studded belt, and hence the Zodiac. 97
enchace serve as a setting for. 98 **sixt . . . degree** Astræa is identified
with the constellation Virgo, the sixth of the zodiacal signs. 99 **her
righteous ballance** the constellation Libra. 100 **groome** servant.
105 **mould** shape.

With which he thresht out falshood, and did truth un-
      fould.°

13

He now went with him in this new inquest,°
      Him for to aide, if aide he chaunst to neede,
      Against that cruell Tyrant, which opprest
      The faire *Irena* with his foule misdeede,
      And kept the crowne in which she should suc-
        ceed.
      And now together on their way they bin,°
      When as they saw a Squire in squallid weed,°
      Lamenting sore his sorowfull sad tyne,°
With many bitter teares shed from his blubbred eyne.°

*After Artegall demonstrates the power of Justice, he is
overpowered by the beauty of the Amazon, Radigund, and
imprisoned by her. When Britomart learns through Talus
of his defeat, she seeks to rescue him. After overcoming
several of Artegall's earlier foes, she arrives at Isis
Church.*

CANTO VII

Britomart comes to Isis Church,
    Where shee strange visions sees:
She fights with Radigund, her slaies,
    And Artegall thence frees.

1

Nought is on earth more sacred or divine,
      That Gods and men doe equally adore,

108 **unfould** reveal. 109 **inquest** quest. 114 **bin** are. 115 **weed**
dress. 116 **tyne** grief. 117 **blubbred eyne** swollen eyes.

    Then this same vertue, that doth right define:
    For th'hevens themselves, whence mortal men
      implore
    Right in their wrongs, are rul'd by righteous lore   5
    Of highest Jove, who doth true justice deale
    To his inferiour Gods, and evermore
    Therewith° containes° his heavenly Common-
      weale:
The skill whereof° to Princes hearts he doth reveale.

    2

Well therefore did the antique world invent,   10
    That Justice was a God of soveraine grace,
    And altars unto him, and temples lent,
    And heavenly honours in the highest place;
    Calling him great *Osyris,*° of the race
    Of th'old Ægyptian Kings, that whylome were;   15
    With fayned colours shading° a true case:
    For that *Osyris,* whilest he lived here,
The justest man alive, and truest did appeare.

    3

His wife was *Isis,* whom they likewise made
    A Goddesse of great powre and soveraranty,   20
    And in her person cunningly did shade°
    That part° of Justice, which is Equity,
    Whereof I have to treat here presently.
    Unto whose temple when as *Britomart*
    Arrived, shee with great humility   25
    Did enter in, ne would that night depart;
But *Talus* mote not be admitted to her part.

    4

There she received was in goodly wize
    Of many Priests, which duely° did attend
    Upon the rites and daily sacrifize,   30

---

8 **Therewith** with justice.   8 **containes** keeps under control.   9 **The skill whereof** the practical knowledge of which.   14 **Osyris** one of the chief Egyptian deities.   16 **shading** obscuring.   21 **shade** represent.   22 **part** side.   29 **duely** properly.

All clad in linnen robes with silver hemd;°
And on their heads with long locks comely
    kemd,°
They wore rich Mitres shaped like the Moone,
To shew that *Isis* doth the Moone portend;°
35 Like as *Osyris* signifies the Sunne.
For that they both like race in equall justice runne.°

5

The Championesse them greeting, as° she could,
  Was thence by them into the Temple led;
  Whose goodly building when she did behould,
40 Borne uppon stately pillours, all dispred°
  With shining gold, and arched over hed,
  She wondred at the workemans passing skill,
  Whose like before she never saw nor red;°
  And thereuppon long while stood gazing still,
But thought, that she thereon could never gaze her
45   fill.

6

Thence forth unto the Idoll they her brought,
  The which was framed all of silver fine,
  So well as could with cunning° hand be wrought,
  And clothed all in garments made of line,°
50 Hemd all about with fringe of silver twine.
  Uppon her head she wore a Crowne of gold,
  To shew that she had powre in things divine;
  And at her feete a Crocodile was rold,
That with her wreathed taile her middle did enfold.

7

55 One foote was set uppon the Crocodile,
  And on the ground the other fast did stand,
  So meaning to suppresse both forged guile,°

---

31 **hemd** edged.   32 **kemd** combed.   34 **portend** signify.   36 **For
. . . runne** Because the moon and the sun are equally regular in their
orbits.   37 **as** as well.   40 **dispred** spread.   43 **red** imagined.   48
cunning skillful.   49 **line** linen.   57 **forged guile** See I. v. 18 for the
crocodile's legendary guile.

And open force: and in her other hand°
    She stretched forth a long white sclender° wand.
    Such was the Goddesse; whom when *Britomart*   60
    Had long beheld, her selfe uppon the land°
    She did prostrate, and with right humble hart,
Unto her selfe° her silent prayers did impart.

8

To which the Idoll as it were inclining,
    Her wand did move with amiable looke,   65
    By outward shew her inward sence desining.°
    Who well perceiving, how her wand she shooke,
    It as a token of good fortune tooke.
    By this the day with dampe° was overcast,
    And joyous light the house of *Jove*° forsooke: 70
    Which when she saw, her helmet she unlaste,
And by the altars side her selfe to slumber plaste.

9

For other beds the Priests there used none,
    But on their mother Earths deare lap did lie,
    And bake° their sides uppon the cold hard stone,   75
    T'enure° them selves to sufferaunce° thereby
    And proud rebellious flesh to mortify.
    For by the vow of their religion
    They tied were to stedfast chastity,
    And continence of life, that all forgon,°   80
They mote the better tend to their devotion.

10

Therefore they mote not taste of fleshly food,
    Ne feed on ought, the which doth bloud con-
        taine,°
    Ne drinke of wine, for wine they say° is blood,

---

58 in ... hand in one hand; possibly, "in her left hand."   **59 sclender**
slender.   **61 land** ground.   **63 her selfe** i.e., Isis.   **66 desining** indicating.   **69 dampe** mist.   **70 the house of Jove** the sky.   **75 bake**
harden.   **76 T'enure** to accustom.   **76 sufferance** patient endur-
ance.   **80 that all forgon** that by abstaining from all things.   **83 the
which ... containe** Cf. Gen. ix. 4: "But flesh with the life thereof,
which is the blood thereof, shall ye not eat."   **84 for wine they say**
The story is told by Plutarch.

85 Even the bloud of Gyants, which were slaine,
    By thundring Jove in the Phlegrean plaine.°
    For which the earth (as they the story tell)
    Wroth with the Gods, which to perpetuall paine
    Had damn'd° her sonnes, which gainst them did
        rebell,
90 With inward griefe and malice did against them swell.

    11

    And of their vitall° bloud, the which was shed
    Into her pregnant bosome, forth she brought
    The fruitfull vine, whose liquor blouddy red
    Having the mindes of men with fury fraught,°
95 Mote in them stirre up old rebellious thought,
    To make new warre against the Gods againe:
    Such is the powre of that same fruit, that nought
    The fell contagion may thereof restraine,
    Ne within reasons rule, her madding° mood containe.

    12

100 There did the warlike Maide her selfe repose,
    Under the wings of *Isis*° all that night,
    And with sweete rest her heavy eyes did close,
    After that long daies toile and weary plight.
    Where whilest her earthly parts with soft delight
105 Of sencelesse sleepe° did deeply drowned lie,
    There did appeare unto her heavenly spright°
    A wondrous vision, which did close implie°
    The course of all her fortune and posteritie.

    13

    Her seem'd,° as she was doing sacrifize
110   To *Isis,* deckt with Mitre on her hed,
        And linnen stole after those Priestes guize,°

86 **the Phlegrean plaine** the home of the Giants.   89 **damn'd** condemned.   91 **vitall** life-giving.   94 **fraught** filled.   99 **madding** frenzied.   101 **Under . . . Isis** under the protecting care of Isis.   105 **sencelesse sleepe** i.e., without sensations; hence, she does not dream but receives a vision.   106 **heavenly spright** heavenly spirit, her Genius; see II. xii. 47.   107 **close implie** express indirectly.   109 **Her seem'd** it seemed to her.   111 **after . . . guize** like the habit of those priests.

All sodainely she saw transfigured
Her linnen stole to robe of scarlet red,
And Moone-like Mitre to a Crowne of gold,
That even she her selfe much wondered   *115*
At such a chaunge, and joyed to behold
Her selfe, adorn'd with gems and jewels manifold.

14

And in the midst of her felicity,
An hideous tempest seemed from below,
To rise through all the Temple sodainely,   *120*
That from the Altar all about did blow
The holy fire, and all the embers strow
Uppon the ground, which kindled privily,
Into outragious° flames unwares° did grow,
That all the Temple put in jeopardy   *125*
Of flaming, and her selfe in great perplexity.

15

With that the Crocodile, which sleeping lay
Under the Idols feete in fearelesse bowre,°
Seem'd to awake in horrible dismay,
As being troubled with that stormy stowre;°   *130*
And gaping greedy wide, did streight devoure
Both flames and tempest: with which growen
    great,
And swolne with pride of his owne peerelesse
    powre,
He gan to threaten her likewise to eat;
But that the Goddesse with her rod him backe did
    beat.   *135*

16

Tho turning all his pride to humblesse° meeke,
Him selfe before her feete he lowly threw,
And gan for grace and love of her to seeke:
Which she accepting, he so neare her drew,

124 **outragious**   violent.   124 **unwares**   suddenly.   128 **fearelesse
bowre** a place where he had no fear.   130 **stowre** tumult.   136
humblesse humbleness.

140   That of his game° she soone enwombed grew,°
             And forth did bring a Lion of great might;
             That shortly did all other beasts subdew.
             With that she waked, full of fearefull fright,
       And doubtfully dismayd through that so uncouth°
             sight.

             17
145   So thereuppon long while she musing lay,
             With thousand thoughts feeding her fantasie,
             Untill she spide the lampe of lightsome° day,
             Up-lifted in the porch of heaven hie.
             Then up she rose fraught with melancholy,
150   And forth into the lower parts did pas;
             Whereas° the Priestes she found full busily
             About their holy things for morrow° Mas:
       Whom she saluting faire, faire resaluted was.

             18
       But by the change of her unchearefull looke,
155   They might perceive, she was not well in plight;°
             Or that some pensivenesse to heart she tooke.
             Therefore thus one of them, who seem'd in sight
             To be the greatest, and the gravest wight,
             To her bespake; Sir Knight it seemes to me,
160   That thorough evill rest of this last night,
             Or ill apayd,° or much dismayd ye be,
       That by your change of cheare° is easie for to see.

             19
       Certes° (sayd she) sith ye so well have spide
             The troublous° passion of my pensive mind,
165   I will not seeke the same from you to hide,
             But will my cares unfolde, in hope to find
             Your aide, to guide me out of errour° blind.

140 **game** amorous play. 140 **enwombed grew** grew pregnant.
144 **uncouth** strange. 147 **lightsome** bright. 151 **Whereas** where.
152 **morrow** morning. 155 **well in plight** in good health. 161
apayd satisfield. 162 **cheare** countenance. 163 **Certes** certainly.
164 **troublous** troublesome. 167 **errour** wandering.

Say on (quoth he) the secret of your hart:
For by the holy vow, which me doth bind,
I am adjur'd,° best counsell to impart   170
To all, that shall require my comfort in their smart.

20

Then gan she to declare the whole discourse°
Of all that vision, which to her appeard,
As well as to her minde it had recourse.°
All which when he unto the end had heard,   175
Like to a weake faint-hearted man he fared,°
Through great astonishment of that strange sight;
And with long locks up-standing, stifly stared
Like one adawed° with some dreadfull spright.
So fild with heavenly fury, thus he her behight.°   180

21

Magnificke° Virgin, that in queint° disguise
Of British armes doest maske thy royall blood,
So to pursue a perillous emprize,°
How couldst thou weene, through that disguized
        hood,°
To hide thy state from being understood?   185
Can from th'immortall Gods ought° hidden bee?
They doe thy linage, and thy Lordly brood;°
They doe thy sire, lamenting sore for thee;
They doe thy love, forlorne in womens thraldome see.

22

The end whereof, and all the long event,°   190
They doe to thee in this same dreame discover.°
For that same Crocodile doth represent
The righteous Knight, that is thy faithfull lover,
Like to *Osyris* in all just endever.

170 **adjur'd** charged.   172 **discourse** narrative.   174 **had recourse**
returned.   176 **fared**   acted.   179 **adawed**   daunted.   180 **behight**
bespoke,   addressed.   181 **Magnificke**   renowned.   181 **queint**
strange.   183 **emprize** enterprise.   184 **hood** mask.   186 **ought** anything.   187 **brood** parentage.   190 **event** issue.   191 **discover** reveal.

195   For that same Crocodile *Osyris* is,
       That under *Isis* feete doth sleepe for ever:
       To shew that clemence oft in things amis,
   Restraines those sterne behests, and cruell doomes of
         his.

       23
   That Knight shall all the troublous stormes asswage,
200   And raging flames, that many foes shall reare,°
       To hinder thee from the just heritage
       Of thy sires Crowne, and from thy countrey
         deare.
       Then shalt thou take him to thy loved fere,°
       And joyne in equall portion of thy realme:
205   And afterwards a sonne to him shalt beare,
       That Lion-like shall shew his powre extreame.
   So blesse thee God, and give thee joyance° of thy
         dreame.

       24
   All which when she unto the end had heard,
       She much was eased in her troublous thought,
210   And on those Priests bestowed rich reward:
       And royall gifts of gold and silver wrought,
       She for a present to their Goddesse brought.
       Then taking leave of them, she forward went,
       To seeke her love, where he was to be sought;
215   Ne rested till she came without relent°
   Unto the land of Amazons, as she was bent.°

       25
   Whereof when newes to *Radigund* was brought,
       Not with amaze,° as women wonted bee,
       She was confused in her troublous thought,
220   But fild with courage and with joyous glee,
       As glad to heare of armes, the which now she

---

200 **reare** cause.   203 **fere** mate.   207 **joyance** enjoyment.   215 **relent** slackening of speed.   216 **bent** determined to do.   218 **Not with
amaze,** etc. In her troubled thought she was not confused with amazement, as women are accustomed to be, but instead was filled . . .

Had long surceast,° she bad to open bold,°
That she the face of her new foe might see.
But when they of that yron man had told,
Which late° her folke had slaine, she bad them forth
    to hold.°   225

26

So there without° the gate (as seemed best)
    She° caused her Pavilion be pight;°
    In which stout *Britomart* her selfe did rest,
    Whiles *Talus* watched at the dore all night.
    All night likewise, they of the towne in fright,   230
    Uppon their wall good watch and ward did keepe.
    The morrow next, so soone as dawning light
    Bad doe away the dampe° of drouzie sleepe,
The warlike Amazon out of her bowre° did peepe.

27

And caused streight a Trumpet loud to shrill,   235
    To warne her foe to battell soone be prest:°
    Who long before awoke (for she ful ill
    Could sleepe all night, that in unquiet brest
    Did closely harbour such a jealous guest)
    Was to the battell whilome ready dight.°   240
    Eftsoones° that warriouresse with haughty crest
    Did forth issue, all ready for the fight:
On th'other side her foe appeared soone in sight.

28

But ere they reared hand, the Amazone
    Began the streight conditions° to propound,   245
    With which she used still to tye her fone;°

---

222 **surceast** given up. From being a warrior, she had become a
wooer of Artegal.   222 **to open bold** to open the gates boldly.   225
late lately. The story is told in Canto v.   225 **forth to hold** to go
forth.   266 **without**   outside.   227 **She**   Radigund.   227 **pight**
placed.   233 **dampe** the "dew" of sleep.   234 **bowre** bedroom.
236 **prest** ready.   240 **whilome ready dight** already dressed.   241
Eftsoones soon afterward.   245 **streight conditions** strict conditions.
As given in Canto iv, these amount to unconditional surrender: the
vanquished must obey the victor's law, and be bound forever to her
teaching.   246 **fone** foes.

To serve her so, as she the rest had bound.
Which when the other heard, she sternly frownd
For high disdaine of such indignity,
250   And would no lenger treat,° but bad them sound.
For her no other termes should ever tie,
Then what prescribed were by lawes of chevalrie.

29

The Trumpets sound, and they together run
With greedy° rage, and with their faulchins°
    smot;
255   Ne either° sought the others strokes to shun,
But through great fury both their skill forgot,
And practicke use° in armes: ne spared not
Their dainty parts, which nature had created
So faire and tender, without staine or spot,
260   For other uses, then they them translated;°
Which they now hackt and hewd, as if such use they
    hated,

30

As when a Tygre and a Lionesse
Are met at spoyling of some hungry pray,°
Both challenge° it with equall greedinesse:
265   But first the Tygre clawes thereon did lay;
And therefore loth to loose° her right away,
Doth in defence thereof full stoutly stond:°
To which the Lion strongly doth gainesay,°
That she to hunt the beast first tooke in hond;
270   And therefore ought it have, where ever she it fond.°

31

Full fiercely layde the Amazon about,
And dealt her blowes unmercifully sore:
Which *Britomart* withstood with courage stout,

---

250 **no lenger treat** no longer negotiate.   254 **greedy** eager.   254
faulchins swords.   255 **Ne either** neither.   257 **practicke use** cunning skill.   260 **translated** turned.   263 **spoyling . . . pray** despoiling
of some prey for which they hunger.   264 **challenge** claim.   266
loose lose.   267 **stond** stand.   268 **gainesay** oppose.   270 **fond**
found.

And them repaide againe with double more.
So long they fought, that all the grassie flore   275
Was fild with bloud, which from their sides did
    flow,
And gushed through their armes, that all in gore
They trode, and on the ground their lives did
    strow,
Like fruitles seede, of which untimely death should
    grow.

32

At last proud *Radigund* with fell despight,°   280
    Having by chaunce espide advantage neare,
    Let drive at her with all her dreadfull might,
    And thus upbrayding said; This token beare
    Unto the man, whom thou doest love so deare;
    And tell him for his sake thy life thou gavest.   285
    Which spitefull words she sore engriev'd° to
        heare,
    Thus answer'd; Lewdly° thou my love
        depravest,°
Who shortly must repent that now so vainely bravest.°

33

Nath'lesse that stroke so cruell passage found,
    That glauncing on her shoulder plate, it bit   290
    Unto the bone, and made a griesly° wound,
    That she her shield through raging smart of it
    Could scarse uphold; yet soone she it requit.°
    For having force increast through furious paine,
    She her so rudely on the helmet smit,   295
    That it empierced to the very braine,
And her proud person low prostrated on the plaine.

34

Where being layd, the wrothfull Britonesse

280 **fell despight** fierce anger.   286 **engriev'd** grieved.   287 **Lewdly**
wickedly.   287 **depravest** defame, by suggesting that he has been
slain by a woman.   288 **bravest** vaunts.   291 **griesly** horrible.   293
requit requited.

Stayd not, till she came to her selfe againe,
300   But in revenge both of her loves distresse,
And her late vile reproch, though vaunted vaine,°
And also of her wound, which sore did paine,
She with one stroke both head and helmet cleft.
Which dreadfull sight, when all her warlike traine
305   There present saw, each one of sence bereft,
Fled fast into the towne, and her sole victor left.

35

But yet so fast they could not home retrate,°
But that swift *Talus* did the formost win;°
And pressing through the preace° unto the gate,
310   Pelmell° with them attonce did enter in.
There then a piteous slaughter did begin:
For all that ever came within his reach,
He with his yron flaile did thresh so thin,
That he no worke at all left for the leach:°
315   Like to an hideous storme, which nothing may
      empeach.°

36

And now by this the noble Conqueresse
Her selfe came in, her glory to partake;°
Where though revengefull vow she did professe,
Yet when she saw the heapes, which he did
      make,
320   Of slaughtred carkasses, her heart did quake
For very ruth,° which did it almost rive,
That she his fury willed him to slake:
For else he sure had left not one alive,
But all in his revenge of spirite° would deprive.

37

325   Tho when she had his execution stayd,
She for that yron prison did enquire,

---

301 **vaine** in vain. 307 **retrate** retreat. 308 **win** overtake. 309
preace throng. 310 **Pelmell** mingling. 314 **leach** surgeon. 315
empeach hinder. 317 **partake** take part in, by conquering the city.
321 **ruth** pity. 324 **spirite** life.

In which her wretched love was captive layd:
Which breaking open with indignant ire,
She entred into all the partes entire.°
Where when she saw that lothly uncouth° sight,   330
Of men disguiz'd° in womanishe attire,
Her heart gan grudge,° for very deepe despight
Of so unmanly maske, in misery misdight.°

38

At last when as to her owne Love she came,
Whom like disguize no lesse deformed had,   335
At sight thereof abasht with secrete shame,
She turnd her head aside, as nothing° glad,
To have beheld a spectacle so bad:
And then too well beleev'd, that which tofore°
Jealous suspect° as true untruely drad,°   340
Which vaine conceipt now nourishing no more,
She sought with ruth to salve his sad misfortunes sore.

39

Not so great wonder and astonishment,
Did the most chast *Penelope* possesse,
To see her Lord,° that was reported drent,°   345
And dead long since in dolorous distresse,
Come home to her in piteous wretchednesse,
After long travell° of full twenty yeares,
That she knew not his favours likelynesse,°
For° many scarres and many hoary heares,   350
But stood long staring on him, mongst uncertaine
        feares.

40

Ah my deare Lord, what sight is this (quoth she)
What May-game° hath misfortune made of you?

329 **partes entire** inward parts.   330 **uncouth** shocking.   331 **disguiz'd** disfigured.   332 **grudge** complain.   333 **misdight** ill-clothed.
337 **nothing** not at all.   339 **tofore** before.   340 **Jealous suspect** her
earlier suspicion that he was not constant in his love.   340 **drad**
dreaded.   345 **her Lord** Ulysses.   345 **drent** drowned.   348 **travell**
travail.   349 **his favours likelynesse** the likeness of his face.   350
For because of.   353 **May-game** laughing-stock.

Where is that dreadfull manly look?° where be
Those mighty palmes, the which ye wont
355   t'embrew°
In bloud of Kings, and great hoastes to subdew?
Could ought on earth so wondrous change have
wrought,
As to have robde you of that manly hew?
Could so great courage stouped have to ought?°
360 Then farewell fleshly force; I see thy pride is nought.

41

Thenceforth she streight into a bowre him brought,
And causd him those uncomely weedes undight;°
And in their steede for other rayment sought,
Whereof there was great store, and armors
bright,
365   Which had bene reft from many a noble Knight;
Whom that proud Amazon subdewed had,
Whilest Fortune favourd her successe in fight,
In which when as she him anew had clad,
She was reviv'd, and joyd much in his semblance°
glad.

42

370 So there a while they afterwards remained,
Him to refresh, and her late wounds to heale:
During which space she there as Princess rained,
And changing all that forme of common weale,
The liberty of women did repeale,
375   Which they had long usurpt; and them restoring
To mens subjection, did true Justice deale:
That all they as a Goddesse her adoring,
Her wisedome did admire, and hearkned to her
loring.°

354 **that dreadfull manly looke** the manly look that arouses dread in others.   355 **t'embrew** to stain.   359 **ought** anything.   362 **weedes undight** clothes to take off.   369 **semblance** appearance.   378 **loring** teaching.

43

For all those Knights, which long in captive shade
 Had shrouded bene, she did from thraldome free; *380*
 And magistrates of all that city made,
 And gave to them great living° and large fee:°
 And that they should for ever faithfull bee,
 Made them sweare fealty to *Artegall.*
 Who when him selfe now well recur'd° did see, *385*
 He purposd to proceed, what so be fall,°
Uppon his first adventure, which him forth did call.

44

Full sad and sorrowfull was *Britomart*
 For his departure, her new cause of griefe;
 Yet wisely moderated her owne smart, *390*
 Seeing his honor, which she tendred chiefe,°
 Consisted much in that adventures priefe.°
 The care whereof, and hope of his successe
 Gave unto her great comfort and reliefe,
 That womanish complaints she did represse, *395*
And tempred for the time her present heavinesse.

45

There she continu'd for a certaine space,
 Till through his want° her woe did more
  increase:
 Then hoping that the change of aire and place
 Would change her paine, and sorrow somewhat
  ease, *400*
 She parted° thence, her anguish to appease.
 Meane while her noble Lord sir *Artegall*
 Went on his way, ne ever howre did cease,
 Till he redeemed had that Lady thrall:°
That for another Canto will more fitly fall. *405*

382 **living** livelihood. 382 **fee** estates. 385 **recur'd** restored. 386
what so be fall whatever may happen. 391 **tendred chiefe** chiefly
cherished. 392 **priefe** proof. 398 **his want** her want of him.
401 **parted** departed. 404 **that Lady thrall** Irena.

The Sixth Booke

OF THE FAERIE QUEENE.

Contayning,

THE LEGEND OF

S. CALIDOR,

OR

Of Courtesie.

1

The waies, through which my weary steps I guyde,
In this delightfull land of Faery,
Are so exceeding spacious and wyde,
And sprinckled° with such sweet variety,
Of all that pleasant is to eare or eye,
That I nigh ravisht with rare thoughts delight,
My tedious travell doe forget thereby;
And when I gin to feele decay of might,
It strength to me supplies, and chears my dulled
spright.

4 **sprinckled** interspersed.

2

Such secret comfort, and such heavenly pleasures,   10
    Ye sacred imps,° that on *Parnasso*° dwell,
    And there the keeping have of learnings
       threasures,
    Which doe all worldly riches farre excell,
    Into the mindes of mortall men doe well,°
    And goodly fury° into them infuse;   15
    Guyde ye my footing, and conduct me well
    In these strange waies, where never foote did
       use,°
Ne none can find, but who was taught them by the
    Muse.

3

Revele to me the sacred noursery
    Of vertue, which with you doth there remaine,   20
    Where it in silver bowre does hidden ly
    From view of men, and wicked worlds disdaine.
    Since it at first was by the Gods with paine°
    Planted in earth, being deriv'd at furst
    From heavenly seedes of bounty° soveraine,   25
    And by them long with carefull labour nurst,
Till it to ripenesse grew, and forth to honour burst.

4

Amongst them all growes not a fayrer flowre,
    Then is the bloosme° of comely courtesie,
    Which though it on a lowly stalke doe bowre,°   30
    Yet brancheth forth in brave nobilitie,
    And spreds it selfe through all civilitie:°
    Of which though present age doe plenteous
       seeme,
    Yet being matcht with plaine Antiquitie,
    Ye will them all but fayned showes esteeme,   35
Which carry colours faire, that feeble eies misdeeme.°

11 **Ye sacred imps** the Muses. 11 **Parnasso** Parnassus. 14 **well**
pour. 15 **fury** poetic "rage." 17 **use** frequent, haunt. 23 **paine**
care. 25 **bounty** goodness. 29 **bloosme** blossom, bloom. 30
bowre lodge. 32 **civilitie** civilization. 36 **misdeeme** cause to misjudge.

5

But in the triall° of true curtesie,
    Its now so farre from that, which then it was,
    That it indeed is nought but forgerie,
40   Fashion'd to please the eies of them, that pas,°
    Which see not perfect things° but in a glas:
    Yet is that glasse so gay,° that it can blynd
    The wisest sight, to thinke gold that is bras.
    But vertues seat is deepe within the mynd,
And not in outward shows, but inward thoughts
45   defynd.°

6

But where shall I in all Antiquity
    So faire a patterne finde, where may be seene
    The goodly praise° of Princely curtesie,
    As in your selfe, O soveraine Lady Queene,
50   In whose pure minde, as in a mirrour sheene,°
    It showes, and with her brightnesse doth inflame
    The eyes of all, which thereon fixed beene;
    But meriteth indeede an higher name:
Yet so° from low to high uplifted is your name.

7

55 Then pardon me, most dreaded Soveraine,
    That from your selfe I doe this vertue bring,
    And to your selfe doe it returne againe:
    So from the Ocean all rivers spring,
    And tribute backe repay as to their King.
60   Right so from you all goodly vertues well°
    Into the rest, which round about you ring,
    Faire Lords and Ladies, which about you dwell,
And doe adorne your Court, where courtesies excell.

---

37 **triall** examination.   40 **pas** go by without attending.   41 **see not perfect things** see things not perfectly. Cf. I Cor. xiii. 12: "For now we see through a glass; darkly."   42 **gay** brilliant.   45 **defynd** to be defined, that is, its essential nature set forth.   48 **praise** ground of praise.   50 **sheene** shining.   54 **Yet so** even so.   60 **well** flow.

*The patron of Courtesy is Calidore, and his pursuit of
the Blatant Beast, a hellish monster whose tongue injures
men and women with shame and slander, becomes the
subject of Book VI. The opening Cantos describe
the nature of his courtesy and his relentless pursuit of the
Blatant Beast. Later Cantos use other stories to show
the nature of discourtesy and the power of the Blatant
Beast to slander lovers. In the four closing Cantos, Spenser
tells how Calidore's pursuit is interrupted by his retreat
into the pastoral world.*

CANTO IX

*Calidore hostes° with Melibœ
    and loves fayre Pastorell;
Coridon envies him, yet he
    for ill rewards him well.*

1

Now turne againe my teme thou jolly swayne,°
    Backe to the furrow which I lately left;
    I lately left a furrow, one or twayne
    Unplough'd, the which my coulter hath not cleft:°
    Yet seem'd the soyle both fayre and frutefull eft,°   5
    As I it past, that were too great a shame,
    That so rich frute should be from us bereft;
    Besides the great dishonour and defame,
Which should befall to *Calidores* immortall name.

2

Great travell° hath the gentle *Calidore*   10
    And toyle endured, sith I left him last
    Sewing° the *Blatant beast,* which I forbore
    To finish then, for other present hast.

Arg. **hostes** is a guest.   1 **thou jolly swayne** the heavenly Muse at her
labors for the poet.   4 **cleft** divided.   5 **eft** afterward.   10 **travell**
travail.   12 **Sewing** pursuing.

Full many pathes and perils he hath past,
Through hils, through dales, throgh forests, and
        throgh plaines
In that same quest° which fortune on him cast,
Which he atchieved to his owne great gaines,
Reaping eternall glorie of his restlesse° paines.

3

So sharply he the Monster did pursew,
        That day nor night he suffred him to rest,
        Ne rested he himselfe but natures dew,°
        For dread of daunger, not to be redrest,
        If he for slouth forslackt° so famous quest.
        Him first from court he to the citties coursed,°
        And from the citties to the townes him prest,
        And from the townes into the countrie forsed,
And from the country back to private farmes he
        scorsed.°

4

From thence into the open fields he fled,
        Whereas the Heardes° were keeping of their
        neat,°
        And shepheards singing to their flockes, that fed,
        Layes of sweete love and youthes delightfull
        heat:
        Him thether eke for all his fearefull threat
        He followed fast, and chaced him so nie,°
        That to the folds, where sheepe at night doe
        seat,°
        And to the litle cots,° where shepherds lie
In winters wrathfull time, he forced him to flie.

5

There on a day as he pursew'd the chace,

16 **that same quest** his quest to capture the Blatant Beast.   18 **restlesse** unceasing.   21 **but natures dew** but only the sleep which
is due nature.   23 **forslackt** neglected.   24 **coursed** pursued.   27
And . . . scorsed He forced the beast to exchange the open country
for private farms.   29 **Heardes** herdsman.   29 **neat** cattle.   33 **nie**
near.   34 **seat** rest.   35 **cots** cotes, shelters.

He chaunst to spy a sort° of shepheard groomes,
    Playing on pypes,° and caroling apace,°
    The whyles their beasts there in the budded
      broomes°   *40*
    Beside them fed, and nipt the tender bloomes:
    For other worldly wealth they cared nought.
    To whom Sir *Calidore* yet sweating comes,
    And them to tell him courteously besought,
If such a beast they saw, which he had thether
    brought.   *45*

6

They answer'd him, that no such beast they saw,
    Nor any wicked feend, that mote offend
    Their happie flockes, nor daunger to them draw:
    But if that such there were (as none they kend)°
    They prayd high God him farre from them to
      send.   *50*
    Then one of them him seeing so to sweat,
    After his rusticke wise,° that well he weend,°
    Offred him drinke, to quench his thirstie heat,°
And if he hungry were, him offred eke to eat.

7

The knight was nothing nice,° where was no need,   *55*
    And tooke their gentle offer: so adowne
    They prayd him sit, and gave him for to feed
    Such homely what,° as serves the simple clowne,°
    That doth despise the dainties of the towne.
    Tho having fed his fill, he there besyde   *60*
    Saw a faire damzell, which did weare a crowne
    Of sundry flowres, with silken ribbands tyde,
Yclad in home-made greene° that her owne hands
    had dyde.

---

38 **sort** band. 39 **pypes** bagpipes. 39 **apace** at a good pace. 40
broomes broom. 49 **kend** knew. 52 **rusticke wise** rural manner.
52 **weend** managed. 53 **his thirstie heat** the heat through which he
thirsts. 55 **nothing nice** not at all fastidious. 58 **what** something.
58 **clowne** countryman. 63 **greene** green garment.

8

Upon a litle hillocke she was placed
65 Higher then all the rest, and round about
  Environ'd with a girland,° goodly graced,
  Of lovely lasses, and them all without°
  The lustie° shepheard swaynes sate in a rout,°
  The which did pype and sing her prayses dew,
70 And oft rejoyce, and oft for wonder shout,
  As if some miracle of heavenly hew°
Were downe to them descended in that earthly vew.

9

And soothly sure° she was full fayre of face,
  And perfectly well shapt in every lim,
75 Which she did more augment with modest grace,
  And comely carriage° of her count'nance trim,°
  That all the rest like lesser lamps did dim:
  Who her admiring as some heavenly wight,
  Did for their soveraine goddesse her esteeme,
  And caroling her name both day and night,
80 The fayrest *Pastorella* her by name did hight.°

10

Ne was there heard, ne was there shepheards swayne
  But her did honour, and eke many a one
  Burnt in her love,° and with sweet pleasing payne
85 Full many a night for her did sigh and grone:
  But most of all the shepheard *Coridon*
  For her did languish, and his deare life spend;°
  Yet neither she for him, nor other none
  Did care a whit, ne any liking lend:°
Though meane her lot, yet higher did her mind
90   ascend.

11

Her whyles Sir *Calidore* there vewed well,

66 **girland** garland. 67 **them all without** all beyond them. 68 **lustie**
joyful. 68 **rout** company. 71 **hew** form. 73 **soothly sure** truly.
76 **carriage** bearing. 76 **count'nance trim** beautiful appearance. 81
hight call. 84 **in her love** for love of her. 87 **spend** wear away.
89 **lend** give.

And markt her rare demeanure,° which him
   seemed
So farre the meane° of shepheards to excell,
As that he in his mind her worthy deemed,
To be a Princes Paragone° esteemed,   95
He was unwares surprisd in subtile bands
Of the blynd boy,° ne thence could be redeemed
By any skill out of his cruell hands,
Caught like the bird,° which gazing still on others
   stands.

12

So stood he still long gazing thereupon,   100
   Ne any will had thence to move away,
   Although his quest° were farre afore him gon;
   But after he had fed, yet did he stay,
   And sate there still, untill the flying day
   Was farre forth° spent, discoursing diversly   105
   Of sundry things, as fell° to worke delay;
   And evermore his speach he did apply
To th'heards, but meant them to the damzels
   fantazy.°

13

By this the moystie° night approching fast,
   Her deawy humour° gan on th'earth to shed,   110
   That warn'd the shepheards to their homes to
      hast
   Their tender flocks, now being fully fed,
   For feare of wetting them before their bed;
   Then came to them a good old aged syre,
   Whose silver lockes bedeckt° his beard and hed,   115
   With shepheards hooke in hand, and fit attyre,
That wild° the damzell rise; the day did now expyre.

---

92 **demeanure** demeanor.   93 **meane** mien, bearing.   95 **Princes
Paragone** mate or match for a prince.   97 **the blynd boy** Cupid.   99
the bird the lark.   102 **quest** the object of his quest.   105 **farre forth**
far.   106 **fell** happened.   108 **fantazy** fancy.   109 **moystie** damp.
110 **deawy humour** mist.   115 **bedeckt** adorned.   117 **wild** bid.

14

He was to weet° by common voice esteemed
    The father of the fayrest *Pastorell*,
120   And of her selfe in very deede so deemed;°
    Yet was not so, but as old stories tell
    Found her by fortune, which to him befell,
    In th'open fields an Infant left alone,
    And taking up brought home, and noursed well
125   As his owne chyld; for other he had none,
That she in tract° of time accompted° was his owne.

15

She at his bidding meekely did arise,
    And streight unto her litle flocke did fare:°
    Then all the rest about her rose likewise,
130   And each his sundrie sheepe with severall° care
    Gathered together, and them homeward bare:
    Whylest everie one with helping hands did strive
    Amongst themselves, and did their labours share,
    To helpe faire *Pastorella,* home to drive
135 Her fleecie flocke; but *Coridon* most helpe did give.

16

But *Meliboæe* (so hight that good old man)
    Now seeing *Calidore* left all alone,
    And night arrived hard at hand, began
    Him to invite unto his simple home;
140   Which though it were a cottage clad with lome,°
    And all things therein meane, yet better so
    To lodge, then in the salvage° fields to rome.
    The knight full gladly soone agreed thereto,
Being his harts owne wish, and home with him did go.

17

145 There he was welcom'd of that honest syre,
    And of his aged Beldame° homely well;°

118 **to weet** to wit, indeed. 120 **deemed** judged to be. 126 **tract**
course. 126 **accompted** accounted. 128 **fare** go. 130 **severall**
separate. 140 **clad with lome** covered with clay. 142 **salvage** savage. 146 **Beldame** wife. 146 **homely well** very simply.

Who him besought himselfe to disattyre,°
And rest himselfe, till supper time befell.
By which home came the fayrest *Pastorell*,
After her flocke she in their fold had tyde,   *150*
And supper readie dight,° they to it fell
With small adoe, and nature satisfyde,
The which doth litle crave contented to abyde.°

18

Tho when they had their hunger slaked well,
And the fayre mayd the table° ta'ne° away,   *155*
The gentle knight, as he that did excell
In courtesie, and well could doe and say,
For so great kindnesse as he found that day,
Gan greatly thanke his host and his good wife;
And drawing thence his speach another way,   *160*
Gan highly to commend the happie life,
Which Shepheards lead, without debate° or bitter
    strife.

19

How much (sayd he) more happie is the state,
In which ye father here doe dwell at ease,
Leading a life so free and fortunate,   *165*
From all the tempests of these worldly seas,
Which tosse the rest in daungerous disease;°
Where warres, and wreckes, and wicked enmitie
Doe them afflict, which no man can appease,
That certes° I your happinesse envie,   *170*
And wish my lot were plast in such felicitie.

20

Surely my sonne (then answer'd he againe)
If happie, then it is in this intent,°
That having small,° yet doe I not complaine
Of want, ne wish for more it to augment,   *175*

147 **disattyre** take off his armor. 151 **dight** prepared. 153 **The . . . abyde** Nature craves little in order to remain content. 155 **table** fare. 155 **ta'ne** taken. 162 **debate** quarreling. 167 **disease** uneasiness. 170 **certes** certainly. 173 **intent** way of understanding. 174 **small** little.

But doe my selfe, with that I have, content;
So taught of nature, which doth litle need
Of forreine helpes to lifes due nourishment:°
The fields my food, my flock my rayment breed;
180 No better doe I weare, no better doe I feed.

21

Therefore I doe not any one envy,
  Nor am envyde of any one therefore;
  They that have much, feare much to loose°
    thereby,
  And store of cares doth follow riches store.
185 The litle that I have, growes dayly more
  Without my care,° but onely to attend it;
  My lambes doe every yeare increase their score,
  And my flockes father daily doth amend° it.
What have I, but to praise th'Almighty, that doth send
    it?

22

190 To them, that list,° the worlds gay showes I leave,
  And to great ones such follies doe forgive,°
  Which oft through pride do their owne perill
    weave,
  And through ambition downe themselves doe
    drive
  To sad decay, that might contented live.°
  Me no such cares nor combrous° thoughts
195   offend,
  Ne once my minds unmoved quiet grieve,°
  But all the night in silver° sleepe I spend,
And all the day, to what I list, I doe attend.

23

Sometimes I hunt the Fox, the vowed foe

178 Of . . . nourishment Of borrowed help for life's proper nourishment.   183 loose lose.   186 care concern.   188 amend restore.
190 list desire.   191 forgive give.   194 that . . . live that otherwise
might have lived contented.   195 combrous troubled.   196 grieve
troubles.   197 silver soft, from the quality of the metal.

Unto my Lambes, and him dislodge° away;   200
Sometimes the fawne I practise° from the Doe,
Or from the Goat her kidde how to convay;
Another while I baytes and nets display,
The birds to catch, or fishes to beguyle:
And when I wearie am, I downe doe lay   205
My limbes in every° shade, to rest from toyle,
And drinke of every brooke, when thirst my throte
    doth boyle.

24

The time was once, in my first prime of yeares,
When pride of youth forth pricked° my desire,
That I disdain'd amongst mine equall peares°   210
To follow sheepe, and shepheards base attire:
For further fortune then I would inquire.°
And leaving home, to roiall court I sought;°
Where I did sell my selfe for yearely hire,
And in the Princes gardin daily wrought:°   215
There I beheld such vainenesse, as I never thought.

25

With sight whereof soone cloyd, and long deluded
With idle hopes, which them doe entertaine,
After I had ten yeares my selfe excluded
From native home, and spent my youth in vaine,   220
I gan my follies to my selfe to plaine,°
And this sweet peace, whose lacke did then
    appeare.
Tho backe returning to my sheepe againe,
I from thenceforth have learn'd to love more
    deare
This lowly quiet life, which I inherite° here.   225

26

Whylest thus he talkt, the knight with greedy eare

200 **dislodge** drive.   201 **practise** lay plans to convey or steal.   206
every any.   209 **forth pricked** urged on.   210 **peares** companions.
212 **inquire** seek.   213 **sought** went.   215 **wrought** worked.   221
plaine lament.   225 **inherite** possess.

Hong still upon his melting mouth° attent;°
Whose sensefull° words empierst° his hart so
   neare,
That he was rapt with double ravishment,
Both of his speech that wrought him great
230   content,
And also of the object of his vew,
On which his hungry eye was alwayes bent;
That twixt his pleasing tongue, and her faire
   hew,°
He lost himselfe, and like one halfe entraunced grew.

27

235 Yet to occasion meanes, to worke his mind,°
And to insinuate° his harts desire,
He thus replyde; Now surely syre, I find,
That all this worlds gay showes, which we
   admire,
Be but vaine shadowes to this safe retyre°
240 Of life, which here in lowlinesse ye lead,
Fearlesse of foes, or fortunes wrackfull° yre,
Which tosseth states, and under foot doth tread
The mightie ones, affrayd of every chaunges dread.°

28

That even I which daily doe behold
245 The glorie of the great, mongst whom I won,°
And now have prov'd, what happinesse ye hold
In this small plot of your dominion,
Now loath great Lordship and ambition;
And wish th'heavens so much had graced mee,
250 As graunt me live in like condition;
Or that my fortunes might transposed bee
From pitch of higher place, unto this low degree.

227 **his melting mouth** the speech which causes Calidore to yield to
emotion.   227 **attent** attentive.   228 **sensefull** sensible.   228 **empierst** pierced.   233 **hew** form.   235 **Yet . . . mind** Yet to bring
about ways to exercise his mind.   236 **to insinuate** to work his way
into   239 **to . . . retyre** compared to this safe retirement.   241
wrackfull destructive.   243 **of . . . dread** of every dread change.
245 **won** live.

29

In vaine (said then old *Meliboe*) doe men
    The heavens of their fortunes fault accuse,
    Sith they know best, what is the best for them: *255*
    For they to each such fortune doe diffuse,°
    As they doe know each can most aptly use.
    For not that, which men covet most, is best,
    Nor that thing worst, which men do most refuse;
    But fittest is, that all contented rest   *260*
With that they hold: each hath his fortune in his brest.

30

It is the mynd, that maketh good or ill,
    That maketh wretch° or happie, rich or poore:
    For some,° that hath abundance at his will,
    Hath not enough, but wants in greatest store;   *265*
    And other, that hath litle, askes no more,
    But in that litle is both rich and wise.
    For wisedome is most° riches; fooles therefore
    They are, which fortunes doe by vowes devize,°
Sith each unto himselfe his life may fortunize.°   *270*

31

Since then in each mans self (said *Calidore*)
    It is, to fashion his owne lyfes estate,
    Give leave awhyle, good father, in this shore
    To rest my barcke, which hath bene beaten late
    With stormes of fortune and tempestuous fate,   *275*
    In seas of troubles and of toylesome paine,
    That whether quite° from them for to retrate
    I shall resolve, or backe to turne againe,
I may here with your selfe some small repose obtaine.

32

Not that the burden of so bold a guest   *280*
    Shall chargefull° be, or chaunge to you at all;

256 **diffuse** send forth.   263 **wretch** wretched.   264 **some** someone.
268 **most** the greatest.   269 **devize** contrive to get.   270 **fortunize**
control his own fortune.   277 **quite** entirely.   281 **chargefull** burdensome.

For your meane food shall be my daily feast,
And this your cabin both my bowre and hall.
Besides for recompence hereof, I shall
285 You well reward, and golden guerdon give,
That may perhaps you better much withall,°
And in this quiet make you safer live.
So forth he drew much gold, and toward him it
drive.°

33

But the good man, nought tempted with the offer
290 Of his rich mould,° did thrust it farre away,
And thus bespake; Sir knight, your bounteous
proffer°
Be farre fro me, to whom ye ill display
That mucky masse,° the cause of mens decay,
That mote empaire my peace with daungers
dread.°
295 But if ye algates° covet to assay
This simple sort of life, that shepheards lead,
Be it your owne: our rudenesse to your selfe aread.°

34

So there that night Sir *Calidore* did dwell,
And long while after, whilest him list remaine,
300 Dayly beholding the faire *Pastorell,*
And feeding on the bayt of his owne bane.
During which time he did her entertaine
With all kind courtesies, he could invent;
And every day, her companie to gaine,
305 When to the field she went, he with her went:
So for° to quench his fire, he did it more augment.

35

But she that never had acquainted beene

---

286 **better much withall** make much better too. 288 **drive** push.
290 **mould** earth. 291 **proffer** offer. 293 **mucky masse** filthy substance. 294 **mote . . . dread** might impair my peace with dread of
danger. 293 **algates** anyhow. 297 **aread** acquire. 306 **So for** so
that.

With such queint° usage, fit for Queenes and
    Kings,
Ne ever had such knightly service seene,
But being bred under base shepheards wings,°   *310*
Had ever learn'd to love the lowly things,
Did litle whit regard his courteous guize,
But cared more for *Colins* carolings
Then all that he could doe, or ever devize:
His layes,° his loves, his lookes she did them all
    despize.   *315*

36

Which *Calidore* perceiving, thought it best
    To chaunge the manner of his loftie looke;°
And doffing his bright armes, himselfe addrest°
In shepheards weed, and in his hand he tooke,
In stead of steelehead speare, a shepheards
    hooke,   *320*
That who had seene him then, would have
    bethought
On° *Phrygian Paris*° by *Plexippus* brooke,
When he the love of fayre *Oenone* sought,
What time° the golden apple was unto him brought.

37

So being clad, unto the fields he went   *325*
    With the faire *Pastorella* every day,
And kept her sheepe with diligent attent,°
Watching to drive the ravenous Wolfe away,
The whylest at pleasure she mote sport and play;
And every evening helping them to fold:°   *330*
And otherwhiles° for need, he did assay
In his strong hand their rugged° teats to hold,

---

308 **queint** elegant, refined.   310 **wings** protection.   315 **layes** songs.
317 **loftie looke** noble appearance.   318 **addrest** dressed.   321–22
would have bethought/On would have called to mind.   322 **Phrygian Paris** See note to II. vii. 55.   324 **What time** when.   327 **attent**
attention.   330 **them to fold** to shut them up in he fold.   331 **otherwhiles** at another time.   332 **rugged** rough.

And out of them to presse the milke: love so much
        could.°

38

Which seeing *Coridon,* who her likewise
335   Long time had lov'd, and hop'd her love to gaine,
      He much was troubled at that straungers guize,
      And many gealous thoughts conceiv'd in vaine,
      That this of all his labour and long paine
      Should reap the harvest, ere it ripened were,
      That made him scoule, and pout, and oft
340   complaine
    Of *Pastorell* to all the shepheards there,
That she did love a stranger swayne then him more
      dere.

39

And ever when he came in companie,
      Where *Calidore* was present, he would loure,°
345   And byte his lip,° and even° for gealousie
      Was readie oft his owne hart to devoure,°
      Impatient of any paramoure:
      Who on the other side did seeme so farre
      From malicing° or grudging his good houre,°
350   That all he could, he graced° him with her,
Ne ever shewed signe of rancour or of jarre.

40

And oft, when *Coridon* unto her brought
      Or° litle sparrowes, stolen from their nest,
      Or wanton° squirrels, in the woods farre sought,
355   Or other daintie thing for her addrest,°
      He would commend his guift, and make the
      best.°

---

333 **love . . . could** love could make him do so much.   334 **loure**
frown.   345 **byte his lip** show vexation.   345 **even** entirely.   346
his . . . devoure to pine away with grief.   349 **malicing** entertaining
malice.   349 **good houre** fortunate time.   350 **graced** showed favor
to.   353 **Or** whether.   354 **wanton** frisky.   355 **addrest** prepared.
356 **make the best** make the best of it.

Yet she no whit his presents did regard,
Ne him could find to fancie in her brest:
This newcome shepheard had his market mard.
Old love is litle worth when new is more prefard.   *360*

41

One day when as the shepheard swaynes together
Were met, to make their sports and merrie glee,
As they are wont in faire sunshynie weather,
The whiles their flockes in shadowes shrouded
        bee,
They fell to daunce: then did they all agree,   *365*
That *Colin Clout°* should pipe as one most fit;
And *Calidore* should lead the ring, as hee
That most in *Pastorellaes* grace did sit.
Thereat frown'd *Coridon,* and his lip closely bit.

42

But *Calidore* of courteous inclination   *370*
Tooke *Coridon,* and set him in his place,
That he should lead the daunce, as was his
        fashion;
For *Coridon* could daunce, and trimly trace.°
And when as *Pastorella,* him to grace,
Her flowry garlond tooke from her owne head,   *375*
And plast on his, he did it soone displace,
And did it put on *Coridons* in stead:
Then *Coridon* woxe frollicke,° that earst seemed dead.

43

Another time, when as they did dispose°
To practise games, and maisteries° to try,   *380*
They for their Judge did *Pastorella* chose;
A garland was the meed of victory.
There *Coridon* forth stepping openly,
Did chalenge *Calidore* to wrestling game:
For he through long and perfect industry,   *385*

366 **Colin Clout** Spenser's name for himself as a poet.   373 **trimly
trace** neatly step.   378 **frollicke** merry.   379 **did dispose** were inclined.   380 **maisteries** competitive feats of strength.

Therein well practisd was, and in the same
Thought sure t'avenge his grudge, and worke his foe
    great shame.

44

But *Calidore* he greatly did mistake;
  For he was strong and mightily stiffe pight,°
390 That with one fall his necke he almost brake,
  And had he not upon him fallen light,
  His dearest joynt he sure had broken quight.
  Then was the oaken crowne by *Pastorell*
  Given to *Calidore,* as his due right;
395 But he, that did in courtesie excell,
Gave it to *Coridon,* and said he wonne it well.

45

Thus did the gentle knight himselfe abeare°
  Amongst that rusticke rout in all his deeds,
  That even they, the which his rivals were,
  Could not maligne him, but commend him
400   needs:°
  For courtesie amongst the rudest breeds
  Good will and favour. So it surely wrought
  With this faire Mayd, and in her mynde the
    seeds
  Of perfect love did sow, that last° forth brought
The fruite of joy and blisse, though long time dearely
405   bought.

46

Thus *Calidore* continu'd there long time,
  To winne the love of the faire *Pastorell;*
  Which having got, he used without crime°
  Or blamefull blot, but menaged so well,
410 That he of° all the rest, which there did dwell,
  Was favoured, and to her grace commended.

389 **mightily stiffe pight** built with great sturdiness.   397 **himselfe
abeare** demean himself.   400 **commend him needs** were obliged to
commend him.   404 **last** at last.   408 **crime** giving occasion for reproach.   410 **of** above.

But what straunge fortunes unto him befell,
Ere he attain'd the point by him intended,
Shall more conveniently in other place be ended.

CANTO X

Calidore sees the Graces daunce,
*   To Colins melody:*
The whiles his Pastorell is led
*   Into captivity.*

1

Who now does follow the foule *Blatant Beast,*
    Whilest *Calidore* does follow that faire Mayd,
    Unmyndfull of his vow and high beheast,°
    Which by the Faery Queene was on him layd,
    That he should never leave, nor be delayd   5
    From chacing him, till he had it attchieved?°
    But now entrapt of love, which him betrayd,
    He mindeth more, how he may be relieved
With grace from her, whose love his heart hath sore
        engrieved.°

2

That from henceforth he meanes no more to sew°   10
    His former quest, so full of toile and paine;
    Another quest, another game in vew
    He hath, the guerdon of his love to gaine:
    With whom he myndes° for ever to remaine,
    And set his rest° amongst the rusticke sort,   15
    Rather then hunt still after shadowes vaine
    Of courtly favour, fed with light report
Of every blaste, and sayling alwaies on the port.°

3 **beheast** command.   6 **till . . attchieved** until he had fulfilled his
vow.   9 **engrieved** grieved.   10 **sew** pursue.   14 **myndes** intends.
15 **set his rest** to take up his permanent abode.   18 **sayling . . . port**
being port-bound.

3

Ne certes mote° he greatly blamed be,
20   From so high step to stoupe unto so low.
        For who had tasted once (as oft did he)
        The happy peace, which there doth overflow,
        And prov'd the perfect pleasures, which doe
            grow
        Amongst poore hyndes,° in hils, in woods, in
            dales,
25   Would never more delight in painted show
        Of such false blisse, as there° is set for stales,°
T'entrap unwary fooles in their eternall bales.°

4

For what hath all that goodly glorious gaze°
        Like to one sight, which *Calidore* did vew?
        The glaunce whereof their dimmed eies would
30   daze,°
        That never more they should endure the shew
        Of that sunne-shine, that makes them looke
            askew.°
        Ne ought in all that world of beauties rare,
        (Save onely *Glorianaes*° heavenly hew
35   To which what can compare?) can it compare;°
The which as commeth now, by course I will declare.

5

One day as he did raunge the fields abroad,
        Whilest his faire *Pastorella* was elsewhere,
        He chaunst to come, far from all peoples troad,°
40   Unto a place, whose pleasaunce° did appere
        To passe° all others, on the earth which were:
        For all that ever was by natures skill
        Devized° to worke delight, was gathered there,

---

19 **Ne certes mote** nor certainly may. 24 **hyndes** rustics. 26 **there**
in the court. 26 **stales** decoys. 27 **in . . . bales** to their eternal woe.
28 **gaze** that which is gazed at, referring to the court with its "world
of beauties rare." 30 **daze** dazzle. 32 **askew** asquint. 34 **Glori-
anaes** Queen Elizabeth's. 35 **compare** rival. 39 **troad** footsteps.
40 **pleasaunce** pleasantness. 41 **passe** surpass. 43 **Devized** de-
signed.

And there by her were poured forth at fill,°
As if this to adorne, she all the rest did pill.°   45

6

It was an hill plaste in an open plaine,
    That round about was bordered with a wood
    Of matchlesse hight, that seem'd th'earth to dis-
        daine,
    In which all trees of honour stately stood,
    And did all winter as in sommer bud,   50
    Spredding pavilions for the birds to bowre,°
    Which in their lower braunches sung aloud;
    And in their tops the soring hauke did towre,
Sitting like King of fowles in majesty and powre.

7

And at the foote thereof, a gentle flud°   55
    His silver waves did softly tumble downe,
    Unmard with ragged mosse or filthy mud,
    Ne mote wylde beastes, ne mote the ruder
        clowne°
    Thereto approch, ne filth mote therein drowne:°
    But Nymphes and Faeries by the bancks did sit,   60
    In the woods shade, which did the waters
        crowne,
    Keeping all noysome° things away from it,
And to the waters fall tuning their accents° fit.

8

And on the top thereof a spacious plaine
    Did spred it selfe, to serve° to all delight,   65
    Either to daunce, when they to daunce would
        faine,°
    Or else to course° about their bases° light;°
    Ne ought there wanted, which for pleasure
        might

44 **at fill** fully.   45 **pill** plunder.   51 **bowre** lodge.   55 **flud** stream.
58 **the ruder clowne** the ignorant rustic.   59 **drowne** sink, fall.
62 **noysome** harmful.   63 **accents** musical stresses.   65 **serve** minister.   66 **faine** desire.   67 **course** run.   67 **bases** the game, "pris-oner's base."   67 **light** quickly.

Desired be, or thence to banish bale:°
So pleasauntly the hill with equall° hight,
Did seeme to overlooke the lowly vale;
Therefore it rightly cleeped° was mount *Acidale.*°

9

They say that *Venus,* when she did dispose°
    Her selfe to pleasaunce, used to resort
Unto this place, and therein to repose
And rest her selfe, as in a gladsome port,°
Or with the Graces there to play and sport;
That even her owne Cytheron,° though in it
She used most to keepe her royall court,
    And in her soveraine Majesty to sit,
She in regard hereof° refusde and thought unfit.

10

Unto this place when as the Elfin Knight
    Approcht, him seemed that the merry sound
Of a shrill pipe he playing heard on hight,
    And many feete fast thumping th'hollow ground,
    That through the woods their Eccho did re-
        bound.
He nigher drew, to weete° what mote it be;
There he a troupe of Ladies dauncing found
Full merrily, and making gladfull glee,
And in the midst a Shepheard piping he did see.

11

He durst not enter into th'open greene,
    For dread of them unwares to be descryde,°
    For° breaking of their daunce, if he were seene;
But in the covert of the wood did byde,
    Beholding all, yet of them unespyde.
There he did see, that° pleased much his sight,

---

69 **bale** grief.   70 **equall** even.   72 **cleeped** called.   72 **Acidale** view
of the valley.   73 **dispose** prepare.   76 **as . . . port** in a pleasant
manner.   78 **Cytheron** Cytheron hill, the haunt of Venus.   81 **in
regard hereof** in comparison with this.   87 **weete** learn.   92 **unwares to be descryde** suddenly to be seen.   93 **For** and for dread of.
96 **that** that which.

That even he him selfe his eyes envyde,
An hundred naked maidens lilly white,
All raunged in a ring, and dauncing in delight.

12

All they without were raunged in a ring,   *100*
    And daunced round; but in the midst of them
    Three other Ladies did both daunce and sing,
    The whilest the rest them round about did
        hemme,°
    And like a girlond did in compasse stemme:°
    And in the middest of those same three, was
        placed   *105*
    Another Damzell, as a precious gemme,
    Amidst a ring most richly well enchaced,°
That with her goodly presence all the rest much
        graced.

13

Looke how the Crowne, which *Ariadne*° wore
    Upon her yvory forehead that same day,   *110*
    That *Theseus* her unto his bridale° bore,
    When the bold *Centaures* made that bloudy fray,
    With the fierce *Lapithes,* which did them dis-
        may;°
    Being now placed in the firmament,
    Through the bright heaven doth her beames dis-
        play,   *115*
    And is unto the starres an ornament,
Which round about her move in order excellent.

14

Such was the beauty of this goodly band,

103 **hemme** enclose.   104 **And . . . stemme** And like a garland en-
compassed them.   107 **enchaced** adorned with figures.   109 **Ariadne**
Theseus escaped from Minos' labyrinth through Ariadne's help, and
they fled together. After their marriage, he abandoned her. Bacchus
brought her the crown that she wears in the sky as the constellation
"Corona Borealis." According to Ovid, Theseus fought in the contest
between the Centaurs and Lapithae at the wedding of Pirithous, not
his own wedding.   111 **bridale** wedding.   113 **dismay** defeat.

Whose sundry parts were here too long to tell:
120 But she that in the midst of them did stand,
Seem'd all the rest in beauty to excell,
Crownd with a rosie girlond, that right well
Did her beseeme.° And ever, as the crew°
About her daunst, sweet flowres, that far did
smell,
125 And fragrant odours they uppon her threw;
But most of all, those three did her with gifts endew.°

15

Those were the Graces,° daughters of delight,
Handmaides of *Venus*, which are wont to
haunt
Uppon this hill, and daunce there day and night:
130 Those three to men all gifts of grace do graunt,
And all, that *Venus* in her selfe doth vaunt,°
Is borrowed of them. But that faire one,
That in the midst was placed paravaunt,°
Was she to whom that shepheard pypt alone,
135 That made him pipe so merrily, as never none.°

16

She was to weete° that jolly Shepheards lasse,
Which° piped there unto that merry rout,
That jolly shepheard, which there piped, was
Poore *Colin Clout* (who knowes not *Colin
Clout*?)
140 He pypt apace, whilest they him daunst about.
Pype jolly shepheard, pype thou now apace°
Unto thy love, that made thee low to lout;°
Thy love is present there with thee in place,
Thy love is there advaunst° to be another Grace.

123 **beseeme** befit. 123 **crew** company. 126 **endew** endow. 127
the Graces the sister goddesses who bestow beauty and charm, and
"all gifts of grace." 131 **vaunt** boast. 133 **paravaunt** pre-eminently.
135 **as never none** as none ever had piped. 136 **to weete** truly
137 **Which** he who. 140 **apace** quickly. 142 **lout** stoop in submission to her. 144 **advaunst** extolled.

17

Much wondred *Calidore* at this straunge sight,   145
 Whose like before his eye had never seene,
 And standing long astonished in spright,
 And rapt with pleasaunce, wist not what to
  weene;°
 Whether it were the traine of beauties Queene,
 Or Nymphes, or Faeries, or enchaunted show,   150
 With which his eyes mote have deluded beene.
 Therefore resolving, what it was, to know,
Out of the wood he rose, and toward them did go.

18

But soone as he appeared to their vew,
 They vanisht all away out of his sight,   155
 And cleane were gone, which way he never
  knew;
 All save the shepheard, who for fell despight°
 Of that displeasure, broke his bag-pipe quight,°
 And made great mone for that unhappy turne.°
 But *Calidore,* though no lesse sory wight,   160
 For that mishap, yet seeing him to mourne,
Drew neare, that he the truth of all by him mote
 learne.

19

And first him greeting, thus unto him spake,
 Haile jolly shepheard, which thy joyous dayes
 Here leadest in this goodly merry make,°   165
 Frequented of these gentle Nymphes alwayes,
 Which to thee flocke, to heare thy lovely layes;
 Tell me, what mote these dainty Damzels be,
 Which here with thee doe make their pleasant
  playes?
 Right happy thou, that mayst them freely see: 170
But why when I them saw, fled they away from me?

148 **wist . . . weene** knew not what to think.   157 **fell despight** fierce
anger.   158 **quight** completely.   159 **turne** event.   165 **merry make**
merry-making.

20

Not I so happy, answerd then that swaine,
 As thou unhappy, which them thence didst
  chace,
 Whom by no meanes thou canst recall againe,
175 For being gone, none can them bring in place,
 But whom they of them selves list so to grace.
 Right sory I, (saide then Sir *Calidore,*)
 That my ill fortune did them hence displace.
But since things passed none may now restore,
180 Tell me, what were they all, whose lacke thee grieves
  so sore.

21

Tho gan that shepheard thus for to dilate;°
 Then wote thou shepheard, whatsoever thou
  bee,
 That all those Ladies, which thou sawest late,
 Are *Venus* Damzels, all within her fee,°
185 But differing in honour and degree:°
 They all are Graces, which on her depend,°
 Besides a thousand more, which ready bee
 Her to adorne, when so she forth doth wend:
But those three in the midst, doe chiefe on her at-
  tend.

22

190 They are the daughters of sky-ruling *Jove,*
 By him begot of faire *Eurynome,*
 The Oceans daughter, in this pleasant grove,
 As he this way comming from feastfull glee,
 Of *Thetis* wedding with *Æacidee,*°
195 In sommers shade him selfe here rested weary.
 The first of them hight mylde *Euphrosyne,*
 Next faire *Aglaia,* last *Thalia* merry:
Sweete Goddesses all three which me in mirth do
  cherry.°

181 **dilate** discourse. 184 **fee** service. 185 **degree** rank. 186 **on
her depend** belong to her. 194 **Æacidee** Peleus, son of Aeacus.
198 **cherry** cheer.

23

These three on men all gracious gifts bestow,
　　Which decke the body or adorne the mynde,　　*200*
　　To make them lovely or well favoured show,
　　As comely carriage,° entertainement° kynde,
　　Sweete semblaunt,° friendly offices that bynde,
　　And all the complements of curtesie:°
　　They teach us, how to each degree and kynde　　*205*
　　We should our selves demeane,° to low, to hie;
To friends, to foes, which skill men call Civility.

24

Therefore they alwaies smoothly° seeme to smile,
　　That° we likewise should mylde and gentle be,
　　And also naked are, that without guile　　*210*
　　Or false dissemblaunce° all them plaine may
　　　　see,
　　Simple and true from covert malice free:
　　And eeke them selves so in their daunce they
　　　　bore,
　　That two of them still froward° seem'd to bee,
　　But one still towards shew'd her selfe afore;°　　*215*
That good should from us goe, then come in greater
　　store.

25

Such were those Goddesses, which ye did see;
　　But that fourth Mayd, which there amidst them
　　　　traced,°
　　Who can aread,° what creature mote she bee,
　　Whether a creature, or a goddesse graced　　*220*
　　With heavenly gifts from heven first enraced?°
　　But what so sure° she was, she worthy was,
　　To be the fourth with those three other placed:

202 **carriage** bearing. 202 **entertainement** reception. 203 **sem-blaunt** demeanor. 204 **all . . . curtesie** All that which perfects courtesy. 206 **ourselves demeane** conduct ourselves. 208 **smoothly** pleasantly. 209 **That** teaching us that. Also line 216. 211 **dissemblaunce** dissembling. 214 **froward** going away from us. 215 **afore** before. 218 **traced** danced. 219 **aread** declare. 221 **enraced** implanted. See Prologue 3. 222 **so sure** for a certainty.

      Yet was she certes° but a countrey lasse,
225 Yet she all other countrey lasses farre did passe.°

26

So farre as doth the daughter of the day,°
    All other lesser lights in light excell,
    So farre doth she in beautyfull array,
    Above all other lasses beare the bell,°
230   Ne lesse in vertue that beseemes her well,
    Doth she exceede the rest of all her race,
    For which the Graces that here wont to dwell,
    Have for more honor brought her to this place,
And graced her so much to be another Grace.

27

235 Another Grace she well deserves to be,
    In whom so many Graces gathered are,
    Excelling much the meane° of her degree;
    Divine resemblaunce,° beauty soveraine rare,
    Firme Chastity, that spight ne blemish dare;°
240   All which she with such courtesie doth grace,
    That all her peres° cannot with her compare,°
    But quite are dimmed, when she is in place.
She made me often pipe and now to pipe apace.

28

Sunne of the world, great glory of the sky,
245   That all the earth doest lighten with thy rayes,
    Great *Gloriana,* greatest Majesty,
    Pardon thy shepheard, mongst so many layes,
    As he hath sung of thee in all his dayes,
    To make one minime° of thy poore handmayd,
250   And underneath thy feete to place her prayse,
    That when thy glory shall be farre displayd
To future age of her this mention may be made.

224 **certes** truly.   225 **passe** surpass.   226 **the daughter of the day**
the evening star.   229 **beare the bell** take the first place.   237 **meane**
average.   238 **Divine resemblaunce** i.e., resembling the divine.   239
ne blemish dare does not dare blemish.   241 **peres** equals.   241
compare rival.   249 **minime** short musical note.

29

When thus that shepherd ended had his speach,
    Sayd *Calidore;* Now sure it yrketh° mee,
    That to thy blisse I made this luckelesse breach,   *255*
    As now the author of thy bale to be,
    Thus to bereave thy loves deare sight from thee:
    But gentle Shepheard pardon thou my shame,
    Who rashly sought that, which I mote not see.
    Thus did the courteous Knight excuse his blame,   *260*
And to recomfort him, all comely meanes did frame.

30

In such discourses they together spent
    Long time, as fit occasion forth them led;
    With which the Knight him selfe did much content,
    And with delight his greedy° fancy fed,   *265*
    Both of his words, which he with reason red;°
    And also of the place, whose pleasures rare
    With such regard° his sences ravished,
    That thence, he had no will away to fare,
But wisht, that with that shepheard he mote dwelling
      share.   *270*

31

But that envenimd sting,° the which of yore,
    His poysnous point deepe fixed in his hart
    Had left, now gan afresh to rancle sore,
    And to renue the rigour° of his smart:
    Which to recure, no skill of Leaches° art   *275*
    Mote him availe, but to returne againe
    To his wounds worker,° that with lovely° dart
    Dinting his brest, had bred his restlesse° paine,
Like as the wounded Whale to shore flies from the
      maine.

---

254 **yrketh** troubles. 265 **greedy** eager. 266 **which . . . red** which
Colin Clout spoke with reason. 268 **With such regard** the sight of
which. 271 **that envenimd sting** i.e., love. 274 **rigour** violence.
275 **Leaches** surgeon's. 277 **To . . . worker** to the one who made his
wounds. 277 **lovely** that arouses love. 278 **restlesse** ceaseless.

32

280 So taking leave of that same gentle swaine,
 He backe returned to his rusticke wonne,°
 Where his faire *Pastorella* did remaine:
 To whome in sort,° as he at first begonne,
 He daily did apply him selfe to donne°
285 All dewfull° service voide of thoughts impure;
 Ne any paines ne perill did he shonne,
 By which he might her to his love allure,
And liking in her yet untamed heart procure.

33

And evermore the shepheard *Coridon,*
290 What ever thing he did her to aggrate,°
 Did strive to match with strong contention,
 And all his paines did closely emulate;
 Whether it were to caroll, as they sate
 Keeping their sheepe, or games to exercize,°
295 Or to present her with their labours° late;
 Through which if any grace chaunst to arize
To him,° the Shepheard streight with jealousie did
  frize.°

34

One day as they all three together went
 To the greene wood, to gather strawberies,
300 There chaunst to them a dangerous accident;
 A Tigre forth out of the wood did rise,°
 That with fell clawes full of fierce gourmandize,°
 And greedy mouth, wide gaping like hell gate,
 Did runne at *Pastorell* her to surprize:°
305 Whom she beholding, now all desolate
Gan cry to them aloud, to helpe her all too late.°

35

Which *Coridon* first hearing, ran in hast
 To reskue her, but when he saw the feend,

281 **wonne** dwelling. 283 **sort** manner. 284 **donne** do. 285 **dew-full** due. 290 **aggrate** gratify. 294 **exercize** carry on. 295 **labours** the product of their labors. 297 **him** Calidore. 297 **frize** freeze. 301 **rise** issue. 302 **gourmandize** greediness. 304 **surprize** seize. 306 **all too late** before it was too late.

Through cowherd feare he fled away as fast,
Ne durst abide the daunger of the end;°   *310*
His life he steemed° dearer then his frend.
But *Calidore* soone comming to her ayde,
When he the beast saw ready now to rend
His loves deare spoile,° in which his heart was
    prayde,°
He ran at him enraged in stead of being frayde.°   *315*

36

He had no weapon, but his shepheards hooke,
To serve the vengeaunce of his wrathfull will,
With which so sternely he the monster strooke,°
That to the ground astonished° he fell;
Whence ere he could recov'r, he did him quell,°   *320*
And hewing off his head, it presented
Before the feete of the faire *Pastorell;*
Who scarcely yet from former feare exempted,
A thousand times him thankt, that had her death
    prevented.

37

From that day forth she gan him to affect,°   *325*
And daily more her favour to augment;
But *Coridon* for cowherdize° reject,
Fit to keepe sheepe, unfit for loves content:°
The gentle heart scornes base disparagement.°
Yet *Calidore* did not despise him quight,   *330*
But usde him friendly for further intent,
That by his fellowship, he colour° might
Both his estate,° and love from skill° of any wight.

38

So well he wood her, and so well he wrought her,°
With humble service, and with daily sute,   *335*

310 **end** issue.   311 **steemed** esteemed.   314 **His . . . spoile:** her
body, the reward his love seeks to possess.   314 **in . . . prayde**
through which his heart was the prey.   315 **frayde** afraid.   318
strooke struck.   319 **astonished** stunned.   320 **quell** kill.   325 **affect** love.   327 **cowherdize** cowardice.   328 **content** pleasure.   329
base disparagement the disgrace of an unequal match.   332 **colour**
disguise.   333 **estate** state.   333 **skill** knowledge.   334 **wrought her**
fashioned her to his will.

That at the last unto his will he brought her;
Which he so wisely well did prosecute,
That of his love he reapt the timely frute,
And joyed long in close felicity:
Till fortune fraught with malice, blinde, and
340 brute,°
That envies lovers long prosperity,
Blew up a bitter storme of foule adversity.

39

It fortuned one day, when *Calidore*
Was hunting in the woods (as was his trade)°
345 A lawlesse people, *Brigants*° hight of yore,°
That never usde to live by plough nor spade,
But fed on spoile and booty, which they made
Upon their neighbours, which did nigh them
  border,
The dwelling of these shepheards did invade,
And spoyld° their houses, and them selves did
350 murder;
And drove away their flocks, with other much dis-
  order.

40

Amongst the rest, the which they then did pray,°
They spoyld old *Melibee* of all he had,
And all his people captive led away,
Mongst which this lucklesse mayd away was
355 lad,°
Faire *Pastorella,* sorrowfull and sad,
Most sorrowfull, most sad, that ever sight,°
Now made the spoile of theeves and *Brigants*
  bad,
Which was the conquest of the gentlest Knight,
360 That ever liv'd, and th'onely° glory of his might.

340 **brute** brutal. 344 **trade** custom. 345 **Brigants** brigands. 345 **hight of yore** called of old. 350 **spoyld** plundered. 352 **pray** prey upon. 355 **lad** led. 357 **sight** sighed. 360 **th'onely** the chief.

41

With them also was taken *Coridon*,
 And carried captive by those theeves away;
 Who in the covert° of the night, that none
 Mote them descry, nor reskue from their pray,°
 Unto their dwelling did them close convay. *365*
 Their dwelling in a little Island was,
 Covered with shrubby woods, in which no way
 Appeard for people in nor out to pas,
Nor any footing fynde for overgrowen gras.

42

For underneath the ground their way was made, *370*
 Through hollow caves, that no man mote dis-
  cover
 For the thicke shrubs, which did them alwaies
  shade
 From view of living wight, and covered over:
 But darkenesse dred and daily night° did hover
 Through all the inner parts, wherein they dwelt. *375*
 Ne lightned was with window, nor with lover,°
 But with continuall candlelight, which delt
A doubtfull sense of things, not so well seene, as felt.

43

Hither those *Brigants* brought their present pray,
 And kept them with continuall watch and ward, *380*
 Meaning so soone, as they convenient may,
 For slaves to sell them, for no small reward,
 To merchants, which° them kept in bondage
  hard,
 Or sold againe. Now when faire *Pastorell*
 Into this place was brought, and kept with gard *385*
 Of griesly° theeves, she thought her self in hell,
Where with such damned fiends she should in dark-
  nesse dwell.

363 **covert** cover. 364 **pray** preying. 374 **daily night** night every
day. 376 **lover** louver. 383 **which** who either. 386 **griesly** horrible.

44

But for to tell the dolefull dreriment,°
      And pittifull complaints, which there she made,
390   Where day and night she nought did but lament
      Her wretched life, shut up in deadly shade,
      And waste her goodly beauty, which did fade
      Like to a flowre, that feeles no heate of sunne,
      Which may her feeble leaves with comfort
         glade.°
395   But what befell her in that theevish wonne,
Will in an other Canto better be begonne.

Two Cantos

OF MUTABILITIE:

Which, both for Forme and Matter, appeare to be

Parcell of some following Book of the

FAERIE QUEENE,

UNDER

THE LEGEND OF

CONSTANCIE.

from CANTO VI

Proud Change *(not pleasd, in mortall things,*
   beneath the Moone, to raigne)
Pretends,° as well of Gods, as Men,
   to be the Soveraine.

1

What man that sees the ever-whirling wheele
   Of *Change,* the which all mortall things doth
      sway,°
   But that therby doth find, and plainly feele,
   How *MUTABILITY* in them doth play
   Her cruell sports, to many mens decay?°   5
   Which that to all may better yet appeare,
   I will rehearse that whylome° I heard say,

Arg. **Pretends** attempts.   2 **sway** rule.   5 **decay** downfall.   7 **that
whylome** what earlier.

How she at first her selfe began to reare,°
Gainst all the Gods, and th'empire sought from them
  to beare.°

2

10 But first, here falleth fittest to unfold
      Her antique race and linage ancient,
      As I have found it registred of old,
      In *Faery* Land mongst records permanent:
      She was, to weet,° a daughter by descent
15   Of those old *Titans,*° that did whylome strive
      With *Saturnes* sonne for heavens regiment.°
      Whom, though high *Jove* of kingdome did de-
        prive,
Yet many of their stemme° long after did survive.

3

And many of them, afterwards obtain'd
20   Great power of *Jove,* and high authority;
      As *Hecaté,*° in whose almighty hand,
      He plac't all rule and principality,
      To be by her disposed diversly,
      To Gods, and men, as she them list divide:
25   And drad *Bellona,*° that doth sound on hie
      Warres and allarums unto Nations wide,
That makes both heaven and earth to tremble at her
        pride.

4

So likewise did this *Titanesse* aspire,
      Rule and dominion to her selfe to gaine;
30   That as a Goddesse, men might her admire,°
      And heavenly honours yield, as to them twaine.°
      And first, on earth she sought it to obtaine;

8 reare raise. 9 beare bear away. 14 to weet truly. 15 Of those
old Titans, etc. The Titans, sons of Uranus, deposed their father and
placed Saturn on the throne. Saturn was deposed in turn by his son
Jove. 16 regiment government, rule. 18 stemme race. 21 Hecaté
goddess of witchcraft. 25 drad Bellona the dreaded goddess of war.
See E. K.'s note to *Shep. Cal.,* Oct. 114. 30 admire wonder at. 31
them twaine i.e., Hecate and Bellona.

Where she such proofe and sad° examples
    shewed
Of her great power, to many ones great paine,
That not men onely (whom she soone sub-
    dewed)   35
But eke all other creatures, her bad dooings rewed.°

5

For, she the face of earthly things so changed,
    That all which Nature had establisht first
    In good estate, and in meet order ranged,°
    She did pervert, and all their statutes burst:°   40
    And all the worlds faire frame° (which none yet
        durst
    Of Gods or men to alter or misguide)
    She alter'd quite, and made them all accurst
    That° God had blest; and did at first provide
In that still happy state for ever to abide.   45

6

Ne shee the lawes of Nature onely brake,
    But eke of Justice, and of Policie;°
    And wrong of right, and bad of good did make,
    And death for life exchanged foolishlie:
    Since which, all living wights have learn'd to die, 50
    And all this world is woxen° daily worse.
    O pittious worke of *MUTABILITIE!*
    By which, we all are subject to that curse,
And death in stead of life have sucked from our
    Nurse.

7

And now, when all the earth she thus had brought 55
    To her behest, and thralled° to her might,
    She gan to cast° in her ambitious thought,
    T'attempt° the empire of the heavens hight,

---

33 **sad** grievous.   36 **rewed** lamented.   39 **in . . . ranged** arranged in
fitting order. 40 **burst** broke. 41 **frame** order. 44 **That** what.
47 **Policie** government. 51 **woxen** grown. 56 **thralled** enslaved.
57 **cast** resolve. 58 **T'attempt** to overthrow.

And *Jove* himselfe to shoulder from his right.
60 And first, she past the region of the ayre,
And of the fire, whose substance thin and slight,
Made no resistance, ne could her contraire,°
But ready passage to her pleasure did prepaire.°

8

Thence, to the Circle° of the Moone she clambe,°
65 Where *Cynthia*° raignes in everlasting glory,
To whose bright shining palace straight she
    came,
All fairely deckt with heavens goodly story;°
Whose silver gates (by which there sate an hory
Old aged Sire, with hower-glasse in hand,
70 Hight *Tyme*) she entred, were he liefe° or sory:
Ne staide till she the highest stage had scand,°
Where *Cynthia* did sit, that never still did stand.

9

Her sitting on an Ivory throne shee found,
Drawne of° two steeds, th'one black, the other
    white,
75 Environd with tenne thousand starres around,
That duly her attended day and night;
And by her side, there ran her Page, that hight
Vesper, whom we the Evening-starre intend:°
That with his Torche, still twinkling like twy-
    light,
Her lightened all the way where she should
80 wend,
And joy to weary wandring travailers did lend:

10

That when the hardy *Titanesse* beheld
The goodly building of her Palace bright,
Made of the heavens substance, and up-held

62 **contraire** oppose.   63 **prepaire** yield.   64 **Circle** sphere.   64
clambe climbed.   65 **Cynthia** goddess of the moon.   67 **story** the
rows of stars.   70 **were he liefe** whether he were glad.   71 **Ne . . .
scand** Nor stopped until she had climbed up to the highest station or
seat.   74 **of** by.   78 **intend** name.

With thousand Crystall pillors of huge hight,   85
 Shee gan to burne in her ambitious spright,
 And t'envie her that in such glorie raigned.
 Eftsoones she cast by force and tortious° might,
 Her to displace; and to her selfe to have gained
The kingdome of the Night, and waters by her
  wained.°   90

11

Boldly she bid the Goddesse downe descend,
 And let her selfe into that Ivory throne;
 For, shee her selfe more worthy thereof wend,°
 And better able it to guide alone:
 Whether to men, whose fall she did bemone,   95
 Or unto Gods, whose state she did maligne,°
 Or to th'infernall Powers, her need give lone°
 Of her faire light, and bounty most benigne,
Her selfe of all that rule shee deemed most condigne.°

12

But shee that had to her that soveraigne seat   100
 By highest *Jove* assign'd, therein to beare
 Nights burning lamp, regarded not her threat,
 Ne yielded ought for favour or for feare;
 But with sterne countenaunce and disdainfull
  cheare,°
 Bending her horned browes, did put her back: 105
 And boldly blaming her for comming there,
 Bade her attonce from heavens coast to pack,°
Or at her perill bide the wrathfull Thunders wrack.°

13

Yet nathemore° the *Giantesse* forbare:
 But boldly preacing-on,° raught forth her hand   110
 To pluck her downe perforce° from off her
  chaire;

88 **tortious** wrongful.   90 **wained** governed.   93 **wend** thought.   96 **maligne** envy.   97 **her . . . lone** she must give.   99 **condigne** worthy. 104 **disdainfull cheare** face full of disdain.   107 **pack** be off.   108 **wrack** destruction.   109 **nathemore** not at all.   110 **preacing-on** advancing.   111 **perforce** violently.

And there-with lifting up her golden wand,
Threatned to strike her if she did with-stand.
Where-at the starres, which round about her
        blazed,
And eke the Moones bright wagon, still did
        stand,
115   All beeing with so bold attempt amazed,
And on her uncouth habit and sterne looke still
        gazed.

14

Meane-while, the lower World, which nothing knew
        Of all that chaunced here, was darkned quite;
120   And eke the heavens, and all the heavenly crew°
        Of happy wights, now unpurvaide of° light,
        Were much afraid, and wondred at that sight;
        Fearing least *Chaos* broken had his chaine,
        And brought againe on them eternall night:
125   But chiefely *Mercury,*° that next doth raigne,°
Ran forth in haste, unto the king of Gods to plaine.°

15

All ran together with a great out-cry,
        To *Joves* faire Palace, fixt° in heavens hight;
        And beating at his gates full earnestly,
130   Gan call to him aloud with all their might,
        To know what meant that suddaine lack of light.
        The father of the Gods when this he heard,
        Was troubled much at their so strange affright,
        Doubting° least *Typhon*° were againe uprear'd,
135 Or other his old foes, that once him sorely fear'd.°

16

Eftsoones the sonne of *Maia*° forth he sent
        Downe to the Circle of the Moone, to knowe

120 **crew** company.   121 **unpurvaide of** unprovided with.   125 **Mercury** the messenger of the gods.   125 **that . . . raigne** because it is the closest planet to the moon according to the Ptolemaic system. 126 **plaine** complaine.   128 **fixt** placed.   134 **Doubting** fearing. 134 **Typhon** one of the Giants who rebelled against Jove.   135 **fear'd** frightened.   136 **the sonne of Maia** Mercury.

The cause of this so strange astonishment,
And why shee did her wonted course forslowe;°
And if that any were on earth belowe   140
That did with charmes or Magick her molest,
Him to attache,° and downe to hell to throwe:
But, if from heaven it were, then to arrest
The Author, and him bring before his presence prest.°

17

The wingd-foot God, so fast his plumes did beat,   145
That soone he came where-as the *Titanesse*
Was striving with faire *Cynthia* for her seat:
At whose strange sight, and haughty hardi-
nesse,°
He wondred much, and feared her no lesse.
Yet laying feare aside to doe his charge,   150
At last, he bade her (with bold stedfastnesse)
Ceasse to molest the Moone to walke at large,°
Or come before high *Jove,* her dooings to discharge.°

18

And there-with-all, he on her shoulder laid
His snaky-wreathed Mace, whose awfull power   155
Doth make both Gods and hellish fiends affraid:
Where-at the *Titanesse* did sternely lower,°
And stoutly answer'd, that in evill hower
He from his *Jove* such message to her brought,
To bid her leave faire *Cynthias* silver bower;   160
Sith shee his *Jove* and him esteemed nought,
No more then *Cynthia's* selfe; but all their kingdoms
sought.

19

The Heavens Herald staid not to reply,
But past away, his doings to relate
Unto his Lord; who now in th'highest sky,   165

139 **her . . . forslowe** delay her accustomed course.   142 **attache**
seize.   144 **prest** immediately.   148 **hardinesse** boldness.   152 **to
. . . large** from walking freely.   153 **her . . . discharge** to clear her
actions from blame.   157 **lower** glower.

Was placed in his principall Estate,°
With all the Gods about him congregate:
To whom when *Hermes*° had his message told,
It did them all exceedingly amate,°
Save *Jove;* who, changing nought his count'nance
    bold,
170 Did unto them at length these speeches wise unfold;

20

Harken to mee awhile yee heavenly Powers;
  Ye may remember since th'Earths cursed seed°
Sought to assaile the heavens eternall towers,
175   And to us all exceeding feare did breed:
  But how we then defeated all their deed,°
Yee all doe knowe, and them destroied quite;
  Yet not so quite, but that there did succeed
  An off-spring of their bloud, which did alite
180 Upon the fruitfull earth, which doth us yet despite.°

21

Of that bad seed is this bold woman bred,
  That now with bold presumption doth aspire
To thrust faire *Phœbe* from her silver bed,
  And eke our selves from heavens high Empire,
185   If that her might were match to her desire:
Wherefore, it now behoves us to advise°
  What way is best to drive her to retire;
  Whether by open force, or counsell wise,
Areed° ye sonnes of God, as best ye can devise.

22

190 So having said, he ceast; and with his brow
  (His black eye-brow, whose doomefull dreaded
    beck°
Is wont to wield the world unto his vow,

---

166 **Estate** throne of state. 168 **Hermes** the Greek name for Mercury. 169 **amate** dismay. 173 **since th'Earths cursed seed** when
the Giants. 176 **all their deed** all that they were capable of doing.
180 **despite** show contempt. 186 **advise** consider. 189 **Areed** counsel me. 191 **beck** nod, indicating command.

And even the highest Powers of heaven to
 check)
Made signe to them in their degrees to speake:
Who straight gan cast° their counsell grave and
 wise.   *195*
Meane-while, th'Earths daughter, thogh she
 nought did reck
Of *Hermes* message; yet gan now advise,
What course were best to take in this hot bold em-
 prize.°

23

Eftsoones she thus resolv'd; that whil'st the Gods
 (After returne of *Hermes* Embassie)   *200*
Were troubled, and amongst themselves at ods,
Before they could new counsels re-allie,°
To set upon them in that extasie;°
And take what fortune time and place would
 lend:
So, forth she rose, and through the purest sky *205*
To *Joves* high Palace straight cast to ascend,
To prosecute her plot: Good on-set boads° good end.

24

Shee there arriving, boldly in did pass;
Where all the Gods she found in counsell close,
All quite unarm'd, as then their manner was. *210*
At sight of her they suddaine all arose,
In great amaze, ne wist what way to chose.
But *Jove,* all fearelesse, forc't them to aby;°
And in his soveraine throne, gan straight dispose°
Himselfe more full of grace and Majestie, *215*
That mote encheare° his friends, and foes mote ter-
 rifie.

25

That, when the haughty *Titanesse* beheld,

195 **cast** deliver. 198 **emprize** enterprise. 202 **re-allie** form again.
203 **extasie** state of astonishment. 207 **boads** bodes. 213 **aby**
abide, remain. 214 **dispose** compose. 216 **encheare** cheer.

All were she° fraught with pride and impudence,
Yet with the sight thereof was almost queld;
220 And inly quaking, seem'd as reft of sense,
And voyd of speech in that drad° audience;
Untill that *Jove* himselfe, her selfe bespake:
Speake thou fraile woman, speake with confi-
         dence,
Whence are thou, and what doost thou here now
         make?°
What idle errand hast thou, earths mansion to for-
225   sake?

26
Shee, halfe confused with his great commaund,
Yet gathering spirit of her natures pride,
Him boldly answer'd thus to his demaund:
I am a daughter, by the mothers side,
230 Of her that is Grand-mother magnifide°
Of all the Gods, great *Earth,* great *Chaos* child:
But by the fathers (be it not envide)°
I greater am in bloud (whereon I build)°
Then all the Gods, though wrongfully from heaven
         exil'd.

27
235 For, *Titan* (as ye all acknowledge must)
Was *Saturnes* elder brother by birth-right;
Both, sonnes of *Uranus:* but by unjust
And guilefull meanes, through *Corybantes*
         slight,°
The younger thrust the elder from his right:
240 Since which, thou *Jove,* injuriously° hast held
The Heavens rule from *Titans* sonnes by might;
And them to hellish dungeons downe hast feld:°
Witnesse ye Heavens the truth of all that I have teld.

218 **All were she** although she were.   221 **drad** dread.   224 **what
. . . make** now what do you intend here.   230 **magnifide** extolled.
232 **envide** begrudged.   233 **build** rest my claim.   238 **Corybantes
slight** To drown the cries of the infant Jove from Saturn who would
have eaten him, the Corybantes beat their shields.   238 **slight** device.   240 **injuriously** wrongfully.   242 **feld** thrown.

28

Whil'st she thus spake, the Gods that gave good eare
    To her bold words, and marked well her grace,   *245*
    Beeing of stature tall as any there
    Of all the Gods, and beautifull of face,
    As any of the Goddesses in place,
    Stood all astonied,° like a sort° of Steeres;
    Mongst whom, some beast of strange and
        forraine race,   *250*
    Unwares is chaunc't,° far straying from his
        peeres:°
So did their ghastly gaze bewray° their hidden feares.

29

Till having pauz'd awhile, *Jove* thus bespake;
    Will never mortall thoughts ceasse to aspire,
    In this bold sort, to Heaven claime to make,   *255*
    And touch celestiall seates with earthly mire?
    I would have thought, that bold *Procrustes*°
        hire,°
    Or *Typhons* fall,° or proud *Ixions* paine,°
    Or great *Prometheus,*° tasting of our ire,
    Would have suffiz'd, the rest for to restraine;   *260*
And warn'd all men by their example to refraine:

30

But now, this off-scum° of that cursed fry,
    Dare to renew the like bold enterprize,
    And chalenge th'heritage of this our skie;
    Whom what should hinder, but that we likewise   *265*
    Should handle as the rest of her allies,
    And thunder-drive° to hell? With that, he shooke

---

249 **astonied** stunned. 249 **sort** herd. 251 **Unwares is chaunc't**
suddenly chances to come. 251 **peeres** companions. 252 **bewray**
reveal. 257 **Procrustes** Procrustes was punished by Theseus, not
Jove, for fitting his victims to a bed by stretching or cutting off their
limbs. 257 **hire** reward, i.e., punishment. 258 **Typhons fall** He was
buried under Mount Etna for attacking Jove. 258 **Ixions paine** He
was tied to a revolving wheel as punishment for trying to rape Juno,
Jove's wife. 259 **Prometheus** For stealing fire from the gods to give
to man, he was tied to a rock where an eagle devours his liver daily.
262 **off-scum** scum. 267 **thunder-drive** with thunder drive.

His Nectar-deawed locks, with which the skyes
And all the world beneath for terror quooke,°
270 And eft° his burning levin-brond° in hand he tooke.

31

But, when he looked on her lovely face,
   In which, faire beames of beauty did appeare,
   That could the greatest wrath soone turne to
      grace
   (Such sway doth beauty even in Heaven beare)
   He staide his hand: and having chang'd his
275   cheare,°
   He thus againe in milder wise began;
   But ah! if Gods should strive with flesh yfere,°
   Then shortly should the progeny of Man
Be rooted out, if *Jove* should doe still° what he can:

32

280 But thee faire *Titans* child, I rather weene,
   Through some vaine errour or inducement light,
   To see that° mortall eyes have never seene;
   Or through ensample of thy sisters might,
   Bellona; whose great glory thou doost spight,°
   Since thou hast seene her dreadfull power
285   belowe,
   Mongst wretched men (dismaide with her
      affright)°
   To bandie Crownes, and Kingdomes to bestowe:
And sure thy worth, no lesse then hers doth seem to
   showe.

33

But wote thou this, thou hardy° *Titanesse,*
290   That not the worth of any living wight
   May challenge ought in Heavens interesse;°

---

269 **quooke** quaked.   270 **eft** then.   270 **levin-brond** bolt of lightning.   275 **cheare** countenance.   277 **with flesh yfere** together with
flesh.   279 **still** always.   282 **that** that which.   284 **spight** envy.
286 **her affright** fear of her.   289 **hardy** bold.   291 **May . . . interesse** May claim any part of Heaven's interest or right.

Much lesse the Title of old *Titans* Right:
For, we by Conquest of our soveraine might,
And by eternall doome of Fates decree,
Have wonne the Empire of the Heavens bright;   *295*
Which to our selves we hold, and to whom wee
Shall worthy deeme partakers of our blisse to bee.

34

Then ceasse thy idle claime thou foolish gerle,
And seeke by grace and goodnesse to obtaine
That place from which by folly *Titan* fell;   *300*
There-to thou maist perhaps, if so thou faine°
Have° *Jove* thy gratious Lord and Soveraigne.
So, having said, she thus to him replide;
Ceasse *Saturnes* sonne, to seeke by proffers°
    vaine
Of idle hopes t'allure mee to thy side,   *305*
For to betray my Right, before I have it tride.

35

But thee, O *Jove,* no equall Judge I deeme
Of my desert, or of my dewfull° Right;
That in thine owne behalfe maist partiall seeme:
But to the highest him, that is behight   *310*
Fathers of Gods and men by equall might;
To weet, the God of Nature, I appeale.
There-at *Jove* wexed wroth, and in his spright
Did inly grudge, yet did it well conceale;
And bade *Dan Phœbus* Scribe her Appellation seale.°   *315*

36

Eftsoones the time and place appointed were,
Where all, both heavenly Powers, and earthly
    wights,
Before great Natures presence should appeare,
For triall of their Titles and best Rights:
That was, to weet, upon the highest hights   *320*

301 **faine** desire.   302 **Have** to have.   304 **proffers** offers.   308 **dew-
full** due.   315 **And . . . seale** And had the scribe, Apollo, seal her
appeal.

Of *Arlo-hill* (Who knowes not *Arlo-hill?*)
That is the highest head (in all mens sights)°
Of my old father *Mole*,° whom Shepheards quill°
Renowmed hath with hymnes fit for a rurall skill.

CANTO VII

Pealing,° from Jove, to Natur's Bar,
  bold Alteration° *pleades*
Large Evidence: but Nature soone
  her righteous Doome areads.°

1

Ah! whither doost thou now thou greater Muse°
  Me from these woods and pleasing forrests bring?
  And my fraile spirit (that dooth oft refuse
  This too high flight, unfit for her weake wing)
5 Lift up aloft, to tell of heavens King
  (Thy soveraine Sire) his fortunate successe,
  And victory, in bigger° noates to sing,
  Which he obtain'd against that *Titanesse,*
That him of heavens Empire sought to dispossesse.

2

10 Yet sith I needs must follow thy behest,
  Doe thou my weaker° wit with skill inspire,
  Fit for this turne; and in my feeble brest
  Kindle fresh sparks of that immortall fire,
  Which learned minds inflameth with desire
15 Of heavenly things: for, who but thou alone,
  That art yborne of heaven and heavenly Sire,

322 **in . . . sights** in the judgment of all men.   323 **my old father
Mole** a mountain in Ireland.   323 **Shepheards quill** Spenser in *Colin
Clouts Come Home Againe*, 1595.   Arg. **Pealing** appealing.   Arg.
Alteration the Titaness, Mutability.   Arg. **her . . . areads** her just
judgment delivers.   1 **thou greater Muse** Clio, the Muse of history.
7 **bigger** louder.   11 **weaker** too weak.

Can tell things doen in heaven so long ygone;
So farre past memory of man that may be knowne.

3

Now, at the time that was before agreed,
    The Gods assembled all on *Arlo* hill;   20
    As well those that are sprung of heavenly seed,
    As those that all the other world doe fill,
    And rule both sea and land unto their will:
    Onely th'infernall Powers might not appeare;
    Aswell for horror of their count'naunce ill,   25
    As for th'unruly fiends which they did feare;°
Yet *Pluto* and *Proserpina* were present there.

4

And thither also came all other creatures,
    What-ever life or motion doe retaine,
    According to their sundry kinds of features;   30
    That *Arlo* scarsly could them all containe;
    So full they filled every hill and Plaine:
    And had not *Natures* Sergeant (that is *Order*)
    Them well disposed by his busie paine,°
    And raunged farre abroad in every border,   35
They would have caused much confusion and
        disorder.

5

Then forth issewed (great goddesse) great dame
        Nature,
    With goodly port and gracious Majesty;
    Being far greater and more tall of stature
    Then any of the gods or Powers on hie: 40
    Yet certes by her face and physnomy,°
    Whether she man or woman inly were,
    That could not any creature well descry:°
    For, with a veile that wimpled° every where,
Her head and face was hid, that mote to none
        appeare.   45

26 **feare** keep in fear of them.   34 **paine** care.   41 **physnomy** countenance.   43 **descry** perceive.   54 **wimpled** covered her in folds.

6

That some doe say was so by skill devized,
    To hide the terror of her uncouth hew,°
    From mortall eyes that should be sore agrized;°
    For that her face did like a Lion shew,
50   That eye of wight could not indure to view:
    But others tell that it so beautious was,
    And round about such beames of splendor threw,
    That it the Sunne a thousand times did pass,°
Ne could be seene, but like an image in a glass.°

7

55 That well may seemen true: for, well I weene
    That this same day, when she on *Arlo* sat,
    Her garment was so bright and wondrous
        sheene,°
    That my fraile wit cannot devize to what
    It to compare, nor finde like stuffe to that,
    As those three sacred *Saints,*° though else most
60   wise,
    Yet on mount *Thabor* quite their wits forgat,
    When they their glorious Lord in strange disguise
Transfigur'd sawe; his garments so did daze° their
      eyes.

8

In a fayre Plaine upon an equall° Hill,
65   She placed was in a pavilion;
    Not such as Craftes-men by their idle° skill
    Are wont for Princes states° to fashion:
    But th'earth her self of her owne motion,°
    Out of her fruitfull bosome made to growe
70   Most dainty trees; that, shooting up anon,
    Did seeme to bow their bloosming° heads full
       lowe,
For homage unto her, and like a throne did shew.

---

47 **uncouth hew** strange form.   48 **agrized** horrified.   53 **pass** surpass.   54 **like . . . glass** i.e., by being reflected.   57 **sheene** brilliant. 60 **those three sacred Saints,** etc. Peter, James, and John, who saw Jesus transfigured on Mount Tabor. See Matt. xvii. 1–8.   63 **daze** dazzle.   64 **equall** even.   66 **idle** vain.   67 **states** canopies.   68 **her selfe . . . motion** i.e., spontaneously.   71 **bloosming** blossoming.

9

So hard it is for any living wight,
 All her array and vestiments° to tell,
 That old *Dan° Geffrey°* (in whose gentle spright   75
 The pure well head of Poesie did dwell)
 In his *Foules parley°* durst not with it mel,°
 But it transferd to *Alane,* who he thought
 Had in his *Plaint of kindes* describ'd it well:
 Which who will read set forth so as it ought,   80
Go seek he out that *Alane* where he may be sought.

10

And all the earth far underneath her feete
 Was dight with flowres, that voluntary grew
 Out of the ground, and sent forth odours sweet,
 Tenne thousand mores° of sundry sent and hew,   85
 That might delight the smell, or please the view:
 The which, the Nymphes, from all the brooks thereby
 Had gathered, which they at her foot-stoole threw;
 That richer seem'd then any tapestry,
That Princes bowres adorne with painted imagery.   90

11

And *Mole* himselfe, to honour her the more,
 Did deck himself in freshest faire attire,
 And his high head, that seemeth alwaies hore
 With hardned frosts of former winters ire,
 He with an Oaken girlond now did tire,°   95
 As if the love of some new Nymph late seene,
 Had in him kindled youthfull fresh desire,
 And made him change his gray attire to greene;
Ah gentle *Mole!* such joyance hath thee well beseene.°

12

Was never so great joyance since the day,   100

74 **vestiments** adornments. 75 **Dan** master. 75 **Dan Geffrey** Chaucer. 77 **Foules parley,** etc. *The Parliament of Fowls* in which Chaucer refers to "Alaine, in the Plaint of Kind," that is, Alanus de Insulis' *De Planctu Naturae.* 77 **mel** meddle. 85 **mores** plants. 95 **tire** dress. 99 **beseene** furnished.

That all the gods whylome assembled were,
 On *Hæmus* hill° in their divine array,
 To celebrate the solemne bridall cheare,
 Twixt *Peleus,* and dame *Thetis* pointed° there;
105 Where *Phœbus* self, that god of Poets hight,
 They say did sing the spousall hymne full cleere,
 That all the gods were ravisht with delight
Of his celestiall song, and Musicks wondrous might.

13

This great Grandmother of all creatures bred
110 Great *Nature,* ever young yet full of eld,°
 Still mooving, yet unmoved from her sted;°
 Unseene of any, yet of all beheld;
 Thus sitting in her throne as I have teld,
 Before her came dame *Mutabilitie;*
115 And being lowe before her presence feld,°
 With meek obaysance° and humilitie,
Thus gan her plaintif Plea, with words to amplifie;°

14

To thee O greatest goddesse, onely° great,
 An humble suppliant loe, I lowely fly
120 Seeking for Right, which I of thee entreat;
 Who Right to all dost deale indifferently,°
 Damning° all Wrong and tortious° Injurie,
 Which any of thy creatures doe to other
 (Oppressing them with power, unequally)°
125 Sith of them all thou art the equall mother,
And knittest each to each, as brother unto brother.

15

To thee therefore of this same *Jove* I plaine,
 And of his fellow gods that faine° to be,

---

102 **On Hæmus hill,** etc. or Mount Pelion upon which King Peleus
married the sea goddess, Thetis. See VI. x. 22. 104 **pointed** appointed. 110 **eld** age. 111 **sted** place. 115 **feld** prostrated. 116
obaysance obeisance. 117 **amplifie** enlarge upon. 118 **onely**
chiefly. 121 **indifferently** impartially. 122 **Damning** condemning.
122 **tortious** wrongful. 124 **unequally** unjustly. 128 **faine** pretend.

That challenge° to themselves the whole worlds
   raign;
Of which, the greatest part is due to me,   130
And heaven it selfe by heritage in Fee:°
For, heaven and earth I both alike do deeme,
Sith heaven and earth are both alike to thee;
And, gods no more then men thou doest
   esteeme:
For, even the gods to thee, as men to gods do seeme.   135

16

Then weigh, O soveraigne goddesse, by what right
   These gods do claime the worlds whole
   soverainty;
And that° is onely dew unto thy might
Arrogate to themselves ambitiously:
As for the gods owne principality,°   140
Which *Jove* usurpes unjustly; that to be
My heritage, *Jove's* self cannot deny,
From my great Grandsire *Titan,* unto mee,
Deriv'd by dew descent; as is well knowen to thee.

17

Yet mauger° *Jove,* and all his gods beside,   145
   I doe possesse the worlds most regiment;°
As, if ye please it into parts divide,
And every parts inholders to convent,°
Shall to your eyes appeare incontinent.°
And first, the Earth (great mother of us all)   150
That only seems unmov'd and permanent,
And unto *Mutability* not thrall;
Yet is she chang'd in part, and eeke in generall.

18

For, all that from her springs, and is ybredde,
   How-ever fayre it flourish for a time,   155

---

129 **challenge** claim.   131 **in Fee** in fee-simple, i.e., absolute posses-
sion.   138 **that** that which.   140 **principality** sovereignty.   145
mauger despite.   146 **the worlds most regiment** the chief rule of the
world.   148 **inholders to convent** inhabitants to convene.   149 **incontinent** immediately.

Yet see we soone decay; and, being dead,
To turne again unto their earthly slime:
Yet, out of their decay and mortall crime,°
We daily see new creatures to arize;
160   And of their Winter spring another Prime,°
Unlike in forme, and chang'd by strange disguise:
So turne they still about, and change in restlesse wise.

19

As for her tenants; that is, man and beasts,
The beasts we daily see massacred dy,
165   As thralls and vassalls unto mens beheasts:
And men themselves doe change continually,
From youth to eld, from wealth to poverty,
From good to bad, from bad to worst of all.
Ne doe their bodies only flit and fly:
170   But eeke their minds (which they immortall call)
Still change and vary thoughts, as new occasions fall.

20

Ne is the water in more constant case;°
Whether those same on high, or these belowe.
For, th'Ocean moveth stil, from place to place;
175   And every River still doth ebbe and flowe:
Ne any Lake, that seems most still and slowe,
Ne Poole so small, that can his smoothnesse
    holde,
When any winde doth under heaven blowe;
With which, the clouds are also tost and roll'd;
Now like great Hills; and, streight, like sluces, them
180   unfold.

21

So likewise are all watry living wights
Still tost, and turned, with continuall change,
Never abyding in their stedfast plights.°
The fish, still floting, doe at randon° range,
185   And never rest; but evermore exchange

158 **mortall crime** sin of mortality, death.   160 **Prime** spring.   172 **case** condition.   183 **plights** states.   184 **randon** random.

Their dwelling places, as the streames them
   carrie:
Ne have the watry foules a certaine grange,°
Wherein to rest, ne in one stead° do tarry;
But flitting still doe flie, and still their places vary.

22

Next is the Ayre: which who feeles not by sense   *190*
   (For, of all sense it is the middle meane)°
To flit still? and, with subtill influence
Of his thin spirit, all creatures to maintaine,
In state of life? O weake life! that does leane
On thing so tickle° as th'unsteady ayre;   *195*
Which every howre is chang'd, and altred cleane°
With every blast that bloweth fowle or faire:
The faire doth it prolong; the fowle doth it impaire.

23

Therein the changes infinite beholde,
   Which to her creatures every minute chaunce;   *200*
Now, boyling hot: streight, friezing deadly cold:
Now, faire sun-shine, that makes all skip and
   daunce:
Streight, bitter storms and balefull countenance,
That makes them all to shiver and to shake:
Rayne, hayle, and snowe do say them sad
   penance,   *205*
And dreadfull thunder-claps (that make them
   quake)
With flames and flashing lights that thousand changes
   make.

24

Last is the fire: which, though it live for ever,
   Ne can be quenched quite; yet, every day,
Wee see his parts, so soone as they do sever,   *210*
To lose their heat, and shortly to decay;

187 **grange** dwelling place.   188 **stead** place.   191 **For . . . meane**
For it serves as the medium for all the senses.   195 **tickle** uncertain.
196 **cleane** entirely.

So, makes himself his owne consuming pray.
Ne any living creatures doth he breed:
But all, that are of others bredd, doth slay;
215   And, with their death, his cruell life dooth feed;
Nought leaving, but their barren ashes, without seede.

25

Thus, all these fower° (the which the ground-work
      bee
Of all the world, and of all living wights)
To thousand sorts of *Change* we subject see:
220   Yet are they chang'd (by other wondrous slights)
Into themselves,° and lose their native mights;
The Fire to Aire, and th'Ayre to Water sheere,°
And Water into Earth: yet Water fights
With Fire, and Aire with Earth approaching
      neere:
225 Yet all are in one body, and as one appeare.

26

So, in them all raignes *Mutabilitie;*
      How-ever these, that Gods themselves do call,
Of them doe claime the rule and soveraity:
As, *Vesta,*° of the fire æthereall;
230   *Vulcan,* of this,° with us so usuall;
Ops,° of the earth; and *Juno* of the Ayre;
Neptune, of Seas; and *Nymphes,* of Rivers all.
For, all those Rivers to me subject are:
And all the rest, which they usurp, be all my share.

27

235 Which to approven° true, as I have told,
      Vouchsafe, O goddesse, to thy presence call
The rest which doe the world in being hold:
As, times and seasons of the yeare that fall:
Of all the which, demand in generall,

---

217 **fower** the four elements. 221 **themselves** each other. 222 **sheere** clear. 229 **Vesta** Roman goddess of the hearth, and hence of fire. 230 **of this** of this earthly fire. 231 **Ops** Roman goddess of agriculture. 235 **approven** prove.

Or judge thy selfe, by verdit° of thine eye, 240
Whether to me they are not subject all.
Nature did yeeld thereto, and by-and-by,°
Bade *Order* call them all, before her Majesty.

28

So, forth issew'd the Seasons of the yeare;
First, lusty° *Spring,* all dight in leaves of flowres 245
That freshly budded and new bloosmes did beare
(In which a thousand birds had built their bowres
That sweetly sung, to call forth Paramours):
And in his hand a javelin he did beare,
And on his head (as fit for warlike stoures)° 250
A guilt engraven morion° he did weare;
That as some did him love, so others did him feare.

29

Then came the jolly *Sommer,* being dight
In a thin silken cassock° coloured greene,
That was unlyned all, to be more light: 255
And on his head a girlond well beseene
He wore, from which as he had chauffed° been
The sweat did drop; and in his hand he bore
A boawe and shaftes, as he in forrest greene
Had hunted late the Libbard° or the Bore, 260
And now would bathe his limbes, with labor heated
    sore.

30

Then came the *Autumne* all in yellow clad,
As though he joyed in his plentious store,
Laden with fruits that made him laugh, full glad
That he had banist hunger, which to-fore° 265
Had by the belly oft him pinched sore.
Upon his head a wreath that was enrold°
With eares of corne, of every sort he bore:

240 **verdit** judgment.   242 **by-and-by** straightway.   245 **lusty** vigorous.   250 **stoures** encounters.   251 **morion** helmet.   254 **cassock**
cloak.   257 **chauffed** heated.   260 **Libbard** leopard.   265 **to-fore**
before.   267 **enrold** wrapped up.

And in his hand a sickle he did holde,
To reape the ripened fruits the which the earth had
270   yold.°

31

Lastly, came *Winter* cloathed all in frize,°
        Chattering his teeth for cold that did him chill,
        Whil'st on his hoary beard his breath did freese;
        And the dull drops that from his purpled bill°
275   As from a limbeck° did adown distill.
        In his right hand a tipped staffe he held,
        With which his feeble steps he stayed still:°
        For, he was faint with cold, and weak with eld;
That scarse his loosed limbes he hable was to weld.°

32

280 These, marching softly, thus in order went,
        And after them, the Monthes all riding came;
        First, sturdy° *March*° with brows full sternly
            bent,
        And armed strongly, rode upon a Ram,
        The same° which over *Hellespontus* swam:
285   Yet in his hand a spade he also hent,°
        And in a bag all sorts of seeds ysame,°
        Which on the earth he strowed as he went,
And fild her womb with fruitfull hope of nourishment.

33

Next came fresh *Aprill* full of lustyhed,°
290   And wanton as a Kid whose horne new buds:
        Upon a Bull he rode, the same° which led

270 **yold** yielded.   271 **frize** a coarse woolen cloth.   274 **bill** nose.
275 **limbeck** a retort used for distilling.   277 **stayed still** always
supported.   279 **weld** move.   282 **sturdy** surly.   282 **First, sturdy
March** In the old calendar, the year began on March 25.   284 **The
same,** etc. The ram with the golden fleece upon which Helle rode to
escape her stepmother, Ino, until she fell into the water that bears her
name, Hellespont; here the constellation Aries. Each month rides,
or is associated with, the constellation of the Zodiac appropriate to
the time at which the sun enters it.   285 **hent** held.   286 **ysame**
together.   289 **lustyhed** lustiness, vigor.   291 **the same,** etc. Jove,
disguised as a bull, carried Europa on his back over the sea to Crete;
here the constellation Taurus.

Europa floting through th'*Argolick* fluds:°
His hornes were gilden all with golden studs
And garnished with garlonds goodly dight
Of all the fairest flowres and freshest buds 295
Which th'earth brings forth, and wet he seem'd
in sight
With waves, through which he waded for his loves
delight.

34

Then came faire *May,* the fayrest mayd on ground,
Deckt all with dainties of her seasons pryde,°
And throwing flowres out of her lap around: 300
Upon two brethrens shoulders she did ride,
The twinnes of *Leda;*° which on eyther side
Supported her like to their soveraine Queene.
Lord! how all creatures laught, when her they
spide,
And leapt and daunc't as they had ravisht
beene!°
And *Cupid* selfe about her fluttred all in greene. 305

35

And after her, came jolly° *June,* arrayd
All in greene leaves, as he a Player° were;
Yet in his time, he wrought as well as playd,
That by his plough-yrons° mote right well
appeare: 310
Upon a Crab° he rode, that him did beare
With crooked crawling steps an uncouth pase,
And backward yode,° as Bargemen wont to fare
Bending their force contrary to their face,
Like that° ungracious crew which faines demurest
grace. 315

292 **th'Argolick fluds** Greek waters, from Argolis in Greece. 299
pryde the most flourishing state. 302 **The twinnes of Leda** Castor
and Pollux, the Gemini. 305 **ravisht beene** been in ecstasy. 307
jolly handsome. 308 **Player** actor. 310 **plough-yrons** plough-
shares. 311 **Upon a Crab** the constellation Cancer. 313 **yode** went.
315 **Like that,** etc. those who walk backwards and bow with affected
politeness as they leave.

36

Then came hot *July* boyling like to fire,
     That° all his garments he had cast away:
     Upon a Lyon raging yet with ire
     He boldly rode and made him to obay:
320   It was the beast° that whylome did forray
     The Nemæan forrest, till th'*Amphytrionide*°
     Him slew, and with his hide did him array;°
     Behinde his back a sithe,° and by his side
Under his belt he bore a sickle circling wide.

37

325 The sixt was *August,* being rich arrayd
     In garment of gold downe to the ground:
     Yet rode he not, but led a lovely Mayd
     Forth by the lilly hand, the which was cround
     With eares of corne, and full her hand was
          found;
330   That was the righteous Virgin,° which of old
     Liv'd here on earth, and plenty made abound;
     But, after Wrong was lov'd and Justice solde,
She left th'unrighteous world and was to heaven
          extold.°

38

Next him, *September* marched eeke on foote:
335   Yet was he heavy laden with the spoyle
     Of harvests riches, which he made his boot,°
     And him enricht with bounty of the soyle:
     In his one hand, as fit for harvests toyle,
     He held a knife-hook; and in th'other hand
340   A paire of waights,° with which he did assoyle°
     Both more and lesse, where it in doubt did stand,
And equall° gave to each as Justice duly scann'd.°

317 **That** so that.   320 **It was the beast,** etc. The Nemean lion slain
by Hercules; here the constellation Leo.   321 **Amphytrionide** Hercules, the reputed son of Amphitruo.   322 **did him array** dressed
himself.   323 **sithe** scythe.   330 **the righteous Virgin** Astræa, the
goddess of justice; here the constellation Virgo.   333 **extold** taken
up. See V. i. 11.   336 **boot** booty.   340 **A paire of waights** a pair of
scales, the sign of Libra.   340 **assoyle** determine.   243 **equall** what
was equitable.   342 **scann'd** judged.

39

Then came *October* full of merry glee:
　　For, yet his noule was totty of the must,°
　　Which he was treading in the wine-fats see,° 345
　　And of the joyous oyle, whose gentle gust°
　　Made him so frollick and so full of lust:°
　　Upon a dreadfull Scorpion he did ride,
　　The same° which by *Dianaes* doom unjust
　　Slew great *Orion:* and eeke by his side 350
He had his ploughing share, and coulter ready tyde.

40

Next was *November,* he full grosse and fat,
　　As fed with lard, and that right well might seeme;
　　For, he had been a fatting° hogs of late,
　　That yet his browes with sweat, did reek and
　　　　steem, 355
　　And yet the season was full sharp and breem;°
　　In planting eeke he took no small delight:
　　Whereon he rode, not easie was to deeme;
　　For it a dreadfull *Centaure°* was in sight,°
The seed of *Saturne,* and faire *Nais, Chiron* hight. 360

41

And after him, came next the chill *December:*
　　Yet he through merry feasting which he made,
　　And great bonfires, did not the cold remember;
　　His Saviours birth his mind so much did glad:
　　Upon a shaggy-bearded Goat he rade, 365
　　The same° wherewith *Dan Jove* in tender yeares,
　　They say, was nourisht by th'*Idæan* mayd;
　　And in his hand a broad deepe boawle he beares;
Of which, he freely drinks an health to all his peeres.

344 **his . . . must** his head was unsteady from drinking new wine.
345 **wine-fats see** wine-vat's sea or liquor. 346 **gust** taste. 347
lust pleasure. 349 **The same,** etc. When Orion boasted that he
could kill any earthly creature, the Earth—here Diana—sent the
scorpion which killed him; here the constellation Scorpion. 354 **a**
fatting fattening. 356 **breem** chill. 359 **Centaure** Sagittarius, the
archer. 359 **sight** appearance. 366 **The same,** etc. The infant Jove
was fed goat's milk by Amalthea, a nymph dwelling on Mount Ida;
here the constellation Capricornus.

42

370   Then came old *January*, wrapped well
      In many weeds to keep the cold away;
      Yet did he quake and quiver like to quell,°
      And blowe his nayles to warme them if he may:°
375   For, they were numbd with holding all the day
      An hatchet keene, with which he felled wood,
      And from the trees did lop the needlesse spray:°
  Upon an huge great Earth-pot steane° he stood;
From whose wide mouth, there flowed forth the
      Romane floud.°

43

And lastly, came cold *February*, sitting
380   In an old wagon, for he could not ride;
      Drawne of two fishes° for the season fitting,
      Which through the flood before did softly slyde
      And swim away: yet had he by his side
      His plough and harnesse fit to till the ground,
385   And tooles to prune the trees, before the pride
  Of hasting Prime did make them burgein°
      round:
So past the twelve Months forth, and their dew places
      found.

44

And after these, there came the *Day*, and *Night*,
      Riding together both with equall pase,
390   Th'one on a Palfrey blacke, the other white;
      But *Night* had covered her uncomely face
      With a blacke veile, and held in hand a mace,
      On top whereof the moon and stars were pight,°
      And sleep and darknesse round about did trace:°
395   But *Day* did beare, upon his scepters hight,
The goodly Sun, encompast all with beames bright.

---

372 **like to quell** as though he were perishing. 373 **may** can. 376
spray branches. 377 **Earth-pot steane** earthen jar; here the constellation Aquarius. 378 **the Romane floud** possibly the Roman Tiber.
381 **Drawne . . . fishes** Drawn by two fishes—the constellation Pisces
—suitable for the season of Lent. 386 **burgein** bud. 393 **pight**
placed. 394 **trace** move.

45

Then came the *Howres,* faire daughters of high *Jove,*
⠀⠀⠀And timely *Night,* the which were all endewed°
⠀⠀⠀With wondrous beauty fit to kindle love;
⠀⠀⠀But they were Virgins all, and love eschewed,⠀⠀⠀*400*
⠀⠀⠀That might forslack° the charge to them fore-
⠀⠀⠀⠀⠀shewed°
⠀⠀⠀By mighty *Jove;* who did them Porters make
⠀⠀⠀Of heavens gate (whence all the gods issued)
⠀⠀⠀Which they did dayly watch, and nightly wake
By even turnes, ne ever did their charge forsake.⠀⠀⠀*405*

46

And after all came *Life,* and lastly *Death;*
⠀⠀⠀*Death* with most grim and griesly visage seene,
⠀⠀⠀Yet is he nought but parting of the breath;
⠀⠀⠀Ne ought to see, but like a shade to weene,
⠀⠀⠀Unbodied, unsoul'd, unheard, unseene.⠀⠀⠀*410*
⠀⠀⠀But *Life* was like a faire young lusty boy,
⠀⠀⠀Such as they faine *Dan Cupid* to have beene,
⠀⠀⠀Full of delightfull health and lively joy,
Deckt all with flowres, and wings of gold fit to employ.

47

When these were past, thus gan the *Titanesse;*⠀⠀⠀*415*
⠀⠀⠀Lo, mighty mother, now be judge and say,
⠀⠀⠀Whether in all thy creatures more or lesse
⠀⠀⠀*CHANGE* doth not raign and beare the greatest
⠀⠀⠀⠀⠀sway:
⠀⠀⠀For, who sees not, that *Time* on all doth pray?°
⠀⠀⠀But *Times* do change and move continually.⠀⠀⠀*420*
⠀⠀⠀So nothing here long standeth in one stay:
⠀⠀⠀Wherefore, this lower world who can deny
But to be subject still to *Mutabilitie?*

48

Then thus gan *Jove;* Right true it is, that these
⠀⠀⠀And all things else that under heaven dwell⠀⠀⠀*425*

398 **endewed** endowed.⠀⠀401 **forslack** delay.⠀⠀401 **fore-shewed** provided.⠀⠀419 **pray** prey.

Are chaung'd of *Time,* who doth them all
    disseise°
Of being: But, who is it (to me tell)
That *Time* himselfe doth move and still compell
To keepe his course? Is not that namely wee°
Which poure that vertue° from our heavenly
    cell,
That moves them all, and makes them changed
    be?
So them we gods doe rule, and in them also thee.

430 (line marker)

49

To whom, thus *Mutability:* The things
    Which we see not how they are mov'd and
      swayd,
Ye may attribute to your selves as Kings,
And say they by your secret powre are made:
But what we see not, who shall us perswade?
But were they so, as ye them faine to be,
Mov'd by your might, and ordred by your ayde;
Yet what if I can prove, that even yee
Your selves are likewise chang'd, and subject unto
    mee?

435, 440 (line markers)

50

And first, concerning her that is the first,°
    Even you faire *Cynthia,* whom so much ye make
Joves dearest darling, she was bred and nurst
On *Cynthus* hill, whence she her name did take:
Then is she mortall borne, how-so ye crake;°
Besides, her face and countenance every day
We changed see, and sundry forms partake,
Now hornd, now round, now bright, now brown
    and gray:
So that *as changefull as the Moone* men use to say.

445, 450 (line markers)

51

Next, *Mercury,* who though he lesse appeare

---

426 **disseise** dispossess. 429 **namely wee** we alone. 430 **vertue** power. 442 **the first** being the planet closest to the earth. 446 **how-so ye crake** however much you boast.

To change his hew, and alwayes seeme as one;
Yet, he his course doth altar every yeare,
And is of late far out of order gone:
So *Venus* eeke, that goodly Paragone,° 455
Though faire all night, yet is she darke all day;
And *Phœbus* self, who lightsome° is alone,
Yet is he oft eclipsed by the way,
And fills the darkned world with terror and dismay.

52

Now *Mars* that valiant man is changed most: 460
For, he some times so far runs out of square,
That he his way doth seem quite to have lost,
And cleane without his usuall sphere to fare;°
That even these Star-gazers stonisht are
At sight thereof, and damne° their lying bookes: 465
So likewise, grim Sir *Saturne* oft doth spare
His sterne aspect, and calme his crabbed lookes:
So many turning cranks° these have, so many crookes.

53

But you *Dan Jove,* that only constant are,
And King of all the rest, as ye do clame, 470
Are you not subject eeke to this misfare?°
Then let me aske you this withouten blame,
Where were ye borne? some say in *Crete* by
name,
Others in *Thebes,* and others other-where;
But wheresoever they comment° the same, 475
They all consent that ye begotten were,
And borne here in this world, ne other can appeare.

54

Then are ye mortall borne, and thrall to me,
Unlesse the kingdome of the sky yee make
Immortall, and unchangeable to be; 480
Besides, that power and vertue which° ye spake,

455 **Paragone** pattern of excellence. 457 **lightsome** radiant. 463
And ... fare And so go entirely outside his usual sphere. 465 **damne**
condemn. 468 **cranks** twists, windings. 471 **misfare** going astray.
475 **comment** devise. 481 **which** of which.

That ye here worke, doth many changes take,
And your owne natures change: for, each of you
That vertue have, or this, or that to make,
485   Is checkt and changed from his nature trew,
By others opposition or obliquid° view.

55
Besides, the sundry motions of your Spheares,
So sundry waies and fashions as clerkes° faine,
Some in short space, and some in longer yeares;
490   What is the same but alteration plaine?
Onely the starrie skie doth still remaine:°
Yet do the Starres and Signes therein still move,
And even it self is mov'd, as wizards saine.°
But all that moveth, doth mutation love:
495 Therefore both you and them to me I subject prove.

56
Then since within this wide great *Universe*
Nothing doth firme and permanent appeare,
But all things tost and turned by transverse:°
What then should let,° but I aloft should reare
500   My Trophee, and from all, the triumph beare?
Now judge then (O thou greatest goddesse trew!)
According as thy selfe doest see and heare,
And unto me addoom° that° is my dew;
That is the rule of all, all being rul'd by you.

57
505 So having ended, silence long ensewed,
Ne *Nature* to or fro° spake for a space,
But with firme eyes affixt,° the ground still
      viewed.
Meane while, all creatures, looking in her face,

486 **obliquid** by the opposition or oblique view of the planets, because the influence of each planet is modified by the position of the
other planets, and depends upon its own position in the sky.   488
clerkes learned men.   491 **remaine** i.e., remains to be examined.
493 **wizards saine** wise men say.   498 **by transverse** athwart.   499
let hinder.   503 **addoom** adjudge.   503 **that** that which.   506 **to or
fro** for or against the question.   507 **affixt** set.

Expecting° th'end of this so doubtfull case,
Did hang in long suspence what would ensew,   *510*
To whether° side should fall the soveraigne
    place:
At length, she looking up with chearefull view,
The silence brake, and gave her doome in speeches
    few.

58

I well consider all that ye have sayd,
And find that all things stedfastnes doe hate   *515*
And changed be: yet being rightly wayd°
They are not changed from their first estate;
But by their change their being doe dilate:°
And turning to themselves at length againe,
Doe worke their owne perfection so by fate: *520*
Then over them Change doth not rule and
    raigne;
But they raigne over change, and doe their states
    maintaine.

59

Cease therefore daughter further to aspire,
And thee content thus to be rul'd by me:
For thy decay° thou seekst by thy desire;   *525*
But time shall come that all shall changed bee,
And from thenceforth, none no more change
    shall see.
So was the *Titaness* put downe and whist,°
And *Jove* confirm'd in his imperiall see.°
Then was that whole assembly quite dismist,   *530*
And *Natur's* selfe did vanish, whither no man wist.

509 **Expecting** awaiting.   511 **whether** which.   516 **wayd** weighed.
518 **dilate** extend.   525 **decay** downfall.   528 **whist** silenced.   529
see seat.

THE VIII CANTO, unperfite.°

1

When I bethinke me on that speech whyleare,°
 Of *Mutability,* and well it way:°
 Me seemes, that though she all unworthy were
 Of the Heav'ns Rule; yet very sooth to say,
5 In all things else she beares the greatest sway.
 Which makes me loath this state of life so tickle,
 And love of things so vaine to cast away;
 Whose flowring pride, so fading and so fickle,
Short *Time* shall soon cut down with his consuming
  sickle.

2

10 Then gin I thinke on that which Nature sayd,
 Of that same time when no more *Change* shall
  be,
 But stedfast rest of all things firmely stayd
 Upon the pillours of Eternity,
 That is contrayr to *Mutabilitie:*
15 For, all that moveth, doth in *Change* delight:
 But thence-forth all shall rest eternally
 With Him that is the God of Sabbaoth hight:°
O! that great Sabbaoth God, grant me that Sabaoths
  sight.°

---

0 **unperfite** imperfect. 1 **whyleare** a while before. 2 **way** weigh,
consider. 17 **the God of Sabbaoth hight** called the God of Hosts.
18 **that Sabaoths sight** sight of that day of eternal rest.

The SIGNET CLASSIC POETRY SERIES presents, in inexpensive format, comprehensive, authoritative, and up-to-date editions of the works of the major British and American poets. Prepared under the general editorship of John Hollander, Professor of English at Hunter College, each volume in the series is devoted to a single poet, and edited by a noted scholar. Included in each volume is an introduction by the individual editor, a bibliography, a textual note, and detailed footnotes. Among the volumes already available are:

SELECTED POETRY OF BROWNING
Edited with Introduction by George Ridenour
This collection includes many old favorites, but preference is shown to Browning's longer works, often omitted in anthologies. George Ridenour is Associate Professor of English at Haverford College, and the author of *Syle of Don Juan,* as well as studies on Browning Byron, and Coleridge. (#CQ313—95¢)

SELECTED POETRY OF KEATS
Edited with Introduction by Paul de Man
A rich sampling of the Romantic poet's works arranged chronologically, including the complete "Endymion" and "Hyperion," as well as many of the shorter poetical works and a selection of the letters. Professor de Man teaches at Cornell University.
(#CQ325—95¢)

SELECTED POETRY OF SHELLEY
Edited with Introduction by Harold Bloom
The complete text of the lyrical drama, "Prometheus Bound," plus such well-known poems as "Ozymandias," "Ode to the West Wind," "To a Skylark," "Adonais," and many others, and two important prose selections, "On a Future State" and "Defense of Poetry." Dr. Bloom is an Associate Professor of English at Yale, and the author of *Shelley's Mythmaking.* (#CQ342—95¢)

SAMSON AGONISTES AND THE SHORTER POEMS OF JOHN MILTON
Edited with Introduction by Isabel Gamble MacCaffrey
"L'Allegro," "Il Penseroso," "Lycidas," a selection of the sonnets, and many other important poems, with an informative introduction by an Associate Professor at Bryn Mawr College and author of *Paradise Lost as Myth.* (#CT323—75¢)

Other Distinguished Poetry in
SIGNET CLASSIC and MENTOR Editions

THE COMPLETE PLAYS OF SHAKESPEARE

The complete plays of Shakespeare are being made available in Signet Classic editions. Under the general editorship of Sylvan Barnet, chairman of the English Department of Tufts University, each volume features a general introduction by Dr. Barnet; special introduction and notes by an eminent Shakespearean scholar; critical commentary from past and contemporary authorities, and when possible, the actual source, in its entirety or in excerpt, from which Shakespeare derived his play. The plays are priced at 50 cents each.

Among the volumes already available are:

KING LEAR, *edited with Introduction and Notes by*
   Russell Fraser, Princeton University.   (#CD160)

MACBETH, *edited with Introduction and Notes by*
   Sylvan Barnet, Tufts University.   (#CD161)

RICHARD II, *edited with Introduction and Notes by*
   Kenneth Muir, University of Liverpool.   (#CD163)

OTHELLO, *edited with Introduction and Notes by*
   Alvin Kernan, Yale University.   (#CD162)

HAMLET, *edited with Introduction and Notes by*
   Edward Hubler, Princeton University.   (#CD169)

HENRY IV, Part I, *edited with Introduction by*
   Maynard Mack, Associate Director of the Yale
   Shakespeare Institute, Yale University.   (#CD283)

HENRY IV, Part II, *edited with Introduction and Notes*
   by Norman N. Holland.   (#CD299)

JULIUS CAESAR, *edited with Introduction and Notes by*
   William and Barbara Rosen, University of
   Connecticut.   (#CD170)

TO OUR READERS: *If your dealer does not have the* SIGNET *and* MENTOR *books you want, you may order them by mail enclosing the list price plus 10¢ a copy to cover mailing.* (New York City residents add 5% Sales Tax. Other New York State residents add 2% plus any local sales or use taxes.) *If you would like our free catalog, please request it by postcard. The New American Library, Inc., P.O. Box 2310, Grand Central Station, New York, N. Y. 10017.*

SIGNET CLASSICS

from Around the World

IDYLLS OF THE KING and a Selection of Poems
by Alfred Lord Tennyson
The famous Arthurian romance and other poetry by the Victorian Poet Laureate. Foreword by George Barker.
(#CT286—75¢)

THE TRAVELS OF MARCO POLO
The enduring record of Marco Polo's thirty-five years of fabulous Eastern travel. Edited with an Introduction by Milton Rugoff.
(#CD97—50¢)

THE INFORMER *by Liam O'Flaherty*
This story of a hunted man who has betrayed his friend to the enemy presents a harshly realistic picture of Ireland divided by the Civil War in the 1920's. Afterword by Donagh McDonagh.
(#CP80—60¢)

CANDIDE, ZADIG and Selected Stories *by Voltaire*
Voltaire satirizes with ruthless wit the social, religious, and human vanities of his day in sixteen biting stories. A new translation with an Introduction by Donald Frame.
(#CD35—50¢)

RESURRECTION *by Leo Tolstoy*
The Russian master's final work tells the story of a young man who seeks salvation by following into exile the girl for whose career in crime he was responsible. Translated by Vera Traill with a Foreword by Alan Hodge.
(#CT63—75¢)

OLIVER TWIST *by Charles Dickens*
Dickens' classic indictment of the orphanages and crime-ridden slums of 19th Century London. Afterword by Edward La Comte.
(#CP102—60¢)

PLATERO AND I *by Juan Ramon Jiminez*
The delightful tale of a poet and his playful donkey by one of Spain's great Nobel Prize winning authors. Translated by William and Mary Roberts, with an Introduction by William Roberts.
(#CP302—60¢)